LOGIC CIRCUITS AND MICROCOMPUTER SYSTEMS

McGraw-Hill Series in Electrical Engineering

Consulting Editor
Stephen W. Director, Carnegie-Mellon University

Networks and Systems
Communications and Information Theory
Control Theory
Electronics and Electronic Circuits
Power and Energy
Electromagnetics
Computer Engineering and Switching Theory
Introductory and Survey
Radio, Television, Radar, and Antennas

Previous Consulting Editors

Ronald M. Bracewell, Colin Cherry, James F. Gibbons, Willis H. Harman,
Hubert Heffner, Edward W. Herold, John G. Linvill, Simon Ramo, Ronald A. Rohrer,
Anthony E. Siegman, Charles Susskind, Frederick E. Terman, John G. Truxal,
Ernst Weber, and John R. Whinnery

Compguter Engineering and Switching Theory

Consulting Editor
Stephen W. Director, Carnegie-Mellon University

Bartee: *Digital Computer Fundamentals*
Bell and Newell: *Computer Structures Readings and Examples*
Clare: *Designing Logic Systems Using State Machines*
Garland: *Introduction to Microprocessor System Design*

Givone: *Introduction to Switching Circuit Theory*
Givone and Roesser: *Microprocessors/Microcomputers: An Introduction*
Hamacher, Vranesic, and Zaky: *Computer Organization*
Hayes: *Computer Organization and Architecture*
Kohavi: *Switching and Finite Automata Theory*
McCluskey: *Introduction to the Theory of Switching Circuits*
Peatman: *Design of Digital Systems*
Peatman: *Digital Hardware Design*
Peatman: *Microcomputer Based Design*
Sandige: *Digital Concepts Using Standard Integrated Circuits*
Scott: *Electronic Computer Technology*
Wiatrowski and House: *Logic Circuits and Microcomputer Systems*
Woollons: *Introduction to Digital Computer Design*

Electronics and Electronic Circuits

Consulting Editor
Stephen W. Director, Carnegie-Mellon University

Angelo: *Electronics: FET's, BJT's, and Microcircuits*
Blatt: *Physics of Electronic Conduction in Solids*
Chirlian: *Electronic Circuits: Physical Principles, Analysis, and Design*
Cornetet and Battocletti: *Electronic Circuits by Systems and Computer Analysis*
Gibbons: *Semiconductor Electronics*
Grinich and Jackson: *Introduction to Integrated Circuits*
Hamilton and Howard: *Basic Integrated Circuits*
Harrison: *Solid State Theory*
Hirth and Lothe: *Theory of Dislocations*
Kubo and Nagamiya: *Solid State Physics*
Meyer, Lynn, and Hamilton: *Analysis and Design of Integrated Circuits*
Millman: *Microelectronics: Digital and Analog Circuits and Systems*
Millman and Halkias: *Electronic Devices and Circuits*
Millman and Halkias: *Electronic Fundamentals and Applications for Engineers and Scientists*
Millman and Halkias: *Integrated Electronics: Analog, Digital Circuits, and Systems*
Millman and Taub: *Pulse, Digital, and Switching Waveforms*
Peatman: *Microcomputer Based Design*
Pettit and McWhorter: *Electronic Switching Timing, and Pulse Circuits*
Ramey and White: *Matrices and Computers in Electronic Circuit Analysis*
Schilling and Belove: *Electronic Circuits: Discrete and Integrated*
Strauss: *Wave Generation and Shaping*
Taub and Schilling: *Digital Integrated Electronics*
Wait, Huelsman, and Korn: *Introduction to Operational and Amplifier Theory Applications*
Wang: *Solid-State Electronics*
Wert and Thompson: *Physics of Solids*
Wiatrowski and House: *Logic Circuits and Microcomputer Systems*
Yang: *Fundamentals of Semi-Conductor Devices*

LOGIC CIRCUITS AND MICROCOMPUTER SYSTEMS

Claude A. Wiatrowski
University of Colorado
Colorado Springs

Charles H. House
Hewlett-Packard Company

McGraw-Hill Book Company

New York St. Louis San Francisco Auckland Bogotá Hamburg Johannesburg
London Madrid Mexico Montreal New Delhi
Panama Paris São Paulo Singapore Sydney Tokyo Toronto

LOGIC CIRCUITS AND MICROCOMPUTER SYSTEMS

2 3 4 5 6 7 8 9 0   DODO   8 9 8 7 6 5 4 3 2 1 0

Library of Congress Cataloging in Publication Data

Wiatrowski, Claude A
   Logic circuits and microcomputer systems.

   (McGraw-Hill series in electrical engineering)
(Computer engineering and switching theory)
(Electronics and electronic circuits)
   Includes index.
   1. Logic circuits.   2. Logic design.
3. Microcomputers.   4. Digital electronics.
I. House, Charles H., joint author.   II. Title.
III. Series.   IV. Series: Computer engineering
and switching theory.   V. Series: Electronics
and electronic circuits.
TK7868.L6W5   621.3815'3   80-10680
ISBN 0-07-070090-7

This book was set in Times Roman by Automated Composition Service, Inc.
The editors were Frank J. Cerra and J. W. Maisel;
the production supervisor was Leroy A. Young.
The drawings were done by Fine Line Illustrations, Inc.
The cover was designed by Mark Weiboldt.
R. R. Donnelley & Sons Company was printer and binder.

CONTENTS

PREFACE

This book presents a modern approach to digital design using both logic circuit and microcomputer implementations. The pace of change in digital systems is extraordinary. New design techniques are constantly needed. Our major goal in writing this book has been to make it as efficient as possible. Outdated material or material of limited usefulness has been omitted. Topics retained have been given space proportional to their current importance.

For these reasons, the practicing engineer can thus use this book to rapidly learn basic logic circuit design and microcomputer application. The professional computer scientist will find that this book furnishes an almost painless way to learn about computer hardware. Professionals not active in the electronics industry might want to supplement our book with a hobbyist book on digital circuits.

The book is suitable for college courses in both logic circuits and microcomputers. Because the book requires no prerequisites, it is especially attractive for computer science courses and lower division engineering courses. On the other hand, the topics included will interest upper division students and skilled engineers. The material in this text could be covered in one semester. We use the book in a two-semester lower-division course augmented with additional material and a heavy lab schedule. The book naturally divides into a semester of logic circuits and a semester of microcomputers.

The first half of the book emphasizes sequential circuit design using the algorithmic-state-machine technique. Read-only-memory implementations are emphasized along with supportive medium-scale integration functions. The second half of the book introduces assembly language programming and microcomputer hardware. Many basic computer concepts are introduced with examples in a real microcomputer (the 8085).

A smaller microcomputer, the 8048, and a larger processor, the 8086, are detailed. The selection of a microcomputer from among the three major categories represented by the 8048, 8085, and 8086 is discussed. A final chapter discusses the development of microcomputer systems, distributed architectures, and testing digital systems.

We hope that a program of study using this text will give the student or professional a firm and *real* understanding of the principles of modern digital system design. No book or course of study can substitute for experience, but an understanding of the basic principles is essential for gaining that experience. We believe that this book plainly presents the basic principles upon which modern digital system design is based. It presents these principles in a realistic framework that ensures an understanding of their applicability.

We'd like to acknowledge the assistance of Stella Sears, Linda Keener, Charles Small, George Mineah, Steve Curtis, and Margaret Wiatrowski.

Claude A. Wiatrowski
Charles H. House

LOGIC CIRCUITS AND
MICROCOMPUTER SYSTEMS

THE ALGORITHMIC STATE MACHINE

The solutions to many engineering problems take the form of a sequence of specific actions. In fact, much of our own life can be described by such a sequence. For example, when we prepare breakfast for ourselves, we follow such a sequence. First, we decide whether we have enough time to fix breakfast so as not to be late for work. If we don't have enough time, we will stop at McDonald's for breakfast. If we do have enough time, we look for all the ingredients needed. If we don't have everything, we'll also have to go out for breakfast. Next, we put a pan on the range, turn up the heat, beat a couple of eggs, and pour them into the pan. Every few seconds we stir the eggs and, at the same time, check to see if they are done to our taste. When they're done, we scoop them onto a plate and eat them. Of course, we would also be performing other sequences of actions simultaneously to ensure that coffee and toast would arrive on the table with our eggs.

You'll notice that the above sequence of actions has two important attributes. First, the sequence depends on time. Actions occur in a particular time order. In fact, some statements of action mention time specifically. For example, we stirred the eggs every few *seconds*. The second important attribute is that alternate actions were performed depending on some decision. For example, we either ate at McDonald's or fixed our own breakfast depending on whether or not we had the ingredients for making breakfast.

The control of traffic at an intersection is an example of an engineering problem that is solved by a sequence of actions. In this case, the sequence of actions is the lighting of traffic signals in a sequence designed to safely control the flow of traffic. Figure 1-1 shows a simple traffic intersection. The letters N, S, E, and W will stand for the traffic lights controlling northbound, southbound, eastbound, and westbound traffic, respectively. In the simplest intersection, the lights controlling north and

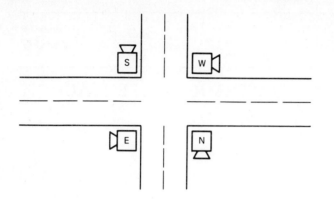

Figure 1-1 Traffic intersection.

southbound traffic will always have identical indications, as will the lights controlling east and westbound traffic.

Since we have to start somewhere, let's pick a safe traffic situation that we know can occur. Let the north and southbound lights be red and the east and westbound lights be green. Next, the east and westbound lights will turn yellow in preparation for changing the flow of traffic through the intersection. The east and westbound lights will turn red as the north and southbound lights turn green. After north and southbound traffic is allowed through the intersection, the north and southbound lights will turn yellow in preparation for another change in traffic flow. Finally, the north and southbound lights will turn red, and the east and westbound lights green. Since this is the condition in which we originally started, we can repeat the described sequence indefinitely.

You should notice that this description of the operation of a traffic light is difficult to follow. It is difficult to visualize the operation of even a simple traffic intersection from such a cumbersome description. For this reason, a sequence of actions is often described by a diagram called a flowchart.

Figure 1-2 is a flowchart for the simple traffic intersection that was previously described. The rectangles are called action blocks, and the actions to be performed are written in these blocks. The action blocks are connected by lines with arrows indicating the sequence in which the actions are to be performed. Often the description of the action is condensed to make the diagram smaller and more easily comprehended. In this case, the notation *NS RED* means that the northbound and southbound lights are set to red. This flowchart explicitly states that the red/green conditions will last for 20 s, while the red/yellow conditions will last for 5 s. Flowcharts are often drawn without time specifications. In this latter case, all action blocks are assumed to take the same amount of time. This time interval must be specified somewhere else and is often called the *CLOCK* interval. You can see that, if we could build a machine that would follow the sequence of Fig. 1-2, that machine could be used to control traffic lights at an intersection. In fact, such a device is called a sequential digital machine, and the design of such a machine with electronic components will be studied in this book. The *controlling* machine and the actual light bulbs of the *controlled* traffic signals are considered separate parts of one system. The actions are also called *OUT-*

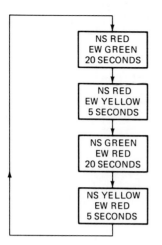

Figure 1-2 Flowchart for traffic intersection.

PUTS since they represent commands to perform an action sent from the sequential machine controller to the controlled traffic lights.

The traffic intersection we've described controls traffic efficiently when the amount of traffic on both streets is approximately equal. If the north-south street had more traffic than the east-west street, the north and southbound lights could have simply been given longer green intervals than the east and westbound lights.

An Algorithm with Inputs

Next, consider an intersection where the north-south street is a major thoroughfare that musn't be stopped unnecessarily. Furthermore, the east-west street is the entrance to a county fairground that has no traffic most of the time. However, when the fairground road is in use, a large number of east and westbound vehicles must be safely moved across the north-south street. One solution to this problem is to install traffic sensors in the pavement of the east-west street, as shown in Fig. 1-3. The traffic signals

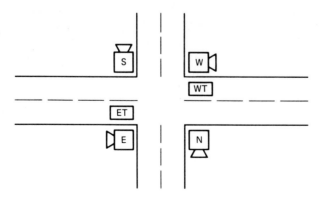

Figure 1-3 Traffic intersection with eastbound and westbound traffic sensors.

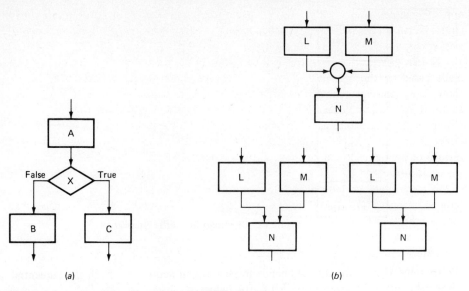

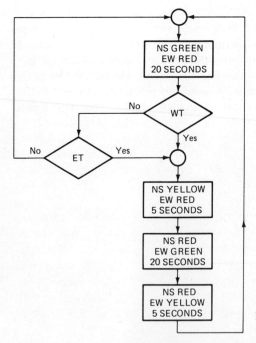

Figure 1-4 (*a*) Conditional branching; (*b*) joining branches.

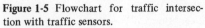

Figure 1-5 Flowchart for traffic intersection with traffic sensors.

normally show green to the major north-south thoroughfare and red to the east-west street. North-south traffic will be stopped only when a vehicle is waiting on the east-west street.

Notice that the solution to this traffic control problem involves a decision to be made based on the condition of the east and westbound traffic sensors. Figure 1-4*a* shows the diamond symbol used on a flowchart to indicate a decision. In Fig. 1-4*a*, action *A* is followed by action *B* only if *X* is false, while action *A* is followed by action *C* only if *X* is true. The decision diamond guides the sequence of actions from *A* to either *B* or *C* depending on the state of *X*. Since the decision merely guides the sequence of actions and is not an action itself, there is no time interval associated with the decision diamond.

If we've split the sequence of actions into two alternative paths, we will probably have to join alternative paths. Figure 1-4*b* shows three notations used in flowcharts to indicate that action *N* will be the next to occur after either action *L* or *M*.

Now we can draw the flowchart for the intersection of Fig. 1-3. Figure 1-5 incorporates two decisions. If neither the east nor westbound traffic sensors indicate a vehicle, the north-south lights will remain green. However, if either sensor indicates a vehicle present, the traffic lights will sequence to allow it to cross. Since the condition of the traffic sensors is sent to the controller that will implement the flowchart of Figure 1-6, these conditions are usually called *INPUTS*. Thus, the electronic circuits we will learn to design have *INPUTS*, on which decisions are based, and *OUTPUTS*, which perform actions. In addition, these circuits have a *CLOCK*, which times their sequencing.

Another Algorithm

Start with the intersection of Fig. 1-1, controlled by the flowchart in Fig. 1-2. Now, we'd like to add an input to allow an emergency vehicle to safely pass through the intersection by stopping traffic in *all* directions. Ignoring the electronic details of the vehicle's radio link, we'll assume that an input called *EMER* exists which, when true, should cause all lights to turn red. In Fig. 1-6 the input *EMER* is tested between every change in the traffic lights. If *EMER* is false, the lights function normally. If *EMER* is true, the lights are all set to red by a new action block that did not appear in the flowchart of Fig. 1-2. After all lights are red, the *EMER* input is tested every 5 s. When *EMER* becomes false (i.e., the emergency vehicle has passed), the normal traffic sequence is resumed.

This solution has one serious drawback. If the emergency vehicle driver pushes his button *just after* one of the 20-s actions is started, almost 20 s will elapse before the lights turn red. Figure 1-7 eliminates this problem by breaking up each 20-s interval into four 5-s intervals. Now, at most, 5 s can elapse between pushing the emergency button and all the traffic lights turning red. Because all action blocks in Fig. 1-7 take the same amount of time (5 s), no time notations are made in the blocks. The notation *CLOCK = 5 SECONDS* at the bottom of the figure indicates the time of each action block in the figure.

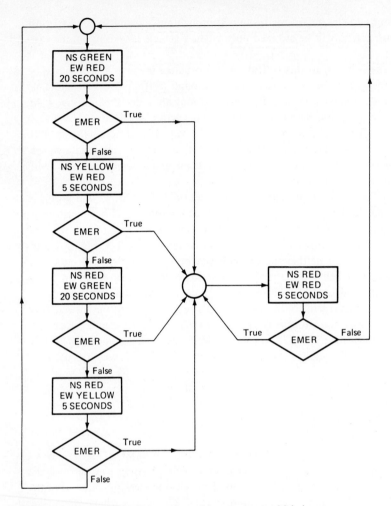

Figure 1-6 Flowchart for intersection with emergency vehicle input.

An Algorithm Definition

The sequence of decisions and actions we have been describing is called an algorithm. Algorithms may be described by plain text, flowcharts, tables, or any other appropriate technique. Any useful algorithm, no matter how it is represented, has certain important characteristics. First, an algorithm must have only a finite number of steps. Note that the traffic light algorithm meets this criteria, even though the entire traffic controlling algorithm repeats forever. The simplest traffic algorithm used only four steps to achieve its solution, even though the solution was to be repeated indefinitely. Second, each step (action or decision) in an algorithm must be precisely and unambiguously defined, as must the order of performing the steps. Third, an algorithm must have one or more outputs. Finally, an algorithm may or may not have inputs,

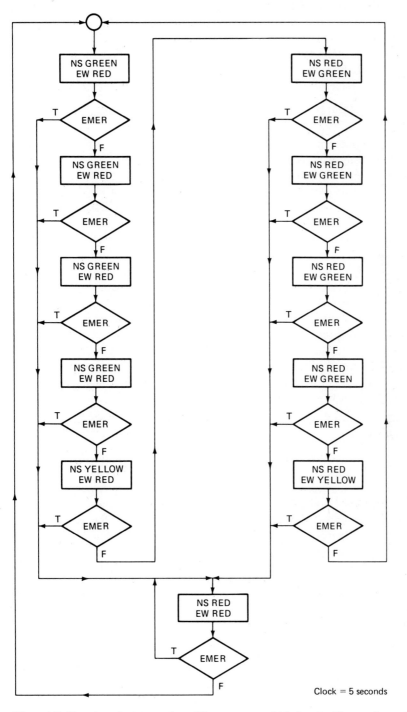

Figure 1-7 Flowchart for intersection with emergency vehicle input with a maximum delay of 5 s.

which it uses in its operation. Although the simplest traffic light controller discussed previously would be said to have no inputs, it does have *time* as an input. Because time is ordinarily an important part of most algorithms we'll be using, it is usually implicitly assumed to be an input.

DIGITAL SOLUTIONS

The task of the engineer is to discover and implement solutions to a problem. We've already discussed a large class of solutions to engineering problems. These solutions are called algorithms, and we have described them with flowcharts. The task of implementing these solutions remains. Not only must we be able to describe the method of controlling traffic at an intersection, but we must also be able to design and build an electronic device to actually perform the function of controlling traffic. One characteristic of all the algorithms we've discussed stands out. Every output or input we've used can be in only two conditions. The green westbound traffic light can be either on or off. The eastbound traffic sensors indicate either the presence or absence of traffic. Algorithms with this characteristic (all inputs and outputs may be in only two conditions) may be implemented by *digital* circuits. Since digital circuits need only recognize and generate two alternative conditions, they are less expensive to fabricate than circuits that must distinguish between hundreds of conditions. In fact, digital circuits that may be used in the solution of any algorithm are mass-produced inexpensively. As we'll see in later chapters, clever techniques exist to design digital implementations of algorithms that are not digital by nature. This is often done to take advantage of inexpensive and reliable digital circuit components.

Digital Signals

Digital circuits are connected to each other and to inputs and outputs with wires that carry digital signals. These signals are electrical voltages that represent the two conditions that the signal may assume. For example, the output wire to the green westbound traffic light may have two conditions. If the light is to be turned on, the wire will transmit a signal of 3.0 V, and, if the light is to be turned off, the wire will transmit a signal of 0.4 V. In real digital circuits, each condition is represented by a range of voltages. By using a range of voltages, the precision required in the circuitry is reduced. For example, the light turned on may be represented by any voltage greater than 2.4 V, and turned off by any voltage less than 0.8 V.

Describing digital signals by referring to voltages is very cumbersome. In addition, different *families* of digital circuits may use different voltages. The two digital signal conditions are often called 1 and 0 both for convenience and to make their description independent of any specific family of circuits. The condition or state specified by 1 usually corresponds to the more-positive voltage, and the state specified by 0 to the less-positive voltage. One common correspondence of condition, voltage, and state is:

Westbound green light	Voltage	State
On	$\geqslant 2.4$	1
Off	$\leqslant 0.8$	0

Binary Numbers

Digital circuits must often represent more than two states. Combinations of 1s and 0s can be used to represent integer numbers. Such a representation is called a binary number. Each digit of the binary number is given a weight equal to a power of 2:

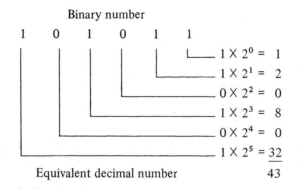

Binary number

1 0 1 0 1 1

$1 \times 2^0 = 1$
$1 \times 2^1 = 2$
$0 \times 2^2 = 0$
$1 \times 2^3 = 8$
$0 \times 2^4 = 0$
$1 \times 2^5 = 32$

Equivalent decimal number   43

This is exactly analogous to decimal numbers, in which each digit is given a weight equal to a power of 10. Just as in the decimal system, the rightmost digit is the least significant digit, with the smallest weight. In a binary system, this is called the least significant bit (LSB). If we can represent integer numbers as combinations of 0s and 1s, we should be able to count in binary. The binary counting sequence and its decimal equivalent are:

Binary				Decimal
0	0	0	0	0
0	0	0	1	1
0	0	1	0	2
0	0	1	1	3
0	1	0	0	4
0	1	0	1	5
0	1	1	0	6
0	1	1	1	7
1	0	0	0	8
1	0	0	1	9
1	0	1	0	10
1	0	1	1	11
1	1	0	0	12
1	1	0	1	13
1	1	1	0	14
1	1	1	1	15

Negative Numbers

One way to represent negative binary integers is called *two's complement*. Consider the 3-bit binary integer 101. This binary number represents the decimal number 5. We want to find a way to represent −5. The next bit to the left of this binary number would have a weight of 2^3 or 8. Change this weight to −8. This does not change the representation for +5, which is still 0101. The number 1011 has a decimal equivalent, which is found to be:

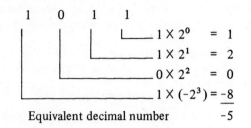

Thus, we have found a way to represent the number -5. In fact, this method will represent other negative numbers. The counting sequence for two's-complement numbers is:

Binary				Decimal
1	0	0	0	-8
1	0	0	1	-7
1	0	1	0	-6
1	0	1	1	-5
1	1	0	0	-4
1	1	0	1	-3
1	1	1	0	-2
1	1	1	1	-1
0	0	0	0	0
0	0	0	1	1
0	0	1	0	2
0	0	1	1	3
0	1	0	0	4
0	1	0	1	5
0	1	1	0	6
0	1	1	1	7

All positive numbers start with a 0 bit, while all negative numbers start with a 1 bit. The binary equivalent of -4 is identical to the binary equivalent of +12. You must know that the number is supposed to be two's complement to interpret it correctly. An easy way to find the negative equivalent of a binary number is to change all the 0s to 1s and 1s to 0s and, then, to increment the resulting number by one. For example, to represent the number -3, we start with the binary equivalent for +3:

$$0011$$

Then, we change all the 1s to 0s and 0s to 1s:

$$1100$$

Finally, we increment the result by one (count up one):

$$1101$$

This is the two's-complement representation of -3. You will see in a later chapter that the two's-complement representation simplifies binary arithmetic.

Representing Time

As previously mentioned, time is an important part of most algorithms. We would like to have a way of representing the manner in which digital signals change with time. Two common representations exist. The first is called a *timing diagram* and is shown in Fig. 1-8. Six digital signals are shown on this diagram, corresponding to the outputs of the simple traffic light controller. Each signal is represented as a horizontal line which may take two positions. The upper position corresponds to the 1 condition, and the lower to the 0 condition. Time is plotted horizontally, increasing to the right. For example, at 25 s, the NS RED turns on, the NS YELLOW turns off, the NS GREEN is off and stays off, the EW RED turns off, the EW YELLOW is off and stays off, and the EW GREEN turns on. By plotting several signals on the same timing diagram, the time relationships among all these signals can be described. A timing diagram for a real operating circuit can be viewed by connecting an instrument called an *oscilloscope* to the circuit. A newer instrument called a *logic-timing analyzer* also displays timing diagrams.

A timing diagram becomes cumbersome for a large number of signals or a long period of time. For that reason, digital signals are often represented in tabular form. Many (but not all!) digital circuits have the characteristic that signals only change at fixed time intervals, called *clock* intervals. The traffic controller of Fig. 1-8 has this characteristic. Signals only change at 5-s intervals. For that reason, we can represent all the information contained in the timing diagram of Fig. 1-8 by listing the states of all the outputs at the beginning of each 5-s interval. Table 1-1 is a table describing

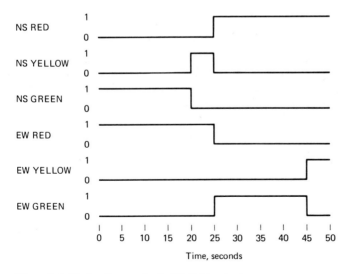

Figure 1-8 Timing diagram for traffic-light output.

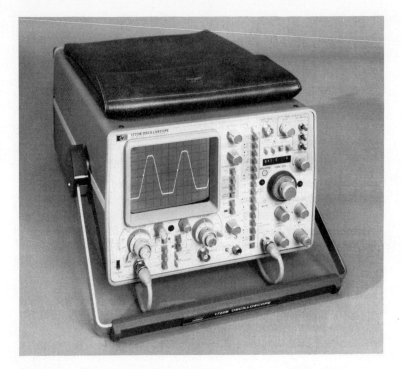

An oscilloscope (*Hewlett-Packard Co.*).

the traffic controller of Fig. 1-8. Since additional signals are merely added columns and additional time intervals are just added rows, very large and complex systems are easily represented in tabular form. However, the tabular description is usually restricted to circuits in which signals change only at regular clock intervals. The tabular representation of a real operating circuit may be viewed by connecting an instrument called a *logic-state analyzer* to the circuit.

Table 1-1 Tabular representation of logic signals

	NS RED	NS YELLOW	NS GREEN	EW RED	EW YELLOW	EW GREEN
0	0	0	1	1	0	0
5	0	0	1	1	0	0
10	0	0	1	1	0	0
15	0	0	1	1	0	0
20	0	1	0	1	0	0
25	1	0	0	0	0	1
30	1	0	0	0	0	1
35	1	0	0	0	0	1
40	1	0	0	0	0	1
45	1	0	0	0	1	0

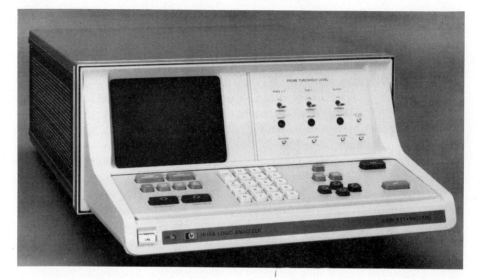

A logic analyzer (*Hewlett-Packard Co.*).

Logic Circuits

Logic circuit elements are usually fabricated from small pieces of silicon as *monolithic integrated circuits*. These integrated circuits (or ICs) are packaged in plastic, ceramic, or metal containers, with leads that allow the various circuits to be interconnected.

Digital ICs are divided into families and subfamilies, according to the electronic circuitry used to implement the device. Compatibility among families and subfamilies may or may not require special conversion circuits. In any case, sets of interconnection rules are developed to assist the designer in interconnecting circuits within and among families. These interconnection rules are available from the manufacturers of the ICs. Standardization within an IC family allows us to concentrate on the function of the circuit without regard to electronic details.

Although thousands of types of digital integrated circuits are manufactured, they may be classified into much fewer general types. In fact, all the algorithms discussed so far may be implemented using only two types of circuits: read-only memories (ROMs) and D flip-flops. Theoretically, all algorithms could be implemented with these two types of digital circuits. However, the many additional types of circuits available offer additional economies in implementations of more complex algorithms.

Circuit Diagrams

Interconnections among logic circuits are specified by a diagram in which they are represented by lines. These lines "connect" symbols representing each logic circuit. Although two conductors are required to complete an electric circuit, only one line is drawn. The other conductor of every electric circuit is assumed to be a *ground* connection, common to all logic circuits. Each logic circuit also requires a *power* connection to a power supply. Neither the power nor ground connections will be shown on diagrams in this book.

D Flip-Flops

A type D flip-flop is a memory circuit. It remembers a single digital signal or bit. In its simplest form, a D flip-flop has two inputs and one output, as shown in Fig. 1-9. The rectangular block represents the type D flip-flop with its inputs labeled D and C and its output labeled Q. The straight lines leading to the block represent wires connecting to other parts of the circuit. These wires carry digital signals to and from the flip-flop. The flip-flop remembers the logic state at its D or data input at the time that its C or clock input makes a transition from a 0 to a 1. The flip-flop remembers this D input state on its Q output and thus makes it available for other circuits to use. The timing diagram of Fig. 1-9 illustrates the operation of this circuit. The clock input is normally a regular periodic signal, like the one shown. It is generated by another electronic circuit, not important to the discussion. The flip-flop *does* something only when a transition from 0 to 1 occurs on its clock input, at times W, X, Y, and Z on the timing diagram. At time W, the state of the D input, a zero, is remembered on the Q output. Even though the D input changes to a 1 later, the Q output remembers the zero and will not change until time X, when a 0-to-1 transition of the clock input occurs. Since the D input is a 1 at time X, a 1 appears on the Q output. At time Y, the Q output remains a 1 because the D input is also a 1. Note that even though the D input changes to a zero, the Q output remains a 1 until the next clock transition at time Z, when Q becomes a zero. Again, to summarize, the Q output remembers the state of the D input that existed when the last 0-to-1 transition occurred on the clock (C) input.

The clock input of the type D flip-flop we are using is *edge-sensitive*. That is, it responds only to the 0-to-1 transition or edge of the clock signal. To distinguish edge-sensitive inputs from other inputs, we will use a small triangle placed inside the circuit symbol next to the edge-sensitive input, as shown in Fig. 1-9.

Actually, the Q output doesn't change until a small time after the clock transition. This time, called *delay time*, is due to the electronic circuitry in the flip-flop. Typical delay times are several nanoseconds (10^{-9} s).

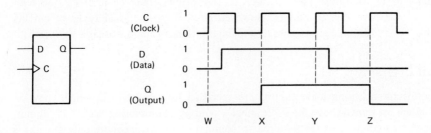

Figure 1-9 Type D flip-flop.

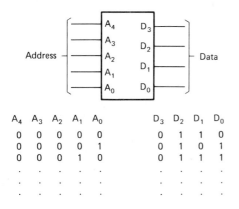

A_4	A_3	A_2	A_1	A_0		D_3	D_2	D_1	D_0
0	0	0	0	0		0	1	1	0
0	0	0	0	1		0	1	0	1
0	0	0	1	0		0	1	1	1
.	.	.	.	.		.	.	.	.
.	.	.	.	.		.	.	.	.

Figure 1-10 Read-only memory.

Read-Only Memories

While type D flip-flops can remember new data at each clock transition, read-only memories (ROMs) remember a preset pattern of data. This pattern is specified when the ROM circuit is manufactured and is unchangeable thereafter. Figure 1-10 shows a ROM represented as a block with connecting wires. The ROM illustrated has five inputs, called address lines, and four outputs, called data lines. There are 32 places in the ROM where 4 bits of data are stored. Each of these 32 places is called a *memory location* or *memory word*. Each memory location is identified by a *memory address*. A memory address is a particular combination of 1s and 0s placed on the address lines of the ROM. Since this ROM has five address lines, 2^5 or 32 combinations of 1s and 0s may be specified as addresses. Placing one such combination of address bits on the address inputs causes data that were stored in that location when the circuit was manufactured to appear on the data lines. For example, in the ROM illustrated, placing 00000 on the address lines causes 0110 to appear on the data lines. You specify the contents of the data word that you want put in each of the memory locations of the ROM. The manufacturer builds those data into the circuit permanently. Notice that

An EPROM is on the left with transparent window and a ROM is on the right (*Hewlett-Packard Co.*).

ROMs have no clock input. The output data simply change as soon after you change the address as the internal electronic circuitry will allow. The time it takes for correct data to appear on the outputs after an address change is called the *access time*. Access time can vary from several nanoseconds (10^{-9} s) to several microseconds (10^{-6} s), depending on the nature of the electronic circuits in the ROM.

A ROM having five address and four data lines is called a 32 × 4 ROM. It has 32 memory locations, each having 4 bits of data. ROMs come in a wide variety of sizes. A ROM having 10 address inputs and 8 data outputs would have 1024 locations (2^{10} memory locations) of 8 bits each. Two common abbreviations are used to specify size. Since 1024 is so close to 1000, the abbreviation K always stands for 1024 when referring to memory circuits. Thus, a 1024 × 8 memory is called a 1K × 8 memory. Since 8 bits is a common unit used by computers, it is given the name *byte*. Thus, a 1024 × 8-bit memory is called a 1K-byte for 1KB memory.

Finally, it should have occurred to you that having a new ROM fabricated with a special pattern is an expensive and time-consuming undertaking. Two kinds of ROMs have been developed to minimize these problems. The first is called a programmable ROM, often called a *PROM*. This kind of ROM is manufactured with either all 1s or all 0s in every bit of every location. A special machine called a PROM programmer allows individual bits to be changed to the opposite state once and only once after the PROM is manufactured. Because all PROMs are identical when they leave the manufacturer, they take advantage of manufacturing economies of scale and are quite inexpensive, even when purchased in small quantities. PROMs allow read-only memories

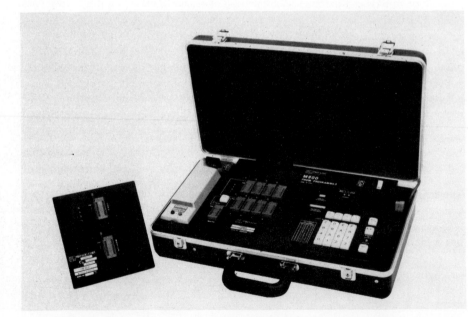

A PROM Programmer. An ultraviolet light for erasing EPROMs is on the left. Sockets for PROMs are in the center. The keyboard allows manual entry of data. PROMs may also be copied from a master PROM (*Pro-Log Corporation*).

to be incorporated in many circuits when small quantities would not justify the cost of manufacturing a specially patterned ROM.

PROMs that can only be programmed once are inconvenient when new digital circuits are being developed in the laboratory. Mistakes are made, specifications change, and new ideas must be continually tried. For this reason, a part called an *erasable programmable read-only memory* or EPROM has been developed. An EPROM is programmed like a PROM. However, it can be erased and returned to its original manufactured state for reprogramming with a new pattern. The EPROM is erased by shining an ultraviolet light onto the circuit through a transparent window in its package.

Hex Notation

Specifying a large ROM with 1s and 0s is very inconvenient. A 1KB ROM would require a 1024-line table, with each line containing 10 address and 8 data bits. One common method of simplifying the specification of large numbers of bits is to use hex notation. Hex notation uses a single character (0-9 and A-F) to specify 1 of 16 possible combinations of 4 bits:

4-bit group				Hex equivalent
0	0	0	0	0
0	0	0	1	1
0	0	1	0	2
0	0	1	1	3
0	1	0	0	4
0	1	0	1	5
0	1	1	0	6
0	1	1	1	7
1	0	0	0	8
1	0	0	1	9
1	0	1	0	A
1	0	1	1	B
1	1	0	0	C
1	1	0	1	D
1	1	1	0	E
1	1	1	1	F

Note that since the *order* of the bits is important, the rightmost bit is always called the least significant, and the leftmost bit the most significant. If the digital signals are given symbolic names (e.g., $A_5, A_4, A_3, A_2, A_1, A_0$), then the least significant bit is almost always the one whose name has the smallest subscript. Groups of more than 4 bits are encoded by dividing the bits into groups of 4, starting from the rightmost or least significant bit, and encoding each group separately. Note that, if the number of bits is not a multiple of 4, zeros are assumed for nonexistent bits. Also, hex numbers are often followed by the letter H to differentiate them from decimal numbers.

$$0000 : 1111 \qquad 0FH$$

$$11 : 0000 : 1110 \qquad 30EH$$

Circuit Parameters

All logic circuits have many electric parameters associated with them. Two important parameters are *fan-out* and *propagation delay*. Fan-out is the specification of the number of inputs to which a given output may be connected. Exceeding the fan-out specification will cause the circuit to malfunction. All logic circuit outputs have a fan-out specification. Propagation delay is the amount of time it takes for a change in an input logic signal to change an output logic signal. Thus, there is a propagation delay between the address inputs and data outputs of a ROM or between the clock input and Q output of a flip-flop. Logic circuits have many other parameters, but these two are the most important. We'll consider other parameters in a later chapter.

IMPLEMENTING A TRAFFIC LIGHT CONTROLLER

We're now ready to design a controller to implement the flowchart of Fig. 1-2. This flowchart is redrawn in Fig. 1-11 with additional blocks added so that all blocks are 5 s long. How should we proceed to use D flip-flops and ROMs to implement an electronic circuit to perform this function? Notice that there are 10 separate action blocks in Fig. 1-11. The controller will sequence through these actions one at a time at each 5-s interval. The controller must obviously remember which of these 10 actions it is currently performing. Four type D flip-flops could remember 1 of 16 different things, by using all possible combinations of 1s and 0s. We could use 10 of those combinations to specify which action block we're currently performing. The flowchart of Fig. 1-11 has a combination of 1s and 0s next to each action block. These 1s and 0s are called *state variables*. These combinations of 1s and 0s are the *states* of the controller and are also listed in the flowchart as hex numbers. Figure 1-12 shows the four type D flip-flops which will remember the current state of the controller. The flip-flop Q outputs are subscripted to differentiate among them. Moreover, the flip-flop labeled Q_0 is the rightmost or least significant state bit in the flowchart of Fig. 1-11. We've connected all the clock inputs together and to a clock generator circuit since we know we will want to change the current state of the machine every 5 s. Let's not worry about from where the next state will come. First, let's determine how to generate the controller's outputs.

Outputs

We must generate six outputs to control the actual light bulbs in the traffic signals. These six outputs are shown in Table 1-2. Each signal is given a name that makes it easy to remember the function of that output. The logic signals to appear on each output are specified by each action block or state of Fig. 1-11. Use the four current state outputs of the flip-flops as address inputs to a ROM, as shown in Fig. 1-13. Store the six outputs corresponding to each of the 10 states in 10 locations of that read-only memory. Table 1-3 specifies the contents of each ROM location and was obtained directly from the flowchart of Fig. 1-11. For example, the first action block in the

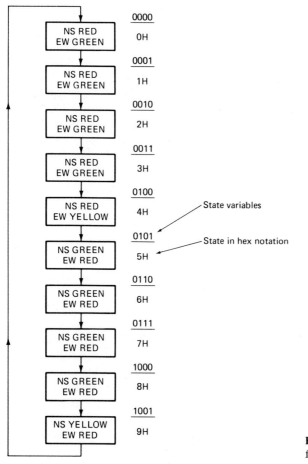

State variables

State in hex notation

Figure 1-11 Flowchart for traffic-light controller.

flowchart corresponds to state 0H. Since the ROM address inputs are connected to the current state outputs in identical order, state 0H also is address 0H in the ROM. We see from the flowchart that we want the north and south red lights on, the east and west green lights on, and all other lights off. We specify the contents of memory location 0H as:

$$
\begin{array}{lll}
D_0 = 0 & \text{or} & NSG = 0 \\
D_1 = 0 & \text{or} & NSY = 0 \\
D_2 = 1 & \text{or} & NSR = 1 \\
D_3 = 1 & \text{or} & EWG = 1 \\
D_4 = 0 & \text{or} & EWY = 0 \\
D_5 = 0 & \text{or} & EWR = 0
\end{array}
$$

Whenever the current state of 0H appears on the four flip-flop outputs, the ROM outputs corresponding to that address will cause the traffic lights to be set to the proper indication. Continuing through all blocks of the flowchart, we generate 10 lines in

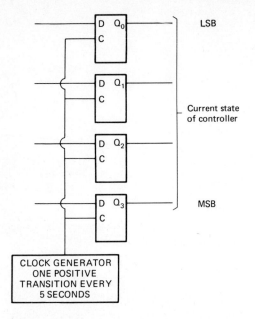

Figure 1-12 Current state register using D flip-flops.

Table 1-3, corresponding to the proper outputs for each of the 10 states. Since four address lines can specify 16 memory locations, six locations of the ROM are not needed for the controller. In Table 1-3, these six unused addresses are specified as all zeros. These locations could be specified as anything because they do not affect the operation of the controller.

Next State

Notice that the D inputs in Fig. 1-13 are not connected to anything. Recall that a type D flip-flop remembers the condition of its D input at the 0-to-1 transition of its clock input. Thus, whatever signals we apply to the D inputs of Fig. 1-13 will become the new state of the controller after the clock transition. We know what this state should be from the flowchart of Fig. 1-11. The transitions from state to state are

Table 1-2 Output signal definitions

Signal abbreviation	If signal is 0	If signal is 1
NSG	NS green is off	NS green is on
NSY	NS yellow is off	NS yellow is on
NSR	NS red is off	NS red is on
EWG	EW green is off	EW green is on
EWY	EW yellow is off	EW yellow is on
EWR	EW red is off	EW red is on

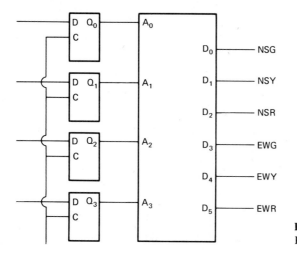

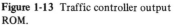

Figure 1-13 Traffic controller output ROM.

indicated by the lines and arrows connecting the states. If we are in state 3H, the line segment directed to state 4H shows us that the next state after 3H should be 4H. Whenever we have 3H as the current state on the Q outputs of the flip-flops, we should have 4H on the D inputs. The next clock transition will cause the next state to be state 4H. We can generate the next state to be applied to the D inputs by storing the next state corresponding to each current state in the ROM, as shown in Fig. 1-14. The four new ROM outputs are the next state to be remembered in the flip-flops after the clock pulse. The 4 additional bits in each ROM location are determined from the

Table 1-3 Traffic controller outputs

State				ROM address	Outputs						ROM contents
Q_3	Q_2	Q_1	Q_0		D_5	D_4	D_3	D_2	D_1	D_0	
0	0	0	0	0H	0	0	1	1	0	0	0CH
0	0	0	1	1H	0	0	1	1	0	0	0CH
0	0	1	0	2H	0	0	1	1	0	0	0CH
0	0	1	1	3H	0	0	1	1	0	0	0CH
0	1	0	0	4H	0	1	0	1	0	0	14H
0	1	0	1	5H	1	0	0	0	0	1	21H
0	1	1	0	6H	1	0	0	0	0	1	21H
0	1	1	1	7H	1	0	0	0	0	1	21H
1	0	0	0	8H	1	0	0	0	0	1	21H
1	0	0	1	9H	1	0	0	0	1	0	22H
				AH	0	0	0	0	0	0	00H
				BH	0	0	0	0	0	0	00H
				CH	0	0	0	0	0	0	00H
				DH	0	0	0	0	0	0	00H
				EH	0	0	0	0	0	0	00H
				FH	0	0	0	0	0	0	00H

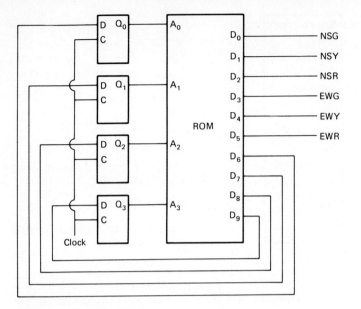

Figure 1-14 Traffic controller.

arrows in the flowchart of Fig. 1-11. If the current state is 6H, then ROM location 6H will contain the next state 0111 in bits D_9, D_8, D_7, and D_6. The next state for each current state is determined to complete the ROM contents of Table 1-4.

Table 1-4 and Fig. 1-14 represent the complete design of a digital controller to control traffic lights at a simple intersection. The controller is a sequential digital

Table 1-4 Traffic controller ROM contents

Current state ROM address	Next state				Outputs						ROM contents
	D_9	D_8	D_7	D_6	D_5	D_4	D_3	D_2	D_1	D_0	
0H	0	0	0	1	0	0	1	1	0	0	04CH
1H	0	0	1	0	0	0	1	1	0	0	08CH
2H	0	0	1	1	0	0	1	1	0	0	0CCH
3H	0	1	0	0	0	0	1	1	0	0	10CH
4H	0	1	0	1	0	1	0	1	0	0	154H
5H	0	1	1	0	1	0	0	0	0	1	1A1H
6H	0	1	1	1	1	0	0	0	0	1	1E1H
7H	1	0	0	0	1	0	0	0	0	1	221H
8H	1	0	0	1	1	0	0	0	0	1	261H
9H	0	0	0	0	1	0	0	0	1	0	022H
AH	0	0	0	0	0	0	0	0	0	0	000H
BH	0	0	0	0	0	0	0	0	0	0	000H
CH	0	0	0	0	0	0	0	0	0	0	000H
DH	0	0	0	0	0	0	0	0	0	0	000H
EH	0	0	0	0	0	0	0	0	0	0	000H
FH	0	0	0	0	0	0	0	0	0	0	000H

machine and could actually be constructed and used to control traffic. It consists of a few simple parts. A group of flip-flops storing the current state (also called the *current state register*) is sequenced to a new state every 5 s by a *clock generator* circuit. A *read-only memory* generates the appropriate *outputs* for each state as well as the *next state* that is to occur after each clock transition.

IMPLEMENTING A TRAFFIC CONTROLLER WITH INPUTS

If we attempt to implement a controller for the flowchart of Fig. 1-5, we'll first draw a flowchart with action blocks of equal time duration, as shown in Fig. 1-15. We can assign a state to each action block and store the appropriate outputs in a ROM. How-

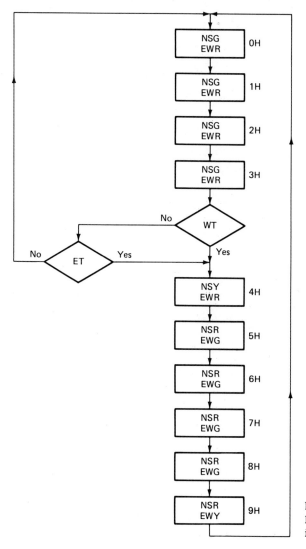

Figure 1-15 Flowchart of traffic-light controller with traffic sensor inputs.

ever, when we come to storing the next state in the ROM, a serious problem arises. The next state after state 3 is *either* state 4 or 0, depending on inputs *ET* and *WT*. The simple traffic controller previously implemented had no inputs. We didn't consider how we'd route the sequence to alternate states, depending on the condition of an input.

The next state now depends on the two inputs *ET* and *WT* as well as the current state Q_3, Q_2, Q_1, and Q_0. The next state will be easily specified for each combination of these six variables, two *inputs* and four *state variables*. By using a ROM with six address inputs, as shown in Fig. 1-16, we can look up the next state for any of the 40 possible combinations of these six digital signals (24 combinations won't occur because the state variables assume only 10 combinations rather than 16). The ROM contents of Table 1-5 are obtained directly from the flowchart of Fig. 1-15. There are four rows in the table for each current state. These four rows correspond to the four possible combinations of *WT* (A_1) and *ET* (A_0). In most cases all four rows are identical, indicating that neither the next states nor the outputs are dependent on the inputs *ET* and *WT*. Only in state 3H are any differences observed because the next state *is* a function of logic signals *ET* and *WT* whenever the controller is in state 3H.

Table 1-5 is long and cumbersome. Since many lines are identical, it seems we should be able to abbreviate this table. Table 1-6 also specifies the ROM's contents. Whenever the condition of an address or data bit doesn't matter, that bit is shown as an X and called a *don't care* bit. Most of the groups of four lines, corresponding to a

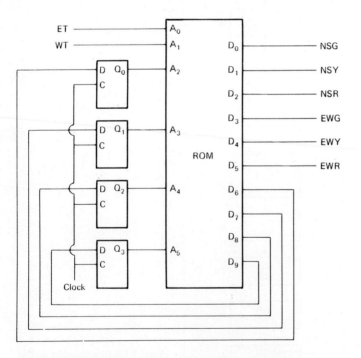

Figure 1-16 Traffic-light controller with traffic sensor inputs.

Table 1-5 ROM contents for traffic controller with traffic sensors

State				WT	ET	Next state				Outputs					
A_5	A_4	A_3	A_2	A_1	A_0	D_9	D_8	D_7	D_6	D_5	D_4	D_3	D_2	D_1	D_0
0	0	0	0	0	0	0	0	0	1	1	0	0	0	0	1
0	0	0	0	0	1	0	0	0	1	1	0	0	0	0	1
0	0	0	0	1	0	0	0	0	1	1	0	0	0	0	1
0	0	0	0	1	1	0	0	0	1	1	0	0	0	0	1
0	0	0	1	0	0	0	0	1	0	1	0	0	0	0	1
0	0	0	1	0	1	0	0	1	0	1	0	0	0	0	1
0	0	0	1	1	0	0	0	1	0	1	0	0	0	0	1
0	0	0	1	1	1	0	0	1	0	1	0	0	0	0	1
0	0	1	0	0	0	0	0	1	1	1	0	0	0	0	1
0	0	1	0	0	1	0	0	1	1	1	0	0	0	0	1
0	0	1	0	1	0	0	0	1	1	1	0	0	0	0	1
0	0	1	0	1	1	0	0	1	1	1	0	0	0	0	1
0	0	1	1	0	0	0	0	0	0	1	0	0	0	0	1
0	0	1	1	0	1	0	1	0	0	1	0	0	0	0	1
0	0	1	1	1	0	0	1	0	0	1	0	0	0	0	1
0	0	1	1	1	1	0	1	0	0	1	0	0	0	0	1
0	1	0	0	0	0	0	1	0	1	1	0	0	0	1	0
0	1	0	0	0	1	0	1	0	1	1	0	0	0	1	0
0	1	0	0	1	0	0	1	0	1	1	0	0	0	1	0
0	1	0	0	1	1	0	1	0	1	1	0	0	0	1	0
0	1	0	1	0	0	0	1	1	0	0	0	1	1	0	0
0	1	0	1	0	1	0	1	1	0	0	0	1	1	0	0
0	1	0	1	1	0	0	1	1	0	0	0	1	1	0	0
0	1	0	1	1	1	0	1	1	0	0	0	1	1	0	0
0	1	1	0	0	0	0	1	1	1	0	0	1	1	0	0
0	1	1	0	0	1	0	1	1	1	0	0	1	1	0	0
0	1	1	0	1	0	0	1	1	1	0	0	1	1	0	0
0	1	1	0	1	1	0	1	1	1	0	0	1	1	0	0
0	1	1	1	0	0	1	0	0	0	0	0	1	1	0	0
0	1	1	1	0	1	1	0	0	0	0	0	1	1	0	0
0	1	1	1	1	0	1	0	0	0	0	0	1	1	0	0
0	1	1	1	1	1	1	0	0	0	0	0	1	1	0	0
1	0	0	0	0	0	1	0	0	1	0	0	1	1	0	0
1	0	0	0	0	1	1	0	0	1	0	0	1	1	0	0
1	0	0	0	1	0	1	0	0	1	0	0	1	1	0	0
1	0	0	0	1	1	1	0	0	1	0	0	1	1	0	0
1	0	0	1	0	0	0	0	0	0	0	1	0	1	0	0
1	0	0	1	0	1	0	0	0	0	0	1	0	1	0	0
1	0	0	1	1	0	0	0	0	0	0	1	0	1	0	0
1	0	0	1	1	1	0	0	0	0	0	1	0	1	0	0
1	0	1	0	0	0	0	0	0	0	0	0	0	0	0	0
1	0	1	0	0	1	0	0	0	0	0	0	0	0	0	0
1	0	1	0	1	0	0	0	0	0	0	0	0	0	0	0
1	0	1	0	1	1	0	0	0	0	0	0	0	0	0	0

Table 1-5 ROM contents for traffic controller with traffic sensors (*Continued*)

A_5	A_4	A_3	A_2	A_1	A_0	D_9	D_8	D_7	D_6	D_5	D_4	D_3	D_2	D_1	D_0
1	0	1	1	0	0	0	0	0	0	0	0	0	0	0	0
1	0	1	1	0	1	0	0	0	0	0	0	0	0	0	0
1	0	1	1	1	0	0	0	0	0	0	0	0	0	0	0
1	0	1	1	1	1	0	0	0	0	0	0	0	0	0	0
1	1	0	0	0	0	0	0	0	0	0	0	0	0	0	0
1	1	0	0	0	1	0	0	0	0	0	0	0	0	0	0
1	1	0	0	1	0	0	0	0	0	0	0	0	0	0	0
1	1	0	0	1	1	0	0	0	0	0	0	0	0	0	0
1	1	0	1	0	0	0	0	0	0	0	0	0	0	0	0
1	1	0	1	0	1	0	0	0	0	0	0	0	0	0	0
1	1	0	1	1	0	0	0	0	0	0	0	0	0	0	0
1	1	0	1	1	1	0	0	0	0	0	0	0	0	0	0
1	1	1	0	0	0	0	0	0	0	0	0	0	0	0	0
1	1	1	0	0	1	0	0	0	0	0	0	0	0	0	0
1	1	1	0	1	0	0	0	0	0	0	0	0	0	0	0
1	1	1	0	1	1	0	0	0	0	0	0	0	0	0	0
1	1	1	1	0	0	0	0	0	0	0	0	0	0	0	0
1	1	1	1	0	1	0	0	0	0	0	0	0	0	0	0
1	1	1	1	1	0	0	0	0	0	0	0	0	0	0	0
1	1	1	1	1	1	0	0	0	0	0	0	0	0	0	0

Table 1-6 Abbreviated ROM contents

A_5	A_4	A_3	A_2	A_1	A_0	D_9	D_8	D_7	D_6	D_5	D_4	D_3	D_2	D_1	D_0
0	0	0	0	X	X	0	0	0	1	1	0	0	0	0	1
0	0	0	1	X	X	0	0	1	0	1	0	0	0	0	1
0	0	1	0	X	X	0	0	1	1	1	0	0	0	0	1
0	0	1	1	0	0	0	0	0	0	1	0	0	0	0	1
0	0	1	1	0	1	0	1	0	0	1	0	0	0	0	1
0	0	1	1	1	0	0	1	0	0	1	0	0	0	0	1
0	0	1	1	1	1	0	1	0	0	1	0	0	0	0	1
0	1	0	0	X	X	0	1	0	1	1	0	0	0	1	0
0	1	0	1	X	X	0	1	1	0	0	0	1	1	0	0
0	1	1	0	X	X	0	1	1	1	0	0	1	1	0	0
0	1	1	1	X	X	1	0	0	0	D_5	0	1	1	0	0
1	0	0	0	X	X	1	0	0	1	0	0	1	1	0	0
1	0	0	1	X	X	0	0	0	0	0	1	0	1	0	0
1	0	1	0	X	X	0	0	0	0	0	0	0	0	0	0
1	0	1	1	X	X	0	0	0	0	0	0	0	0	0	0
1	1	0	0	X	X	0	0	0	0	0	0	0	0	0	0
1	1	0	1	X	X	0	0	0	0	0	0	0	0	0	0
1	1	1	0	X	X	0	0	0	0	0	0	0	0	0	0
1	1	1	1	X	X	0	0	0	0	0	0	0	0	0	0

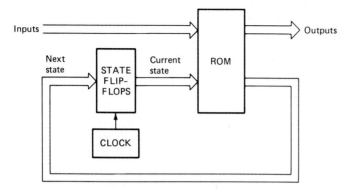

Figure 1-17 Sequential digital machine.

single state in Table 1-5, may be abbreviated as a single line in Table 1-6. The abbreviated table is useful while the design is in progress. A complete table is usually generated to program a PROM after the design has been completed.

Figure 1-16 incorporates all the features required of any digital logic circuit. Although we'll study many different approaches to logic circuits other than Fig. 1-16, they all accomplish the same function as this simple state flip-flop and ROM controller. Figure 1-17 shows a generalized diagram of a digital logic circuit. Many controller circuits are built exactly in this fashion. It is very important that you really understand the operation of this circuit before proceeding.

BLOCK DIAGRAMS

Most real digital circuits are so complex that they must be divided into simpler subcircuits. Numbers of small circuits are easier to design than one large circuit. A *block*

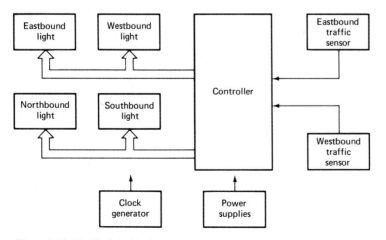

Figure 1-18 Traffic-light block diagram.

diagram shows these subcircuits (blocks) and their interconnections. Block diagrams are an aid to planning and understanding the operation of large digital systems. Even a simple system like the traffic lights has a block diagram shown in Fig. 1-18. Note that multiple signals are represented by broad lines and the number and nature of these signals have not yet been specified. The next step in the design process would be to specify these signals connecting the blocks.

The arrangement of the blocks and their interconnection is a very important part of the design process. Especially in large digital systems, *the arrangement of the block diagram will have more effect on cost and performance than the design of the circuitry in each block.* The block diagram and the algorithm design are the most creative part of designing a digital system.

THE FORMAL ALGORITHMIC STATE MACHINE

Returning to the individual circuit block, we see the digital control circuit we will use is represented by the generalized controller of Fig. 1-17 and the definitions of all its inputs and outputs. Once you decide to use the general model of the digital sequential machine for your solution and define all the inputs and outputs of that machine, you are in a position to describe the algorithm to be used as the solution to the problem. The description of the algorithm may be plain text, a flowchart, or any other convenient technique. After describing the algorithm, the actual circuit may be implemented. The implementation amounts to connecting the ROMs, flip-flops, inputs, and outputs in an appropriate manner and specifying the contents of the ROM to implement the algorithm desired.

In order to minimize design errors, we will formalize some of the techniques we've been using. First, we will formalize the notation for input and output signals. Then the flowchart notation will be more rigorously specified and the flowchart renamed the ASM chart.

Input and Output Signals

Previously, we gave input and output signals names to distinguish them from each other and to make it easy to remember what each signal did. These names are called *mnemonics.* The meaning of each output signal was defined in a table, like Table 1-2. Since this table requires additional effort to generate and must be referenced often while reading circuit drawings, we'd like to find a way to include this information in the mnemonic itself. The signal naming system we will use is the same as that used by Clare.[1] We shall put one additional letter ahead of the mnemonic. If this first letter is an *H*, the action specified by that mnemonic is performed when the associated digital signal is a 1 (high). If the first letter is an *L*, the action specified by that mnemonic occurs when the signal is a 0 (low). For example, the mnemonic *HNSG*

[1]Christopher R. Clare, *Designing Logic Systems Using State Machines*, McGraw-Hill, New York, 1973, pp. 8–9.

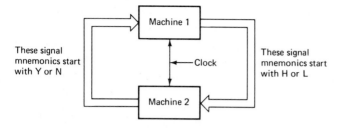

Figure 1-19 Interconnected sequential machines.

means that the north-south green light is on whenever this signal is a 1. The mnemonic *LEWG* means that the east-west green light is on whenever this signal is a 0. By adding this single letter to each output mnemonic, we are able to tell if the action occurs when the signal is a 1 or if the action occurs when the signal is a 0.

To distinguish inputs from outputs, we'll use two different letters for input signals. If an input signal mnemonic is preceded by a *Y*, the condition specified by the mnemonic is true when the signal is a 1. If the mnemonic is preceded by an *N*, the condition specified is true when the signal is a 0. For example, the mnemonic *YWT* means that there is westbound traffic present if this signal is a 1. The mnemonic *NEMER* means that the emergency button is pushed if this signal is a 0.

Now we are able to distinguish between input and output signals and, at the same time, precisely define their operation. Two more complications arise when two digital controllers are connected to each other, as shown in Fig. 1-19. Since the output of one machine is the input of the other, we obviously can't keep our input and output naming convention if each signal is to have only one name. The signals starting with *Y* or *N* will be inputs of machine 1 but outputs of machine 2. Likewise, the signals starting with *H* or *L* will be outputs of machine 1 but inputs of machine 2. This naming difficulty causes no problems because the action of the signals with respect to the two machines is well-defined.

A more important characteristic of two interconnected digital controllers is shown in Fig. 1-20. The input of machine 2, called *HRST*, is also an output of machine 1. Machine 1 makes this signal a 1 (*asserts* it) during machine 1's state 4. Note that *HRST*

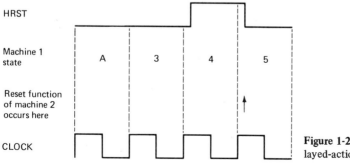

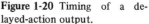

Figure 1-20 Timing of a delayed-action output.

changes a small time after the clock transition, as we've discussed previously. There-fore, *machine 2 cannot respond to this input until the next clock transition.* Thus, the function specified by the signal *HRST* will not be performed by machine 2 until machine 1 is in state 5. Although the signal *HRST* was asserted by machine 1 in state 4, the function associated with *HRST* was not performed until machine 1 reached state 5. This delayed action will occur any time the output of one sequential machine is the input to another and both machines use the same clock signal. This was not the case for the outputs of the traffic light controller. These outputs caused the traffic lights to turn on immediately. The output and the action caused by it were simul-taneous. To distinguish immediate from delayed-action outputs, we will prefix im-mediate outputs with the letter *I*. Thus, a mnemonic for the traffic light controller output would be *IHEWG*. No prefix is added for delayed-action outputs because they are usually more numerous than immediate-action outputs. The prefix *I* only makes sense on the mnemonic of an output signal.

Synchronous and Asynchronous Inputs

Since an input to an ASM (algorithmic state machine) may come from any number of sources, it may change state (0 to 1 or 1 to 0) at any time. These inputs are called asynchronous because they are not synchronized with the clock transitions of the ASM. Asynchronous inputs may cause many problems in an ASM, as will be discussed in a later chapter. To simplify the current discussion, we will assume that all inputs to our ASMs will be synchronous. That is, all inputs can only change state just after the clock transition. Any input, such as a traffic sensor, that is not inherently synchro-nized with a clock, will be assumed to have additional internal circuitry to synchronize it to the clock transitions.

ASM Charts

An ASM chart is simply a flowchart describing a sequential digital machine. ASM charts were first described by Clare.[1] An ASM chart is drawn following a set of simple but precise rules. A *state box* is drawn for each machine state, as shown in Fig. 1-21. The outputs for that state are listed inside the box. The name of the state is encircled and placed to either side of the box. This allows the state to be referenced by name even before the particular combination of state variables representing that state is

[1] Clare, *Designing Logic Systems Using State Machines*, pp. 16–19.

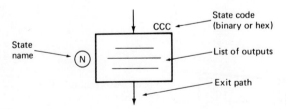

Figure 1-21 ASM state box.

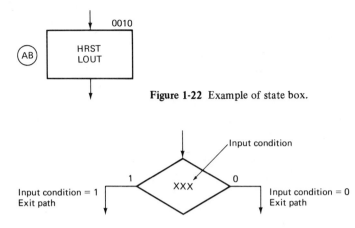

Figure 1-22 Example of state box.

Figure 1-23 Decision diamond.

assigned. This combination of state variables is called the *state code* and is written in hex or binary on top of the state box. Finally, the line drawn from the state box, indicating the path to the next state, is called the *exit path*. Figure 1-22 is an example of a state box. It shows a state named *AB*, which has outputs *HRST* and *LOUT*. The state code for this state is 0010.

ASM charts also have decision diamonds, just like flowcharts. Figure 1-23 shows a decision diamond. The input to be tested is drawn inside the diamond. The diamond exits are always marked 0 and 1. Since 0 and 1 refer to actual digital signal values, there can be no confusion arising from words such as TRUE, FALSE, YES, or NO. Note that a 1 will correspond to the true condition only if the input mnemonic begins with a *Y*. If the input mnemonic begins with an *N*, the true condition will be represented by the 0 branch.

An *ASM block* consists of a single state box and all the decision diamonds connected to its exit path. Figure 1-24 is an example of such an ASM block. Each exit path

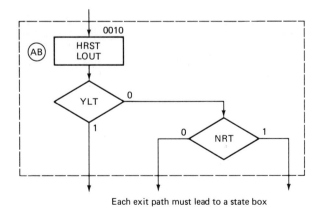

Each exit path must lead to a state box

Figure 1-24 ASM block.

must lead to a state box. Since only state boxes have a time period associated with them, *each ASM block represents a single time period or clock interval.* An ASM block shows the current state, its outputs, and the conditions for each next-state path. Thus, each ASM block completely defines all the rows of a ROM table corresponding to a single current state.

Conditional Outputs

In our previous examples, input decisions were made only to determine which of several next-state paths would be followed. In other words, only the next-state entries were different for each input combination in the ROM table. The outputs for a given current state were always the same, regardless of the inputs. This is an unnecessary restriction. The outputs of a single state could easily be made different for each input combination simply by specifying them differently for each row in the ROM table. Outputs that depend on inputs are shown on an ASM chart by a *conditional output box.* Figure 1-25 shows the symbol for a conditional output box. The line entering the box *always* comes from a decision diamond specifying the condition required for these outputs to occur. The conditional outputs are listed in the box and can cause immediate or delayed actions, just like the outputs listed in a state box.

Figure 1-26 shows an example of an ASM block with a conditional output. The output *HRST* always occurs in state *AC*; so *HRST* is listed in the state box. The output *LOUT* only occurs in state *AC* if *NRT* is 0; so *LOUT* is listed in a conditional output box in the exit path corresponding to *NRT* = 0. *Conditional output boxes have no additional time associated with them. Only state boxes have a time interval associated with them.* In the example of Fig. 1-26, the conditional output *LOUT* occurs in the same time period in which *HRST* occurs. All conditional outputs in an ASM block occur in the state time of the single state box in that block.

Let's look at three possible timing diagrams for the ASM chart of Fig. 1-26. These timing diagrams are shown in Fig. 1-27. In Fig. 1-27*a*, the input *NRT* is 1 during state *AC*. The conditional output *LOUT* is not asserted, and the next state is *AE*. *HRST* is always asserted in state *AC*. In Fig. 1-27*b*, input signal *NRT is* asserted during state *AC*. Conditional output *LOUT* will be low during state *AC*, and the next state will be *AD*.

Now, study Fig. 1-27*c*. In this timing diagram we have purposefully made *NRT* asynchronous. Changing *NRT* in the middle of state *AC* simply changes the address sent to the ROM. As soon as the ROM looks up this new address, the conditional output will change. Thus, the conditional output will also be asynchronous if it de-

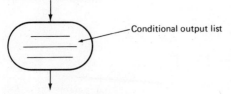

Figure 1-25 Conditional output box.

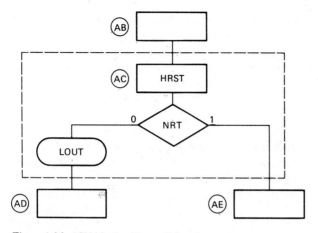

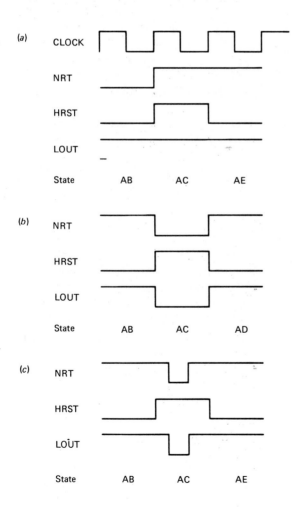

Figure 1-26 ASM block with conditional output.

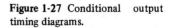

Figure 1-27 Conditional output timing diagrams.

pends on an asynchronous input. However, the transition out of state *AC* is made at the next clock transition. Since the input *NRT* has returned to a 1 by this clock transition, the next state will be *AE*. Because *NRT* was asynchronous, the machine asserted *LOUT* and went to state *AE*, even though this seems impossible from the ASM chart in Fig. 1-26.

Problems and Abbreviations

Each exit path from an ASM block leads to only one state. In addition, the decision structure of the block must not indicate two or more simultaneous exit paths for any set of inputs. Since the actual machine can only be in one state at a time, an ASM chart that specifies two next states would be meaningless. Never divide an exit into two or more paths without using a decision diamond. On occasion, it is convenient to divide an exit path for conditional outputs, as shown in Fig. 1-28. Both of the ASM blocks in Fig. 1-28 perform the same function. In each case only one next state can be specified, regardless of the inputs. The form of Fig. 1-28*a* is not recommended except for the most simple cases, like the one illustrated. Although two next states can't be simultaneously specified, two conditional outputs can be specified simultaneously. Figure 1-28*a* will work because all exit paths converge to the same next state. The form of Fig. 1-28*b* is preferred because it *ensures* that only one next state is specified and will always unambiguously specify conditional outputs in more complex charts.

Two abbreviations are commonly used in ASM charts. First, the dotted line around each ASM block is omitted. This causes no problems since an ASM block always

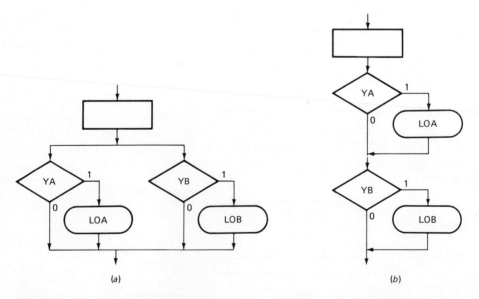

(a)   *(b)*

Figure 1-28 *(a)* Parallel paths for conditional outputs. *(b)* Series paths for conditional outputs (preferred).

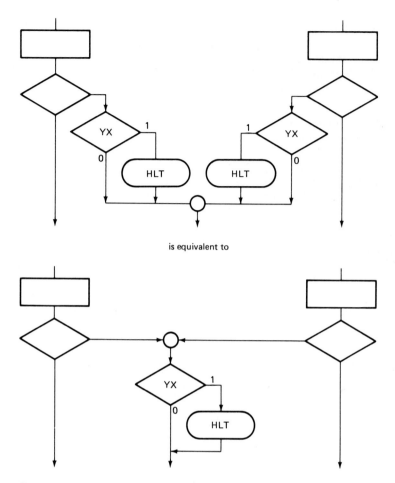

Figure 1-29 Sharing decisions and conditional outputs.

consists of a single state box and all decision diamonds and conditional output boxes in its exit paths. Second, decision diamonds and conditional output boxes may be shared among ASM blocks, as shown in Fig. 1-29. This abbreviation *does not affect the implementation* in any way. It simply reduces the amount of drawing required for the ASM chart.

DESIGN PROCEDURE FOR ASMS

The design procedure for ASMs may be summarized as follows:

1. Write a specification of the problem to be solved.
2. Translate this specification into an overall flowchart if necessary to clarify operation.

3. Develop a block diagram of the system including signal definitions.
4. Implement each block in the block diagram.
   a. Develop the algorithm for each block, either in written or flowchart form.
   b. Translate these algorithms into ASM charts.
   c. Implement the ASM charts with logic circuits.

In order to show you how all the procedures we've discussed so far fit into this framework, let's work an example following the steps outlined above.

A DESIGN EXAMPLE FOR AN AUTOMATED BANK TELLER

The problem to be solved is to design an automated bank teller that will dispense cash if a customer enters a correct account number and a correct amount. This written description corresponds to step one in the general design procedure. A simple, overall flowchart may be drawn, as shown in Fig. 1-30, to complete step 2 of the procedure. This flowchart tells us several things about the elements of the block diagram. First, since the customer must enter the account number and amount, the teller must be able to prompt the customer to enter these numbers. Thus, the block diagram of Fig. 1-31 includes three lighted messages that are used to prompt the customer. Second, the flowchart shows that not only must numbers be entered by the customer, but also that those numbers must be compared to determine their validity. Thus, the block diagram has a comparator circuit associated with the keyboard, used to enter the

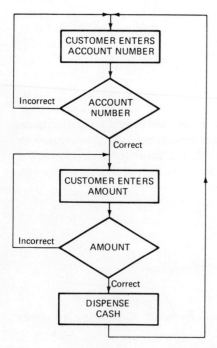

Figure 1-30 Overall flowchart for bank teller.

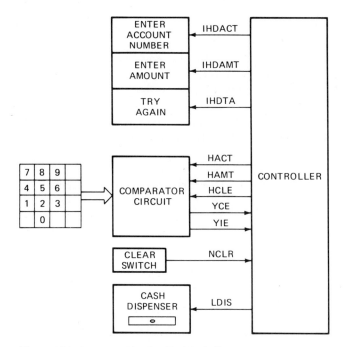

Figure 1-31 Automated bank teller block diagram.

numbers. Third, the flowchart dispenses cash, which implies that a cash dispenser must appear on the block diagram. Fourth, you should notice from the overall flowchart that the ASM could "get stuck" in the middle of a transaction if the customer fails to complete his transaction. A *CLEAR* switch is included in the block diagram so that a new customer can force the teller to start a new transaction, even if the last transaction was never completed. Finally, a controller block connects to all the other blocks to sequence the overall operation of the bank teller. This arrangement of blocks in which a controller block directs the operation of input blocks (keyboard and clear switch), output blocks (displays and cash dispenser), and processing blocks (comparator) is very common. We can complete step 3 of the general design procedure by specifying the various signals that connect the blocks together:

IHDACT. Display "Enter Account Number."
IHDAMT. Display "Enter Amount."
IHDTA. Display "Try Again."
HACT. Set comparator to accept the account.
HAMT. Set comparator to accept the amount.
YCE. A correct entry has been made.
YIE. An incorrect entry has been made.
HCLE. Resets both *YCE* and *YIE* to 0.
LDIS. Dispense the cash.
NCLR. The clear switch has been pressed.

All outputs of the controller must be continuously asserted as long as that action is desired. For example, *HAMT* must be a 1 as long as the customer is supposed to be entering the amount. If neither *YCE* nor *YIE* is asserted, no entry has been made or an entry is in progress. After a correct entry, *YCE* remains a 1. After an incorrect entry, *YIE* remains a 1. Asserting *HCLE* will reset either or both *YIE* and *YCE* to 0. The clock period is very short, say 50 ms. It is short enough that the message may be lighted simultaneously with asserting the corresponding comparator control signal. Even though the comparator control signal is delayed-action, the customer can't see the message and respond to it in such a short time as 50 ms. Now, we can proceed to step 4, which tells us to implement each block. We'll only implement one block in this example, the controller block. Figure 1-32 is a flowchart describing the algorithm to be implemented by the controller block. It is *not* an ASM chart, but merely serves as a guide to develop such a chart. We could have used a written description for the controller algorithm if it had seemed more appropriate.

The flowchart in Fig. 1-32 and the logic signal specifications given previously

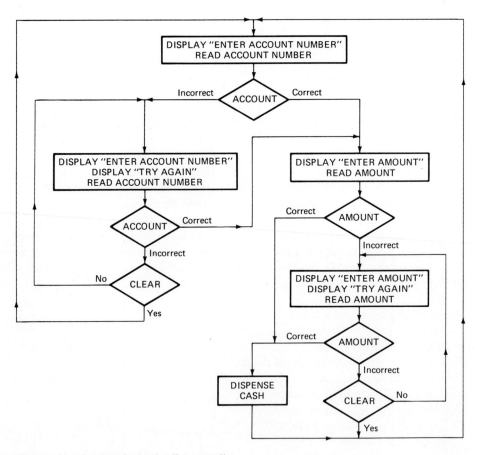

Figure 1-32 Flowchart for bank teller controller.

Table 1-7 Chart to convert algorithm to ASM chart for bank teller without conditional outputs

State	Outputs	YCE	YIE	NCLR	Next state	Comments
A Read account number	HACT, IHDACT	0 1 0	0 X 1	X X X	A C B	Display and read account number if no entry Correct entry Incorrect entry
B Try again to read account number	HACT, IHDACT IHDTA	1 0 0	X X X	X 1 0	C B D	Correct entry No entry or incorrect entry, stay here Clear switch pressed
D Clear YIE and YCE before new account number	HCLE	X	X	X	A	Extra state needed to reset YIE and YCE Reset occurs on clock edge that causes transition to state A
C Clear YIE and YCE before amount entry	HCLE	X	X	X	E	Same as state D except that read amount is next state
E Read amount	HAMT, IHDAMT	1 0 0 0	X 0 0 1	X 1 0 X	F E A G	Correct entry, go get cash Display and read amount if no entry Clear switch pressed. State D not needed because YIE = YCE = 0 Incorrect amount entered
F Dispense cash and clear YIE and YCE	LDIS, HCLE	X	X	X	A	Dispense cash and go back to get another account
G Try to read amount again	HAMT, IHDAMT IHDTA	1 0 0	X X X	X 1 0	F G D	Correct entry, dispense cash No entry or another incorrect entry Clear switch pressed

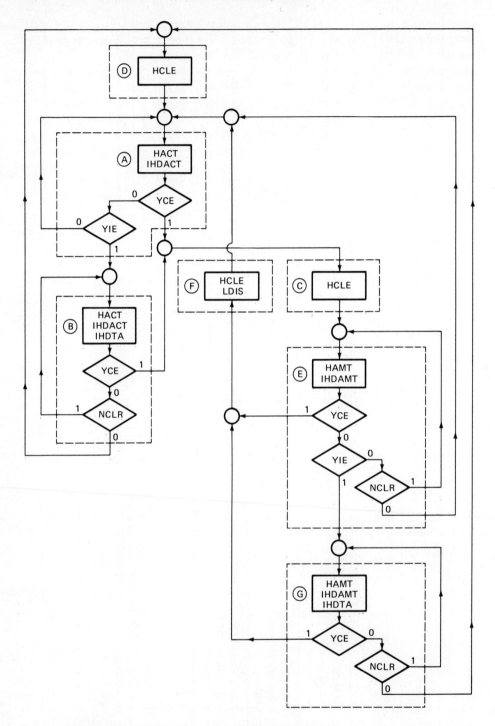

Figure 1-33 ASM chart for bank teller without conditional outputs.

must now be merged to form an ASM chart. Let's assume that we desire to implement this algorithm without conditional outputs. The thought process used in developing the ASM chart is shown in Table 1-7. We start in a state easily determined from the algorithm specification. In this case, there obviously must be an initial state to read the account number entered by the customer and it must have outputs *HACT* and *IHDACT*. Note that we are trying to *implement a sequence of outputs* required; so both state and outputs appear first in our chart. After we've listed state and outputs, we list inputs so that the next state can be determined. Although we have three inputs, all combinations need not be listed as several "don't care" conditions exist. For exam-

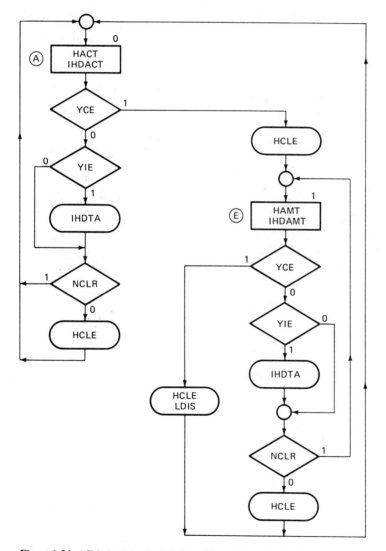

Figure 1-34 ASM chart for bank teller with conditional outputs.

ple, if $YCE = 1$, that is, a correct entry has been made, we need not worry about the clear switch or the incorrect-entry inputs. In the process of filling out the next-state information for state A, we determine a need for two additional states. State C is required for a correct entry, while state B is required for an incorrect entry. The next step is to list these new states and their outputs, which may, in turn, give rise to additional states. Eventually, no new states will be required (since an algorithm has a finite number of steps) and the chart will be finished. Table 1-7 may be immediately drawn as the ASM chart of Fig. 1-33. The intermediate step of generating Table 1-7 may not always be necessary. You may find it easier to draw only the chart of Fig. 1-33, especially if the algorithm is short and simple. Even if you draw the ASM chart directly, you still use the thought process represented by Table 1-7. Before we continue, you should notice that we needed two states C and D to do nothing but assert $HCLE$ one clock transition ahead of the state in which YIE and YCE must be reset. Since $HCLE$ is a delayed-action output, these additional states were needed to assure that the previous comparator outputs were cleared before a new decision was made.

How would the controller block change if we were to allow conditional outputs? Figure 1-34 shows the bank-teller ASM chart using conditional outputs where appropriate. Conditional output boxes were used to assert $IHDTA$ when an incorrect entry was made. The "TRY AGAIN" display will be lighted without requiring additional states. A conditional output box is also used to assert $LDIS$ when the cash is to be dispensed. Conditional output boxes were used to assert $HCLE$. In this way, the same clock transition that causes the next state to occur will also reset YCE and YIE when desired. This saves the extra states C and D in Fig. 1-33 needed to assert $HCLE$ before the comparator inputs were changed. Figure 1-35 is the timing diagram for the bank teller without conditional outputs. State C must be added to ensure that $HCLE$ is asserted one state before state E in order to reset YCE at the correct time. The timing diagram of a bank teller using conditional outputs is shown in Fig. 1-36. The input YCE can cause the conditional output $HCLE$ to occur *while still in state A*. An additional state C is not needed to ensure that YCE will be reset at the beginning of state E.

Finally, only specifying the ROM contents completes our design procedure. Figure 1-37 and Table 1-8 show the implementation of the controller with conditional

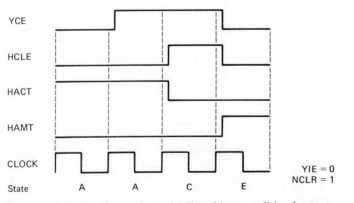

Figure 1-35 Timing diagram for bank teller without conditional outputs.

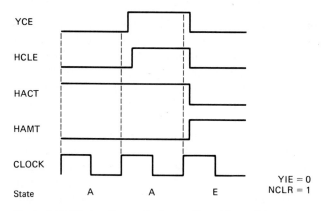

Figure 1-36 Timing diagram for bank teller with conditional outputs.

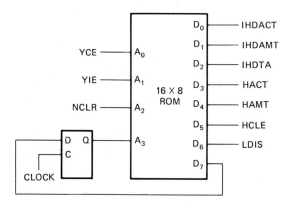

Figure 1-37 Bank teller with conditional outputs.

Table 1-8 ROM contents of bank teller with conditional outputs

Current state A_3	NCLR A_2	YIE A_1	YCE A_0	Next state D_7	LDIS D_6	HCLE D_5	HAMT D_4	HACT D_3	IHDTA D_2	IHDAMT D_1	IHDACT D_0
0	X	X	1	1	1	1	0	1	0	0	1
0	1	0	0	0	1	0	0	1	0	0	1
0	1	1	0	0	1	0	0	1	1	0	1
0	0	0	0	0	1	1	0	1	0	0	1
0	0	1	0	0	1	1	0	1	1	0	1
1	X	X	1	0	0	1	1	0	0	1	0
1	1	0	0	1	1	0	1	0	0	1	0
1	1	1	0	1	1	0	1	0	1	1	0
1	0	0	0	0	1	1	1	0	0	1	0
1	0	1	0	0	1	1	1	0	1	1	0

outputs. This example is a good illustration of the advantages of conditional outputs. The controller without conditional outputs has six states, requiring three flip-flops and a 64×10 read-only memory. The controller with conditional outputs has only two states, requiring one flip-flop and a 16×8 read-only memory!

DESIGN CRITERIA

In many respects, you now know all there is to know about designing digital circuits. The rest of this book will cover other implementation techniques used to reduce development effort or circuit cost. You now understand the basic principles of digital design, although you might have difficulty recognizing what you've learned if you immediately turned to the section of this book on microcomputers. Since the rest of this book will be devoted to "refinements" of the basic ASM, we should logically ask the question: What makes any additional technique we might learn an "improvement"? What are the criteria by which we may judge digital designs? This is a very difficult question to answer because criteria for good designs have changed over the years and are changing right now.

When all electronic components were expensive, good design techniques focused on reducing the number of components required. The Karnaugh maps of the next chapter were among many techniques developed to systematically reduce the number of components required. With the advent of the integrated circuit, the electronic components themselves were essentially "free." The cost of a system was related to packaging and interconnection costs (as well as the cost of power supplies, cooling fans, testing, and many other peripheral factors). With the advent of microcomputers and other large integrated circuits, the cost of *developing* the digital system is likely to be paramount. Our criteria for "good" digital system design will consist of only two factors (in order of importance):

1. Minimize the cost of development
2. Minimize the cost of the hardware of each system while maintaining the required level of performance

While these criteria seem obvious, their application is not always simple. For example, a large portion of the cost of development usually consists of the cost of finding mistakes in the original design (called debugging). It pays to take extra care (and spend additional time and money) with the initial design because these extra costs are more than made up by the lessened cost of debugging. This book will continually stress *systematic* design procedures, even at the expense of additional circuit cost, just to reduce design costs.

Even the hardware cost criteria are not obvious. Testing and repairing digital systems often account for a large part of hardware cost. It may pay to add additional interconnections and circuitry to reduce the cost of testing and repairing the system.

PROBLEMS

1-1 (*a*) Count in binary and hex from 0 to 31 decimal. List the binary and hex numbers equivalent to each decimal number on the same line.

(*b*) Count in two's-complement binary from −16 to +15 decimal. List the binary number equivalent to each decimal number on the same line.

1-2 Figure P1-1 shows a D flip-flop and a partial timing diagram.

(*a*) Fill in the output in the timing diagram as it would be seen on an oscilloscope.

(*b*) Make a table listing both D input and Q output as would be generated by a logic-state analyzer.

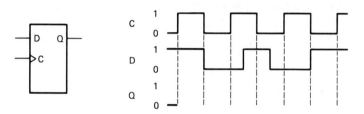

Figure P1-1 D flip-flop timing diagram.

1-3 Figure P1-2 shows a ROM and a partial timing diagram. The contents of this ROM are:

A_2	A_1	A_0	D_1	D_0
0	0	0	0	0
0	0	1	1	1
0	1	0	1	0
0	1	1	1	1
1	0	0	1	1
1	0	1	0	1
1	1	0	0	0
1	1	1	0	0

(*a*) Complete the timing diagram by filling in the outputs.

(*b*) Make a table listing only the outputs D_1 and D_0 as they would be seen on a logic-state analyzer.

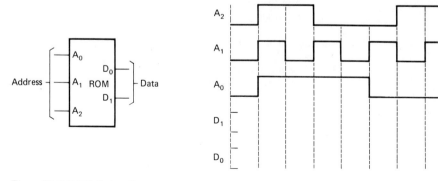

Figure P1-2 ROM timing diagram.

1-4 Consider a traffic intersection combining traffic sensors as described in Fig. 1-5 and an emergency-vehicle input as described in Fig. 1-7.

    (*a*) Draw a circuit diagram and ASM chart for this controller.

    (*b*) Make a ROM contents table and convert it to hex.

1-5 Figure P1-3 is a diagram of a very simple rapid-transit system with three stations.

    (*a*) Draw an ASM chart and circuit diagram that will move a train back and forth over the line, stopping at each station for 10 s. Track sensor inputs *A*, *B*, and *C* correspond to each station. The train must stop within 2 s of receiving a track sensor input to keep from overshooting the platform. The conductor has an override button which causes an input *NOVER* to become true whenever he wants to extend the 10-s loading delay to load more passengers. You'll use three outputs: Move East (*HEAST*), Move West (*HWEST*), and Stop Moving (*STOP*).

    (*b*) Make a complete ROM contents table for this controller.

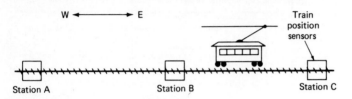

Figure P1-3 Commuter railroad.

1-6 Figure P1-4 shows a more complex rapid-transit system with an additional station (*D*) on a branch line. The train should alternate trips to *A* and *D* along the main line and branch line, respectively. Of course, it stops at *B* on each trip.

    (*a*) Draw the ASM chart and circuit diagram for this transit system, following the additional operating specifications of Prob. 1-5. Besides one additional track sensor input *D*, you'll need two more outputs *HMAIN* and *HBRANCH* to throw the switch.

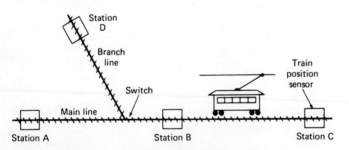

Figure P1-4 Commuter railroad with branch line.

1-7 A washing machine controller is to be constructed. The controller has the following inputs:

YHOT. 1 if hot/cold switch specifies hot water wash
NSTRT. 0 to start washing; 1 to stop, even in midcycle
YFULL. 1 if water filled to top
YEMPTY. 1 if water completely empty
YTIME. 1 if timer indicates done

    The controller must operate the following outputs:

HHOT. 1 to select hot water
     0 to select cold water

LPUMP. 0 to turn on water pump
HFILL. 1 to direct water into washer
      0 to direct water out of washer
LAG. 0 to agitate wash and start timer, set *YTIME* to 0
LSPIN. 0 to spin wash and start timer, set *YTIME* to 0

When the controller receives a start signal, it fills the washer with the correct temperature of water and agitates until the timer indicates it is done. It empties the soapy water and fills the washer with cold rinse water and agitates again until the timer indicates it is done. Finally, it spins the clothes dry after emptying the rinse water. Draw the ASM chart for this controller. Use conditional outputs.

1-8 Draw an ASM chart with correct input and output mnemonics to implement an ordinary traffic light with an emergency input. The emergency input sets both the EW and NS lights to red as before. However, when the emergency button is released, the traffic lights continue sequencing *from the state in which they were when the emergency button was pressed.* The easiest way to accomplish this is to use conditional outputs.

1-9 Design a controller with two inputs and one output. The inputs are *YA* and *YB*. The output is *HT*. This controller responds only to 0-to-1 *transitions* on its inputs. The output *HT* sets to a 1 if a 0-to-1 transition occurs on *YA*. The output resets to a 0 if a 0-to-1 transition occurs on *YB*.

TWO

BOOLEAN FUNCTIONS AND GATES

In this chapter you'll learn a different technique for generating the same logic signals that were obtained from a ROM in the last chapter. Instead of ROMs you'll use logic circuits called gates. Gates are used instead of ROMs for three reasons:

1. Gates are usually faster than ROMs and are used for highest-speed digital circuitry.
2. Gates may be less expensive than ROMs for very small ASMs.
3. Gates are often used to supplement a ROM, usually reducing the size of ROM required.

Gate circuitry is more difficult to design, more expensive to build and test, and less flexible than ROM circuitry. The operation of gates may be described by *boolean algebra*, which is the next topic we discuss.

Logical Connectives

Logical or boolean connectives are operations performed on variables which may assume the value of 0 or 1. A variable which can assume only two values is called a *boolean variable*. Since digital signals can only assume two values, you can see that we'll be able to make a one-to-one correspondence between boolean variables and digital signals.

The AND Connective

The logical *AND* connective is symbolized by a dot between the boolean variables to be ANDed:

$$A \cdot B$$

An equal sign is used to assign the value of this expression or *function* to another variable:

$$C = A \cdot B$$

The value of boolean variable C is made equal to the AND function of variables A and B. However, we still don't know the value of this function. The expression $A \cdot B$ is 1 only if *both A and B* are 1. This may be expressed in tabular form:

$$C = A \cdot B$$

C	A	B
0	0	0
0	0	1
0	1	0
1	1	1

These tables are often called *truth tables*. More than two variables may be ANDed together:

$$F = A \cdot B \cdot C$$

The value of the resulting expression is 1 only if all the variables are 1. For the example above, F is 1 only if A is 1 *and B* is 1 *and C* is 1. The AND function is often abbreviated by omitting the dots:

$$ABC = A \cdot B \cdot C$$

If a variable has more than one letter, it must be separated by parentheses if the dots are omitted:

$$(RST)BC = RST \cdot B \cdot C$$

The OR Connective

The logical *OR* connective is symbolized by a plus sign between the variables to be ORed:

$$C = A + B$$

The expression $A + B$ is a 1 if A is a 1 *or B* is a 1 *or* both A and B are 1.

$$C = A + B$$

C	A	B
0	0	0
1	0	1
1	1	0
1	1	1

More than two variables may be ORed together:

$$F = A + B + C$$

The value of the resulting expression is 1 if one or more of the variables are one. In the example above, F is 1 when *at least* one of the variables A, B, or C is 1.

Logical Inversion

Logical *inversion* is symbolized by a horizontal line drawn over the variable to be inverted:

$$C = \overline{A}$$

The above expression is read *C equals A inverted* or *C equals A bar* or *C equals not A* or *C is the complement of A*. The value of the expression is 1 when A is 0 and is 0 when A is 1.

$$C = \overline{A}$$

C	A
1	0
0	1

Complex Expressions

The logical connectives may be used together in complex expressions. Parentheses are used to group subexpressions when confusion might exist. For example, the expression

$$F = A + (B \cdot C)$$

is different from the expression

$$F = (A + B) \cdot C$$

A common abbreviation is to omit parentheses when they surround an AND connective. For example, the following are equivalent:

$$A + (B \cdot C) = A + BC$$

As an example, let's evaluate the following function:

$$F = \overline{A + BC}$$

Of course, this is an abbreviation for the expression

$$F = (\overline{A + (B \cdot C)})$$

Evaluate this expression by listing all possible combinations of the three variables A, B, and C in a table. Then, evaluate and tabulate each subexpression, starting from the innermost parentheses.

A	B	C	BC	A + BC	F
0	0	0	0	0	1
0	0	1	0	0	1
0	1	0	0	0	1
0	1	1	1	1	0
1	0	0	0	1	0
1	0	1	0	1	0
1	1	0	0	1	0
1	1	1	1	1	0

In this case, we evaluate $B \cdot C$ first, then $A + BC$ and, finally, invert $A + BC$ to get F.

Logical Expressions from Tables

Any boolean expression can be evaluated as described in the previous section. It would be much more useful to be able to find a logical expression corresponding to a given table. Since we can generate a table of ROM contents from an ASM chart, we should like to be able to write the logical expressions corresponding to each ROM data output in that table. As an example, let's use the ROM contents for the simple traffic light controller which is shown in Table 2-1. Notice that we have renamed the state variables in this table. For example, state variable A_3 is now called D. This was done to simplify writing the expressions we shall generate. There are two methods we can use to get different but equivalent expressions for each of these ROM outputs. These methods are called sum of products and product of sums.

Table 2-1 Traffic controller ROM

Current state													
A_3 D	A_2 C	A_1 B	A_0 A	D_9	D_8	D_7	D_6	D_5	D_4	D_3	D_2	D_1	D_0
0	0	0	0	0	0	0	1	0	0	1	1	0	0
0	0	0	1	0	0	1	0	0	0	1	1	0	0
0	0	1	0	0	0	1	1	0	0	1	1	0	0
0	0	1	1	0	1	0	0	0	0	1	1	0	0
0	1	0	0	0	1	0	1	0	1	0	1	0	0
0	1	0	1	0	1	1	0	1	0	0	0	0	1
0	1	1	0	0	1	1	1	1	0	0	0	0	1
0	1	1	1	1	0	0	0	1	0	0	0	0	1
1	0	0	0	1	0	0	1	1	0	0	0	0	1
1	0	0	1	0	0	0	0	1	0	0	0	1	0
1	0	1	0	0	0	0	0	0	0	0	0	0	0
1	0	1	1	0	0	0	0	0	0	0	0	0	0
1	1	0	0	0	0	0	0	0	0	0	0	0	0
1	1	0	1	0	0	0	0	0	0	0	0	0	0
1	1	1	0	0	0	0	0	0	0	0	0	0	0
1	1	1	1	0	0	0	0	0	0	0	0	0	0

Canonical Sum of Products

One boolean expression represents one output of the ROM. In Table 2-2, we've listed the state variables and ROM output D_7 for which we intend to find a logical expression. The expression we will find is called a *canonical sum of products* (SOP), although it has nothing to do with ordinary arithmetic. We start by finding each row in which the output D_7 is a 1. There are four such rows. For each of these rows, we write the AND expression of *all* four input variables that is 1 for that row. For example, the row corresponding to state 2 has an output of 1 for D_7. The variables in that row have the values $D = 0$, $C = 0$, $B = 1$, and $A = 0$. Thus, the AND expression that is 1 for that set of variables' values is:

$$\overline{D} \cdot \overline{C} \cdot B \cdot \overline{A}$$

Note that this expression is 1 for this particular combination of variables' values and *only* for this combination. Since there are four 1s in the D_7 column, we find four AND expressions, as shown in Table 2-3. These expressions are:

$$\overline{D} \cdot \overline{C} \cdot \overline{B} \cdot A$$
$$\overline{D} \cdot \overline{C} \cdot B \cdot \overline{A}$$
$$\overline{D} \cdot C \cdot \overline{B} \cdot A$$
$$\overline{D} \cdot C \cdot B \cdot \overline{A}$$

Each of these expressions will evaluate to a 1 only for that combination of input variable values corresponding to one of the four rows in which D_7 is a 1. You can see we've written four AND expressions each of which generates a single 1 output of D_7. Since we want a *single* expression whose output is 1 whenever *any* of these 4 individual

Table 2-2 Sum of products for D_7

D	C	B	A	D_7	AND function
0	0	0	0	0	
0	0	0	1	1	$\overline{D}\overline{C}\overline{B}A$
0	0	1	0	1	$\overline{D}\overline{C}B\overline{A}$
0	0	1	1	0	
0	1	0	0	0	
0	1	0	1	1	$\overline{D}C\overline{B}A$
0	1	1	0	1	$\overline{D}CB\overline{A}$
0	1	1	1	0	
1	0	0	0	0	
1	0	0	1	0	
1	0	1	0	0	
1	0	1	1	0	
1	1	0	0	0	
1	1	0	1	0	
1	1	1	0	0	
1	1	1	1	0	

$$D_7 = \overline{D}\overline{C}\overline{B}A + \overline{D}\overline{C}B\overline{A} + \overline{D}C\overline{B}A + \overline{D}CB\overline{A}$$

**Table 2-3 All SOP expressions for
traffic controller**

$$D_9 = \overline{D}CBA + D\overline{C}\overline{B}\overline{A}$$
$$D_8 = \overline{D}C\overline{B}A + \overline{D}C\overline{B}\overline{A} + \overline{D}CB\overline{A} + \overline{D}CB\overline{A}$$
$$D_7 = \overline{D}\overline{C}\overline{B}A + \overline{D}\overline{C}B\overline{A} + \overline{D}CBA + \overline{D}CB\overline{A}$$
$$D_6 = \overline{D}\overline{C}B\overline{A} + \overline{D}C\overline{B}\overline{A} + \overline{D}C\overline{B}\overline{A} + \overline{D}CB\overline{A} + D\overline{C}\overline{B}\overline{A}$$
$$D_5 = \overline{D}\overline{C}B\overline{A} + \overline{D}C\overline{B}\overline{A} + \overline{D}CB\overline{A} + D\overline{C}\overline{B}\overline{A} + D\overline{C}\overline{B}\overline{A}$$
$$D_4 = \overline{D}C\overline{B}\overline{A}$$
$$D_3 = \overline{D}\overline{C}\overline{B}\overline{A} + \overline{D}\overline{C}B\overline{A} + \overline{D}C\overline{B}\overline{A} + \overline{D}CB\overline{A}$$
$$D_2 = \overline{D}\overline{C}\overline{B}\overline{A} + \overline{D}\overline{C}B\overline{A} + \overline{D}CB\overline{A} + \overline{D}C\overline{B}\overline{A} + \overline{D}CB\overline{A}$$
$$D_1 = D\overline{C}\overline{B}\overline{A}$$
$$D_0 = \overline{D}\overline{C}\overline{B}A + \overline{D}C\overline{B}\overline{A} + \overline{D}CBA + D\overline{C}\overline{B}\overline{A}$$

expressions is a 1, we will simply OR all four expressions together. Remember that an OR function is a 1 whenever any of its variables is a 1. We can now write the logical expression for D_7:

$$D_7 = \overline{D}\overline{C}\overline{B}A + \overline{D}\overline{C}B\overline{A} + \overline{D}CBA + \overline{D}CB\overline{A}$$

This expression is a 1 for the four input variable combinations for which D_7 should be a 1 and is a 0 otherwise. We can write SOP expressions for each of the 10 ROM outputs, as shown in Table 2-3.

Canonical Product of Sums

Another expression we can find from a truth table is the *canonical product of sums* (POS). To find the POS expression, we find all rows in the table that are 0 (rather than 1 as we did for SOP). Next we find the OR function that evaluates to 0 for each input combination for which D_7 is 0. This is shown in Table 2-4. For example, D_7 is 0 for the variable combination $D = 0$, $C = 1$, $B = 0$, and $A = 0$. The OR expression of all four variables that is 0 for these variables' values is:

$$D + \overline{C} + B + A$$

This expression is 0 for this combination of variables' values and only for this combination. We find a similar expression for each row in which D_7 is 0. Now we have 12 expressions, each of which is 0 for a single row of the table for D_7. Since we need a *single* expression which is 0 whenever any of these 12 expressions is 0, we simply AND the 12 expressions together, as shown in Table 2-4. You'll notice that, although this POS expression is equivalent to the SOP expression, it is much more complex. This is because the function D_7 has many more 0s than 1s.

Several techniques can be used to reduce the complexity of logical expressions. In this chapter we will examine *boolean identities* and *Karnaugh maps* (K maps).

Table 2-4 Product of sums for D_7

D	C	B	A	D_7	OR function
0	0	0	0	0	$D + C + B + A$
0	0	0	1	1	
0	0	1	0	1	
0	0	1	1	0	$D + C + \overline{B} + \overline{A}$
0	1	0	0	0	$D + \overline{C} + B + A$
0	1	0	1	1	
0	1	1	0	1	
0	1	1	1	0	$D + \overline{C} + \overline{B} + \overline{A}$
1	0	0	0	0	$\overline{D} + C + B + A$
1	0	0	1	0	$\overline{D} + C + B + \overline{A}$
1	0	1	0	0	$\overline{D} + C + \overline{B} + A$
1	0	1	1	0	$\overline{D} + C + \overline{B} + \overline{A}$
1	1	0	0	0	$\overline{D} + \overline{C} + B + A$
1	1	0	1	0	$\overline{D} + \overline{C} + B + \overline{A}$
1	1	1	0	0	$\overline{D} + \overline{C} + \overline{B} + A$
1	1	1	1	0	$\overline{D} + \overline{C} + \overline{B} + \overline{A}$

$$D_7 = (D + C + B + A)(D + C + \overline{B} + \overline{A})(D + \overline{C} + B + A)(D + \overline{C} + \overline{B} + \overline{A})$$
$$(\overline{D} + C + B + A)(\overline{D} + C + B + \overline{A})(\overline{D} + C + \overline{B} + A)(\overline{D} + C + \overline{B} + \overline{A})$$
$$(\overline{D} + \overline{C} + B + A)(\overline{D} + \overline{C} + B + \overline{A})(\overline{D} + \overline{C} + \overline{B} + A)(\overline{D} + \overline{C} + \overline{B} + \overline{A})$$

BOOLEAN IDENTITIES

Boolean expressions may be simplified by a formal algebra. Boolean algebra is described by Hill and Peterson.[1] Rather than proceed with a similar, rigorous treatment of boolean algebra, we will present several important boolean identities and demonstrate their use. Important boolean identities are summarized in Table 2-5. Any of these identities may be proved correct by evaluating the expressions on both sides of the equal sign for all possible variable combinations. You'll notice that the identities are arranged in two columns. Identities opposite each other are called *duals*. That is, one identity may be derived from the other by exchanging AND and OR symbols, and 0s and 1s.

According to the distributive laws in Table 2-5, boolean expressions may be factored in two ways. The first way seems familiar because it is analogous to arithmetic factoring (as if the symbols + and · stood for addition and multiplication):

$$A \cdot (B + C) = (A \cdot B) + (A \cdot C)$$

The second way seems unfamiliar since it would not be correct if we interpreted the symbols + and · as arithmetic rather than as logical connectives:

$$A + (B \cdot C) = (A + B) \cdot (A + C)$$

[1] Fredrick J. Hill and Gerald R. Peterson, *Switching Theory and Logical Design*, 2d ed., John Wiley & Sons, New York, 1974, chap. 4.

Table 2-5 Boolean identities

Identities involving one variable

$\overline{(\overline{A})} = A$	$\overline{(\overline{A})} = A$
$A + 0 = A$	$A \cdot 1 = A$
$A + 1 = 1$	$A \cdot 0 = 0$
$A + A = A$	$A \cdot A = A$
$A + \overline{A} = 1$	$\overline{A} \cdot A = 0$

Commutative, associative, and distributive laws

$A + B = B + A$	$AB = BA$
$A + B + C = (A + B) + C = A + (B + C)$	$ABC = (AB)\,C = A\,(BC)$
$(AB) + (AC) = A\,(B + C)$	$(A + B)\,(A + C) = A + (BC)$

Identities involving two or more variables

$A + (AB) = A$	$A\,(A + B) = A$
$(A + \overline{B})\,B = AB$	$(A\overline{B}) + B = A + B$
$AB + \overline{A}C + BC = AB + \overline{A}C$	$(A + B)\,(\overline{A} + C)\,(B + C) = (A + B)\,(\overline{A} + C)$

De Morgan's laws

$\overline{(A + B + C \cdots)} = \overline{A} \cdot \overline{B} \cdot \overline{C} \cdot \ldots$	$\overline{ABC \cdots} = \overline{A} + \overline{B} + \overline{C} + \cdots$

Using the first form above, the SOP expression for D_7 may be written as

$$D_7 = \overline{DC}\,(\overline{B}A + B\overline{A}) + \overline{D}C\,(\overline{B}A + B\overline{A})$$

Notice we still have a common factor and can apply the first form of factoring twice to get

$$D_7 = (\overline{DC} + \overline{D}C)\,(\overline{B}A + B\overline{A})$$
$$= \overline{D}\,(\overline{C} + C)\,(\overline{B}A + B\overline{A})$$

From Table 2-5, we know that $\overline{C} + C$ is always 1, so that

$$D_7 = \overline{D} \cdot 1 \cdot (\overline{B}A + B\overline{A})$$

Now 1 ANDed with any variable is just that variable so that

$$D_7 = \overline{D}\,(\overline{B}A + B\overline{A})$$

As you might expect, considerable practice is required to determine which identities to use to reduce a complex boolean expression. Also, several different but equivalent reductions might be possible. For these reasons, formal boolean manipulations are usually used for quick reduction of simple expressions. More systematic methods are used for complex expressions. One useful systematic method is the Karnaugh map.

KARNAUGH MAPS

Examine the logical expression

$$\overline{A}BC + \overline{A}B\overline{C}$$

Note that it can be factored into

$$\overline{A}B\,(C + \overline{C})$$

which is simply reduced to

$$\overline{A}B$$

In other words, we have been able to eliminate the variable C entirely and combine two terms into one. We were able to eliminate the variable C because all the other variables *except* C were identical in both terms. We could factor out all the identical variables and find a $C + \overline{C}$ term remaining.

An analogous situation exists for the logical expression

$$(\overline{A} + B + C)\,(\overline{A} + B + \overline{C})$$

which can be factored to

$$(\overline{A} + B) + C \cdot \overline{C}$$

From Table 2-5, we note that $C \cdot \overline{C}$ is always 0, and 0 ORed with any variable is simply that variable. Then, this expression can be reduced to

$$(\overline{A} + B)$$

We've again been able to eliminate one variable completely because the original two terms differed in only one variable.

Karnaugh maps (K maps) are figures on which boolean expressions may be plotted. K maps are arranged so that terms that differ by only a single variable are plotted adjacently. We showed above that terms that differ in only one variable may be combined and the differing variable eliminated. We will find that, because adjacent terms on a K map differ by only one variable, simplified expressions may be written directly from these maps. The K maps for two, three, four, and five variables are shown in Figs. 2-1, 2-2, 2-3, and 2-4, respectively. Each square is given a decimal number corresponding to a specific combination of variable values, as listed in each figure. In addition, a bracket and letter denote those areas of the map where a particular variable is 1. For example, in Fig. 2-3, the B and bracket denote that the variable B is a 1 in squares 3, 2, 7, 6, 15, 14, 11, and 10. The variable B is a zero in the remaining squares. As a convention in this book, we'll use the first occurring letter of the alphabet as the least significant variable on a K map. That is, the binary number formed by a particular combination of the variables $DCBA$ corresponds to the decimal numbers used on the

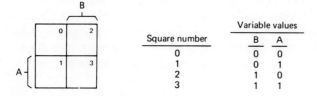

Figure 2-1 Two-variable Karnaugh map.

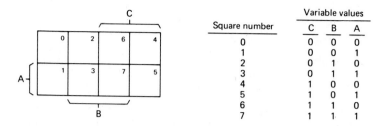

Square number	Variable values		
	C	B	A
0	0	0	0
1	0	0	1
2	0	1	0
3	0	1	1
4	1	0	0
5	1	0	1
6	1	1	0
7	1	1	1

Figure 2-2 Three-variable Karnaugh map.

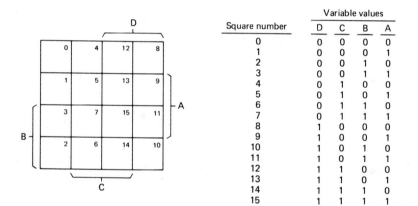

Square number	Variable values			
	D	C	B	A
0	0	0	0	0
1	0	0	0	1
2	0	0	1	0
3	0	0	1	1
4	0	1	0	0
5	0	1	0	1
6	0	1	1	0
7	0	1	1	1
8	1	0	0	0
9	1	0	0	1
10	1	0	1	0
11	1	0	1	1
12	1	1	0	0
13	1	1	0	1
14	1	1	1	0
15	1	1	1	1

Figure 2-3 Four-variable Karnaugh map.

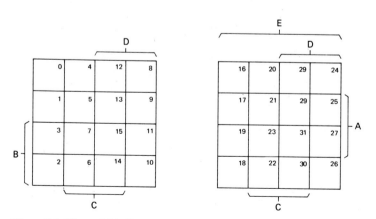

Figure 2-4 Five-variable Karnaugh map.

maps. If $DCBA = 1101$, that variable combination corresponds to square 13 on the K map. We'll use this four-variable K map as an example from here on. Adjacent squares on the map differ by only one variable. Thus, squares 7 and 3 differ only in variable C, squares 7 and 5 in variable B, squares 7 and 15 in variable D, and squares 7 and 6 in variable A. Diagonals are *not* considered adjacent and differ by more than one variable. Thus, squares 7 and 13 are *not* adjacent as they differ in both variables B and D. Squares along the edges of the map are also adjacent to the square along the opposite edge. Thus, square 1 is adjacent to square 9 besides 0, 5, and 3. Also, square 2 is adjacent to squares 0 and 10, as well as 3 and 6.

Using the K Map

Let's use function D_7 from Table 2-1 as an example. We'll enter a 1 into each square on a K map where the function D_7 happens to be 1. That is, each square corresponding to a variable combination that should make D_7 a 1 will have a 1 marked in it, as shown in Fig. 2-5. Since squares 1 and 5 each have a 1 in them and are adjacent, we know that the AND expressions for these 1s will differ by only a single variable. We'll circle these adjacent 1s to indicate that we should be able to combine these terms into a single AND expression with one less variable. Similarly, we'll do the same to squares 2 and 6. Now we can write a reduced expression simply by reading it off the K map! Squares 1 and 5 tell us that D_7 should be 1 if $B = 0$ (both squares are outside the B bracketed area), if $A = 1$ (both squares are inside the A bracketed area), and if $D = 0$ (both squares are outside the D bracketed area). The AND expression that is a 1 for this combination of variable values is:

$$A\bar{B}\bar{D}$$

Note that the variable C does not appear because the area circled (squares 1 and 5) is half inside and half outside of the area bracketed by C. The circle around squares 2 and 6 represents the term

$$\bar{A}\bar{B}\bar{D}$$

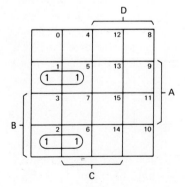

Figure 2-5 Karnaugh map for traffic light D_7.

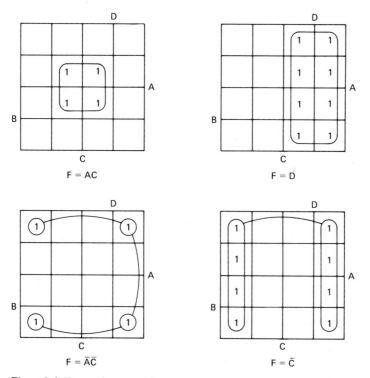

Figure 2-6 Karnaugh maps with groups having more than two terms.

These expressions are ORed together to generate a function that is 1 whenever any of the AND expressions is 1. This is the reduced SOP expression for D_7:

$$D_7 = \overline{A}B\overline{D} + A\overline{B}\overline{D}$$

K maps are even more versatile. Any group of *four* mutually adjacent squares can be combined into one term with two-fewer variables, any group of *eight* mutually adjacent squares into one term with three-fewer variables, etc. Figure 2-6 shows some examples of combining more than two squares. In each case, the boolean expression may be read from the K map by analyzing the circled areas. If the circled area is completely contained in the area bracketed by a variable, that variable will appear in the AND expression. If the circled area is completely outside an area bracketed by a variable, that variable will appear complemented in the AND expression. If a circled area overlaps areas bracketed and not bracketed by a variable, that variable will not appear in the AND expression.

K-Map Product of Sums

The result obtained in the example above was a sum-of-products representation. A product-of-sums representation can be obtained by plotting the 0s on the K map,

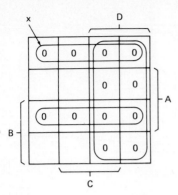

Figure 2-7 Product of sums Karnaugh map for D_7.

rather than the 1s of the function. Figure 2-7 shows the 0s of D_7 plotted and adjacent 0s circled in groups. Note that we've circled each 0 at least once and four of the 0s are in two groups. We wanted to circle as large a group as we possibly could to eliminate the most variables and have the fewest terms. It doesn't hurt to circle a square twice; if two terms of the function are 0, the function will still be 0. Likewise, we may circle 1s twice on a SOP map if it is advantageous to do so.

The group of 0s marked X in Fig. 2-17 tells us that we need an OR function that is 0 whenever $B = 0$ and $A = 0$. This function is:

$$A + B$$

Note that C and D do not appear because this group overlaps both the $C = 0$ and $C = 1$ areas and the $D = 0$ and $D = 1$ areas. Be careful to notice that in the POS solution, a 0 group *inside* a variable area causes that variable to appear in the expression *with* an inversion. This is exactly opposite to the SOP solution, in which a 1 group appearing *inside* a variable area causes that variable to appear *without* an inversion. Complete the expressions for the remaining two groups, and AND them together to get a function that is zero whenever any OR expression is zero. This is the reduced POS expression for D_7:

$$D_7 = (A + B)(\overline{A} + \overline{B})(\overline{D})$$

This is much simpler than the original POS expression for D_7 which had 12 terms, each having four variables.

The Best K Map

Often there are several ways to circle K-map groups. Each way may be equally acceptable, subject to a few rules:

1. Every term must be circled at least once, even if it is the only term in the circle, as shown in Fig. 2-8.
2. Circled groups must contain 2, 4, 8, 16, etc., terms that are mutually adjacent. Some *incorrect* groups are shown in Fig. 2-9.

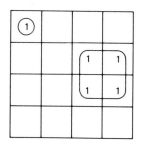

Figure 2-8 Karnaugh map with a group having only one term.

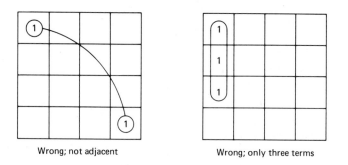

Wrong; not adjacent   Wrong; only three terms

Figure 2-9 Karnaugh maps with incorrect groups.

3. Circled groups should be as large as possible, as shown in Fig. 2-10, even if a term must be in more than one group.
4. Once all the terms are circled in as large a group as possible, do not add additional groups, as shown in Fig. 2-11.

A good starting point is to circle all terms for which only one choice of group exists.

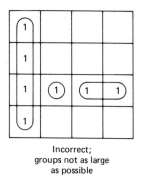

Incorrect;
groups not as large
as possible

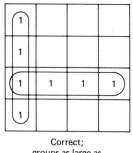

Correct;
groups as large as
possible even if terms
are circled twice

Figure 2-10 Karnaugh map group size.

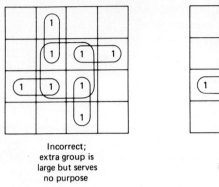

Incorrect;
extra group is
large but serves
no purpose

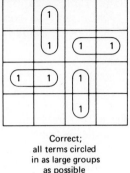

Correct;
all terms circled
in as large groups
as possible

Figure 2-11 Redundant group.

Don't Cares on K Maps

You'll remember that, in the traffic controller of Table 2-1, all states were not used. States AH to FH weren't required to implement the traffic light. We arbitrarily assigned the contents of the ROM words associated with these states to be 0s. These table entries are really don't cares, and not 0s, and should be entered on the K map as don't cares. Don't cares are represented by the letter X on a K map. This is shown in Fig. 2-12 for D_7. Since we really don't care what these values are, we will assign values to them so that we can enlarge existing groups on the K map.

In Fig. 2-12, we will assign the value 1 to boxes 14 and 10 so that we can expand the bottom group to include four terms. This will eliminate an additional variable from one AND expression. We'll leave the don't cares in boxes 12, 13, and 15 as 0s; so we need not add additional groups to include them. We don't actually change the X's on the map. We just know that we can add them to groups when convenient (10 and 14), but also can leave them uncircled when convenient (12, 13, and 15). The expression for D_7 in Fig. 2-12 is the same as that for D_7 in Fig. 2-5 for those input combinations that are actually used by the traffic light controller. These expressions are *not* equivalent for input combinations 10 and 14.

$$D_7 = A\overline{B}\overline{D} + \overline{A}B$$

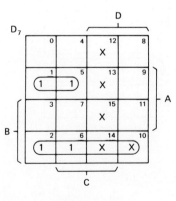

Figure 2-12 Karnaugh map don't cares.

Now we can derive boolean expressions from tables and use K maps to reduce those expressions. However, reduced boolean expressions are little use to us unless we can implement them with logic circuits. We could have simply stored the original table in a ROM.

GATES

Logic circuits exist that implement boolean connectives. In fact, the three basic connectives we've used are available as integrated circuits. The *AND gate* generates a logic signal output that is a 1 only if all its inputs are 1s. The *OR gate* generates a logic signal output that is a 1 whenever one or more of its inputs are a 1. The *inverter* generates a 1 output whenever its single input is a 0 and a 0 output whenever its input is a 1. The symbols for these circuits are shown in Fig. 2-13. Just as the AND and OR connectives could be applied to more than two inputs, AND and OR gates can have two or more inputs. Electrical, physical, and economic factors restrict the number of inputs available on a single gate. For one common logic family, 13 inputs are available on one gate, but two, three, and four input gates are much more common. The number of inputs of a gate is called the *fan in*.

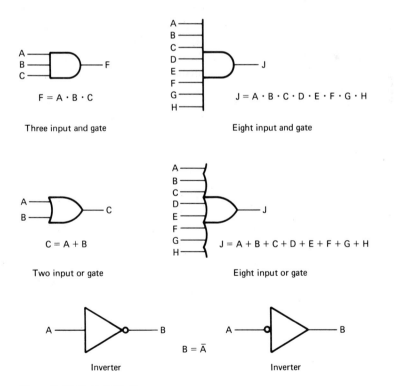

Figure 2-13 Gate symbols.

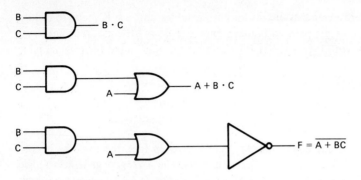

Figure 2-14 Implementing logical expressions with gates.

Gates and inverters can be used to implement logical expressions directly. Consider the expression

$$F = \overline{(A + (BC))}$$

Just as when evaluating logical expressions, we start implementing boolean expressions from the innermost parentheses. In this case, the function BC is implemented first with an AND gate, as shown in Fig. 2-14. Next, this BC output is connected to an OR gate, along with A, to form $A + BC$. Finally, an inverter forms the complement of the output of the OR gate to generate the desired function. Figure 2-15 shows another example. Note several important techniques used in this diagram. First, the inverters for the input variables are drawn to the side to make the drawing more readable. Each inverter output is labeled to indicate to what inputs on the diagram it is connected. Second, even though $\overline{D}$ is used twice, only one inverter is needed as its output may be connected to two inputs. A single output may be connected to several inputs; the maximum number of inputs is specified by the fan out of the logic circuit family. Usually 10 or more inputs may be connected to a single output. Third, two functions F and G are generated. They share a common term $\overline{A}B$, which need be implemented only once.

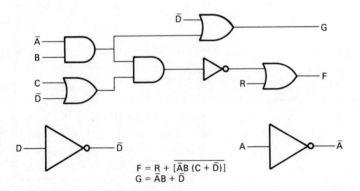

$$F = R + [\overline{A}B (C + \overline{D})]$$
$$G = \overline{A}B + \overline{D}$$

Figure 2-15 Gate-realization example.

Gate Implementation of a ROM

Since our logical expressions originally were obtained from a ROM table, a gate realization of these expressions should work the same as the ROM specified by the original table. Consider the ROM specified by Table 2-1. To implement this table with gates, draw the K maps corresponding to each of the 10 functions. Each function corresponds to one of the ROM outputs D_0 to D_9. Reduce the K maps using either SOP or POS. The K maps are shown in Fig. 2-16. The SOP functions are:

$$D_9 = ABC\overline{D} + \overline{A}\overline{B}\overline{C}D$$

$$D_8 = AB\overline{C}\overline{D} + \overline{A}C\overline{D} + \overline{B}C\overline{D}$$

$$D_7 = A\overline{B}\overline{D} + \overline{A}B\overline{D}$$

$$D_6 = \overline{A}D + \overline{A}\overline{B}\overline{C}$$

$$D_5 = BC\overline{D} + AC\overline{D} + \overline{B}\overline{C}D$$

$$D_4 = \overline{A}BC\overline{D}$$

$$D_3 = \overline{C}\overline{D}$$

$$D_2 = \overline{C}\overline{D} + \overline{A}B\overline{D}$$

$$D_1 = A\overline{B}\overline{C}D$$

$$D_0 = BC\overline{D} + AC\overline{D} + \overline{A}\overline{B}CD$$

Draw the gate realizations, shown in Fig. 2-17, corresponding to each of these reduced expressions. Since the gate realization of Fig. 2-17 should behave identically to the ROM, we should be able to connect the gates to inputs, outputs, and flip-flops, as shown in Fig. 2-18, to implement a traffic light controller. The ROM and gate realizations are identical for all input combinations that are actually used. Unused input combinations had 0 outputs in the ROM realization. Unused input combinations could have been specified as don't cares and assigned a value of either 0 or 1, as convenient, in the gate realization. If we had used don't cares, these two "equivalent" circuits would *not* behave identically if a combination of unused state variables were to accidentally occur.

Designing a gate implementation requires many more steps than designing an equivalent ROM implementation. In addition, many logic circuits need to be interconnected in the gate implementation, while only a single ROM circuit may be all that is needed in the alternate implementation. Then, why should gate implementations be used? Several factors enter into this decision. Some are tabulated in Table 2-6. Often, cost is most important. Especially for very simple circuits, a gate realization may be less expensive than a ROM. Computing cost is very difficult and must include fabrication, power supply, cooling, testing, and other costs that are attributable to each implementation. These associated costs may vary widely and are often quite large in relation to the cost of the logic circuits themselves. For this reason, comparing parts costs alone is not sufficient.

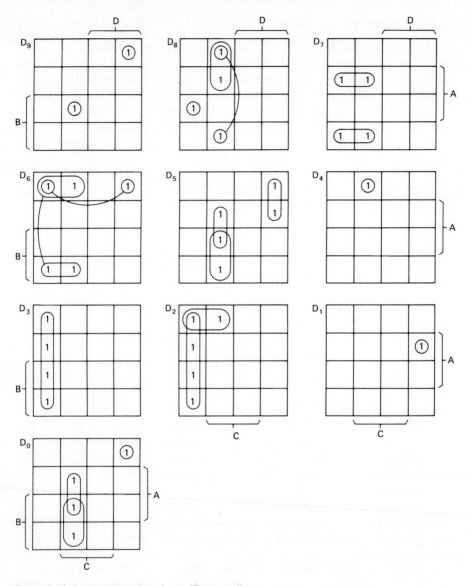

Figure 2-16 Reduced functions for traffic controller.

Trends in most factors affecting the choice between gate and ROM realizations are favoring the use of ROMs. However, gates are often used in conjunction with ROMs to reduce the cost of the ROM-implemented circuit. Gates may be used to reduce the number of ROM outputs required. This is especially important since the number of ROM outputs available is often a multiple of 4 or 8. Thus, a ROM implementation requiring 10 outputs often must be implemented with a 12- or even 16-output ROM. We've seen that the size, and cost, of a ROM are strongly related to the

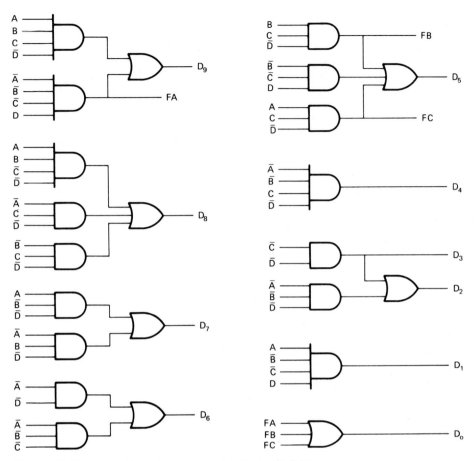

Figure 2-17 Gate realizations of logic expressions for traffic light.

number of inputs or address lines. Eliminating only one address input of a ROM will reduce the size of the ROM by half. Later, we will learn how to use gates to reduce both the number of address inputs and the number of data outputs required of a ROM.

Symbology and Graphical Techniques

A small circle like that used in the inverter symbol may be appended to any logic circuit symbol's input or output. The new circuit performs a new function. The input or output with the circle (called an *inversion bubble*) behaves as if an inverter were connected to that signal. Figure 2-19 shows some examples of this notation. Also, the type D flip-flop shown has an additional output called $\overline{Q}$. Many flip-flops have the complement of the output signal Q available. This often eliminates an additional external inverter. In order to implement a circuit with available parts, it is often necessary to move, add, or delete inverters or inversion bubbles, as shown in Fig. 2-20.

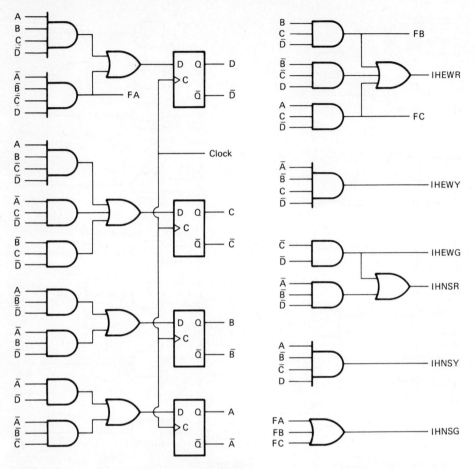

Figure 2-18 Complete traffic-light controller using gates.

In Fig. 2-20a, an inversion bubble is moved from a gate output to a gate input (or vice-versa), without changing the function F which is generated. As long as one inversion occurs between the AND gate output and the OR gate input connected to it, the function F will remain the same. However, the intermediate variable available on the wire connecting the two gates will change, as shown in the drawing.

Table 2-6 ROM vs gate implementation

	ROM	Gate
Design	Simple	Complex
Fabrication	Easy	Difficult
Maintenance	Easy	Difficult
Cost	May be more	May be less
Speed	May be slower	May be faster

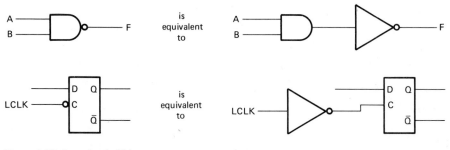

Figure 2-19 Inversion bubbles.

Since a logic variable inverted twice is simply that same original variable, we may add or delete *two* inversions at a time in any logic connection without changing circuit operation. Figure 2-20*b* shows two circuits for generating the function *G* that differ only by a double inversion. Although the function *G* remains unchanged, the intermediate variable *is* different. Finally, anything we've been doing with inversion bubbles may also be done with inverters, as shown in Fig. 2-20*c*.

Two common logic circuits are NAND and NOR gates, as shown in Fig. 2-21. These combinations of an AND and of an OR gate with inverters connected to their outputs are so common that they've been given special names: NAND and NOR gates, respectively. In fact, logic circuits fabricated with this integral inverter are more common than simple AND or OR gates.

Often, it is useful to use an AND gate instead of an OR gate, or vice-versa. For example, it may be desirable to use all of one type of gate to minimize parts stocking

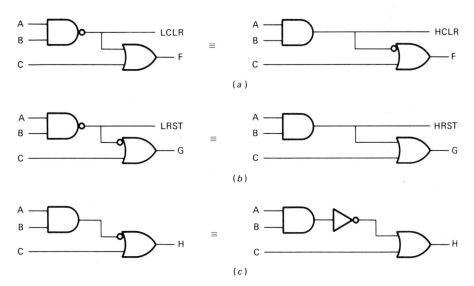

Figure 2-20 (*a*) Moving inversion bubbles. (*b*) Adding/deleting inversion bubbles. (*c*) Adding/deleting inverters.

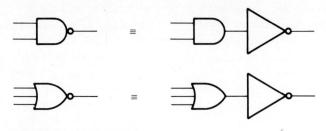

Figure 2-21 NAND and NOR gates.

requirements or simplify assembly or maintenance. Two boolean identities, called *De Morgan's laws*, allow us to substitute AND for OR gates, or vice-versa. These identities are:

$$\overline{(A + B + C + \ldots)} = \overline{A} \cdot \overline{B} \cdot \overline{C} \cdot \ldots$$

$$\overline{ABC \cdots} = \overline{A} + \overline{B} + \overline{C} + \cdots$$

Although these identities may be applied to the logical expressions directly, a simple graphical method exists to use these identities directly on the circuit diagram. To change an AND gate to an OR gate, first change the gate symbol to the OR-gate shape and then add inversion bubbles to the output and all inputs of that gate. To change an OR gate to an AND gate, first change the gate symbol to the AND-gate shape and then add inversion bubbles to the output and all inputs of that gate. After all gates have been changed to the type desired, you can manipulate inversion bubbles and inverters as described previously to obtain the desired circuit.

We desire to implement the standard SOP circuit of Fig. 2-22*a* with all NAND

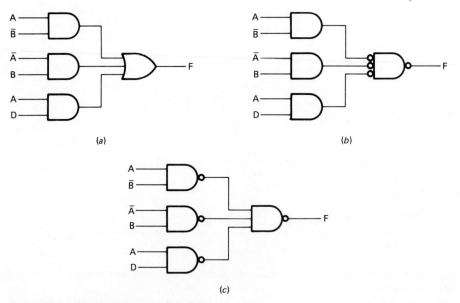

Figure 2-22 All NAND gate sum of products.

gates. Since we know that the OR output gate will have to change to an AND gate, we first apply the graphical version of De Morgan's law to get Fig. 2-22*b*. We change the gate symbol from OR to AND and add inversion bubbles to all inputs and outputs. This *does not* change the function of this gate. Next, notice that to obtain all NAND gates, move three inversion bubbles, as shown in Fig. 2-22*c*. Starting with the same SOP circuit in Fig. 2-23*a*, we obtain an all-NOR-gate realization in Fig. 2-23*c*. Draw this circuit more simply, as in Fig. 2-23*d*, by changing the input variables. Figure 2-23*d* also makes more physical sense since most input variables will be available in both true and complemented forms (e.g., from the Q and $\overline{Q}$ outputs of a flip-flop). Input variables that are not available in the sense desired are best inverted aside in the circuit diagram, as has been described previously. You can see now why NAND and NOR gates are so common. It is easy to change a SOP realization (or POS) to an all-NAND- or all-NOR-gate implementation.

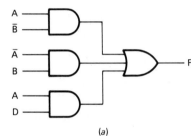

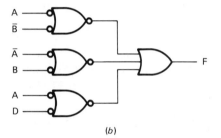

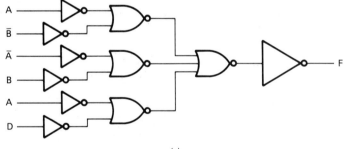

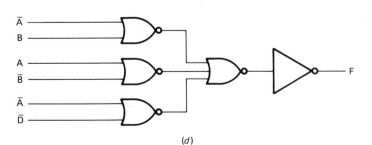

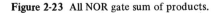

Figure 2-23 All NOR gate sum of products.

(a)   (b)   (c)   (d)

Figure 2-24 Alternate symbols for NAND and NOR gates.

You should also see that every gate circuit may be represented by two different symbols. Alternate symbols for NAND and NOR gates are shown in Fig. 2-24. These symbols are identical in meaning, and either may be used to indicate the same physical circuit. The choice of symbol is usually made to best describe the operation of the circuit. For example, in Fig. 2-24a, this NAND symbol tells us that the output will be 0 only when all inputs are 1s. However, the NAND symbol of Fig. 2-24b is more descriptive of a circuit whose output should be 1 when either or both inputs are 0. *Both of these circuits perform the same logic function.* The first symbol indicates that the gate generates an active low signal only when two active high signals are both asserted. The second symbol indicates that the gate generates an active high signal whenever either of two active low inputs is asserted.

Figure 2-24c and d are analogous for the NOR gate. The gate of Fig. 2-24c generates an active low signal if either of two active high signals is asserted. The same gate in Fig. 2-24d generates an active high signal when both its active low inputs are asserted.

Although either symbol for a gate would be correct on a circuit diagram, a circuit diagram is easier to understand if the symbol corresponding to the action desired is used. For example, consider the circuit of Fig. 2-25a. The function of this circuit is not obvious. Figure 2-25b describes the function more clearly. The designer had wanted an active high output when all 16 active high inputs were asserted. Since only

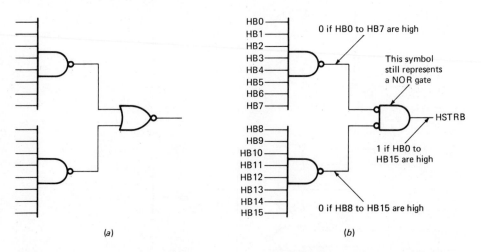

(a)   (b)

Figure 2-25 (a) 16-bit coincidence detector. (b) More meaningful symbology for coincidence detector.

8-input NAND gates were available, two of these were combined with a NOR gate to perform the same function as a 16-input AND gate. The symbols in Fig. 2-25*b* clearly show that the designer was implementing a 16-input AND function.

Wired OR and Wired AND

Usually, the operation of a gate circuit is undefined if the *outputs* of two or more gates are connected directly together. This is the case for many logic gates: interconnecting their outputs does not generate a meaningful digital signal. However, some logic families (e.g., emitter-coupled logic or ECL) allow two or more outputs to be interconnected to generate a meaningful signal. Two such AND gates are interconnected in Fig. 2-26. The logic function generated by interconnecting these two outputs is the OR function. Thus, this connection is often called the *wired OR*. Other logic families may implement a *wired AND* function when interconnected as shown in Fig. 2-27. Notice that you cannot determine if a wired function is an AND or an OR from the circuit diagram alone. The data sheet for the gates being used must be consulted to determine the function implemented. Most logic families have at least a few types of gates that may be wire ORed or ANDed, even if the majority of gates in the family may not be so connected. For example, the transistor-transistor logic (TTL) family does not allow for interconnection of its outputs. However, a few TTL gates exist which can be interconnected to implement the wired AND function.

Although wired functions may seem very desirable because they save one entire gate, disadvantages sometimes limit their usefulness. Connecting gate outputs together usually *reduces* the fan out below that of *either* gate alone. If two gates, each with a fan out of 10, are wire ANDed, the combined circuit may be able to drive only nine inputs. Also, connecting gate outputs together will slow the propagation of logic signals through those gates. As will be seen in a later chapter, increasing the delay through gating circuits will slow the maximum speed at which an ASM using those gating circuits can operate. Finally, testing a circuit using wired functions may be very difficult. If 10 gate outputs are wired together, it is impossible to determine which of

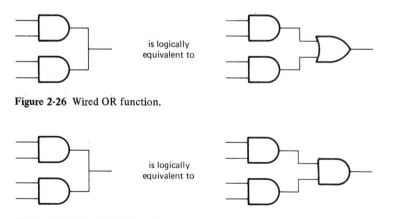

Figure 2-26 Wired OR function.

Figure 2-27 Wired AND function.

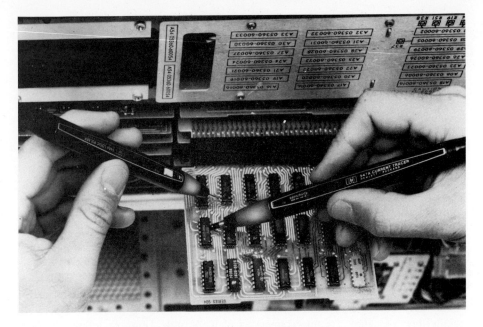

A current probe is on the right and a logic probe is on the left (*Hewlett-Packard Co.*).

the 10 is malfunctioning from measuring their single output logic voltage level! A *current probe* allows the current in the wire to each individual output to be sensed, even if the outputs are connected together. Even so, wired functions are often implemented so that gate outputs may be individually disconnected to facilitate testing.

Finally, flip-flop outputs are almost never connected together. Connecting flip-flop outputs together is ambiguous. It is not clear if the unchanged flip-flop output state is an input to the wired function or if the wired function actually changes the flip-flop's state.

PROBLEMS

2-1 Evaluate the following logical expressions for all combinations of variables.
  (a) $F_1 = \overline{A} + B + \overline{C}$
  (b) $F_2 = (\overline{A})\,(\overline{B})\,(\overline{C})$
  (c) $F_3 = \overline{A} + \overline{B} + \overline{C}$
  (d) $F_4 = \overline{A\,B\,C}$
  (e) $F_5 = ABC + \overline{(\overline{B} + \overline{C})}$

2-2 Consider the function specified by Table P2-1.
  (a) Find the canonical SOP expression for this function.
  (b) Find the canonical POS expression for this function.
  (c) Find the reduced SOP expression, using a K map.
  (d) Find the reduced POS expression, using a K map.

2-3 Reduce the K maps of Fig. P2-1 to the simplest SOP expressions.

2-4 Reduce the K maps of Fig. P2-1 to the simplest POS expressions.

Table P2-1 Function table

D	C	B	A	F
0	0	0	0	0
0	0	0	1	1
0	0	1	0	0
0	0	1	1	0
0	1	0	0	1
0	1	0	1	0
0	1	1	0	1
0	1	1	1	0
1	0	0	0	0
1	0	0	1	1
1	0	1	0	0
1	0	1	1	0
1	1	0	0	1
1	1	0	1	1
1	1	1	0	1
1	1	1	1	0

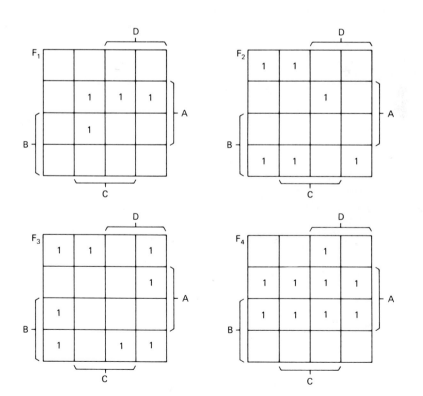

Figure P2-1 Karnaugh map for Prob. 2-6.

2-5 Draw circuit diagrams that implement the following logical expressions with AND gates, OR gates, and inverters.

(a) $AB + CD$

(b) $\overline{AB} + A\overline{B}$

(c) $(\overline{A}\overline{B} + AB)D + CE$

(d) $(\overline{A}\overline{B} + C)(D + E)$

2-6 Repeat Prob. 2-5 using:

(a) Only NAND gates and inverters

(b) Only NOR gates and inverters

2-7 Design two circuits to implement the flowchart of Fig. P2-2.

(a) Draw the circuit for a ROM controller, and specify the ROM contents.

(b) Draw the circuit for a gate controller.

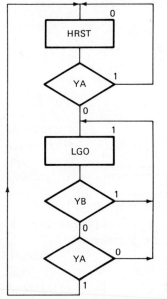

Figure P2-2 ASM chart for Prob. 2-7.

2-8 Design a gate controller for Prob. 1-9.

2-9 The K maps in Fig. 2-16 could have don't cares in positions 10, 11, 12, 13, 14, and 15 because these states were used in the ASM. Determine the minimum SOP representation for these 10 functions if the don't cares are included.

2-10 (a) Assume you are using a logic family that has wired ANDs. Repeat Prob. 2-6a, using the wired AND function.

(b) Assume you are using a logic family that has wired ORs. Repeat Prob. 2-6b, using the wired OR function.

THREE

MSI AND LSI CIRCUITS

Examining many digital circuits, we should notice that similar circuitry and similar algorithms are used repeatedly. These functions are so common that they are manufactured as standard integrated circuits that may be incorporated into any digital system. The economies of scale reduce the cost of these mass-produced parts, regardless of the type of system in which they are used. Thus, the many computers manufactured help reduce the cost of traffic light controllers, and vice-versa. More importantly, these commonly used functions are preengineered. The cost of designing these circuits may be amortized over millions of individual parts. This significantly reduces digital system development costs.

We have already examined three types of mass-produced parts: gates, flip-flops, and ROMs. Gates and flip-flops are called small-scale integrated (SSI) circuits because they contain relatively few electronic components. In this chapter, we'll be primarily concerned with medium- and large-scale integrated (MSI and LSI) circuits. These larger circuits are advantageous because they allow complex functions to be preengineered and mass-produced. Before we examine common MSI circuits and their uses, we shall introduce digital signal busses.

BUS NOTATION

Often digital signals are grouped together for a common purpose. On a circuit diagram they appear as parallel signal lines, running together to various circuits. These signals are collectively called a bus. Because busses are difficult to draw and require a great amount of space on the diagram and their drawings can be confusing and difficult to follow, a shorthand notation has been developed. In Fig. 3-1, both the state variables ($SV0$ to $SV3$) and the next-state function ($NS0$ to $NS3$) are drawn as busses. Each

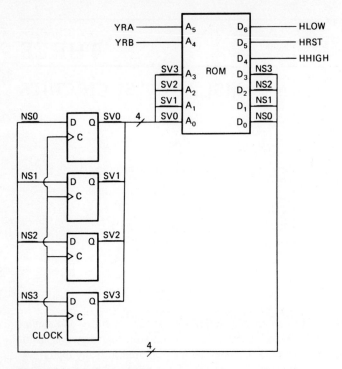

Figure 3-1 Notation for bus.

group of signals or bus is drawn as a single line. The number 4 adjacent to the slash mark indicates that this single line actually represents four digital signals. These signals must be separated whenever they connect to a logic circuit and plainly marked at these connections with their mnemonics.

DATA BUSSES

One common digital bus is the data bus. In Fig. 3-2, an 8-bit data bus allows data (say, 8-bit binary numbers) to be passed among three different ASMs. Control signals determine the origin and destination of data. Data must be transmitted bidirectionally over the same eight wires among three different ASMs. Two circuit techniques may be used to accomplish this data transfer.

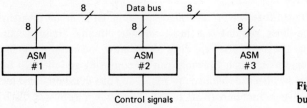

Figure 3-2 Bidirectional data bus.

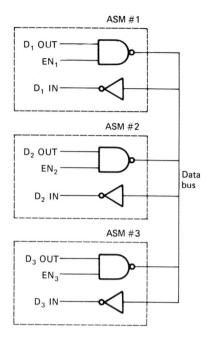

Figure 3-3 Wired AND data bus.

In Fig. 3-3, a wired AND function is used to allow more than one output to con-nect to a single wire of the 8-bit data bus. Each ASM may receive data from the bus through the inverter or may transmit data by enabling its NAND gate. This circuit is redrawn in Fig. 3-4a to explicitly show the wired AND function. Applying De Morgan's laws as shown in Fig. 3-4b, we obtain the circuit of Fig. 3-4c. From this last circuit, it is easy to see that each ASM may gate its data onto the bus, which will be received by all other ASMs, if it enables its AND gate. Only one ASM at a time may enable a transmitting AND gate. The bus acts as an OR function (because of De Morgan's laws), even though a wired AND is actually implemented. In fact, this kind of data bus is often called a wired OR bus, even if the wired AND function is actually being used, as in this case. We mentioned in Chap. 2 that wired functions slow down the digital signal's propagation through the gates that have their outputs connected together. To speed up the operation of data busses, a new kind of logic circuit was developed to replace the wired function. This new kind of logic circuit is called a *three-state* circuit.

A three-state circuit is identical to its ordinary circuit counterpart except for its output. A three-state inverter is shown in Fig. 3-5. It is an ordinary inverter with a logic-controlled switch in its output lead. When the three-state enable signal is a 0, the switch is open and the inverter output is disconnected. This condition is not a logic 0 or a logic 1, it is a third state called a *high-impedance* or *high-Z* state. Since we may now disconnect logic circuit outputs internally, we may fabricate a data bus as shown in Fig. 3-6. As long as only one three-state enable signal is asserted, only one inverter is connected to the bus allowing the ASM to send data to the others. This bus is not a wired AND or OR because only one output is really connected to the bus at

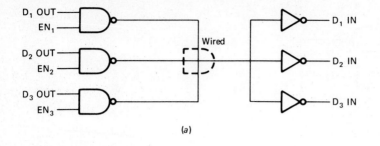

(a)

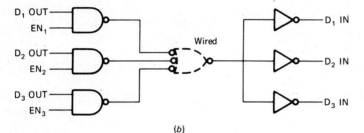

(b)

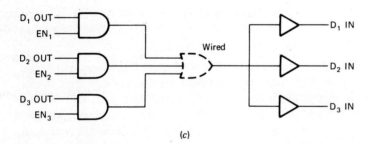

(c)

Figure 3-4 (a) Wired AND. (b) De Morgan's law. (c) Equivalent circuit.

any time. The other outputs are disconnected by switches located in the digital circuits.

MULTIPLEXERS

A *multiplexer* (also called a data selector) is a group of gates that can be used to selectively route data from several inputs to one output. Figure 3-7 is a four-line to one-

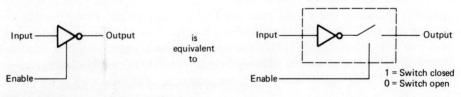

Figure 3-5 Inverter with three-state output.

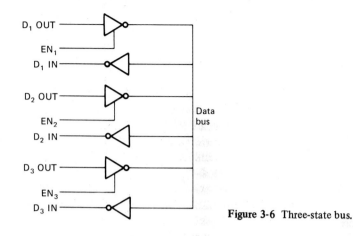

Figure 3-6 Three-state bus.

line multiplexer. The logic signal on any one of the four data inputs D_0 through D_3 can be made to appear on output Y. The signal to appear at Y is selected by inputs A and B. For example, if $B = 1$ and $A = 0$, signal 2 would appear on output Y. The complete logic table for this circuit appears in Table 3-1. Multiplexers are commonly available as MSI circuits. Figure 3-8 is the MSI circuit symbol for the multiplexer of Fig. 3-7. This MSI multiplexer has an extra output W, which is the complement of Y and is simply included for convenience. In addition, a *STROBE* (also called an

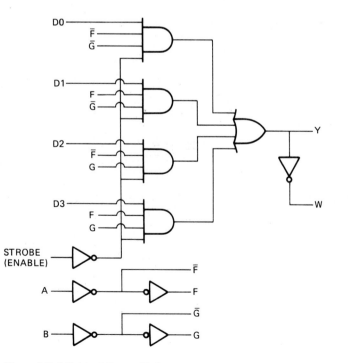

Figure 3-7 4-line to 1-line multiplexer.

Table 3-1 Logic table for multiplexer

STROBE	B	A	Y	W
1	X	X	0	$\overline{1}$
0	0	0	D_0	$\overline{D_0}$
0	0	1	D_1	$\overline{D_1}$
0	1	0	D_2	$\overline{D_2}$
0	1	1	D_3	$\overline{D_3}$

$ENABLE$) signal input will set the output Y to 0, regardless of any data input. This $STROBE$ input may also control a three-state output in some multiplexers. One or more independent multiplexers may be included in a single MSI circuit. Commonly available combinations are:

Single.	16 line to 1 line
Single.	8 line to 1 line
Dual.	4 line to 1 line
Quadruple.	2 line to 1 line

One of the more important uses of a multiplexer is to select input conditions to be tested by an algorithmic state machine. Four input conditions must be tested in the ASM of Fig. 3-9. A multiplexer is used to connect these four inputs to a single ROM address input. The select inputs of the multiplexer are connected to the state variables so that a different input may be tested in each state.

In state number	A_0 is connected to
0	YINP
1	NFOR
2	NFOR
3	YINP
4	0
5	NRST
6	NFOR
7	YMAX

The selected input is the condition to be tested in that state, as specified by an ASM chart. Since no input must be tested in state 4, multiplexer input D_4 is permanently

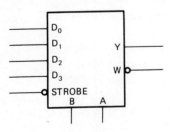

Figure 3-8 MSI multiplexer symbol.

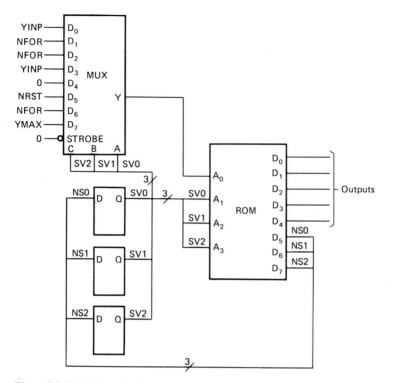

Figure 3-9 Multiplexer for input conditions.

connected to a 0. Without a multiplexer, a 128×8 ROM would've been required. With a multiplexer, a 16×8 ROM is required. This saving in ROM size is not without disadvantages, however. There can be only one decision diamond after each state box in the ASM chart because only one input is connected to the ROM in each state. Additional states may have to be added to the original ASM chart to test multiple inputs. Additional flip-flops may be required to implement these states. The ASM will respond to input changes more slowly because it will have to sequence through more states.

Multiplexers can still be used to advantage even if more than one input must be tested simultaneously. The machine in Fig. 3-10 is similar to the previous example, except that two multiplexers are used so that two inputs may be tested in each state. This increases the ROM size to 32×8, which is still far short of the original 128×8 ROM. A very complex ASM may have dozens of inputs to be tested. Seldom must more than two or three be tested simultaneously. In these cases, multiplexing is a necessity for it reduces the ROM size by orders of magnitude.

One more problem exists with our multiplexing scheme. For large numbers of states, the size of the multiplexer becomes excessive. For example, if our ASM had 7 state flip-flops, our multiplexing scheme would require 128-input multiplexers. One hundred and twenty-eight inputs would be needed, even if only a few input signals must be multiplexed. An alternative multiplexer connection is shown in Fig. 3-11.

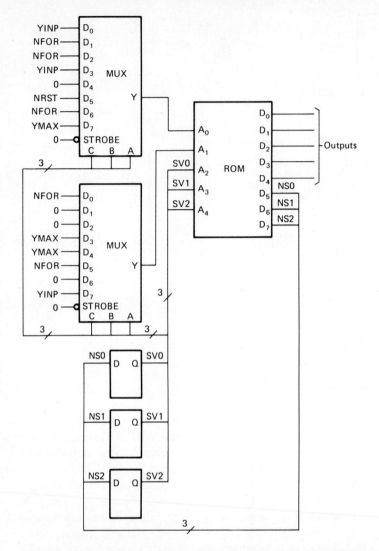

Figure 3-10 Using two multiplexers to test up to two conditions simultaneously.

The input selected by the multiplexer is controlled by ROM outputs, rather than the current state variables. In this way, the multiplexers need only be large enough to connect once to each required input. The ROM can be programmed to select any input in any state. In fact, multiple multiplexers may or may not be the same size. Some inputs that are tested very often may be routed to the ROM directly, without being multiplexed.

We've added three flip-flops to save the state of the multiplexer select lines. If we had tried to connect *SMA*, *SMB*, and *SMC* directly back to the multiplexer, we should have discovered that the circuit would probably malfunction. Remember that

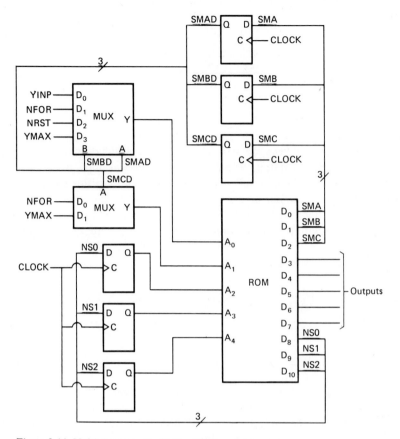

Figure 3-11 Multiplexers controlled by ROM outputs.

we assumed that all ROM address changes caused by state variable or input changes would be synchronous with the clock. If we had not added the three flip-flops in the select lines, a change in the select signals could change the ROM address asynchronously. This, in turn, could change the select signals, which could asynchronously change the address signals. This could change the select signals back again, etc. Thus, even without a clock transition, the circuit would repetitively change its outputs at some rate determined by the propagation delays of the ROM and multiplexer.

Although the three flip-flops synchronize the multiplexer select signals with the clock, they also delay the action of *SMA*, *B*, and *C* by one clock pulse. We shall have to assert the select signals one state early in the ASM chart.

Multiplexing ASM Inputs

A small tram shown in Fig. 3-12 must be automated. The tram car is to travel back and forth over the line, stopping for 10 s at each station. Three sensors A, B, and C sense the tram at the three stations. The tram must stop within 1 s of actuating a

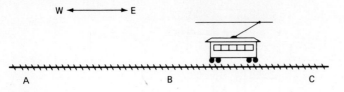

Figure 3-12 Tram.

sensor. An override button will keep the tram stopped whenever the button is pushed while the train is stopped at a station. The ASM chart for this example is shown in Fig. 3-13. Note that, at most, one input is tested in each state. For this reason, we should be able to multiplex the four inputs into one ROM address line. Since six flip-flops are required, we'll choose to control the multiplexer with ROM outputs. If we controlled the multiplexer with the 6 state variables, we'd need a 64-input multiplexer. The implementation of this controller is shown in Fig. 3-14. Two ROM outputs are used to select one of four inputs to be tested.

SMB	SMA	Input to be tested
0	0	YA
0	1	YB
1	0	YC
1	1	YOVER

The multiplexer select signals must be asserted in the state before they are needed because they actually reach the multiplexer after the next clock pulse loads them into the synchronizing flip-flops. The controller with multiplexer requires a 128×11 ROM (a total of 1408 bits), while a controller without the multiplexer would require a 1024×9 ROM (a total of 9216 bits).

Expanding Multiplexers

Multiplexers may be combined to form larger multiplexers in two ways. In Fig. 3-15, two 16-input, three-state output multiplexers are combined to form one 32-input multiplexer. The most significant selection bit, bit E, is used to enable the three-state output of one or the other multiplexer. Multiplexer outputs may be multiplexed, as shown in Fig. 3-16. Here, four 16-input multiplexers are cascaded to form a 64-input multiplexer. One of the outputs of the 16-input multiplexer is selected by a 4-input multiplexer connected to the most significant bits E and F.

Generating Logic Functions with Multiplexers

A multiplexer may be used to generate an arbitrary logic function. This use of multiplexers is advantageous when the function would involve a complex gating structure that would be difficult to design and implement. Multiplexer generation of functions

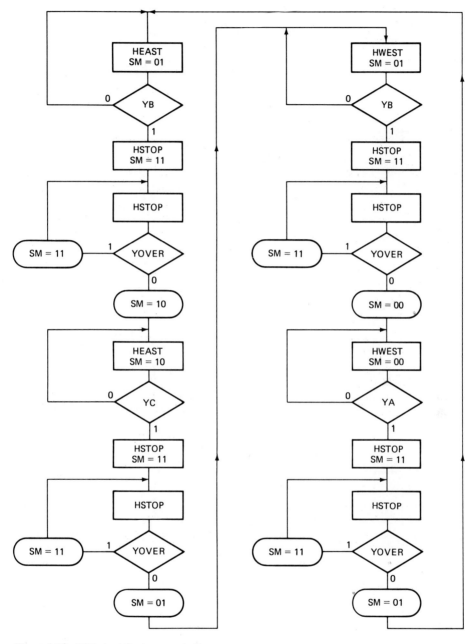

Figure 3-13 ASM chart for tram controller.

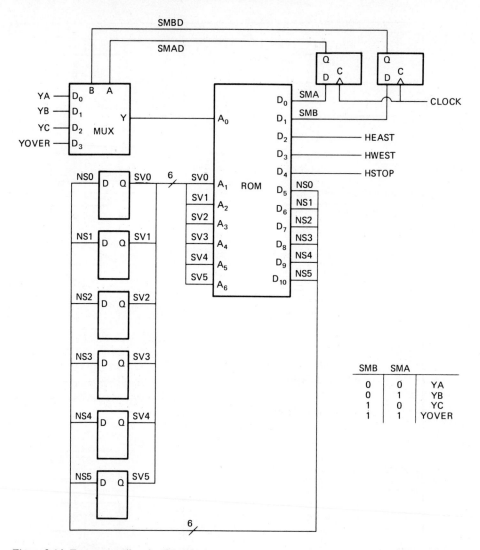

Figure 3-14 Tram controller circuit.

is often useful when a few auxiliary functions must be generated in a ROM ASM. The multiplexer implementation is easily designed and the same single integrated-circuit multiplexer will generate *any* logic function.

A multiplexer can generate any logic function of $n + 1$ input variables if the multiplexer has n select inputs. Thus, an eight-input multiplexer can generate any logic function of up to four variables. A logic function of four variables is shown in Table 3-2. The most significant 3 bits of this function are connected to the select inputs of the multiplexer in Fig. 3-17. Thus, each multiplexer data input D_0 through D_7 corresponds to two lines of the function in Table 3-2. Looking at the first two lines of

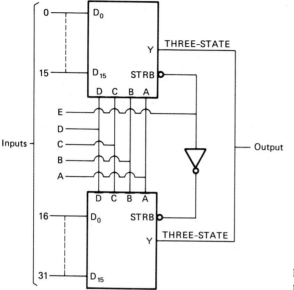

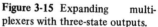

Figure 3-15 Expanding multiplexers with three-state outputs.

this table, we notice that, when D_0 is selected by inputs Z, Y, and X, the output F is identical to input W. We connect D_0 to input W on the circuit diagram. When D_1 is selected, the function F is always 1, independent of input W. Input D_1 is connected to 1 on the circuit diagram. For each pair of lines on the function table, we connected the corresponding multiplexer input to W, $\overline{W}$, 0, or 1 as required to generate the proper function.

Table 3-2 Function of four variables

Multiplexer input	Z	Y	X	W	F
D_0	0	0	0	0	0
	0	0	0	1	1
D_1	0	0	1	0	1
	0	0	1	1	1
D_2	0	1	0	0	0
	0	1	0	1	0
D_3	0	1	1	0	0
	0	1	1	1	1
D_4	1	0	0	0	1
	1	0	0	1	0
D_5	1	0	1	0	1
	1	0	1	1	1
D_6	1	1	0	0	0
	1	1	0	1	1
D_7	1	1	1	0	1
	1	1	1	1	0

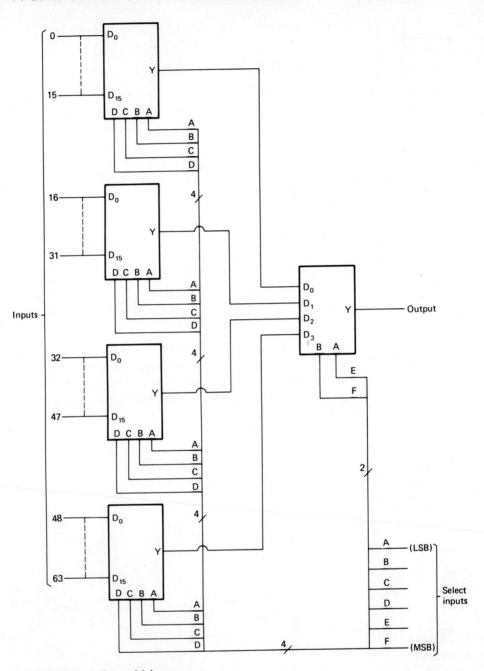

Figure 3-16 Cascading multiplexers.

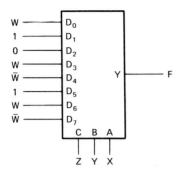

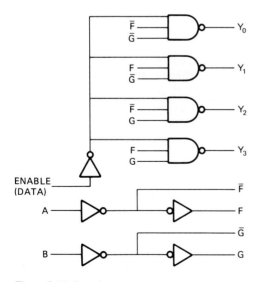

Figure 3-17 Boolean function implemented with multiplexer.

DECODERS

Another common MSI circuit is the *decoder* (also called a *demultiplexer*). A decoder is an arrangement of gates that allows a single enable or data input to be sent to several destinations. A decoder circuit along with its MSI symbol is shown in Fig. 3-18. This is a two-line to four-line decoder (also called a one out of four). Two select inputs A and B determine which of four outputs Y_0 through Y_3 will be connected to the enable or data input.

Enable	*B*	*A*	Y_3	Y_2	Y_1	Y_0
1	X	X	1	1	1	1
0	0	0	1	1	1	0
0	0	1	1	1	0	1
0	1	0	1	0	1	1
0	1	1	0	1	1	1

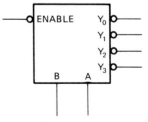

Figure 3-18 Decoder.

Decoders are available in several sizes, packaged one or more in each integrated circuit. Common sizes are:

Single.   4 line to 16 line
Single.   4 line to 10 line
Single.   3 line to 8 line
Dual.   2 line to 4 line

One common use of the decoder does not use the data input. With the enable or data input of Fig. 3-18 permanently connected to a 0, all but one of the decoder's outputs will be 1. A single output will be selected by inputs A and B. Many times, outputs from algorithmic state machines are mutually exclusive. That is, only one of several outputs can occur at one time. For example, only one color traffic light in each direction may be lighted at one time. Since two digital signals can specify four conditions, we can use a decoder, as shown in Fig. 3-19, to generate three traffic light control signals from only two ROM outputs.

HNSB	HNSA	ILNSG	ILNSY	ILNSR
0	0	1	1	1
0	1	0	1	1
1	0	1	0	1
1	1	1	1	0

The ASM can turn on only one light at a time. This restriction is entirely acceptable for the control of most intersections. A simple traffic light controller using this technique is shown in Fig. 3-20. Only four ROM outputs are required, rather than the six that would have been required without the decoders. The ROM was a 16 × 10 and has been reduced to a 16 × 8 through the use of decoders. This is not as dramatic an improvement as was obtained with multiplexers since saving one output line doesn't save as many bits in the ROM as saving one address line. ROMs with any number of address lines desired are easily obtainable. However, ROMs are usually manufactured with outputs in multiples of 4 or even 8. For the original traffic controller, a 16 × 12 ROM would have been used, even though only a 16 × 10 was required. Thus, requiring two-fewer outputs would probably save 4 ROM output bits in the implementation. A decoder is a necessity when *many* mutually exclusive outputs must be controlled. In fact, when many outputs are required, it may be useful to try to set up the ASM chart

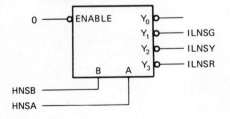

Figure 3-19 MSI decoder used to generate traffic-light control signals.

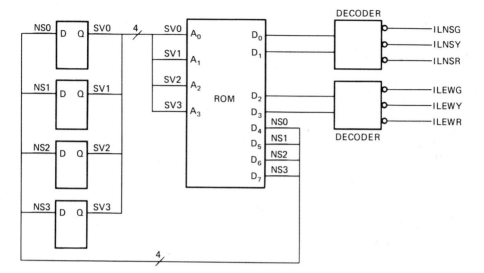

Figure 3-20 Traffic-light controller with decoders.

so that outputs can be made mutually exclusive even if they are not intrinsically mutually exclusive. If this can be done, a decoder could be used to save a large number of ROM output bits. Just as in the case of the input multiplexer, additional states required to sequentially activate outputs could negate the advantages of decoding by requiring more state variables (and a much bigger ROM) or by slowing down the operation of the ASM.

REGISTERS

A register is a group of flip-flops with a common clock input, just like the flip-flops we've been using to store state variables. Groups of such flip-flops in multiples of 4 or 8 are manufactured as MSI circuits, as shown in Fig. 3-21. One important variation is shown in Fig. 3-22. The register shown here has an enable input. When the enable input is a 0, the contents of the register do not change, even though clock pulses continue. The register does not change because the AND gates marked *B* are enabled so that the signals at the outputs of the flip-flops are routed back to their inputs. Only if the enable input is a 1 will AND gates *A* be enabled and new data be stored in the register.

A register with an enable input is a sequential circuit that remains in its current state when its enable input is a 0 and changes to the state specified by its data inputs when its enable input is 1. The enable input of such a register may be connected to the output of an ASM controller. This ASM will control the flow of data into that register.

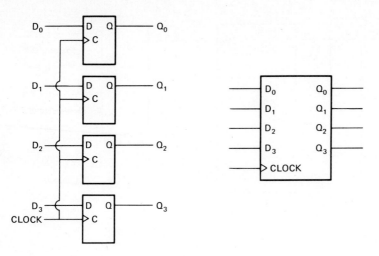

Figure 3-21 4-bit register and MSI circuit symbol.

Simultaneous Sampling with a Register

Multiplexing inputs to an ASM may present another problem not yet mentioned. Often inputs *must* be tested simultaneously. If tested in sequence, the first inputs tested might change their state before the last inputs are tested. An ASM with multiplexed inputs, as shown in Fig. 2-23a, performs a test on YA in state X and a test on

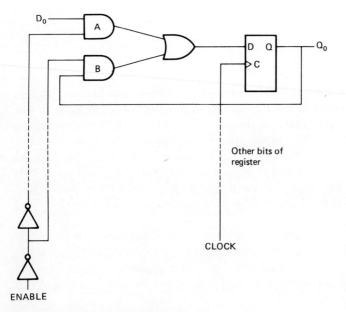

Figure 3-22 Register with enable inputs.

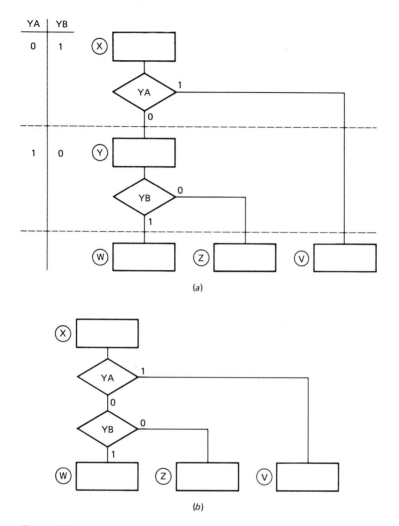

Figure 3-23 (*a*) Inputs changing during sequential testing. (*b*) Simultaneous testing.

YB in state *Y*. If the inputs change between these two states as shown, the next state will be *Z*. Input *YA* is 0 in state *X*, while input *YB* is 0 in state *Y*. State *Z* will be the next state, even though both inputs were never zero simultaneously! A simultaneous test, as might be performed without multiplexed inputs, is shown in Fig. 3-23*b*. In this case, the next state will be *W* if the input during state *X* is 01. The next state will be *V* if the input is 10. In *neither* case will the next state be *Z*, as it was when the inputs were sequentially tested.

If it is necessary to test more than one input whose possible changes between sequential tests would cause an ASM to behave incorrectly, those inputs could all be stored in a register at *one* time to be tested sequentially later. In Fig. 3-24, a 4-bit register is used to store a "snapshot" of four inputs. Whenever the ROM output en-

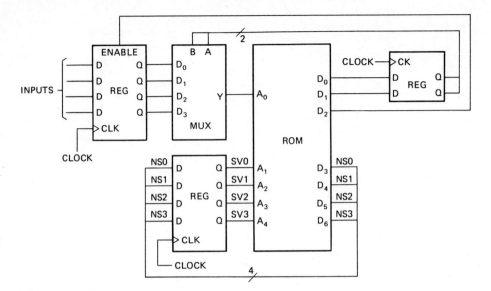

Figure 3-24 ASM using one MSI register to simultaneously save inputs and another MSI register for the state variables.

ables this register, the four input conditions are stored in the register at the next clock pulse *simultaneously*! Since these four inputs were stored at the same time, the ASM can now test them sequentially and be certain that these conditions did actually occur simultaneously at the time the register was enabled.

Expanding Outputs with a Register

ASM outputs may be stored in registers, as shown in Fig. 3-25. Using registers to store these outputs may be desirable for two reasons. First, many outputs may be obtained with a small ROM. These outputs do *not* have to be mutually exclusive, as was necessary when a decoder was used. Second, the ASM can store an output based on some decision and then completely forget about that output until it must be changed again. Without output storage registers, the ASM might have to use many extra states to remember which outputs to keep asserted long after the decision to assert that output had been reached.

In Fig. 3-25, data for register W are output from the ROM to the D inputs of all four registers. Simultaneously, the select code for register W is output to the decoder, along with the enable signal. The decoded enable signal is sent to register W so that, on the next clock pulse, the ROM data are loaded into register W. The other three registers X, Y, and Z are loaded sequentially with their data in the same manner. All four registers will retain the data stored in them as long as the ASM does not output a decoder enable signal. In this case, only 7 output bits were needed for 16 outputs. Unlike a simple decoder, these outputs need not be mutually exclusive, but can be any combination of 0s and 1s. However, all outputs cannot be made to *change* simul-

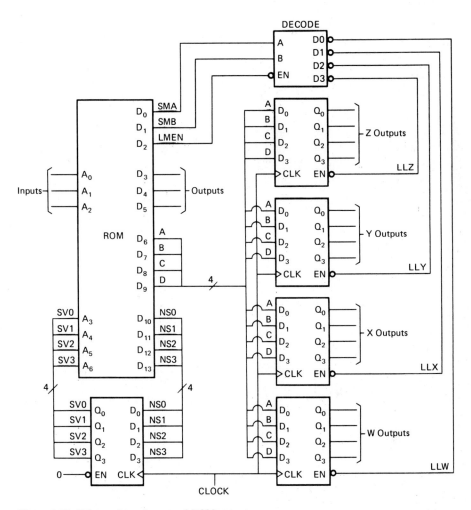

Figure 3-25 Using registers to expand ROM outputs.

taneously. The four outputs of register W will change first, followed by the outputs of X, then Y, and then Z.

COUNTERS

An ASM that repeatedly outputs the same output sequence is called a counter. The most common type of counter outputs the binary sequence. MSI counters are usually implemented as 4-bit counters. As we'll see later, several 4-bit MSI counters may be connected together to build larger counters. The simple 4-bit counter shown in Fig. 3-26 contains four flip-flops and associated gates, which together implement an ASM

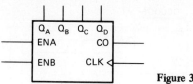

Figure 3-26 MSI counter.

that counts in the sequence shown. The counter remains in the same state as long as either enable input is 0. If both enables are 1, the counter counts at each clock pulse. The current state is output to four wires, labeled Q_A, Q_B, Q_C, and Q_D. A fifth output labeled CO is a 1 only when the current state is 1111 *and* both enables are a 1.

ENA	ENB	Current state				Next state				CO
		Q_D	Q_C	Q_B	Q_A	Q_D	Q_C	Q_B	Q_A	
0	0	q_D	q_C	q_B	q_A	q_D	q_C	q_B	q_A	0
0	1	q_D	q_C	q_B	q_A	q_D	q_C	q_B	q_A	0
1	0	q_D	q_C	q_B	q_A	q_D	q_C	q_B	q_A	0
1	1	0	0	0	0	0	0	0	1	0
1	1	0	0	0	1	0	0	1	0	0
1	1	0	0	1	0	0	0	1	1	0
1	1	0	0	1	1	0	1	0	0	0
1	1	0	1	0	0	0	1	0	1	0
1	1	0	1	0	1	0	1	1	0	0
1	1	0	1	1	0	0	1	1	1	0
1	1	0	1	1	1	1	0	0	0	0
1	1	1	0	0	1	1	0	1	0	0
1	1	1	0	1	0	1	0	1	1	0
1	1	1	0	1	1	1	1	0	0	0
1	1	1	1	0	0	1	1	0	1	0
1	1	1	1	0	1	1	1	1	0	0
1	1	1	1	1	0	1	1	1	1	0
1	1	1	1	1	1	0	0	0	0	1

The CO output can be used to connect two 4-bit counters together to make an 8-bit counter. In Fig. 3-27, MSI counter X is the least significant (rightmost) 4 bits of an

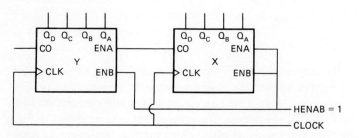

Figure 3-27 8-bit counter.

Table 3-3 Counting sequence for 8-bit counter

Counter Y					Counter X				
CO	Q_D	Q_C	Q_B	Q_A	CO	Q_D	Q_C	Q_B	Q_A
0	1	1	0	1	0	0	0	0	0
⋮	⋮	⋮	⋮	⋮	⋮	⋮	⋮	⋮	⋮
0	1	1	0	1	1	1	1	1	1
0	1	1	1	0	0	0	0	0	0
⋮	⋮	⋮	⋮	⋮	⋮	⋮	⋮	⋮	⋮
0	1	1	1	0	1	1	1	1	1
0	1	1	1	1	0	0	0	0	0
⋮	⋮	⋮	⋮	⋮	⋮	⋮	⋮	⋮	⋮
1	1	1	1	1	1	1	1	1	1
0	0	0	0	0	0	0	0	0	0
⋮	⋮	⋮	⋮	⋮	⋮	⋮	⋮	⋮	⋮

8-bit counter, while MSI counter Y is the most significant 4 bits. The CO output of X is connected to one of the enable inputs of Y. The letters CO stand for *carry output* and indicate that counter X has reached the largest value it can represent (i.e., 1111). The next clock pulse will set counter X back to 0000, but will also increment counter Y. The counting sequence is shown in Table 3-3. Counter Y will count because its *ENB* is connected to the CO output of counter X. Every time counter X reaches its maximum value, its CO output will signal Y that Y should add 1 to its 4 most significant bits on the next clock pulse. MSI counters have two enable inputs so that one may be used to connect multiple MSI counters together, while the other is used to enable and disable the entire counter (*HENA* in Fig. 3-27). You'll also notice that CO from counter Y occurs in exactly the right place to signal a third counter to count so that a 12-bit counter could be built. Counters have additional inputs to make them more useful. The counter in Fig. 3-28 has a clear and a load input. Both of these inputs are high when the counter is counting. If the clear input is low, the counter's next state will be 0000. The next clock pulse to occur after the clear input becomes a 0 will clear the counter's outputs to 0000. The counter will resume counting only on the first clock pulse after the clear input becomes a 1.

If the load input becomes a 0, the next clock pulse will load the four counter flip-flops with the data on inputs D, C, B, and A. In other words, the counter will act as a register as long as the load input is a 0. At each clock pulse, the datum present at input D will be stored at output Q_D, C at Q_C, B at Q_B, and A at Q_A. The counter resumes counting from the state last specified by D, C, B, and A when the load input returns to a 1.

Time Delays with a Counter

One use of a counter is to implement delays longer than one clock cycle in an ASM. You'll remember that the simple traffic light controller required 10 states. Six of those

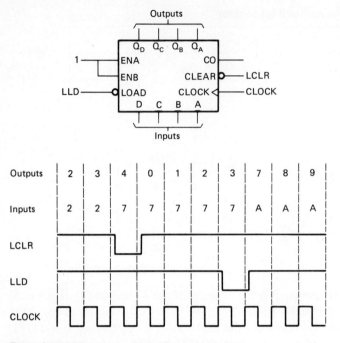

Figure 3-28 MSI counter with load and clear inputs.

states were simply used to delay outputs a longer time than one clock period. The traffic light controller is redrawn in Fig. 3-29, using a counter to implement this time delay. The delay counter is loaded by output *LCLD* (LOW COUNTER LOAD) on the same clock pulse that causes the ASM to enter the red/green states. These are the states marked 1 and 3 in the ASM chart of Fig. 3-30. The carry output of the delay counter is an input to the ASM. While the ASM is in the red/green states, the counter is counting. When the counter finally reaches 1111, the *CO* output signals the ASM to proceed to the next state. You'll notice that the ASM now requires only 4 states instead of 10. We have designed a circuit that does not require the ASM to count with its state flip-flops. Instead, the ASM uses an auxiliary MSI counter. Because counting is such a common requirement, MSI counters are mass-produced. It is economically advantageous to use an MSI counter rather than build the counting function into the ASM by adding state variables and ROM bits. In addition, less design effort will be required using the MSI counter.

Figure 3-31 shows both the timing diagram and state analyzer representation of the traffic controller. The counter's state is shown as a decimal number. Asserting output *LCLD* during state 0 causes the counter to be set to 12 during state 1. The counter counts to 15, at which time the *CO* output becomes 1. On the next clock pulse the ASM tests *CO* and proceeds to state 2. By setting the counter to 12 we were able to have the ASM remain in state 1 for four clock periods. The binary number 1100, which represents 12, is also the two's-complement representation of -4. Thus, the counter can also be thought of as counting down from -4, as shown in Table 3-4.

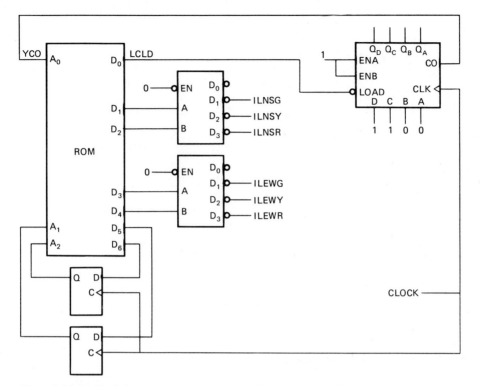

Figure 3-29 Traffic-light controller using counter for delay.

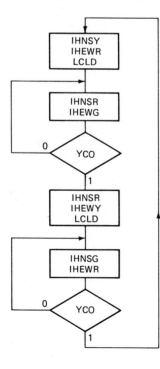

Figure 3-30 ASM chart for traffic light using delay counter.

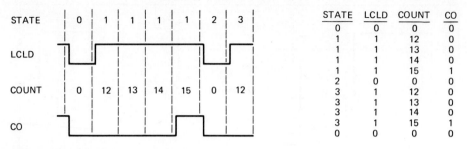

STATE	LCLD	COUNT	CO
0	0	0	0
1	1	12	0
1	1	13	0
1	1	14	0
1	1	15	1
2	0	0	0
3	1	12	0
3	1	13	0
3	1	14	0
3	1	15	1
0	0	0	0

Figure 3-31 Traffic-light controller sequencing.

The delay is easily changed by changing the binary number connected to the counter data inputs. The binary number 0000 will cause a delay of 16 clock periods, while 1111 will cause the ASM to remain in states 1 and 3 for only one clock period. These inputs might be connected to switches to allow a traffic engineer to set the time. Rather than using multiple counters if we need more than one delay period, the counter's data inputs may be connected to the ASM's ROM outputs, as shown in Fig. 3-32. The delay counter may be loaded with different initial values from the ROM, for different delays.

State Sequencing with a Counter

Many of the ASM charts we've drawn had several states following each other sequentially. Few branches occurred to other states. The simple traffic light controller had no decisions at all. By assigning states in numerical order, we should be able to use a counter for the state register since the next state will always be one greater than the current state. Figure 3-33 shows a circuit and ASM chart for a traffic light controller using this technique. The *CO* output of the state counter is connected to the load input of the counter through an inverter. The next state after state 15 will be loaded

Table 3-4 Interpreting the count as a two's-complement (negative) number

State	LCLD	Count	CO
0	0	0	0
1	1	−4	0
1	1	−3	0
1	1	−2	0
1	1	−1	1
2	0	0	0
3	1	−4	0
3	1	−3	0
3	1	−2	0
3	1	−1	1
0	0	0	0

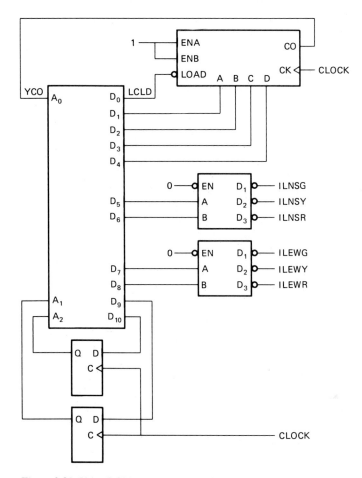

Figure 3-32 Using ROM outputs to set delay.

from the counter's data inputs. In this example, we specified the next state as 6. The counter will cycle through the 10 states needed to implement the traffic light controller. Limited branching could be implemented by connecting one or more counter data inputs to external input conditions. The flexibility of this branching arrangement is very limited.

In Fig. 3-34, the counter's load and data inputs are connected to ROM outputs. Any next state may now be specified for branching from any current state. The ASM chart in Fig. 3-35 shows how this may be done. States 0 through 9 follow sequentially, and the state variable counter simply counts through these states. In state 9, a branch must be made on the condition of input YI. If YI is 0, the counter will be allowed to increment to state 10. However, if YI is a 1, the counter must be set to state 14. This is done by asserting outputs $SV = 1110$ to the counter's data input and asserting $LSVLD$ (LOW STATE VARIABLE LOAD). These conditional outputs will cause the counter to be loaded with 14 on the next clock pulse. Thus, we've caused the branch

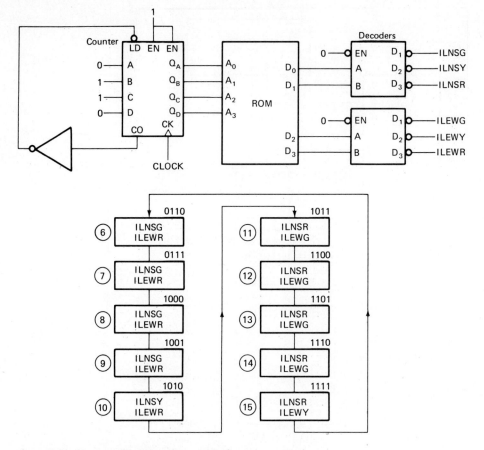

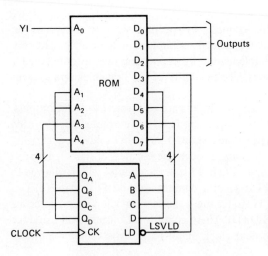

Figure 3-33 Simple traffic light using counter for state sequencing.

Figure 3-34 Loading an arbitrary next state when using a counter for the state register.

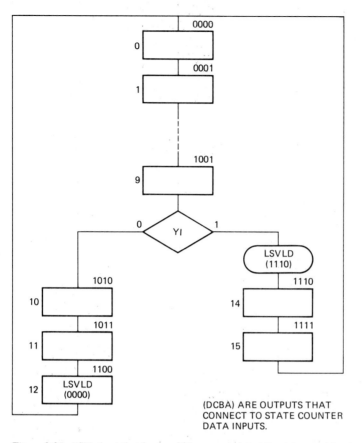

Figure 3-35 ASM chart that loads arbitrary next state into state variable counter.

to occur from state 9 to state 14. The counter's sequence may also be changed unconditionally. For example, in state 12, *LSVLD* and *SV* = 0000 cause the next state to always be state 0.

You should have noticed by now that implementing this controller without a next-state counter would've required four ROM outputs to specify the next state. With a next-state counter it requires five outputs. Hardly a bargain! Loading a state counter from ROM outputs is only advantageous when those ROM outputs can be used for other purposes as well. In Fig. 3-36, four data lines are also used to load three output registers, as well as state branches. Thus, this ASM has 12 outputs and 16 states. This would ordinarily require 16 ROM outputs: 12 outputs and 4 next-state variables. By using a state counter and output latches, all sharing the same ROM data outputs, only 8 outputs are required from the ROM. Finally, just as in past examples of multiplexing and demultiplexing, branching with next-state counters is liable to require extra states. If too many extra states are required, more state variables may be needed, which would partially negate the advantages of this scheme.

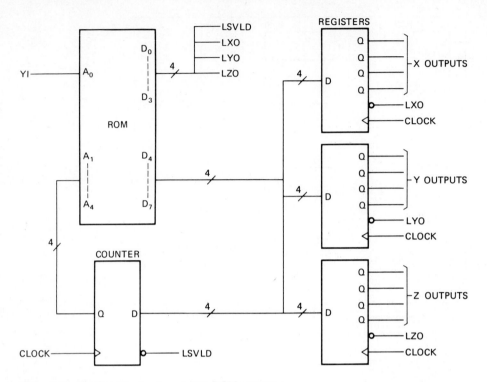

Figure 3-36 Sharing output and next state ROM outputs.

SHIFT REGISTERS

Another common MSI circuit is a shift register. A simplified shift register is shown in Fig. 3-37. It is composed of four flip-flops. At each clock pulse, the datum on Q_C is transferred to Q_D, the datum on Q_B to Q_C, the datum on Q_A to Q_B, and the datum on input SI to Q_A. In this way, a new datum is stored at Q_A, while all previous data are shifted toward the most significant bit Q_D. The datum that was stored at Q_D is lost (unless, of course, something else is connected to Q_D).

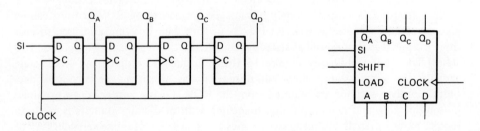

Figure 3-37 Shift register.

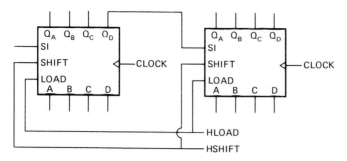

Figure 3-38 Cascaded MSI shift registers.

An actual MSI shift register has several additional useful inputs, as shown in Fig. 3-37. The *SHIFT* input must be high for the shift register to move data; otherwise data will remain stored in their original flip-flops, even though clock pulses continue. The *LOAD* input allows data present on the A, B, C, and D inputs to be stored at Q_A, Q_B, Q_C, and Q_D, respectively, at the next clock transition.

MSI shift registers may be cascaded when longer shift registers are needed. In Fig. 3-38, two 4-bit MSI shift registers are connected together to form an 8-bit shift register. The datum that would've been lost from Q_D of the least significant register is shifted to Q_A of the most significant register.

Serial Data Communication

Very often, two ASMs must communicate with each other. In Fig. 3-39, ASM1 has eight outputs that must be sent to ASM2. In addition, ASM1 sends a signal, *HREADY*, to ASM2 to indicate that the eight outputs have been changed and ASM2 may now test them. Besides the clock, nine wires are required to interconnect the two ASMs. Interconnections are often expensive, especially if they pass through mechanical connectors or travel over long distances.

These same two ASMs may communicate as described above using only *two* interconnections, as shown in Fig. 3-40. Two shift registers are used to send and receive 8 bits of data over a single wire. ASM1 outputs 8 bits of data to *SR1* and asserts *HLOAD* to load these data into the shift register's eight flip-flops. Next, ASM1 outputs *HSHFT*, which causes a bit of data from *SR1* to be shifted into *SR2*. After eight clock pulses, the data from *SR1* have been transferred to *SR2* and ASM1 stops outputting *HSHFT*.

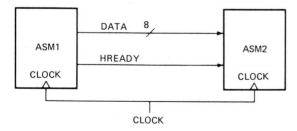

Figure 3-39 Parallel data transmission.

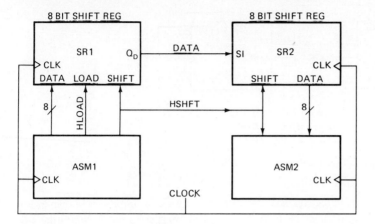

Figure 3-40 Serial data transmission.

Since ASM2 can test *HSHFT*, it now knows that the data shifting operation has been completed and it can test the data available to it from *SR2*.

Although we've saved interconnections, we have paid a penalty in the speed of the data transfer. In Fig. 3-39, data were transferred in 1 clock period, while, in Fig. 3-40, 10 clock periods were required (1 to load *SR1*, 8 to shift, and 1 to transfer from *SR2* to ASM2). This trade-off of speed and number of interconnections is common to all *timeshared* or *serial* systems, like the serial data transmission system just described. Serial data transmission systems are common and very sophisticated. Often only one wire is required for data transmission; the "clock" and "shift" signals are cleverly added to the data.

A TRAFFIC LIGHT CONTROLLER USING MSI CIRCUITS

Let's design a traffic light controller using MSI circuits. This intersection normally allows only north-south traffic through. Only when east and westbound traffic sensors are activated will the traffic lights change to halt north-south traffic. In addition, an emergency input sets all lights to red. When the emergency input is released, the lights should return to the north-south green condition after a delay. The delay is to allow a following emergency vehicle to activate the emergency input, so that the lights will remain red continuously. The times associated with each traffic light condition should be easily changed.

A circuit diagram of such a controller is shown in Fig. 3-41. The circuit is a ROM/flip-flop ASM. The next-state register is a counter. Branching is accomplished by loading the counter from four ROM data outputs. These data outputs are shared with both an output register and another counter, used as a delay timer. Decoders are used to reduce the number of output bits required. A two-line to one-line multiplexer connects either the timer output or east-west sensor as a branch input. The emergency

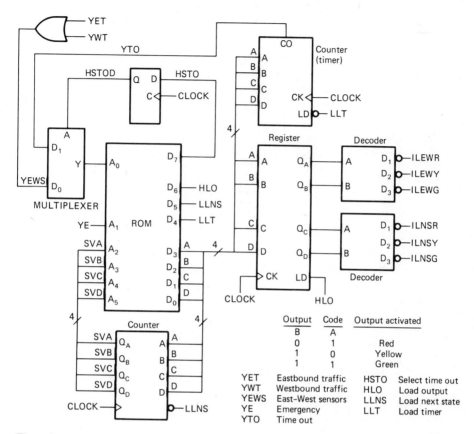

Figure 3-41 Traffic-light controller circuit.

input is not multiplexed. Finally, a simple OR gate combines the east and westbound sensors.

The ASM chart for this controller is shown in Fig. 3-42. Since four data outputs from the ROM are shared by the next-state counter, the timer counter, and the output register, extra states must be added to perform some functions sequentially. For example, state 0000 changes the output register, state 0001 sets the timer, and state 0010 tests for branches. These three functions must be performed sequentially because each requires use of the same ROM data outputs they all share. Since YTO and $YEWS$ are multiplexed, an additional state, 0011, must be added to test $YEWS$. This additional state delays changing the traffic lights by one clock cycle. Thus, the timer constant in state 0001 provides one less delay cycle than the constant in state 1000. The timer constants specified will cause 20-s green lights and 5-s yellow lights, using the 1.25-s clock specified. Don't forget that *all* states between output register changes must be included when calculating delays. The ROM contents for this circuit are specified in Table 3-5. Data outputs are listed as don't cares when these outputs aren't used. However, some value must be specified when the ROMs are programmed.

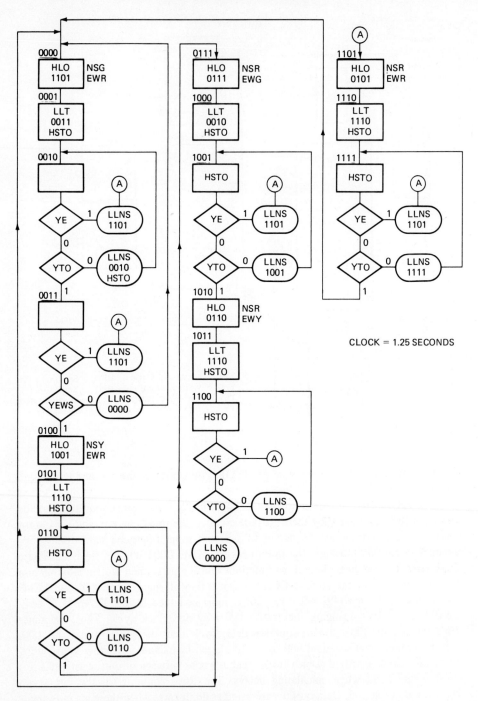

Figure 3-42 ASM chart for traffic-light controller.

Table 3-5 Traffic light control ROM contents

Current state				YEWS									
				YE	YTO	HSTO	HLO	LLNS	LLT	D	C	B	A
A_5	A_4	A_3	A_2	A_1	A_0	D_7	D_6	D_5	D_4	D_3	D_2	D_1	D_0
0	0	0	0	X	X	0	1	1	1	1	1	0	1
0	0	0	1	X	X	1	0	1	0	0	0	1	1
0	0	1	0	1	X	0	0	0	1	1	1	0	1
0	0	1	0	0	0	1	0	0	1	0	0	1	0
0	0	1	0	0	1	0	0	1	1	X	X	X	X
0	0	1	1	1	X	0	0	0	1	1	1	0	1
0	0	1	1	0	0	0	0	0	1	0	0	0	0
0	0	1	1	0	1	0	0	1	1	X	X	X	X
0	1	0	0	X	X	0	1	1	1	1	0	0	1
0	1	0	1	X	X	1	0	1	0	1	1	1	0
0	1	1	0	1	X	1	0	0	1	1	1	0	1
0	1	1	0	0	0	1	0	0	1	0	1	1	0
0	1	1	0	0	1	1	0	1	1	X	X	X	X
0	1	1	1	X	X	0	1	1	1	0	1	1	1
1	0	0	0	X	X	1	0	1	0	0	0	1	0
1	0	0	1	1	X	1	0	0	1	1	1	0	1
1	0	0	1	0	0	1	0	0	1	1	0	0	1
1	0	0	1	0	1	1	0	1	1	X	X	X	X
1	0	1	0	X	X	0	1	1	1	0	1	1	0
1	0	1	1	X	X	1	0	1	0	1	1	1	0
1	1	0	0	1	X	1	0	1	1	X	X	X	X
1	1	0	0	0	0	1	0	0	1	1	1	0	0
1	1	0	0	0	1	1	0	0	1	0	0	0	0
1	1	0	1	X	X	0	1	1	1	0	1	0	1
1	1	1	0	X	X	1	0	1	0	1	1	1	0
1	1	1	1	1	X	1	0	0	1	1	1	0	1
1	1	1	1	0	0	1	0	0	1	1	1	1	1
1	1	1	1	0	1	1	0	1	1	X	X	X	X

EXCLUSIVE OR GATES

The exclusive OR function (XOR) is a simple logical connective, like the AND and OR connectives. It is represented by the OR sign encircled:

$$F = A \oplus B$$

The function F is a 1 when either A or B is a 1 but is not a 1 when both A and B are 1:

$$F = A \oplus B$$

A	B	F
0	0	0
0	1	1
1	0	1
1	1	0

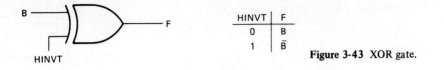

HINVT	F
0	B
1	$\bar{B}$

Figure 3-43 XOR gate.

Although generally useful, the XOR function has two especially common applications. The symbol for the XOR gate is shown in Fig. 3-43. The XOR *selectively* inverts the bit B in this diagram. One input, *HINVT*, is thought of as a control signal which can invert bit B if the control signal is a 1. This property of selective inversion is often used to invert an entire binary word, as shown in Fig. 3-44.

The output of an XOR gate is 0 whenever both inputs are identical. Thus, XOR gates can be used to compare single bits or groups of bits to determine equality. A *digital comparator* implemented with XOR gates is shown in Fig. 3-45. The output *HEQL* is 1 if all the bits of word F are equal to the corresponding bits of word G. Digital comparators are also available as single integrated circuits and usually include $F > G$ and $F < G$ outputs, besides an $F = G$ output. In the case of the inequalities, F and G are usually interpreted as positive binary numbers.

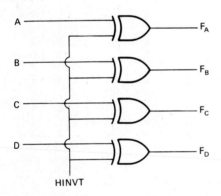

Figure 3-44 Selective inversion.

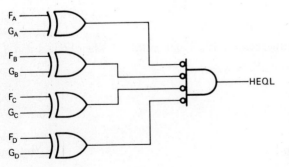

Figure 3-45 Digital comparator.

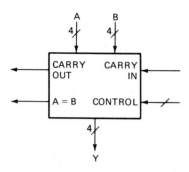

Figure 3-46 Arithmetic logic unit.

ARITHMETIC LOGIC UNITS

Another common MSI circuit is the arithmetic logic unit (ALU). An ALU generates logic functions of many inputs. Some sophisticated ALUs may also contain registers since data registers are almost always used with ALUs. We'll consider only those ALUs without registers. The diagram of Fig. 3-46 is representative of most ALUs. An output word Y is generated as some function of input words A and B. The function to be performed is specified by the control inputs. This function may be addition, subtraction, negation, shifting, bit-by-bit ANDing or ORing, and many others. The connections labeled *CARRY IN* and *CARRY OUT* allow multiple ALUs to be interconnected so that any word length for A, B, and Y may be accommodated. An $A = B$ output allows testing for equality. The ALU is controlled by an ASM and usually must have one or more external data storage registers, as shown in Fig. 3-47. Most digital systems, including computers, use an ALU and registers controlled by an ASM to perform arithmetic computations. Binary arithmetic will be discussed in detail in a later section of this book.

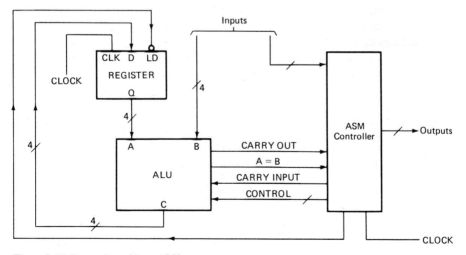

Figure 3-47 Processing with an ALU.

The ALU is a very general processing element. For simpler problems, a simpler processing element could be substituted for the ALU of Fig. 3-47. For example, if only addition were required, an MSI *adder* circuit could be substituted for the ALU of Fig. 3-47. The arrangement of circuit elements or *architecture* shown in Fig. 3-47 is very common. Although subject to many variations, it is characterized by data, stored in registers, being changed by a processing element under the control of an ASM.

LSI CIRCUITS

Large-scale integrated circuits contain very large numbers of circuits, thousands of flip-flops and gates. We have already used one LSI circuit, the read-only memory. In the last half of this book, we will use LSI circuits, almost exclusively, to design micro-computer systems. Let us examine some common LSI circuits.

Read-Only Memory

Although we have been using ROMs in our designs, one additional input often is included in a ROM that we haven't discussed. This input is called output enable, shown in Fig. 3-48, and is used to enable three-state outputs incorporated into the ROM. ROM outputs may need to be disabled when they are connected to a common data bus with other memories.

If one ROM doesn't have a sufficient number of outputs, two can be easily combined, as shown in Fig. 3-49. In this circuit, two 1KB ROMs have their address inputs paralleled, forming a 1K X 16 read-only memory. If we need more *address* inputs, the problem of combining ROMs is not as simple. The output enable input may be used to expand the number of words, as shown in Fig. 3-50. The most significant address bit is used to enable the three-state outputs of either one ROM or the other. The three-state outputs of one ROM are connected or bussed to the corresponding output bits of the other ROM. The MSB of the address selects one of the two ROMs to be connected to the output signals. Each ROM is again 1KB. Combined this way, they form a 2KB read-only memory. One ROM responds to addresses 000H to 3FFH, while the other ROM responds to addresses 400H to 7FFH.

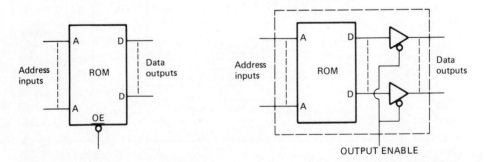

Figure 3-48 ROM with three-state outputs.

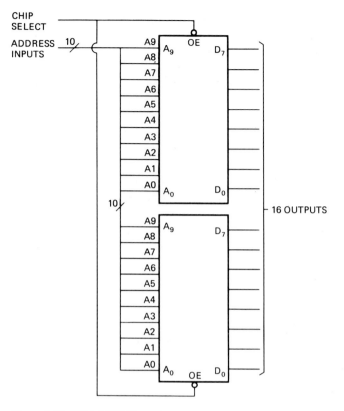

Figure 3-49 1K × 16 ROM.

Read-Write Memory

Often large amounts of data must be remembered in a digital system. Although individual registers could be used to store these data, read-write memory (RWM) is usually a better alternative. An RWM circuit is simply a large number of flip-flops fabricated on a single integrated circuit. Each flip-flop or group of flip-flops is assigned an address and may be changed or sensed whenever it is addressed. Changing a word in RWM is called *writing*. Sensing a word is called *reading*. In Fig. 3-51, notice that this RWM has four data inputs and four outputs. Thus, the states of four flip-flops may be sensed or changed at one time. The RWM circuit contains 1024 flip-flops; so that eight address inputs must determine which one of 256 groups of four flip-flops may be selected. Each group is called a word; so this is a 256-word RWM with each word containing 4 bits. This is represented by the notation 256 × 4. Three control signals are also required for operation of this RWM. An output enable (*OE*) turns on the three-state outputs of the RWM, to allow the data selected at the address inputs to appear on the four outputs. A write (*WR*) signal causes the addressed flip-flops in the circuit to be changed to the state of the four data inputs. Finally, a chip-select (*CS*) signal enables or disables all functions (both read and write) for this integrated circuit, which allows

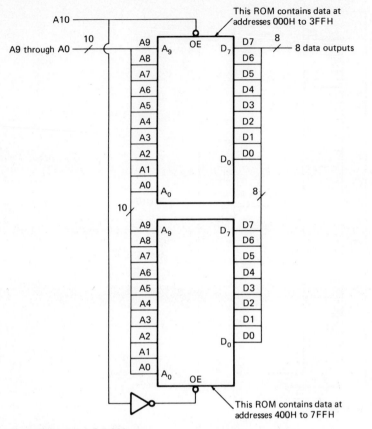

Figure 3-50 2K × 8 ROM.

for expansion by adding additional RWM circuits. Figure 3-52 shows an RWM using four 256 × 4 RWM circuits interconnected to form a 512-byte or 512 × 8 read-write memory. RWM integrated circuits are available in a wide variety of sizes including:

$$4 \times 4$$

$$16 \times 1$$

$$16 \times 4$$

$$256 \times 1$$

$$256 \times 4$$

$$1024 \times 1$$

$$1024 \times 4$$

$$4096 \times 1$$

$$16384 \times 1$$

$$65536 \times 1$$

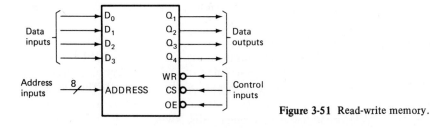

Figure 3-51 Read-write memory.

In addition, performance, which is usually measured by propagation delay and power supply requirements, varies greatly. Considerable effort is often necessary to specify an optimum RWM circuit.

There are many timing parameters associated with RWMs. The data sheet for the RWM must be consulted to ensure that no timing restriction is violated. It is important to know that the write function of an RWM is *not* edge-triggered. As long as the write and chip-select inputs are asserted, the data at the RWMs inputs will affect the con-

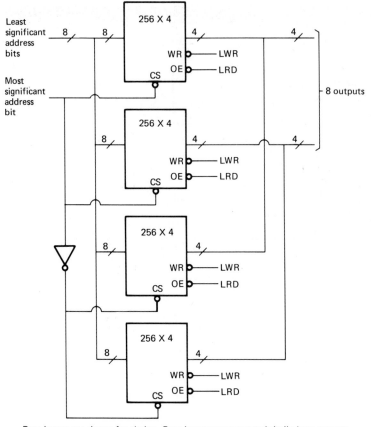

Data inputs not shown for clarity. Data inputs are connected similarly to outputs.

Figure 3-52 512 × 8 RWM.

tents of the memory flip-flops. The RWM must not be enabled to write data inputs until both address and data inputs are stable for a period sufficiently long to ensure they are properly recognized by the RWM. Figure 3-53 shows a read-write memory and its timing diagram. The chip-select input of the RWM is connected to the clock so that the RWM is enabled only in the *last* half of each ASM cycle. Address, data, and control inputs of the RWM change during the *first* half of the ASM cycle because they are either ROM outputs or other signals controlled by ROM outputs. Almost one half of a clock cycle occurs between changing the RWM's inputs and enabling the RWM. This half clock period is calculated to allow sufficient time for all address, data, and control signals to be properly recognized by the RWM.

The RWMs we have been discussing are all *static* RWMs. Another type of RWM is the *dynamic* RWM. Dynamic RWMs allow more bits to be fabricated onto a single integrated circuit. However, dynamic memories forget the data that have been stored in them unless they are periodically *refreshed*. Refreshing is accomplished by making sure that each memory cell is written or read periodically. This refresh period is specified by the manufacturer of the RWM and is usually around 2 ms. Also, dynamic RWMs are constructed so that only a small fraction of memory words must be

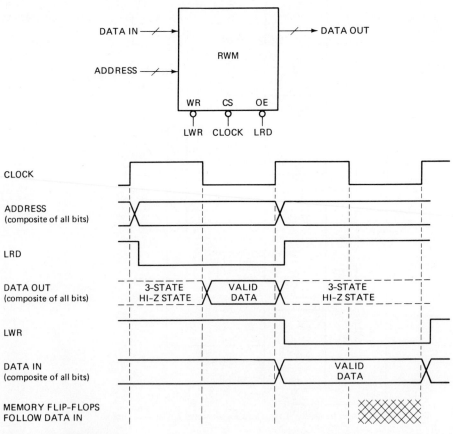

Figure 3-53 RWM timing.

periodically addressed to refresh all the memory words. For example, only 64 memory bits must be addressed to completely refresh a 4096 × 1 RWM.

Finally, RWMs are often called RAMs (random-access memories). We didn't use the term RAM since read-only memories are also random access. The term RAM is very commonly used for a read-write memory for historical reasons.

Programmable Logic Arrays

A ROM is a standardized part that is fabricated in quantity at low cost. However, when used in an ASM, it is often inefficient. Many entries in the ROM will be identical owing to don't cares in the input-variable specification. A gate implementation of next-state and output functions may be made very efficient by appropriate use of K maps or other reduction techniques. However, a gate implementation may not be standardized and fabricated as an integrated circuit unless a very large number of circuits are required. A compromise exists between these two extremes in the form of a programmable logic array (PLA). A PLA is designed to regularize the sum-of-products form of logic functions so that a "standard" SOP may be fabricated as an integrated circuit. In fact, PLAs are commonly available as FPLAs (field programmable logic arrays) that can be programmed after manufacture, much like a PROM. A typical PLA is shown in Fig. 3-54. It consists of 48 AND gates, each with 14 inputs. Each input

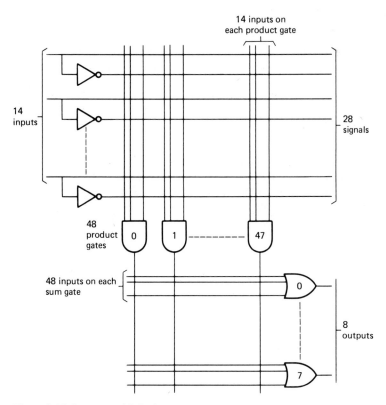

Figure 3-54 Programmable logic array.

Table 3-6 PLA specification for product gate 41

Product Gate	D_{13}	D_{12}	D_{11}	D_{10}	D_9	D_8	D_7	D_6	D_5	D_4	D_3	D_2	D_1	D_0	Q_7	Q_6	Q_5	Q_4	Q_3	Q_2	Q_1	Q_0
41	0	0	X	X	X	X	1	0	1	X	X	X	X	1	1	–	–	1	–	–	1	1

may be connected to one of 14 input variables or to the complement of that variable or not be connected at all. In this way, up to 48 product terms may be generated by the PLA. Eight 48-input OR gates generate eight output functions. Each of these 48 inputs may be connected or not connected to 1 of the 48 product terms. This circuit will generate any eight functions of up to 14 variables with the restriction that a maximum of 48 different product terms are allowed. A ROM that generated any eight functions of 14 variables would require $2^{14} \times 8$ or 131,072 bits. A PLA is specified by listing the input combination corresponding to each of the 48 product terms and the outputs asserted by that product. Thus, the specification shown in Table 3-6 means that, whenever $D_{13} = D_{12} = D_6 = 0$ and $D_7 = D_5 = D_0 = 1$, then outputs Q_7, Q_4, Q_1, and Q_0 will be 1. Physically, this table entry means that AND gate number 41 has six inputs connected to $\overline{D_{13}}, \overline{D_{12}}, D_7, \overline{D_6}, D_5$, and D_0. The output of AND gate 41 is connected to inputs on OR gates corresponding to outputs Q_7, Q_4, Q_1, and Q_0.

There are two ways to design with PLAs. Generating a next-state and output table for a ROM-implemented ASM usually creates many don't care inputs. It is these don't cares that make a ROM implementation inefficient. However, don't care conditions need not be implemented in a PLA. If the number of lines of our next-state and output table is less than the number of PLA product terms, each line may be implemented as a product term in the PLA. In other words, each line (don't cares and all) of the next-state and output table corresponds to one line of the PLA specification.

If a number of entries of the next-state and output table exceeds the number of product terms available, the functions can be placed on K maps in the hope that the number of distinct product terms needed will be reduced when the K maps are reduced. The remaining product terms can then be programmed into the PLA directly.

Don't forget that all the MSI circuits previously discussed in conjunction with ROMs may be applied to a PLA implementation. Thus, a multiplexer can reduce the number of inputs required or a decoder may be used to increase the number of outputs.

PROBLEMS

3-1 Design a 24-bit multiplexer using three 8-input multiplexers. Design the multiplexer twice, once using each technique shown in the text.

3-2 Use multiplexers to implement the functions in Prob. 2-5. Use the smallest multiplexer possible.

3-3 Decoders can be expanded, as well as multiplexers:

(a) Design a 32-output decoder, using two 16-output decoders.

(b) Design a 16-output decoder, using *only* 4-output decoders.

3-4 (*a*) Assume you have 4-bit MSI counters, each with two enable inputs and a carry output. Design a 12-bit binary counter, using three of these MSI circuits.

(*b*) Assume that the above counters each have *LOAD* and *CLEAR* inputs. Show how these inputs should be interconnected so that the entire 12-bit counter will load or clear simultaneously.

3-5 Assume you have 8 bits of data on eight separate wires. You must design a circuit to output these 8 bits in serial form, repeatedly. One bit should follow another at each clock edge with no pause.

(*a*) Design a circuit using a shift register.

(*b*) Design a circuit using a multiplexer.

3-6 Repeat Prob. 1-5. Use a decoder for the outputs. Use a counter for the state register.

3-7 Repeat Prob. 3-6. Now, add a multiplexer for inputs.

3-8 Repeat Prob. 3-7. Now add another counter for timing the tram stopped state.

3-9 Repeat Prob. 1-7. Use MSI parts as needed. Be sure to use a multiplexer for inputs. Add a separate counter to perform the cycle timing function (which was just assumed to exist in Prob. 1-7). You do not have to draw the ASM chart, but you should be sure that it is *possible* to draw an ASM chart based on your solution to Prob. 1-7.

FOUR

MORE IMPLEMENTATIONS

In the last chapter, we studied several MSI circuits that also happened to be ASMs themselves. In this chapter, we'll look at the counter circuit both because of its own importance as a circuit element and because it will serve as an example to introduce new topics. These topics are JK flip-flops, ASM coupling, hang-up states, and initialization.

COUNTERS AND FLIP-FLOPS

A counter is designed exactly like any ASM. The ASM chart for a simple eight-state counter is shown in Fig. 4-1. The outputs and state variables have been made identical in each state to eliminate the need for any output functions. The outputs are simply the state variables. In a ROM implementation, only next-state ROM outputs would be required. In a gate implementation, only next-state gating would be required. This counter has no enable or other inputs. It counts continuously as long as clock signals are applied. The circuit for this counter, using D flip-flops, is shown in Fig. 4-2. Even in this simple 3-bit counter, the next-state gating is becoming complex, especially for the more significant bits. In fact, counters implemented with D flip-flops having more than 4 or 5 bits require intolerable amounts of gating. Another type of flip-flop, called a *JK flip-flop*, can be used to reduce the number of gating circuits required.

JK Flip-Flops

The symbol for a positive edge-triggered JK flip-flop is shown in Fig. 4-3. The abbreviated Next-State Table 4-1 is easily understood; so we'll use it to explain the operation of this circuit. The table heading Q^{t+1} is the Q output after the clock transition,

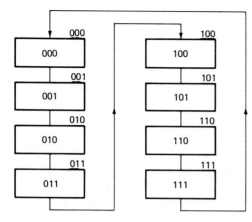

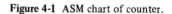

Figure 4-1 ASM chart of counter.

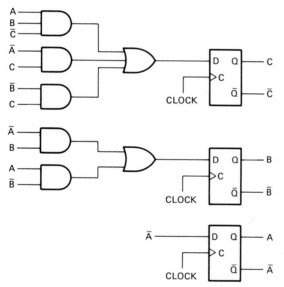

Figure 4-2 Counter with D flip-flops.

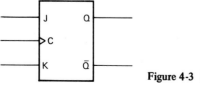

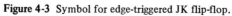

Figure 4-3 Symbol for edge-triggered JK flip-flop.

**Table 4-1 Next-state table
for JK flip-flop**

J	K	Q^{t+1}
0	0	Q^t
1	0	1
0	1	0
1	1	$\overline{Q^t}$

while the entry Q^t represents the Q output before the clock pulse occurred. If both the J and K inputs are 0 when a clock transition occurs, the Q output remains the same, $Q^{t+1} = Q^t$. If $J = 1$ and $K = 0$, the Q output will become 1 at the next clock transition. If $J = 0$ and $K = 1$, the Q output will become 0 at the next clock transition. Finally, if both the J and K inputs are 1, the output will assume the opposite state at the clock transition, $Q^{t+1} = \overline{Q}^t$. This last behavior, changing to the opposite state regardless of the current state, is called *toggling*. A flip-flop is often required to toggle so that the connection of a JK flip-flop in Fig. 4-4 is also called a *type T* or *toggle flip-flop*. A toggle flip-flop remains unchanged as long as its T input is a 0 and toggles to alternate states on each clock transition when its T input is a 1.

You can already see that the JK flip-flop is more versatile than the D flip-flop. Only two operations are possible with the D flip-flop. These are setting the D flip-flop's output to 1 and resetting its output to 0. Four operations are possible with the JK flip-flop. Besides the operations of setting or resetting its output at each clock transition, the JK flip-flop may also toggle or remain in the same state. It is these two additional operations that we will use to our advantage.

In Table 4-2, we've tabulated the inputs necessary to cause each possible next state for each possible current state. If the Q output is 0 and we desire that it remain 0 after the clock transition, we have two choices of inputs. If we select inputs $J = 0$

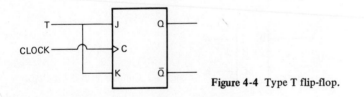

Figure 4-4 Type T flip-flop.

**Table 4-2 JK inputs required for flip-flop state
state changes**

Original state	Next state	J	K
0	0	0	X
0	1	1	X
1	0	X	1
1	1	X	0

and $K = 0$, the flip-flop will remain in its original state of $Q = 0$. If we select inputs $J = 0$ and $K = 1$, the flip-flop will reset to state $Q = 0$. Either way, the state after the clock transition will be $Q = 0$. Notice that all four possible state transitions may be accomplished in two ways. These alternatives will allow us to enter don't cares on our K maps, which may allow us to simplify the next-state gating.

Designing with JK Flip-Flops

The next-state table for the simple 3-bit counter of Fig. 4-1 is shown in Table 4-3. The next-state columns are not marked D_C, D_B, and D_A because we shall use JK, not D, flip-flops to implement this counter. For simplicity, we'll consider only the next-state function of flip-flop C, as shown in Table 4-4. We've listed the current state and the C flip-flop's next state. We desire to specify the J_C and K_C inputs to flip-flop C. At state 0 on the table, flip-flop C is a 0 and must remain so. Table 4-2 indicates that the J input must be 0 and K can be a don't care in order to keep the flip-flop output at 0 if its current output is 0. We enter those inputs in the line of Table 4-4 corresponding to the transition from state 0. At state 3 in Table 4-4, a 0-to-1 transition of flip-flop C

Table 4-3 Next-state table for eight-state counter

Current state			Next state		
C	B	A	C^{t+1}	B^{t+1}	A^{t+1}
0	0	0	0	0	1
0	0	1	0	1	0
0	1	0	0	1	1
0	1	1	1	0	0
1	0	0	1	0	1
1	0	1	1	1	0
1	1	0	1	1	1
1	1	1	0	0	0

Table 4-4 Determining JK inputs for flip-flop C

Current state					
C^t	B^t	A^t	C^{t+1}	J_C	K_C
0	0	0	0	0	X
0	0	1	0	0	X
0	1	0	0	0	X
0	1	1	1	1	X
1	0	0	1	X	0
1	0	1	1	X	0
1	1	0	1	X	0
1	1	1	0	X	1

Table 4-5 Determining JK inputs for eight-state counter

Current state			Next state			Flip-flop inputs					
C^t	B^t	A^t	C^{t+1}	B^{t+1}	A^{t+1}	J_C	K_C	J_B	K_B	J_A	K_A
0	0	0	0	0	1	0	X	0	X	1	X
0	0	1	0	1	0	0	X	1	X	X	1
0	1	0	0	1	1	0	X	X	0	1	X
0	1	1	1	0	0	1	X	X	1	X	1
1	0	0	1	0	1	X	0	0	X	1	X
1	0	1	1	1	0	X	0	1	X	X	1
1	1	0	1	1	1	X	0	X	0	1	X
1	1	1	0	0	0	X	1	X	1	X	1

causes us to enter $J_C = 1$ and $K_C = X$. At state 4, the C flip-flop remains a 1 and we enter $J_C = X$ and $K_C = 0$. At state 7, a 1-to-0 transition of flip-flop C requires an entry of $J_C = X$ and $K_C = 1$. In this way, we can determine the correct logic function for each of the six inputs of the three flip-flops, as shown in Table 4-5. Each of these functions is transferred to a K map in Fig. 4-5. These functions may be considerably

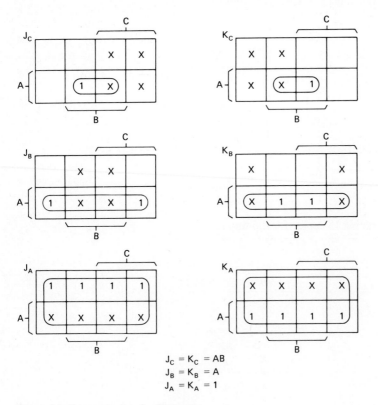

$$J_C = K_C = AB$$
$$J_B = K_B = A$$
$$J_A = K_A = 1$$

Figure 4-5 Karnaugh maps for JK inputs.

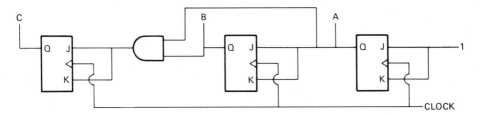

Figure 4-6 Eight-state counter using JK flip-flops.

simplified because of many don't cares. Also, the *J* and *K* inputs of each flip-flop just happen to be equal to the same boolean function! The counter of Fig. 4-6, using JK flip-flops, is considerably simpler than the equivalent counter of Fig. 4-2, using type D flip-flops.

Another JK Counter

Every JK implementation is not as simple and symmetric as the example above. The above example was particularly simple because it was a binary counter and had a total number of states equal to a power of 2. However, many JK implementations are often simpler than D implementations. Let's consider a binary counter with five states. Its next states and the *J* and *K* inputs needed to establish them are tabulated in Table 4-6. Transferring these functions to the K maps of Fig. 4-7, we specify states 5, 6, and 7 as don't cares since these states are unused. The circuit of Fig. 4-8 is a five-state counter using JK flip-flops. Although not as simple as the eight-state counter, this circuit is simpler than a D flip-flop implementation.

JK Flip-Flops and the General ASM

The JK design technique described above for ASM counters applies equally well to any ASM. The use of JK flip-flops will often lead to simpler next-state gating than an equivalent D flip-flop implementation. In the previous counter examples, no gates were required to generate the output functions. When output gating is required, it will be identical in both the JK and D implementations. Finally, JK flip-flops are almost always *undesirable* when used with a ROM for generating next-state functions. The JKs

Table 4-6 Determining JK inputs for five-state counter

Current state			Next state			Flip-flop inputs					
C^t	B^t	A^t	C^{t+1}	B^{t+1}	A^{t+1}	J_C	K_C	J_B	K_B	J_A	K_A
0	0	0	0	0	1	0	X	0	X	1	X
0	0	1	0	1	0	0	X	1	X	X	1
0	1	0	0	1	1	0	X	X	0	1	X
0	1	1	1	0	0	1	X	X	1	X	1
1	0	0	0	0	0	X	1	0	X	0	X

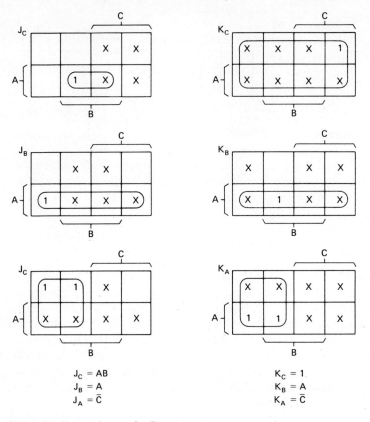

$$J_C = AB$$
$$J_B = A$$
$$J_A = \bar{C}$$

$$K_C = 1$$
$$K_B = A$$
$$K_A = \bar{C}$$

Figure 4-7 Karnaugh maps for five-state counter.

will require twice the number of next-state outputs from the ROM than the D flops require. The cost of the ROM is not dependent on the function implemented, but does increase as the number of output bits increases. The JK implementation's don't cares are of no use with the ROM.

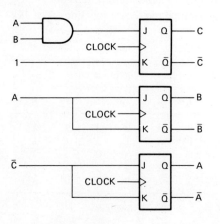

Figure 4-8 Five-state counter.

COUPLING ASMs

ASMs must often be coupled or interconnected. Designing a very large digital system is simplified by dividing the system into smaller parts, each of which is a separate ASM. The method of interconnecting ASMs that we've been using is called *synchronous coupling*. We have simply connected the output of one ASM to the input of another. Figure 4-9 shows two 4-bit counters coupled this way. The carry output of the least significant counter is connected to the enable input of the most significant counter. If these counters are binary counters, the carry output will be 1 when the least significant counter is 1111. This enables the most significant counter so the same clock pulse will reset the least significant counter to 0000 *and* make the most significant counter count up by one. *Synchronous coupling is usually the best way to couple ASMs.*

Synchronous coupling does have drawbacks. First, extra inputs are required. Each extra input doubles the size of the ROM in a ROM implementation or complicates the gating in a gate implementation. Second, cascading multiple ASMs in this way *may* slow the maximum rate at which they will operate. Consider the counters of Fig. 4-9. Each time a carry output is generated, it is delayed by the output logic of the following counter. The carry output of the last counter in a 12-bit cascade will be delayed by 3 times the propagation delay of a single counter's output logic. Since the next clock transition must not occur until the last carry is correctly generated, these propagation delays limit the speed at which this counter will operate.

Several alternatives to synchronous coupling exist. The important alternatives are *asynchronous coupling* and *gated-clock coupling*.

Asynchronous Counters

Even using JK flip-flops to advantage, synchronous counters of many bits will have complex gating structures to generate the next state. Studying the timing diagram for a

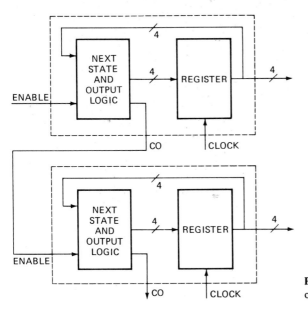

Figure 4-9 Synchronous coupling of MSI counters.

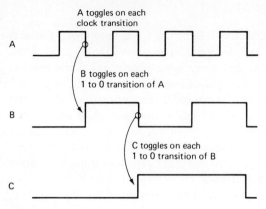

A toggles on each
clock transition

A

B toggles on each
1 to 0 transition of A

B

C toggles on each
1 to 0 transition of B

C

Figure 4-10 Binary counting sequence.

binary counter in Fig. 4-10, note that each bit toggles at the same time the next least significant bit makes a 1-to-0 transition. If we use a 1-to-0 transition of a bit to toggle the next most significant bit, we should be able to build a counter requiring no gating! We will use transitions of outputs to clock flip-flops, rather than a common clock signal. A circuit in which all flip-flops do not have their clock lines driven in synchronism is called an *asynchronous* circuit. A 3-bit counter using this technique is shown in Fig. 4-11. This asynchronous counter consists of three JK flip-flops connected as type T or toggle flip-flops. A 1-to-0 transition on any Q output causes the next most significant bit to toggle. The $\overline{Q}$ output is actually connected to the next most significant clock input because these positive edge-triggered flip-flops are toggled by a 0-to-1 transition. Unlike the synchronous counter, all outputs do not change simultaneously. For example, let's assume that $Q_C = Q_B = Q_A = 1$ and a clock transition occurs. This will cause the Q_A flip-flop to toggle, after a short delay, through the electronic circuitry of the flip-flop. The $\overline{Q_A}$ output will change state from 0 to 1, causing the Q_B flip-flop to change state after another short delay. This will, in turn, cause the Q_C flip-flop to change after another short delay. Because the flip-flops change sequentially, this type of counter is often called a *ripple counter*. As we'll see later, the short delay through each flip-flop can cause malfunctions of circuitry connected to the counter or, at the very least, degrade performance.

Asynchronous Coupling

Since small synchronous counters are easily implemented, it would be advantageous to connect small synchronous counters together asynchronously. A 5-bit counter may be

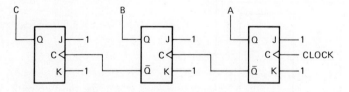

Figure 4-11 Asynchronous counter.

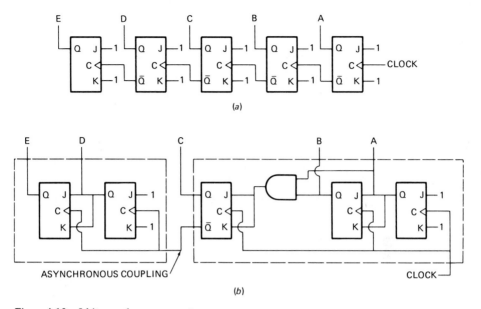

(a)

(b)

Figure 4-12a 5-bit asynchronous counter.
Figure 4-12b 5-bit counter using two asynchronously coupled synchronous counters.

implemented in several ways. As a completely synchronous ASM, it would require considerable gating. Two simpler alternatives are shown in Fig. 4-12. The 5-bit ripple counter in Fig. 4-12a is the simplest circuit but requires five flip-flop delays between a clock transition and a change of the most significant flip-flop Q_E. The alternate circuit shown in Fig. 4-12b consists of a 3-bit synchronous counter coupled asynchronously to a 2-bit synchronous counter. The most significant counter is clocked whenever the most significant bit of the least significant counter changes from a 1 to 0. Only two flip-flop delays occur between a clock transition and a change in the most significant bit Q_E. Output C changes one flip-flop delay after the clock. Output E changes one flip-flop delay after output C.

It should be obvious to you that one reason we worry about reducing delays is because we might want to operate the circuit at as high a clock rate as possible. For example, if we're building a digital computer, we'd like to solve problems as fast as possible. Using our 5-bit ripple counter would require waiting at least five flip-flop delays between clock transitions so that all five outputs have a chance to change.

Output Races

Suppose that we desire to connect gating to the outputs of the 3-bit ripple counter of Fig. 4-11. The timing diagram for this counter is shown in Fig. 4-13, along with the outputs of three AND gates we might use to decode particular counter states. Note that short undesired outputs occur on these AND gates in addition to the desired outputs. Because the three state variables change in sequence, the three flip-flop outputs momentarily assume *combinations that are not the actual next state*. For exam-

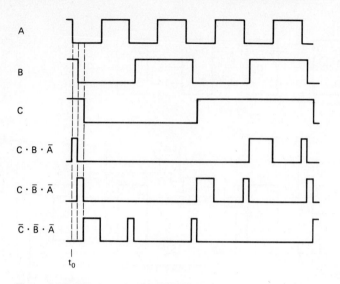

Figure 4-13 Output races when decoding an asynchronous counter.

ple, at time t_0, the circuit should make a transition from state 7 to state 0. In reality, flip-flop A changes first so that state 6 seems to momentarily occur. Flip-flop B changes next so that state 4 seems to momentarily occur. Finally, flip-flop C changes so that state 0 occurs. The decoding gates for states 6 and 4 will have momentary undesired outputs. These undesired outputs are called *output races*. Output races even occur in completely synchronous circuitry. Even though all flip-flops of a synchronous circuit are clocked simultaneously, each flip-flop will have a different propagation delay so that their outputs do not change exactly simultaneously. We will study problems such as races in detail in a later chapter. Note that even in our asynchronous ASM counter, where these output races are more pronounced, no difficulties will be encountered as long as these outputs are inputs to another ASM connected to the same clock. This clock must be slow enough that all outputs with races reach their correct value before the next clock transition. If outputs with races are used as immediate outputs or as inputs to another ASM which is connected to a different clock, the output races will be sensed as real outputs.

Gated-Clock Coupling

One more technique can be used to couple counters or other ASMs together. By selectively turning the clock of a counter on or off, we can cause it to count only when desired. Since the same clock is being used to change all the flip-flop's states, all outputs will change within one flip-flop delay. A 5-bit counter is formed by cascading a 2- and 3-bit counter, as shown in Fig. 4-14. The $A = 1$ and $B = 1$ state of the 2-bit counter is used to gate the clock to the 3-bit counter. For proper operation of this circuit, the gated clock *GCLK* must have two properties. It must be generated so that

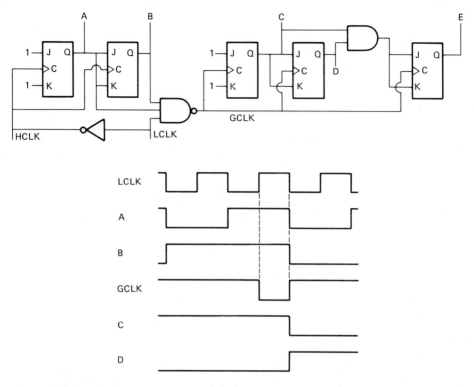

Figure 4-14 Coupling counters with a gated clock.

the circuitry it is driving is clocked at the same time as the other flip-flops in the system. Also, it must be generated in the *last half of the clock cycle* so that any state variables connected to the clock gate inputs have as much time as possible to reach their correct values before a gated-clock pulse is generated. A gated clock may be generated in four ways, as shown in Fig. 4-15. *Only one of these is correct for any given circuit.* If ever in doubt, remember the following two rules.

1. The edge of the gated clock causing a state transition must cause this transition simultaneously with other nongated state transitions in the circuit.
2. The edge described above must always be the second or trailing edge of the gated-clock pulse.

The same clock signal is not really used for the gated and nongated flip-flops of Fig. 4-14. These two signals will differ in time by the *difference* in propagation delay between the inverter generating *HCLK* and the gate generating *GCLK*. This is the reason we generated *HCLK* by inverting *LCLK*. If we had generated *LCLK* by inverting *HCLK*, the *HCLK* and *GCLK* transitions would differ by the *sum* of the inverter and gate delays.

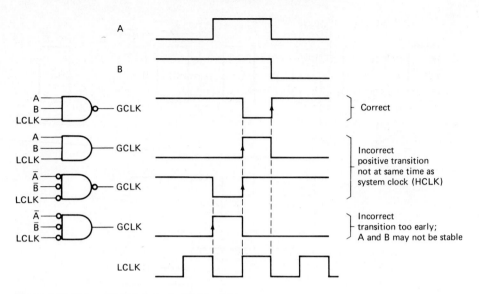

Figure 4-15 Generating gated clocks for Fig. 4-14.

Selection of Coupling Technique

These three coupling techniques apply to interconnection of any ASM, as well as counters. The following table describes the important considerations involved in selection of a coupling technique.

Asynchronous coupling

1. Used in counters with very long count sequences
2. Used when cost is paramount
3. Not used with immediate outputs, unless special provisions made to eliminate output races

Gated-clock coupling

1. Used with MSI devices that do not have an integral enable input. The clock to the MSI device must be turned off to disable it.
2. Used with complex functions made from individual gates and flip-flops that would become hopelessly complex if enabling logic were included in next-state circuitry
3. Not used when highest speed is required

Synchronous coupling
Generally recommended in all cases

HANDSHAKING

Often more than 1 bit of information must be transferred between ASMs. A common requirement, shown in Fig. 4-16, is transferring multiple bits between ASMs. These bits may represent a number or the code for a function to be performed or many other things. In a previous chapter, we have transferred data between ASMs, using a data-valid signal to indicate to the the the receiving ASM that data were present. In Fig. 4-16, a data-available signal ($HDAV$) indicates to the receiving ASM that data are available. Also, a data-accepted signal ($HDAC$) indicates to the sending ASM that the data have been accepted. The operation of these signals is called a *handshake* and is shown in the timing diagram of Fig. 4-16.

At time t_0, ASM1 has data read to be sent to ASM2. ASM1 asserts $HDAV$ to notify ASM2 that new data must be transferred. When ASM2 tests and recognizes that $HDAV$ is asserted, ASM2 stores (or tests) the data sent to it and asserts $HDAC$ at t_1 to tell ASM1 that it has accepted this data byte. ASM1 makes $HDAV$ false at t_2, indicating that valid data are no longer being sent. Finally, ASM2 makes $HDAC$ false at t_3 to prepare for another data transfer at t_4.

ASM1 transmits new data only after it recognizes an $HDAC$ transition from true to false, indicating completion of the last data transfer. ASM1 leaves $HDAV$ true until it recognizes an $HDAC$ transition from false to true, indicating that the data were accepted. ASM2 accepts data only when it recognizes an $HDAV$ transition from false to true. ASM2 acknowledges a transfer complete only when it recognizes an $HDAV$ transition from true to false. The handshake sequence assures that ASM2 accepts each data byte before another is transmitted. A data byte cannot be missed, nor can it be read twice, as long as the handshake sequence is followed. The handshake sequence does not rely on synchronism between the clocks of the two ASMs and will work even if each ASM has a different clock.

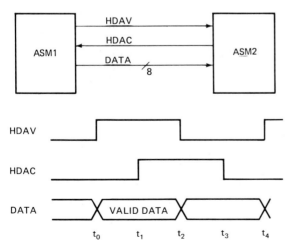

Figure 4-16 Handshaking.

HANG-UP STATES AND SYSTEM INITIALIZATION

Let's implement the six-state counter whose ASM chart and K maps are shown in Fig. 4-17. Note that the counting sequence we chose caused a particularly simple implementation, shown in Fig. 4-18. States 2 and 5 were not used; so we specified all entries corresponding to these states to be don't cares. Since we have no control over the initial state of the counter when power is first applied to the circuit, either of these unused states could occur at that time. Returning to Fig. 4-17, we can calculate the next states if the current state is either 2 or 5. If the counter is in state 2, we find the next state by looking in square 2 of the K maps of Fig. 4-17. The next state will be $D_C = 1, D_B = 0$, and $D_A = 1$ or state 5. If the counter is in state 5, its next state will be state 2. If the counter is in state 2, it will count to state 5. If the counter is in state 5, it will count to state 2. The ASM chart of Fig. 4-19 describes the counter's behavior in states 2 and 5. If the circuit starts in state 2 or 5, it will just alternate between these states. It will never count as we designed it! Any ASM that has fewer states than the maximum allowed by the number of state variables can have undesirable sequences

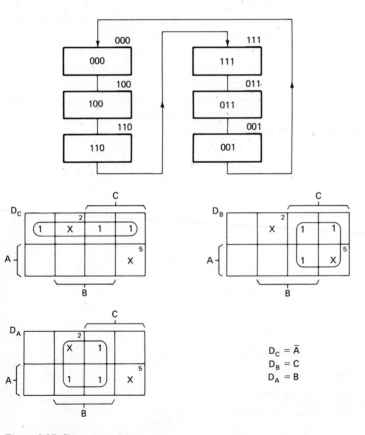

Figure 4-17 Six-state counter.

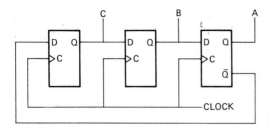

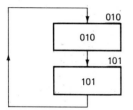

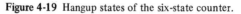

Figure 4-18 Six-state counter schematic.

Figure 4-19 Hangup states of the six-state counter.

like this one. Any unused state that doesn't eventually lead back to a desired state is called a *hang-up state*.

System Initialization

One way to make sure hang-up states are not entered when power is applied is to specify the first state explicitly, as shown in Fig. 4-20. Often, the first state must be specified anyway for functional reasons. For example, we couldn't have a computer start in the "erase disk memory state" when power is first applied. Specifying the first state on the ASM chart is done by simply noting this state with the words "power on" or "initialize," as shown in Fig. 4-20. Implementing this notation is more difficult. A signal (*LPWRON*) indicating that power has just been applied must be generated in the power supply of the logic circuit. This signal may be used in several ways to

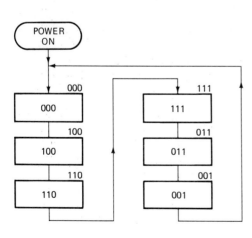

Figure 4-20 Initializing the ASM chart.

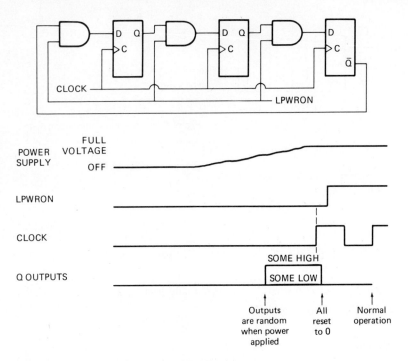

Figure 4-21 Initializing by modifying flip-flop inputs.

preset the state variables. In Fig. 4-21 each flip-flop is given additional input gating to allow *LPWRON* to set the *D* inputs to the desired next state. The first clock pulse to be generated clocks this state into the flip-flops. The simple gating shown is possible because we've picked 000 as our first state. More complex gating might be necessary for other initial states. In general, the all-0s and all-1s states are easiest to use as the first state after power is applied. In Fig. 4-22 we've saved input gating by noting that we can set only one *D* input to 0 and let three clock transitions propagate this 0 to the three flip-flop outputs. Propagating the initialization signal may be inconvenient or time-consuming with many ASMs. This technique is naturally suited to shift register implementations, such as this example. This technique could be the only one possible if these flip-flops were part of an MSI or LSI circuit and external connections were not available.

The most common initialization technique uses *direct clear* and *direct preset* inputs found on many flip-flops and MSI circuits containing flip-flops. These inputs, shown on a D flip-flop in Fig. 4-23, are usually immediate-acting. They do not depend on the clock input for operation. If the preset input is low, the *Q* output will immediately become 1 (and $\overline{Q}$ will become 0). If the clear input is low, the *Q* output will immediately become 0 (and $\overline{Q}$ will become 1). If both clear and preset are low, the operation of the circuit is unpredictable. Both clear and preset must be high just before and during a clock pulse if the clock transition is to have a predictable effect on the flip-flop's output. In Fig. 4-24, the direct clear inputs of the three flip-flops are held

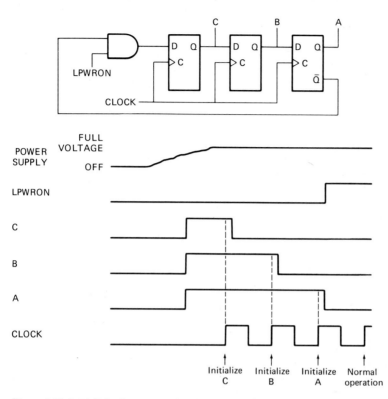

Figure 4-22 Initializing by propagating through ASM.

low by *LPWRON* until after power is applied. After the clear inputs are brought to a 1, the clock is started.

Self-Clearing Logic

Even though we have now made sure that our original six-state counter will start in the correct state, we have no guarantee that it will stay in that sequence. Environmental conditions such as excessive electric noise could cause the circuit to accidentally and erroneously enter state 2 or 5. It would alternate between these two states until we removed and reapplied power. To avoid this malfunction, we will design the circuit

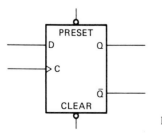

Figure 4-23 Type D flip-flop with direct preset and direct clear.

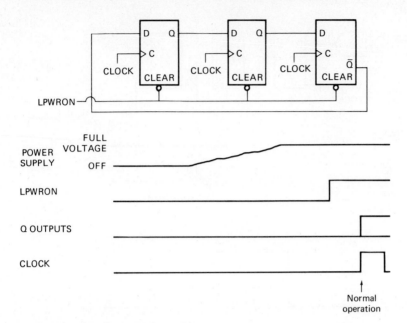

Figure 4-24 Initializing with direct inputs

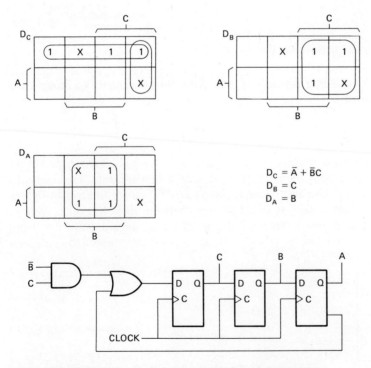

$$D_C = \bar{A} + \bar{B}C$$
$$D_B = C$$
$$D_A = B$$

Figure 4-25 Modified K-maps and circuit to eliminate hang-up states.

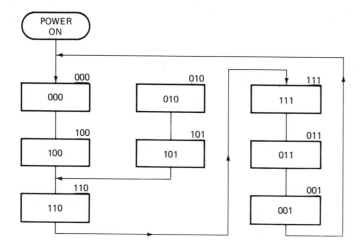

Figure 4-26 ASM chart for six-state counter with initialization and without hangup states.

so that all unused states will eventually lead back to a desired state. If electric noise should ever disturb its operation, the malfunction would last only momentarily, until the circuit sequenced back to a desired state. *Never design a logic circuit with hang-up states!* The K maps for our counter are redrawn in Fig. 4-25. Only now we would like to change the next state corresponding to a current state of 2 or 5. One simple alternative is to change the interpretation of the don't care of D_C from a 0 to a 1, as shown. This complicates the expression for D_C and adds two gates to our implementation, also shown in Fig. 4-25. However, the ASM chart for this circuit in Fig. 4-26 has no hang-up states. If the circuit is accidentally put in state 2 or 5, it will eventually return to state 6, where it will continue the correct counting sequence.

PROBLEMS

4-1 Design counters using JK flip-flops for the following sequences.

    (*a*) 00, 01, 11

    (*b*) 00, 11, 01

    (*c*) 01, 11, 00

4-2 Design a five-state counter using D flip-flops to perform identically to the JK flip-flop counter of Fig. 4-8.

4-3 Draw a circuit to synchronously couple three 4-bit counters, like those shown in Fig. 4-9. Devise a coupling scheme that *does not* cascade delays through each counter's output logic.

    Hint: You can only use the least significant counter's carry output since only this carry output occurs one propagation delay after the clock.

4-4 Add an enable input to the asynchronous counter of Fig. 4-11 in the simplest way possible. Do *not* gate the clock.

4-5 Figure P4-1 shows three other possible configurations for the counter of Fig. 4-14. Draw the correct gated-clock logic for each.

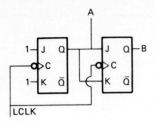

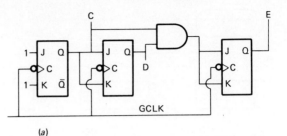

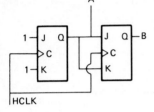

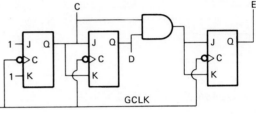

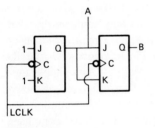

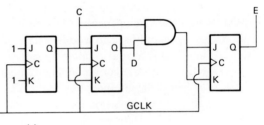

Figure P4-1 Gated clock configurations.

4-6 Design a six-state counter, using JK flip-flops for the ASM chart of Fig. 4-17.

4-7 Consider the counter of Prob. 4-6. It is called a Moebius counter and has several useful properties.

(*a*) Design a decoder of each of the six states. What do these decoders have in common? Can you find a simple rule for decoding a state without having to resort to K maps?

(*b*) What additional gating would be required to stop the counter when it reached a particular state?

Hint: It is a single gate and does not require decoding states.

(*c*) If the three flip-flops had different delays, would output races occur in the decoding of part (*a*)? Explain your answer.

CHAPTER FIVE

CLOCKS AND SIGNALS

The clock signal of any sequential machine is very important. Up to now we have been ignoring the details of the clock signal, assuming that it had any attributes necessary for proper operation of the ASM. Actually, generating and distributing clock signals in an ASM is a complex subject.

Clock Skew

Since digital systems are often very large, the situation depicted in Fig. 5-1 usually occurs. Here, the number of flip-flops is so large that the clock circuit cannot drive all of them directly. In this example, two inverters are used to drive the clock lines. Some of the flip-flop clock inputs are connected to each inverter. The signal propagation delays through these two inverters are probably different. Usually only maximum delay times are specified for logic circuits. Any individual circuit may have a delay considerably less than the maximum. The delay through any logic circuit is dependent on the number of other circuits connected to it. If one inverter drove 10 clock inputs and the other drove 5 inputs, their propagation delays would be different, even if both inverters were electrically identical. Also, as seen in the last chapter, gating the clock also causes unequal clock delays.

Does the fact that the clocks of two flip-flops occur at different times cause problems? In the simple 2-bit shift register of Fig. 5-2, clock inputs are driven by two different sources. The clock of the first flip-flop X occurs later than the clock of the second flip-flop Z. The timing diagram in Fig. 5-2 shows data shifted through the register correctly. Because $CLKA$ is later than $CLKB$, data are shifted properly from flip-flop X to flip-flop Z. In fact, whenever information is transferred from a later clock to an earlier clock, the information transfer will take place correctly. However, if information is transferred from an earlier to a later clock, the transfer could occur

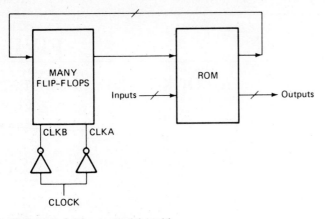

Figure 5-1 A large sequential machine.

incorrectly. In Fig. 5-3, flip-flop X is clocked by the earlier clock. Flip-flop X changes to a 1 so early that the later clock $CLKB$ stores this 1 into flip-flop Z on the current clock transition and not on the next clock transition! Both flip-flops are loaded with the same datum simultaneously. The circuit fails to function as a shift register.

Circuits can seldom be arranged to always transfer information from a later to an earlier clock. Even in the simple counter of Fig. 5-4, data transfers must occur in both directions. Data are transferred from a later to an earlier clock, and vice-versa.

Before we can calculate the maximum delay permitted for $CLKB$ of Fig. 5-3 without causing a malfunction, we need the definitions of the timing specifications of a flip-flop. The following definitions are illustrated in Fig. 5-5 for a type D flip-flop.

Setup time, t_S.   The setup time is the time that an input must have valid data *before* a clock transition if the flip-flop is to recognize it reliably.

Hold time, t_H.   The hold time is the time that an input must remain correct *after* a clock transition if the flip-flop is to recognize it reliably.

Propagation delay, t_P.   The propagation delay is the time that occurs between the clock transition and an output change caused by that clock transition.

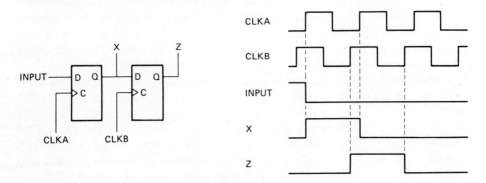

Figure 5-2 Correct data transfer from a later to an earlier clock.

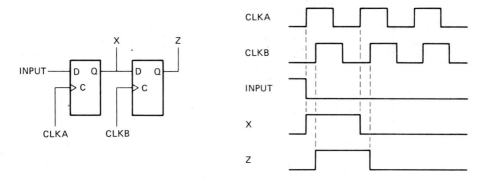

Figure 5-3 Incorrect data transfer from an earlier to later clock.

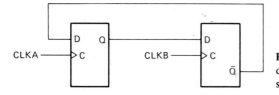

Figure 5-4 Simple counter that requires data transfers in both directions between skewed clocks.

Propagation delay is sometimes dependent on the direction of the output transition. For example, if the Q output makes a transition from 1 to 0, the propagation delay for a high-to-low transition t_{PHL} may be 25 ns. However, the propagation delay, if the output is making a low-to-high transition t_{PLH} may be 40 ns. Normally, maximum propagation delays are specified by the manufacturer. Also, typical propagation delays are specified. Typical delays are simply specifications averaged for a large number of circuits.

The difference in time between two clock signals is called *clock skew* and is computed as shown in Fig. 5-6. Here, a datum is being transferred from an earlier to a later clock, and the circuit could malfunction. To prevent the same datum from being stored in both flip-flops simultaneously, output X must not change until after the hold

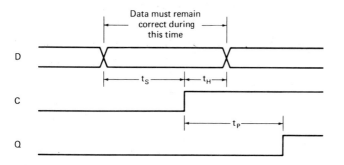

t_S Setup time
t_H Hold time
t_P Propagation delay

Figure 5-5 Timing specification for a D flip-flop.

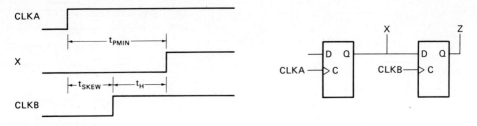

Figure 5-6 Calculation of clock skew.

time of flip-flop Z. The maximum allowable clock skew is easily read from the timing diagram as the *minimum propagation delay minus the hold time*. This calculation is correct for the worst-case situation of flip-flops connected directly to each other. If we add any gates between the flip-flops, the maximum allowable clock skew increases, as shown in Fig. 5-7. Often the hold time is guaranteed to be zero (i.e., the input may change simultaneously with the clock); so the maximum clock skew is equal to the minimum propagation delay. If the shortest (quickest) path in the circuit from one flip-flop to another also contains gates, you may add the *minimum* propagation delay of these gates to the clock-skew calculation. This will increase the allowable clock skew. *Minimum* gate propagation delays are seldom specified. You could estimate a minimum from the maximum and typical specifications. It is safest to assume a minimum of zero if none is specified.

What can be done if the calculated maximum allowable clock skew is exceeded by the difference in delays expected from the clock driving circuits? Several alternatives are possible. Clock driving circuits with shorter maximum delays will decrease the

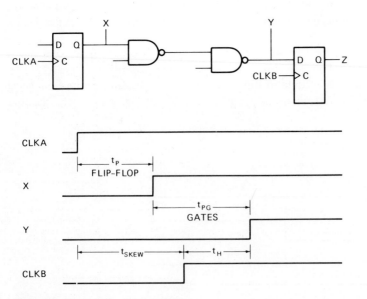

Figure 5-7 Clock skew with gate delays.

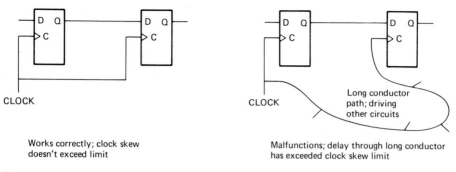

Works correctly; clock skew
doesn't exceed limit

Malfunctions; delay through long conductor
has exceeded clock skew limit

Figure 5-8 Logic signal delays through long conductors.

absolute delays and, more importantly, decrease the maximum *difference* in delays. This is because the maximum difference occurs if one clock driver operates with the guaranteed maximum delay while another has zero delay. The difference is simply the guaranteed maximum. Using gates or inverters fabricated on the same integrated circuit as clock drivers will reduce delay variations. Equalizing the number of inputs connected to each driving circuit output will also tend to equalize delays. Of course, you can add additional delay (e.g., two inverters) between flip-flops to increase the minimum propagation delay and increase allowable clock skew. As will be seen in the next section, this could decrease the speed at which your circuit will operate. Adding extra components will certainly increase cost and decrease circuit reliability. Finally, in very-high-speed digital circuits, even the delay in the wires themselves could cause the circuit to malfunction, as shown in Fig. 5-8. Interconnection delays vary, but a common rule of thumb is 6 ns/m for printed-circuit wiring.

Clock Rate

Every ASM implementation has a maximum clock rate, above which the circuit will not operate reliably. This maximum clock rate is determined by the time required for a change in flip-flop outputs to be converted to the next state and appear at the flip-flop inputs. The maximum-rate calculation for the simple ROM/register ASM, shown in Fig. 5-9, proceeds as follows. A clock pulse transition causes the flip-flop outputs to

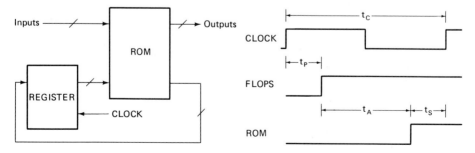

Figure 5-9 Maximum-operating-frequency calculation.

change after a propagation delay t_P. These flip-flop output changes are address inputs to the ROM. The outputs of the ROM change to their new values after the propagation delay or access time t_A of the ROM. These output changes are the next state and must appear at the flip-flop inputs no later than the worst-case setup time before the next clock transition. Thus, the time between clock transitions has a minimum value for proper operation.

$$t_C \geq t_P + t_A + t_S$$

The maximum clock rate or frequency is the reciprocal of the minimum period:

$$f_{MAX} = \frac{1}{t_C}$$

The calculation for maximum clock rate is performed identically if gates are used instead of a ROM. The longest delay path through the gating structure must be used to calculate the maximum propagation delay expected through the gates t_{PG}. The minimum clock period is obtained by using the gate propagation delay instead of the ROM access time.

$$t_C \geq t_P + t_{PG} + t_S$$

No matter how complex the digital circuit, you can always find the minimum clock period by looking for the *maximum delay* for a clock-induced flip-flop change to appear at a flip-flop input in time to be properly recognized at the next clock transition. This maximum delay may not be easily found in a complex circuit.

Clock Rate for Asynchronously Coupled Circuitry

In the simple counter of Fig. 5-10, each flip-flop is asynchronously coupled to the previous flip-flop. Since flip-flop A must change before B changes and B must change

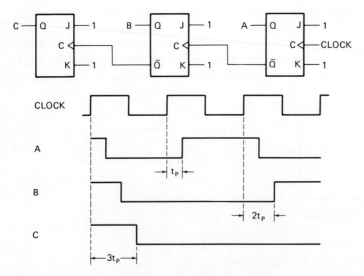

Figure 5-10 Propagation delays in an asynchronous counter.

before C can change, three flip-flop propagation delays will be required between the clock transition and the change in the output of flip-flop C. Flip-flop C behaves as if it has a propagation delay of $3t_P$. It is this longer, apparent propagation delay that must be used in maximum-clock-rate calculations for this circuit. Similarly, flip-flop B will have an apparent propagation delay of $2t_P$. However, since all three flip-flops do not change at each clock pulse, the time required to reach a new state varies, as shown in Fig. 5-10. Even so, we shall almost always have to consider the maximum flip-flop propagation delay to be $3t_P$ whenever using this counter in an ASM.

Clock Rate for a Gated Clock

Consider the ASM of Fig. 5-11. Both a normal positive transition clock $HCLK$ and a gated clock $GCLK$ are generated. Signals that gate the clock are created by combining flip-flop outputs with gates or a ROM. All these signals that enable the clock gate must have reached their correct state by the time $LCLK$ becomes a 1 and enables the clock gate. Since these gating signals are generated by the ASM, we can easily calculate the minimum time t_{C1} that $LCLK$ must remain low. In Fig. 5-11, $HCLK$ clocks the ASM's flip-flops after a delay through the inverter t_I. The flip-flop outputs will change after a propagation delay t_P, and the gating signals will change after a gate delay t_{PG} (or t_A if using a ROM). The clock gating signals must appear before $LCLK$ becomes a 1. Writing this statement as an inequality gives us the constraint on t_{C1}.

$$t_{C1} \geqslant t_I + t_P + t_{PG}$$

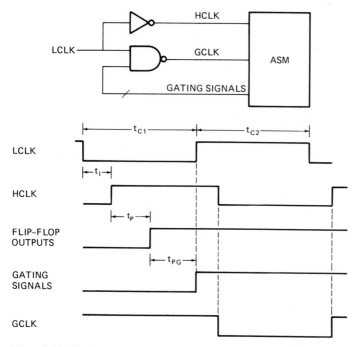

Figure 5-11 Maximum clock rate with gated clock.

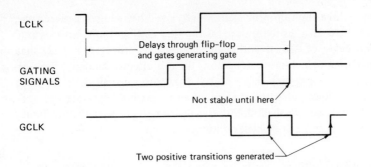

Figure 5-12 Gated clock malfunction caused by exceeding maximum rate.

If we are using a symmetric clock signal (i.e., $t_{C1} = t_{C2}$), then the minimum clock period $t_C = 2t_{C1}$.

$$t_C \geqslant 2(t_I + t_P + t_{PG})$$

This additional factor of 2 can potentially halve the maximum operating frequency of the circuit! If gated clocks must be used and operating speed is important, two approaches may be used to prevent the maximum operating speed from being halved. First, any delay associated with generating the gating signals should be as small as possible. The clock inverter and those flip-flops and gates that generate the clock gating signals should be faster than the other logic circuits in the system. Second, since our timing restriction really only applied to t_{C1}, when *LCLK* is low, we can reduce t_{C2} to increase the operating speed of the circuit without violating the inequality for t_{C1}. However, t_{C2} cannot be made arbitrarily small for two reasons. First, the flip-flops in the ASM have a specified minimum clock-pulse width, below which proper operation is not guaranteed. Second, very narrow signal pulses are difficult to generate and distribute for electrical reasons.

If we were to violate the minimum-time restriction for t_{C1}, the situation of Fig. 5-12 might arise. The gating signals do not become completely stable until well past the point at which *LCLK* enables the clock gate. As a result, two positive transitions occur on the gated clock, where only one is desired.

Gate-Implemented ASM Timing Example

A very simple ASM is shown in Fig. 5-13. The timing specifications for the parts used are tabulated in Table 5-1. We'd like to calculate maximum allowable clock skew and the maximum operating frequency for this circuit. The maximum clock skew is the smallest propagation delay between any two flip-flops minus the hold time. In this simple example, the shortest path is easily found. The smallest delay will obviously occur through gate C. We have the minimum propagation delay specified for the flip-flops, but, unfortunately, not for the gates. A conservative design could assume no delay in gate C so that

$$t_{SKEW} \leqslant t_{PMIN} - t_H$$

$$\leqslant 10 - 5 = 5 \text{ ns}$$

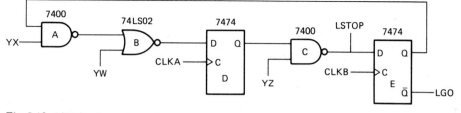

Fig. 5-13 ASM for timing example.

To calculate the maximum operating frequency, we must calculate the maximum delay through the longest path. This path is easily spotted as the connection through gates A and B. We know that the output of gate A will move in the opposite direction from the outputs of flip-flop E and gate B since A and B are inverting gates. If flip-flop E makes a 0-to-1 transition, the circuit delay will be:

$$t_{PLHE} + t_{PHLA} + t_{PLHB}$$
$$25 \quad + \quad 15 \quad + \quad 20$$
$$60 \text{ ns}$$

If flip-flop E makes a 1-to-0 transition, then the delay will be:

$$t_{PHLE} + t_{PLHA} + t_{PHLB}$$
$$40 \quad + \quad 22 \quad + \quad 20$$
$$82 \text{ ns}$$

The longest delay will be 82 ns, so that the clock period will be:

$$t_C \geqslant 82 \text{ ns} + t_S$$
$$\geqslant 82 + 20 \text{ ns}$$
$$\geqslant 102 \text{ ns}$$

The maximum clock frequency is:

$$f_{MAX} = \frac{1}{102 \text{ ns}} = 9.8 \text{ MHz}$$

Table 5-1 Component timing specifications

Part		t_{PLH}			t_{PHL}	
	Min	Typ	Max	Min	Typ	Max
7400		11	22		7	15
74LS02		10	20		10	20
7474	10	14	25	10	20	40
7474: Setup Time t_S = 20						
Hold Time t_H = 5						

Note: All times are in nanoseconds.

Other Calculations for the ASM

The ASM in Fig. 5-13 has inputs and outputs. The timing constraints for these inputs and outputs must be calculated so that other engineers desiring to connect or *interface* to this circuit will be able to do so. For example, if this circuit were implemented as an MSI circuit, it would be drawn as shown in Fig. 5-14 and timing specifications would be given for all inputs and outputs.

Each input will require both setup and hold specifications. The setup time of an input will be the setup time of the flip-flop affected by that input plus the maximum gate delay between the input and the flip-flop. If an input affects more than one flip-flop, use the longest setup time of all those calculated. Setup time will now be dependent on the transition direction of the input because the gates used have delays that depend on the transition direction.

The setup time for a low-to-high transition on input YX is given by

$$t_{SLHX} = t_{SD} + t_{PLHB} + t_{PHLA}$$

$$= 20 + 20 + 15$$

$$= 55 \text{ ns}$$

The setup time for a high-to-low input transition is:

$$t_{SHLX} = t_{SD} + t_{PHLB} + t_{PLHA}$$

$$= 20 + 20 + 22$$

$$= 62 \text{ ns}$$

If one setup time t_{SX} is to be specified for convenience, it should be the larger of the two times calculated.

$$t_{SX} = 62 \text{ ns}$$

The hold time on an input will be equal to the hold time of the flip-flop affected by that input *minus* the minimum propagation delays of any gates between the input and the flip-flop.

To calculate the hold time for input YW, we must assume a minimum propagation delay for gate B. If we're conservative and choose to assume 0 ns for this delay, the hold time of this input is just equal to the hold time of the flip-flop.

$$t_{HW} = t_H = 5 \text{ ns}$$

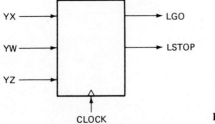

Figure 5-14 ASM of Fig. 5-13 as an MSI circuit.

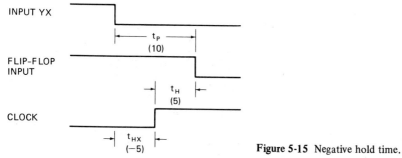

Figure 5-15 Negative hold time.

We can assume the minimum delay for gate B to be 2 ns. Now the hold time could be specified as:

$$t_{HW} = 5 - 2 = 3 \text{ ns}$$

If many gates are connected between an input and a flip-flop, the hold time could become negative. Assume that gates A and B in Fig. 5-13 each have a minimum propagation delay of 10 ns. The hold time of input YW will be:

$$t_{HW} = t_{HD} - t_{PG}$$

$$= 5 - 10 = -5 \text{ ns}$$

This negative hold time is shown in the timing diagram of Fig. 5-15. Input YW may actually change 5 ns *before* the clock without a circuit malfunction. Since at least 10 ns are required to propagate this change through gates A and B, the change will arrive at the D input of flip-flop D no earlier than 5 ns *after* the clock.

Finally, we must specify the propagation delays for the outputs. These delays will be equal to the maximum flip-flop delays plus any gate delays.

$$t_{PLHSTOP} = t_{PLHC} + t_{PHLD}$$

$$= 22 + 40 = 62 \text{ ns}$$

$$t_{PHLSTOP} = t_{PHLC} + t_{PLHD}$$

$$= 15 + 25 = 40 \text{ ns}$$

The timing specifications for the circuit of Fig. 5-13 are summarized in Table 5-2.

READ-WRITE-MEMORY TIMING

Read-write memory is most easily interfaced to an ASM as shown in Fig. 5-16. Since the chip-select input is activated in the last half of the clock cycle, RWM timing is somewhat similar to a gated clock. RWM timing is divided into *read-cycle timing* and *write-cycle timing*. We'll first discuss all the timing specifications of an RWM. Then we'll show how they are related to the ASM interface of Fig. 5-16. Finally, we will

Table 5-2 Timing specifications for the ASM of Fig. 5-13

Setup times	Inputs		
	X	W	Z
t_{SLH}	55	40	35
t_{SHL}	62	40	42
Hold times			
t_H		5*	

	Outputs			
	LSTOP		LGO	
Propagation delays	Max	Min	Max	Min
t_{PLH}	62	10*	25	10
t_{PHL}	40	10*	40	10

Note: All times in nanoseconds
*These calculations conservatively assume 0 ns as the minimum gate propagation delay.

give a numerical example for a real RWM circuit. Since memory nomenclature is not standardized, we will use Intel Corporation's nomenclature for a 2101A RWM.

Read-Cycle Timing

Six timing specifications are required for read-cycle timing.

Read-cycle time, T_{RC}.   This time is specified as a minimum and is the shortest time possible to complete a read cycle. It is measured between changes of address inputs. Cycle time is a composite of other timing parameters and is a measure of memory performance.

Access time, T_A.   This time is specified as a maximum. It is the time required for valid data to appear on the memory's data outputs after an address change.

Chip-enable to output time, T_{CO}.   This time is specified as a maximum. It is the time

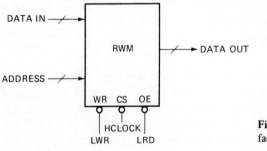

Figure 5-16 Read-write memory interface.

required for the three-state data outputs to be enabled after the chip-select (also called chip-enable) input is asserted.

Output enable time, T_{OE}. This time is specified as a maximum. It is the time required for the three-state data outputs to be enabled after the output enable input is asserted.

Data-false time, T_{DF}. This time is specified as a maximum. It is the time required for the three-state outputs to be disabled. It is measured from whichever input, chip-select or output enable, becomes false first.

Data-valid-after-address-change time, T_{OH}. This time is specified as a minimum. It is the time data will remain valid after an address change.

The timing diagram for the read cycle of the RWM of Fig. 5-16 is shown in Fig. 5-17. Uppercase T represents timing parameters associated with the RWM itself. Lowercase t represents timing parameters of the ASM interfaced to this memory. These latter parameters are:

t_{PA}. The propagation delay from the clock edge until the address arrives at the memory.

t_{PRD}. The propagation delay from the clock edge until the read signal arrives at the memory.

t_S. The setup time of the flip-flops that will save or test the data output from memory.

t_H. The hold time of the flip-flops that will save or test the data output from memory.

Several timing constraints may be seen in Fig. 5-17. The address must arrive in sufficient time to allow output data to reach the ASM's data flip-flops at or before their setup time:

$$t_{PA} + T_A + t_S \leqslant t_{CLK}$$

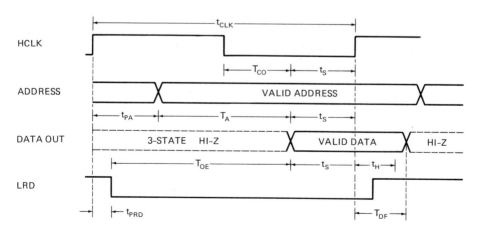

Figure 5-17 Read cycle timing.

The read signal must reach the output enable input soon enough to enable the tristate outputs before the setup time of the ASM's data storage flip-flops:

$$t_{\text{PRD}} + T_{\text{OE}} + t_S \leqslant t_{\text{CLK}}$$

The chip-select input is asserted by the clock. Chip select must occur soon enough to enable the tristate outputs also:

$$T_{\text{CO}} + t_S \leqslant \frac{t_{\text{CLK}}}{2}$$

The three inequalities above must all be satisfied. Thus, the inequality requiring the largest value of t_{CLK} will constrain the speed of operation of the RWM.

Data output from the memory must remain correct until after the hold time of the flip-flops that are to read those data:

$$T_{\text{DF}} \geqslant t_H$$

This inequality must be satisfied for proper operation.

Write-Cycle Timing

Seven parameters are required to specify write-cycle timing

Write-cycle time, T_{WC}.   This time is specified as a minimum. It is the smallest time in which a write cycle can be completed. It is analogous to read-cycle time and is a measure of memory performance.

Address to write time, T_{AW}.   This time is specified as a minimum. It is the shortest time after an address change that the memory's write circuitry can be enabled. If the write circuitry is enabled earlier, the memory may write into the wrong address. The write circuitry is enabled by the last signal asserted of either the chip-select or the write signal.

Chip-select to write time, T_{CW}.   This time is specified as a minimum. This memory is *not* edge-triggered. It remembers the data present on its inputs when the write signal becomes false. This time is the minimum time that chip select must be asserted before the write signal becomes false.

Write pulse time, T_{WP}.   This time is specified as a minimum. It is the minimum time that the write signal must be asserted.

The above definitions for T_{CW} and T_{WP} assume that the write signal will become false before the chip select. Since the write circuitry is activated by the AND function of the write and chip-select signals, their timing specifications may be interchanged. Thus, T_{CW} could be the time that the write signal must be asserted before the chip select becomes false. T_{WP} would become the minimum time that the chip select must be asserted. This latter interpretation is used in the ASM interface of Fig. 5-18.

Write recovery time, T_{WR}.   This time is specified as a minimum. It is the time the address must be held correct after the write signal becomes false (or chip-select signal if that becomes false first).

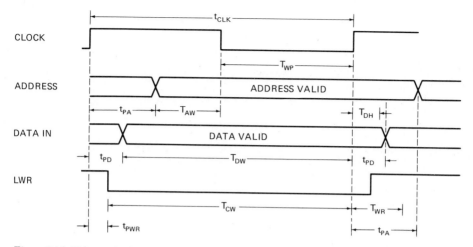

Figure 5-18 Write cycle timing.

Data setup time, T_{DW}.　This time is specified as a minimum. It is the time the data must be correct before the write signal becomes false (or chip-select signal if it becomes false first).

Data hold time, T_{DH}.　This time is specified as a minimum. It is the time the data must be correct after the write signal becomes false (or chip-select signal if it becomes false first).

The memory write cycle for the **RWM** of Fig. 5-16 is shown in Fig. 5-18. Two additional **ASM** parameters will be required for the write cycle.

t_{PD}.　The propagation delay from the clock edge until data are correct at the memory data inputs.

t_{PWR}.　The propagation delay from the clock edge until the write signal arrives at the memory.

Several timing constraints may be read from Fig. 5-18. The address must reach the memory sufficiently soon to prevent data from being written into the wrong memory location:

$$t_{PA} + T_{AW} \leqslant \frac{t_{CLK}}{2}$$

The write signal must reach the memory at least T_{CW} before the chip-select signal becomes false.

$$t_{PWR} + T_{CW} \leqslant t_{CLK}$$

The chip-select input must be at least a write-pulse width long.

$$T_{WP} \leqslant \frac{t_{CLK}}{2}$$

The data must arrive sufficiently soon to be properly recognized by the RWM:

$$t_{PD} + T_{DW} \leqslant t_{CLK}$$

Thus, we have four inequalities. All must be satisfied; so one inequality will limit the minimum clock time allowed.

Additionally, the hold time requirement of the memory must be satisfied:

$$t_{PD} \geqslant T_{DH}$$

Finally, the address must remain stable after the chip-select signal becomes false:

$$T_{WR} \leqslant t_{PA}$$

Memory Timing Example

Table 5-3 lists the timing parameters of an Intel 2101A-2 RWM. Also listed are timing parameters of the ASM controlling the RWM. The read clock cycle is governed by three inequalities given previously:

Address delay

$$t_{PA} + T_A + t_S \leqslant t_{CLK}$$
$$40 + 250 + 20 \leqslant$$
$$310 \text{ ns} \leqslant$$

Read signal delay

$$t_{PRD} + T_{OE} + t_S \leqslant t_{CLK}$$
$$40 + 130 + 20 \leqslant$$
$$190 \text{ ns} \leqslant$$

Chip-select delay

$$T_{CO} + t_S \leqslant \frac{t_{CLK}}{2}$$
$$180 + 20 \leqslant$$
$$400 \text{ ns} \leqslant t_{CLK}$$

Since all three inequalities must be satisfied, we must limit the clock period to be:

$$t_{CLK} \geqslant 400 \text{ ns}$$

Finally, we should check the hold-time inequality for the read cycle:

$$T_{DF} \geqslant t_H$$
$$180 \geqslant 5 \text{ ns}$$

The hold time is easily satisfied.

Table 5-3 Memory timing example parameters

2101A-2 read-cycle parameters	
T_{RC}	250 ns
T_A	250 ns
T_{CO}	180 ns
T_{OE}	130 ns
T_{DF}	180 ns
T_{OH}	40 ns

2101A-2 write-cycle parameters	
T_{WC}	170 ns
T_{AW}	20 ns
T_{CW}	150 ns
T_{WP}	150 ns
T_{WR}	0 ns
T_{DW}	150 ns
T_{DH}	0 ns

ASM parameters	
t_{PA}	40 ns
t_{PRD}	40 ns
t_S	20 ns
t_H	5 ns
t_{PD}	40 ns
t_{PWR}	40 ns

Four inequalities control the write clock cycle.

Address delay

$$t_{PA} + T_{AW} \leqslant \frac{t_{CLK}}{2}$$

$$40 + 20 \leqslant$$

$$120 \text{ ns} \leqslant t_{CLK}$$

Write signal delay

$$t_{PWR} + T_{CW} \leqslant t_{CLK}$$

$$40 + 150 \leqslant$$

$$190 \text{ ns} \leqslant$$

Chip-select width

$$T_{WP} \leqslant \frac{t_{CLK}}{2}$$

$$150 \leqslant$$

$$300 \text{ ns} \leqslant t_{CLK}$$

Data delay

$$t_{\rm PD} + T_{\rm DW} \leqslant t_{\rm CLK}$$

$$40 + 150 \leqslant$$

$$190 \text{ ns} \leqslant$$

The write clock cycle must be greater than or equal to 300 ns to satisfy all these inequalities. The data hold time inequality must be checked:

$$t_{\rm PD} \geqslant T_{\rm DH}$$

$$40 \geqslant 0 \text{ ns}$$

The address hold inequality must also be satisfied:

$$T_{\rm WR} \leqslant t_{\rm PA}$$

$$0 \leqslant 40 \text{ ns}$$

Both inequalities are easily satisfied.

Memory Performance Improvement

Since both read and write timing inequalities must be satisfied, the system in the previous example must operate with a 400 ns or longer clock cycle. This is considerably slower than $T_{\rm RC}$ of 250 ns or $T_{\rm WC}$ of 170 ns. The RWM is operating below its capability because of the simple interface we've chosen. Since the second half of the read cycle limits the timing, we could expect to improve system speed by using an asymmetric clock signal. The chip-select delay inequality of the read cycle constrained the *low part* of the clock cycle to be not less than 200 ns. Let's tabulate our timing restrictions in Table 5-4. We can easily see from this table that we can shorten the entire clock cycle to 310 ns. We must also be sure that the high part of the cycle is greater than 60 ns, while the low part must be greater than 200 ns. Since it is easier to gener-

Table 5-4 Memory performance restrictions

	Clock cycle		
Inequality	High part	Low part	Entire
Read cycle			
Address delay			310
Read signal delay			190
Chip-select delay		200	
Write cycle			
Address delay	60		
Write signal delay			190
Chip-select width		150	
Data delay			190

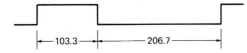

Figure 5-19 Maximum performance clock signal for memory interface.

ate asymmetric clocks in which each part is related by a common multiple, we'll choose 103.3 ns for the high part of the clock cycle and 206.7 ns for the low part, as shown in Fig. 5-19. The entire clock cycle is 310 ns, while each part of the cycle meets the timing restrictions of Table 5-4. The system's performance has been increased by almost 25 percent.

NOISE IN CIRCUIT IMPLEMENTATIONS

All the digital signals we have used in this book have been ideal. They have always caused the action desired. Real digital signals are far from ideal. They are corrupted by interference from many sources. All this interference is collectively called *noise* and can cause particularly vexing circuit malfunctions. A noise malfunction may not be continuous. It may occur only occasionally. The circuit may malfunction every hour, every day, or a few times each year. It may malfunction only with particular data inputs or only on alternate Thursdays. Immunity to these malfunctions is accomplished by careful logical, electric, and physical design. We will discuss noise problems and their solutions without much electric engineering. For those who desire a more technical treatment, an excellent synopsis of digital noise problems and their solutions is found in Blakeslee.[1]

Noise Margin

The manufacturers of digital ICs guarantee *worst-case* voltages for both 0 and 1 logic levels. For example, let's consider the logic family called *TTL* (transistor-transistor logic). The output of a TTL circuit is guaranteed to be greater than 2.4 V if a logic 1 is being represented. However, an input of a TTL circuit will recognize any voltage greater than 2.0 V as a logic 1. The difference between the *output level* of 2.4 and the *input threshold* of 2.0 V is the *noise margin* of 0.4 V. A TTL 0 output is guaranteed to be less than 0.4 V, while a TTL input recognizes any voltage less than 0.8 V as a 0. The 0-level noise margin for TTL is also 0.4 V. Any TTL system will tolerate up to 0.4 V of interference on its signals before that system malfunctions. This noise margin is very important for a great amount of noise is present in most complex digital systems. Without noise margins, it would be difficult or impossible to construct reliable digital systems.

The worst-case guaranteed output levels are specified for *rated* fan out. A TTL gate with a maximum fan out of 10 is guaranteed to have outputs greater than 2.4 and less than 0.4 V only when connected to no more than 10 inputs. Most digital circuits

[1] Thomas R. Blakeslee, Digital Design with Standard MSI and LSI, John Wiley & Sons, New York, 1975, chap. 10.

will work better than their worst-case specification. A TTL circuit might have actual output levels of 0.2 and 3.6 V. Such a circuit might work even if its fan-out rating is exceeded or if more than 0.4 V of noise is present on its data lines. For this reason, *successful operation of a circuit does not mean the circuit has been correctly designed.* Many poorly designed and poorly constructed circuits will work correctly. Unfortunately, such a circuit may work correctly *only* with a particular "better-than-normal" IC or *only* with a specific power supply voltage or *only* at a particular temperature or *only* when Saturn is in conjunction with Mars! Manufacturers' worst-case ratings are *carefully* specified to include effects of temperature, fan out, power supply voltage, etc. *Always design to the worst-case specifications.* Never violate fan-out or propagation delay specifications. *Measure* the noise to make sure it is less than the worst-case noise margin. Even though these extra steps require time to be performed, the overall cost of your design will be reduced because fewer problems will occur in production or use of your circuit.

Transmission Lines

Ideally, a wire should carry a digital signal from one circuit to another without changing that signal in any way. Unfortunately, real interconnections do change digital signals considerably. A wire carrying a fast digital signal acts like a *transmission line*. It will be impossible to completely explain transmission lines without advanced electric engineering. Instead, we will try to explain their operation intuitively.

Digital signals travel along transmission lines at a finite speed. This *propagation velocity* is about 0.169 m/ns for the printed-circuit wiring used for most digital circuits. Propagation velocity is almost always specified by giving its reciprocal or propagation time of 5.9 ns/m (1.8 ns/ft). Transmission lines also have a *characteristic impedance* Z_0. This impedance is the ratio of the voltage to the current of the propagating signal and is about 50 to 200 Ω for printed-circuit connections. When a signal propagating down a transmission line reaches the end of that line, several things may happen. If the transmission line has a resistor equal to Z_0 connected to its receiving end, the signal will simply stop propagating. This situation is as close as we can come to ideal signal transmission. All we must consider is the 5.9-ns/m propagation time of the signal.

Most digital signal connections are terminated by gate inputs. Not only are gate input impedances not equal to Z_0, but gate inputs are nonlinear. That is, the gate input impedance is a function of the voltage applied to that input. When a digital signal reaches a gate input, part of the signal is reflected backwards toward the source. Since the source is usually a gate output which also does not have an impedance of Z_0, the reflected signal will be reflected again when it reaches the source. The signal will be reflected back and forth between the source and receiving ends. The amplitude of the reflected signal is reduced at each reflection. Eventually, the reflections will no longer be visible, and both ends of the wire will have the same stable logic level. Transmission-line reflections in a digital system are called *ringing* and appear as shown in Fig. 5-20 if viewed on an oscilloscope.

Everything we've said about transmission lines has been simplified. Different kinds of gate inputs and outputs will have different kinds of nonlinear impedances. Each

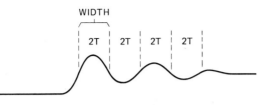

WIDTH

2T = Round–trip wire delay   **Figure 5-20** Ringing.

physical discontinuity in the transmission line will be a discontinuity in impedance that will produce a reflection. These discontinuities include multiple paths, logic circuit inputs connected along the wire, and connectors through which the interconnection passes. This myriad of reflections will produce a signal much more complex than Fig. 5-20.

Effect of Reflections

Reflections occur both on clock lines and other signal lines. Reflections on clock lines can cause a flip-flop to be clocked twice. Assume the ringing of Fig. 5-20 appeared on the clock input of a flip-flop. That flip-flop would be clocked twice if the amplitude of the ringing exceeded the clock input threshold and the width of the ringing exceeded the minimum pulse width of the flip-flop's clock input. How could we prevent the flip-flop from being clocked twice? One technique we could use would be to reduce the width of the ringing so that it would be less than the minimum pulse width required to clock the flip-flop. The ringing width is equal to the time required for a *round trip* of the signal on the transmission line. Making the transmission line shorter will reduce the width of the ringing. To ensure that the ringing is less than the minimum clock-pulse width, we can make all our interconnections shorter than

$$\text{maximum length} = \frac{\text{minimum clock-pulse width}}{2 \text{ (propagation time)}}$$

For the 7474 flip-flop used in a previous example, the minimum clock-pulse width is 30 ns:

$$\text{maximum length} = \frac{30 \text{ ns}}{2 \text{ (5.9 ns/m)}}$$

$$= 2.54 \text{ m}$$

If no clock line exceeds 2.54 m, the width of the ringing will not exceed 30 ns and will not clock the flip-flop incorrectly.

Especially for fast-logic families, the restriction on clock line length may be intolerably short. The only solution possible when using very fast logic may be reducing the amplitude of the reflections. This can be done by modifying the impedance of gate outputs and inputs to more closely match the Z_0 of the transmission line. Often, this technique involves inserting a resistor in series with the driver output and another resistor in parallel with the receiving end of the transmission line. Selection of values of these resistors is beyond the scope of this book. Again, the interested reader is advised to start by looking at Blakeslee.[1]

The same sort of problems occur with signal lines as with clock lines. However, an additional solution is available for curing noise on signal lines. Ringing occurs right after a signal transition and will eventually die away. We can delay the next clock transition sufficiently so that the amplitude of any ringing on signal lines will be small and not cross the logic threshold voltage. If possible, we should always design circuits to operate below their maximum possible speed. More problems will occur as a circuit operates closer to its limit of correct operation. We can use an *effective propagation velocity* of digital signals that includes reflection effects. The effective propagation velocity will depend on output impedances, input impedances, and other impedance discontinuities. Since signal wires usually are shorter and have fewer discontinuities than clock wires, we can approximate reflection effects by considering only output and input impedances. This means that we can specify effective propagation velocities for logic families. For example, *Schottky TTL* (STTL) signals will be sufficiently close to correct levels when they first arrive at the end of a transmission line. Thus, the effective propagation time of STTL signals is:

$$T_{STTL} = 5.9 \text{ ns/m}$$

On the other hand, standard TTL signals will not reach correct values at the receiving end until three trips over the transmission line (from source to receiver to source to receiver). The effective propagation time of TTL signals will be 3 times slower:

$$T_{TTL} = 17.7 \text{ ns/m}$$

A logic system built with TTL would operate more slowly than a STTL system for *two* reasons. First, STTL internal propagation delays are less than TTL delays. Second, the wire propagation delays of STTL will appear to be one-third those of the TTL system. This is because the amplitude of a TTL signal at the end of a transmission line does not become correct until the signal makes three trips on the interconnection.

Other Noise Sources

Each TTL circuit has both a power and ground connection. These two connections complete the electrical circuit for logic signals between ICs. For example, if a flip-flop output goes from 1 to 0, current will flow *into* the flip-flop output. This current comes from the inputs of gates connected to this flip-flop's output. Every electrical circuit requires two wires. The ground wire of the flip-flop returns current to the gates which supplied the current going into the flip-flop output. If the ground wire was constructed identically to the signal wire, they would both have the same impedance. Since they have the same current flowing in them, any voltage change in the flip-flop's output would be divided equally between the two wires, as shown in Fig. 5-21. Until reflections subsided, the ground wire would become more positive by half the output

[1] Blakeslee, Digital Design with Standard MSI and LSI, pp. 262-266.

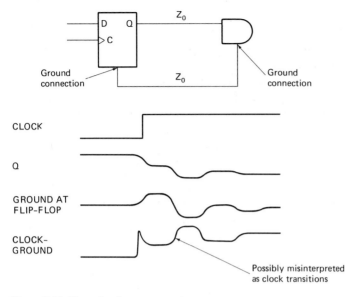

Figure 5-21 Ground noise.

voltage change and the signal wire would only change halfway from 1 to 0. Moving the ground wire more positive has exactly the same effect as moving all other flip-flop signal wires more negative. Figure 5-21 also shows the *difference* between the clock and ground signals. Even though the clock driver is not changing, the flip-flop could be clocked again because its clock input *is* changing with respect to the flip-flop's ground! Actually, the situation is worse than this. While the flip-flop output is changing, a *large* momentary current surge passes through the flip-flop from power supply to ground. This current surge adds to the return current in the ground wire and raises the ground potential even more positive. Worse yet, this same current surge acts to reduce the power supply voltage to the flip-flop. This could cause the flip-flop to forget its state! For any of these malfunctions to occur, the round-trip propagation delay on the power and ground connections must be longer than the flip-flop's minimum clock-pulse width. Unfortunately, this requirement is easily satisfied for TTL and faster-logic families. The power and ground wires are often the longest in the system.

The solution to this problem of power and ground noise is reduction of the impedance of the power and ground connections. The voltage change on the flip-flop's output divides between signal and ground wires in proportion to their impedance. Reducing the impedance of the ground wire will reduce the voltage change appearing on it. Reducing the impedance of the power and ground connections is accomplished in two ways. First, impedance-lowering *capacitors* are added between power and ground connections. Often, as many as one capacitor for each two or three ICs are used. Second, the geometry of the power and ground conductors is made different from that of the signal wires. Many wide conductors are used to distribute power and

A printed circuit board showing wide power and ground conductors and bypass capacitors. (*Hewlett-Packard Co.*)

ground in a grid. Wide power conductors will have a lower impedance than narrower signal conductors. Paralleling many conductors in a grid parallels and reduces their impedance. In extreme cases of very-high-speed logic and signals, the power and ground connections are almost solid sheets of copper called power and ground planes. Four-layer printed circuits, shown in Fig. 5-22, are needed to provide these additional planes.

One other important noise source is common to all digital circuits. Conductors act

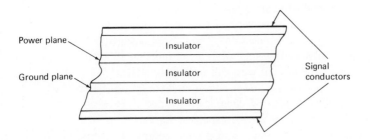

Figure 5-22 Side view of four-layer printed circuit.

Two sides of a printed circuit board showing right angle conductors. (*Hewlett-Packard Co.*)

as both transmitting and receiving antennae. Signal changes can travel between adjacent conductors, even if no physical connection exists! This is called *crosstalk*. Power and ground planes minimize crosstalk. Lowering the impedance of signal wires also minimizes crosstalk. Multilayer printed circuit boards are expensive. Conductor width is limited by available space on the printed circuit. Fortunately, two-sided printed circuits can be designed to have little crosstalk because signal wires that are not changing can act as a ground plane for those that are changing. Conductors at right angles have minimum crosstalk. Conductors on opposite sides of a printed circuit are placed at right angles. Not only is crosstalk between sides minimized, but the conductors on one side act as a ground plane for those on the other side. Long parallel conductors have the worst crosstalk. Ground conductors placed between long parallel conductors will act as a shield to minimize crosstalk.

Since crosstalk is the transmission of signal *changes* between conductors, it must be avoided on clock lines at all cost. Crosstalk on signal wires appears immediately after a clock transition. If the clock speed is sufficiently slow, the crosstalk will have disappeared by the next clock transition. This is another reason we want to operate a circuit at a speed less than the maximum speed.

Other Logic Families

Each logic family has noise problems peculiar to it. Faster logic like *ECL* (emitter-coupled logic) will aggravate the problems already mentioned. Slower-logic families like *CMOS* (complementary metal oxide silicon) have fewer problems. In fact, CMOS is so slow that none of these noise problems usually occurs. The transmission lines in a CMOS circuit may be modeled as capacitors. The effective propagation velocity is slowed as a gate output has to charge up more capacitance from increased wire length or additional gate inputs.

Conservative Design

Many noise calculations must be approximate. For this reason, it is best to design digital circuits conservatively. Conservative noise design may be summarized as follows:

1. Use the slowest-logic family possible.
2. Design to worst-case specifications.
3. Do not operate logic at the limit of its speed.
4. Use short conductors.
5. Use low-impedance signal conductors (as wide as possible).
6. Use even-lower-impedance power and ground conductors (capacitors and wide conductors in a grid).
7. Use ground and power planes if 5 and 6 are inadequate.
8. *Measure* the noise to be sure it is less than the worst-case noise margin.

PROBLEMS

5-1 The ASM shown in Fig. P5-1 uses the components specified in Table P5-1.
    (*a*) Calculate the maximum clock skew.
    (*b*) Calculate the maximum operating frequency.
    (*c*) Calculate the setup and hold time specification for input *YON*.
    (*d*) Calculate the propagation delay specifications for outputs *LX* and *HY*.

Table P5-1 Component parameters for problems

	t_{PLH}		t_{PHL}	
	Min	Max	Min	Max
7400		22		15
7404		22		15
7408		27		19
7410		22		15
7420		22		15
7474	10	25	10	40
74109	4	16	9	28
74LS139		27		38
74163 CO	23	35	23	35
74163 Q	17	25	19	29

	t_S	t_H
7474	20	5
74109	10	6
74163 Data	15	0
74163 Enable	20	0
74163 Load	25	0
74163 Clear	20	0

Note: All times in nanoseconds

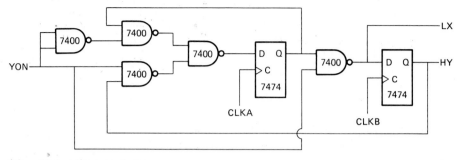

Figure P5-1 ASM for Prob. 5-1.

5-2 The ASM of Fig. P5-2 uses a ROM with a maximum access time of 75 ns and a minimum access time of 25 ns.

(a) Calculate the maximum allowable clock skew.

(b) Calculate the maximum operating frequency.

(c) Calculate the setup and hold times of the inputs.

(d) Calculate the propagation delay of the outputs.

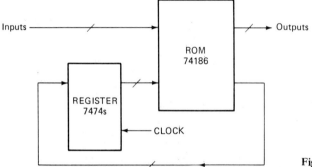

Figure P5-2 ASM for Prob. 5-2.

5-3 The ASM of Fig. P5-3 is the same as the ASM of Fig. P5-2 except that it includes a *synchronizing register.* This register ensures that inputs presented to the ROM will change only at each clock transition, even if these inputs come from sources not synchronized with the system clock. Calculate the setup and hold times for this circuit's inputs.

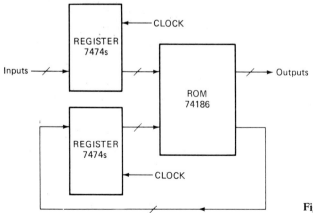

Figure P5-3 ASM for Prob. 5-2.

5-4 Consider the ASM in Fig. P5-4. Its state register is a 3-bit asynchronous counter. The counter stops counting when it reaches 111. It can be started only by external input *LSTRT*. What is the maximum clock frequency at which this circuit will correctly operate? Use the component specifications in Table P5-1.

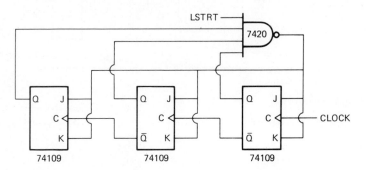

Figure P5-4 Asynchronous counter ASM.

5-5 Consider the grated-clock ASM of Fig. 4-14. Will clock skew between *HCLK* and *GCLK* cause faulty operation? What is the allowable clock skew? What is the maximum skew attributable to the clock drivers? What is the maximum clock rate of this circuit? Assume the NAND gate is a 7410, the AND gate is a 7408, the inverter is a 7404, and the flip-flops are 74109s. The specifications for these components are shown in Table P5-1.

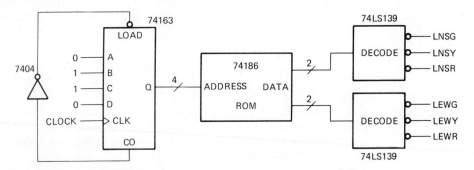

Figure P5-5 Traffic-light controller.

5-6 The circuit of Fig. P5-5 is the simplest traffic light controller. It uses a counter for state register and has no branches in its ASM chart. What is the maximum clock rate of this circuit? Use component parameters in Table P5-1.

5-7 The RWM interface example in this chapter did not use the memory to its full speed capability. Even using an asymmetric clock, the memory write cycle was longer than it might be. Worse yet, the entire ASM was constrained to a 310 ns clock. Design an interface from ASM to RWM that will shorten the write cycle.

Hint: Try dividing the memory cycle into more than one ASM cycle.

CHAPTER SIX

ASYNCHRONOUS INPUTS AND ASMS

In previous chapters, we have always assumed that external inputs to the ASM will change synchronously with the clock. Inputs were assumed to change just after the clock transition (along with the state variables), which allows sufficient time for the effect of input changes to arrive at state flip-flop inputs before the next clock transition. Inputs will be synchronous if they are outputs of another ASM using the same clock signal. Many times, synchronism will not exist. For example, an input could be generated by another ASM which is timed by a different clock signal. Often, inputs are generated by pushbuttons or other physical events which have no time relationship to any clock signal. An input not synchronized with the ASM clock is called an *asynchronous input*. What problems arise when an asynchronous input is connected to a synchronous ASM? One obvious problem is that any output of the ASM that is a function of *both* the current state *and* an asynchronous input will, itself, be asynchronous. An asynchronous input change will simply propagate through the output ROM or gating. If asynchronous outputs (that change at times other than clock transitions) must be avoided, the ASM chart can have no conditional outputs that depend on asynchronous inputs.

Figure 6-1 shows a conditional output *IHLD* which depends on an asynchronous input *YX* while in state 12. You can see that *IHLD* follows the asynchronous changes of *YX*. *IHLD* is an immediate output; so any changes between clock transitions will cause the *IHLD* function to occur. In the timing diagram of Fig. 6-1, the *IHLD* function would occur twice. The next state would be state 13. The ASM chart of Fig. 6-1 indicates that *IHLD* should occur once and always should be followed by state 14!

Transition Races

Asynchronous inputs can cause a much more serious problem: erroneous next states. A simple ASM is shown in Fig. 6-2. The single input *YI* is an asynchronous input.

171

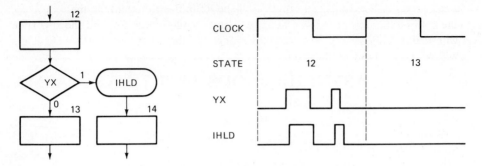

Figure 6-1 Asynchronous output caused by asynchronous input.

Assume that the ASM is in state 00 and asynchronous input *YI* changes state just before the next clock transition. In fact, the input changes so close to the clock transition that the new next state from ROM outputs D_2 and D_1 arrives after the worst-case setup time of the flip-flops. Setup time specified is for the worst flip-flop expected. Flip-flops A and B may have quite different setup times, as long as neither is larger than the worst-case specification. Thus, the A flip-flop, the B flip-flop, both flip-flops, or neither flip-flop might recognize this late next-state change.

Let's use a specific example to demonstrate the way in which the circuit could malfunction. If $YI = 0$ and the current state is 00, the next state should be 10. Suppose that YI changes from a 0 to a 1 late in the clock cycle, so late that both flop inputs change after the worst-case setup time. If both flops do not recognize this change, the next state will still be 10. The operation of the ASM is correct. The input change occurred too late to be recognized. However, it is very likely that one or both flip-flops will have an actual setup time less than the worst-case setup time specification. If both flip-flops recognize the change, the next state will be 01 and the ASM is still functioning correctly. Because both flip-flops operate better than specification, the late input

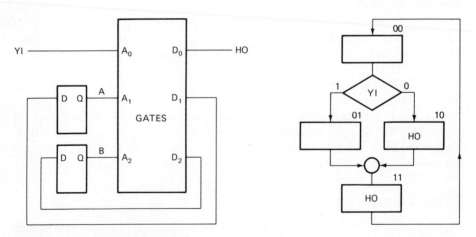

Figure 6-2 ASM with transition race.

change is correctly recognized. However, if the B flip-flop is better than the A flip-flop, the B flip-flop might recognize the state change, while A will not, and the next state will be 00! If the A flop recognizes the change and the B flop does not, the next state will be 11. In both of these last cases, the actual next state was incorrect for either $YI = 0$ or 1. The ASM chart does not even *have* an exit path from state 00 to states 00 or 11!

Not only can setup time differences cause transition races, but differences in propagation times of next-state variables can also cause transition races. Propagation-delay differences can be quite large in gate implementations. A transition race can be avoided by modifying either the ASM chart or the circuit. In Fig. 6-3, asynchronous input YI affects only one state variable B. If input YI changes from 0 to 1 late in the clock cycle, this change may be recognized and the next state will be 01. If the change is not recognized, the next state will be 11. Since the A flip-flop is always a 1 in each of these next states, it doesn't matter if A does or doesn't recognize the change as it will be 1 in either case! Since only the B flip-flop changes, the next state can be only one of the two correct next states. Transition races may be avoided by assigning next states so that all decisions on asynchronous inputs affect only one state flip-flop. In a complex ASM with many asynchronous inputs, additional state flip-flops may be required to follow this rule.

An alternative solution is changing the circuit to ensure that state changes occur only at the beginning of a clock cycle. In Fig. 6-4, a synchronizing register has been added to the circuit to assure that changes in YI will only be sent to the ROM just after a clock transition. Any state assignment will work properly in this ASM because YI is synchronized with the system clock before being used to select the next state. In a complex ASM this latter solution may eliminate extra state flip-flops, required to meet the state assignment criteria of the former solution. Even though synchronizing flip-flops are required, the total number of flip-flops could be less in a complex ASM. In addition, conditional outputs depending on asynchronous inputs will now be synchronized with the clock. No ROM address input is asynchronous; so no output will be asynchronous. Most importantly, the time and cost of designing this circuit with a synchronizing register is less because states can be arbitrarily assigned. In a complex

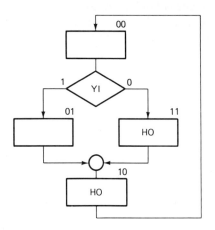

Figure 6-3 ASM without transition races by changing state assignment.

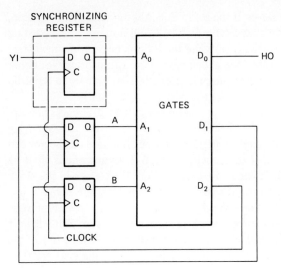

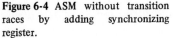

Figure 6-4 ASM without transition races by adding synchronizing register.

ASM, the regularized design of the synchronizing register is much quicker than a specialized state assignment.

Output Races

In an earlier chapter, we saw that nonsimultaneous changes of flip-flop outputs caused undesirable ASM output signals, called output races. The solution proposed for this problem was to restrict the ASM to only one state variable change at each transition. This solution usually requires additional state variable flip-flops and next-state functions. Design is time-consuming and much more difficult if both output *and* transition races must be eliminated through state assignment. When using gates, we can simplify our state assignment criteria for eliminating output races. In order to eliminate races an output change should be *caused* by only one state variable change (even if more than one state variable is changing). State-assignment solutions to races are still cumbersome and time-consuming. The best output-race solution is not to have critical immediate outputs that will respond to the short pulses produced by output races. After all, if a circuit will respond to a short digital pulse produced by an output race, it will also respond to a short pulse produced by electric noise!

Sometimes an immediate output without output races *must* be generated. These outputs can be generated easily in two ways, without resorting to state assignment changes. In Fig. 6-5, a synchronizing register assures that output races will not appear on immediate outputs. These flip-flops only change at clock transitions after output races have disappeared. These "immediate" outputs are delayed one clock cycle from their occurrence on the ASM chart. The ASM chart may have to be modified to account for this delay.

A solution that does not delay outputs is shown in Fig. 6-6. Immediate-acting outputs are enabled only during the second half of the clock cycle, after the output

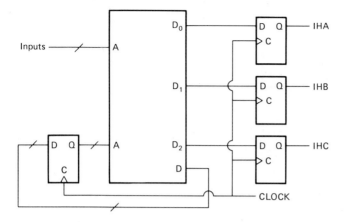

Figure 6-5 Resynchronizing outputs to eliminate races.

races have disappeared. The immediate outputs occur where they appear in the ASM chart, but only during the last half of each clock cycle.

In general, immediate outputs are best used only for slowly responding physical devices (like light bulbs) that do not act quickly enough to be affected by output races.

Hazards

Even in a race-free ASM, outputs may still have unwanted signals. In Fig. 6-7, a simple circuit generates an immediate output *IHO* from three state variables C, B, and A. The output *IHO* should be a 1 for state $C = B = A = 1$ and should also be a 1 for state $C = A = 1$ and $B = 0$. Since the transition between these two states involves the change of only one state variable, no output races can occur. Yet, the output on the timing diagram shown in Fig. 6-7 momentarily becomes 0, even though it should remain 1.

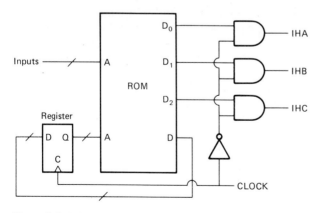

Figure 6-6 Gating outputs to remove races.

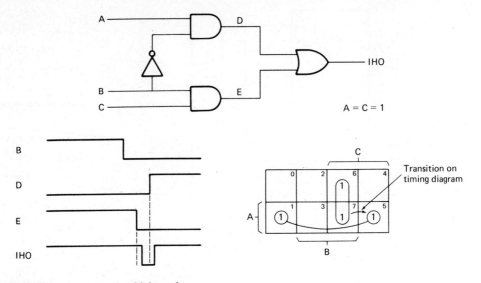

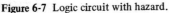

Figure 6-7 Logic circuit with hazard.

You'll notice that this extraneous pulse or *glitch* is caused by the extra delay introduced by the inverter in the circuit. Of course, all the gates and inverters will have different delays, and circuit operation will be unpredictable. Operation will depend on the individual logic circuits used. This erroneous signal does not depend on the state variable assignment. It is only a function of the particular gate implementation of the logic function. Worse yet, you can expect four kinds of hazards, one for each possible output transition, as shown in Fig. 6-8. Fortunately, it has been proved that a two-level logic (sum-of-products or product-of-sums) circuit is free of all hazards if it is free of hazards for the 1-to-1 transition.

It is necessary for us to know how to detect and correct hazards that occur for the 1-to-1 transition, shown in Fig. 6-7. In this circuit, state variable B acts to *select* one of two gates. Each gate implements a product function that is 1 for a particular set of inputs. The hazard occurs because function E returns to a 0 before function D becomes a 1. Thus, the output OR gate momentarily has all 0 inputs. This hazard-

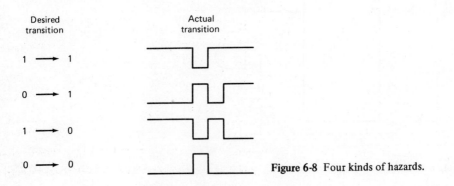

Figure 6-8 Four kinds of hazards.

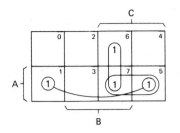

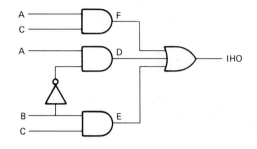

Figure 6-9 Circuit without hazard.

causing transition can be seen on the K map of Fig. 6-7. It is a transition between adjacent squares that are in different groups. In other words, it is a transition involving the change of only one variable between one product gate and another. To avoid this hazard, we must make sure that no allowable state transition changing only one variable "switches" between two different product functions. We must encircle such transitions in a single group on the K map, as shown in Fig. 6-9. No hazard occurs because a new product function generates intermediate variable F, which remains a 1 during the former hazard-causing transition. The output F of this new gate is a 1 for both states 5 and 7 and prevents *IHO* from returning to 0 even momentarily. Since this is a two-level (sum-of-products) circuit free of hazards for all 1-to-1 transitions, we can be confident it is free of all hazards for other transitions as well.

Another example is shown in Fig. 6-10. Looking at the K map for the output function shown, we discover two possible locations where a single variable change (adjacent squares) would "switch" from one product group to another. These are

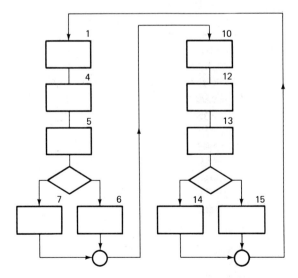

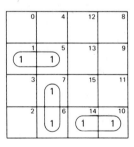

Output function

Figure 6-10 Hazard example.

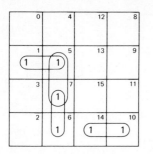

Figure 6-11 Hazard example solution.

between squares 5 and 7, and between squares 6 and 14. However, looking at the ASM chart, we discover that no transition can occur between states 6 and 14. The hazard-free implementation is shown in the K map of Fig. 6-11, in which both squares 5 and 7 have been concluded in a product function.

Hazard elimination is an easier design task than race elimination, although hazard elimination requires extra gates. As with output races, hazards will cause circuit malfunctions only if they appear on immediate outputs. The synchronizing technique of Fig. 6-5 or gating technique of Fig. 6-6 will eliminate hazards as well as races from critical immediate outputs.

ROMs and Glitches

The circuit designer has no control over the internal configuration of a ROM, other than specifying its contents. Hazards potentially exist in all ROM outputs. The output of a ROM *must* be assumed to be unpredictable while its address inputs are changing. Immediate outputs that must not have extraneous short pulses *must* be gated or synchronized. Since all state variables and inputs are used as ROM address bits, any change of inputs or state variables must be assumed to potentially affect all the outputs during such a change. This is true even if the ASM chart does not show explicit dependence of the output on those inputs or state variables that are changing. Thus, asynchronous inputs should *always* be synchronized before becoming ROM address inputs. State-assignment race solutions should not be attempted with ROM implementations.

It may seem that gate design is more flexible in some respects than ROM design. However, the ROM circuit design is, and must be, more structured. This "structure" actually reduces design time and cost, while making circuit operation more reliable. Also, the structured ROM design is often less expensive to build and repair. The "flexiblility" of a gate design only increases design time and cost and greatly increases the chance for error. Many of the problems caused by races and hazards are especially vexing. These timing problems depend on the timing parameters of specific individual components and on unspecified asynchronous inputs. Although modern instrumentation, especially the logic-state analyzer, makes it possible to locate intermittent timing problems, such troubleshooting is still a time-consuming and expensive operation. The best design is a conservative design that does not allow the possibility of errors.

ASYNCHRONOUS ASMS

In the simple gate/flip-flop ASM, the clocked flip-flops act as delays to prevent the next state from reaching the gate inputs until after all current state outputs have stabilized. A new current state at the ROM address inputs causes a new next state to appear at the ROM data outputs. This new next state appears on the D inputs of the next-state register. This new next state does not appear on the flip-flop's outputs until they are clocked. The delay through the state register, caused by the clock period, ensures that the new next state is correct and stable. Since the next-state gates have an inherent propagation delay, could we use only these gate delays instead of a periodic clock to build a working ASM, as shown in Fig. 6-12? Figure 6-12 is a completely asynchronous ASM with no clock to control timing. A new current state at the gate inputs causes a new next state to appear at the gate outputs after a short delay. This new next state becomes the current state immediately. The next-state outputs are simply connected directly to the current state inputs. Since no clock exists, all inputs and outputs must be asynchronous.

Since gate delays are highly variable, we should expect extremely difficult design problems with transition and output races and hazards. In fact, design is so difficult that it is often divided into classes. One such division includes three classes: pulse, fundamental, and level mode.[1] In a *pulse-mode* circuit, each input must be a pulse (either from 0 to 1 to 0 or vice-versa). Pulses must be long enough to allow the circuit to operate and must not occur simultaneously or so close together that the circuit doesn't stabilize between them. In other words, one input changes from 0 to 1 to 0 (a pulse to 1), and a new current state becomes stable after some gate delay. Another input change may not occur until this current state is stable. A *fundamental-mode* circuit allows inputs to be levels, but transitions between levels must not occur simultaneously (nor too close together) on two or more inputs. Again, one input changes, either from 0 to 1 or from 1 to 0, and a new current state becomes stable after some gate delay. Another input change may not occur until this state is stable. A *level-mode* circuit allows any input transition at any time. A level-mode circuit is the most general of all and, of course, the most difficult to design. Pulse, fundamental, and level modes are methods of operation of a circuit. Obviously, any circuit can be excited by inputs

---

[1] Fredrick J. Hill and Gerald R. Peterson, *Switching Theory and Logical Design*, 2d ed., John Wiley & Sons, New York, 1974, chaps. 11, 13.

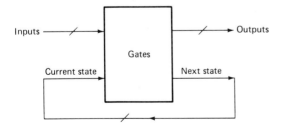

Figure 6-12 Asynchronous ASM.

that conform to these three operation modes. By restricting inputs in pulse- and fundamental-mode operation, we simplify the design process for an asynchronous circuit.

Because of the difficulties in designing asynchronous ASMs, they are seldom used when they can be avoided. Extremely simple and cost-sensitive logic circuits may have to be asynchronous (e.g., children's toys) in order to eliminate the cost of a clock. Even in very cost-sensitive circuits, the trend is away from asynchronous circuitry and toward a custom integrated circuit implementing a synchronous ASM (e.g., a TV game). Changes in the economics of production and design of circuits as well as the increased complexity of most digital circuits have reduced the importance of asynchronous circuitry.

Flip-flops themselves are asynchronous circuits for they do not contain an internal clock. For example, an edge-triggered D flip-flop is an asynchronous ASM with two inputs D and C and two outputs Q and $\overline{Q}$. Thus, integrated-circuit designers must be able to design classical asynchronous ASMs to implement flip-flops. Usually, a limited number of standard flip-flops are designed and their operation verified thoroughly. These standard flip-flop designs are used as building blocks for designing more complex ICs as synchronous circuits.

Although we will not discuss classical asynchronous ASM design, we will describe the way in which small asynchronous circuits are often designed to complement synchronous circuits. Small asynchronous circuits are commonly used to simplify designs and to implement functions difficult for synchronous circuitry.

SR Flip-Flops

Most simple asynchronous circuits are not designed by starting with the model of Fig. 6-12. Asynchronous circuits are usually designed using flip-flops as building blocks. Besides using edge-triggered JK and D flip-flops, another flip-flop, called the *SR* or *set-reset flip-flop*, is commonly used. This flip-flop is an unclocked flip-flop, which also happens to be the simplest example of the classical asynchronous ASM of Fig. 6-12. An SR flip-flop operates like the direct clear and direct preset inputs we used in an earlier chapter for system initialization.

The symbol for one type of SR flip-flop is shown in Fig. 6-13a. Both the S and R inputs normally rest at 0. With these inputs both 0, the flip-flop is stable, remembering the output resulting from its last change. If input S becomes a 1 while R remains a 0, the flip-flop will set so that $Q = 1$ and $\overline{Q} = 0$. Even if S now returns to 0, the flop will remain in the *set state*. If input R becomes 1 while S remains 0, the flop will reset so that $Q = 0$ and $\overline{Q} = 1$. The flip-flop will remember this *reset state*, even if R returns to 0. The condition $S = R = 1$ is not allowed.

An SR flip-flop is easily implemented with two gates, as is shown in Fig. 6-13b. The circuit is drawn so that it can be easily compared to Fig. 6-11. It is an asynchronous ASM because its next-state output is connected directly back to its current state inputs. Two NOR gates generate the next state from two inputs and the single current state bit. Assume that the circuit starts with $Q = 0$ and $\overline{Q} = 1$, and $YS = YR = 0$. Because Q and YS are both 0 inputs to gate A, $\overline{Q}$ will be 1. If $\overline{Q} = 1$ (regardless of YR),

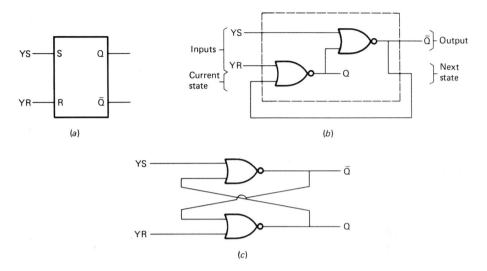

(a)

(b)

(c)

Figure 6-13(*a*) Symbol for SR flip-flop. (*b*) Implementation of SR flip-flop. (*c*) Implementation of SR flip-flop as commonly drawn.

then Q must be 0. Now, let $YS = 1$. This input forces $\overline{Q} = 0$ through gate A. $\overline{Q}$ is an input to gate B and forces $Q = 1$. Even after YS has returned to 0, $Q = 1$ will hold $\overline{Q} = 0$, which will in turn hold $Q = 1$ so that the flip-flop remembers its new state! An exactly analogous sequence describes the operation of the reset input. The SR flip-flop implementation is most often drawn as shown in Fig. 6-13*c*. A similar (but not identical) flip-flop can be made using NAND gates instead of NOR gates.

Although SR flip-flops can remember the last occurrence of two inputs, some kind of synchronization is required between the input sources to assure that both inputs do not simultaneously occur. This synchronization need not be electric. In Fig. 6-14, an SR flip-flop is connected to two mechanical switches. The flip-flop may be connected to an indicator in another room or to a synchronous ASM that controls door motion. It seems as though no synchronization exists between S and R inputs.

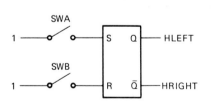

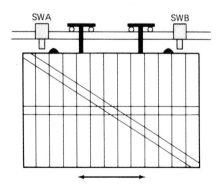

Figure 6-14 SR flip-flops controlled by door switches.

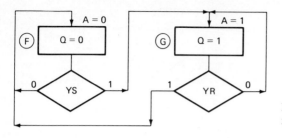

Figure 6-15 ASM chart for SR flip-flop.

However, the switches are mounted next to the sliding door so that only one switch can be activated at a time. This circuit changes state when the door is moved left or right and remembers the direction in which the door was moved.

Asynchronous State Machine Design

Is there a regularized way to design asynchronous ASMs? An ASM chart for the SR flip-flop is shown in Fig. 6-15. The flip-flop is reset in state F. A reset pulse would not affect state or output; so no decision diamond is shown for YR. If YS became a 1, the flip-flop would set and go to state G. A YR input would send the flip-flop back to state F. Let's call the current state A and the next state Q. We can complete the Next-State Table 6-1 directly from the ASM chart of Fig. 6-15. The next-state function Q is placed on a K map in Fig. 6-16. Since inputs YS and YR may not be 1 simultaneously, we put don't cares in squares 3 and 7 of the K map. A standard sum-of-products reduction is shown in Fig. 6-16, along with a change to NOR gates using De Morgan's laws. Finally, the ASM is completed by connecting the next-state output Q back to the current state input A.

The ASM chart of Fig. 6-15 adequately represented the asynchronous ASM to be implemented. This will not always be the case for more complex asynchronous ASMs. The inputs of a synchronous ASM are sensitive to logic levels, rather than logic-level transitions. A decision made on input YX depends only on the state of YX at the time of decision. It doesn't matter when YX changed to its current level nor how many times YX may have changed before. In an asynchronous ASM, input transitions are very important. Input transitions cause the ASM to change state. At least some inputs of an asynchronous ASM must cause state changes when they change. No clock signal

Table 6-1 Next state for SR flip-flop

Current state	Inputs		Next state
A	YS	YR	Q
0	0	X	0
0	1	0	1
1	X	0	1
1	0	1	0

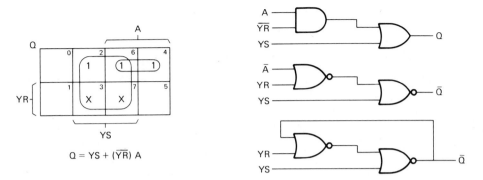

Figure 6-16 Implementation of SR flip-flop from ASM chart.

exists and *only* an input change can cause a state change. Some decision diamonds on an asynchronous ASM chart are more than decisions. At least one of the diamonds after each state box represents the occurrence of the input that actually causes the state change. This input takes the place of the clock.

How can we show a state change dependent on an input transition? Two alternatives are available to us. In Fig. 6-17a, output *HO* should be a 1 only after a 0-to-1 transition on input *YX*. Input *YX* is a 1 in state *A*. If input *YX* changes to a 0, the ASM proceeds to state *B*. States *A* and *B* are identical except for input *YX*. States *A*

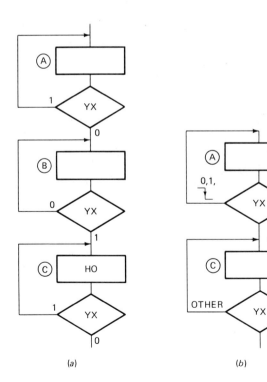

Figure 6-17(*a*)   Transition-sensitive ASM chart by adding states. (*b*) Transition-sensitive ASM chart by notation.

and B have identical values of state variables. What was formerly one state has been split into two state boxes on the ASM chart. Thus, this ASM chart includes the inputs as well as the state variables in its "states." Why? As long as we are in state *B*, we can be sure that $YX = 0$. The transition from $YX = 0$ to $YX = 1$ can be represented by the decision diamond leading to state *C*. Figure 6-17*a* is only a notational convenience. The number of state variables has not changed. Only the number of state boxes has increased! If this ASM had many inputs, you can see that the number of state boxes would become very large. An alternative notation avoids this problem. The ASM chart in Fig. 6-17*b* performs the same actions as the ASM chart in Fig. 6-17*a*. Transitions are now represented by arrows. Up arrows represent transitions from 0 to 1. Down arrows represent transitions from 1 to 0. Thus, the ASM changes from state *A* to state *C* if input *YX* makes a transition from 0 to 1. Four symbols may now be used with decision diamonds. These symbols are 0, 1, up arrow, and down arrow.

The notation of Fig. 6-17*a* is most convenient for classical asynchronous ASM design and produces a circuit like that in Fig. 6-12. Many small asynchronous ASMs are designed using edge-triggered flip-flops as building blocks. The notation of Fig. 6-17*b* is more convenient when designing asynchronous ASMs incorporating edge-triggered flip-flops.

Time-Oriented Design

The design of simple asynchronous ASMs may be considered to be time, rather than state, oriented. Often the input specification for such an ASM is a timing diagram or word description of the time order in which inputs may be expected. Edge-triggered flip-flops are often useful in implementing such designs. The simplest such use of an edge-triggered flip-flop is shown in Fig. 6-18. A single type D edge-triggered flip-flop

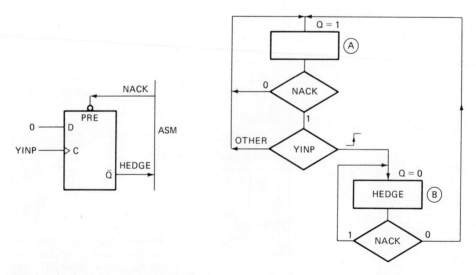

Figure 6-18 Asynchronous edge detector.

is used to detect a 0-to-1 transition on input *YINP*. This transition resets the flip-flop, which signals the ASM connected to it that a positive edge has occurred. The ASM acknowledges that the signal *HEDGE* has been received by momentarily asserting *NACK* in order to set the flip-flop to prepare to receive another edge. The *YINP* decision has been implemented with the transition-sensitive clock input of the flip-flop. The *NACK* decision has been implemented with the level-sensitive preset input.

Small asynchronous ASMs are commonly found in computer interfaces. Often, data and the destination address of that data are multiplexed on a common bus. In Fig. 6-19, a destination address from a computer is decoded from the common bus. The destination address allows the computer to select one peripheral among a group. If the computer peripheral device shown is to be the recipient of the data to be sent, *YADDR* will be 1 and *YASTB* (address strobe) will cause the ASM to change to the

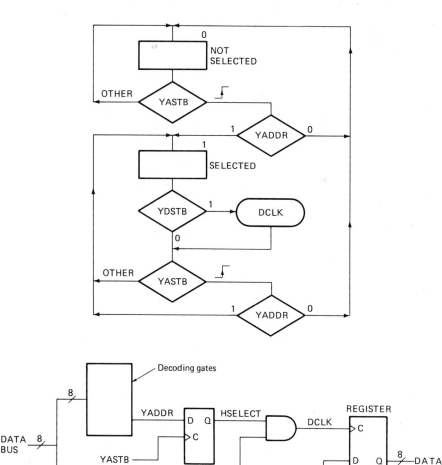

Figure 6-19 Asynchronous ASM for demultiplexing address selection and data from common bus.

selected state. Successive signals on *YDSTB* (data strobe) will cause data on the bus to be stored into this device's data register by *DCLK*. The signal *DCLK* is a conditional output of this ASM. Even though *DCLK* may be output several times, the ASM will not change state until *YASTB* makes a transition. This is indicated by the up arrow next to the *YASTB* decision. Only when the computer desires to send data to a different peripheral will it send another address and *YASTB*. Now *HSELECT* will be 0 if the new address selects a different peripheral, and *YDSTB* will not affect this peripheral's data register.

Asynchronous Design with Edge-Triggered Flip-Flops

Unfortunately, no regularized method exists for designing circuits like those in Figs. 6-18 and 6-19. Generalizations about the use of flip-flop inputs will help the partially intuitive task of designing these circuits.

Flip-flop inputs may be divided into three categories: edge-sensitive, delayed level-sensitive and immediate level-sensitive. Most flip-flops have one *edge-sensitive* input, the clock input. The clock input must be used to implement input-transition-caused state changes. For example, state changes in Fig. 6-19 are caused by positive transitions on input *YASTB*. Thus, input *YASTB* is connected to the flip-flop's clock input. *Delayed level-sensitive* inputs are those level-sensitive inputs that are sensed only at a clock transition. The *D*, *J*, and *K* inputs of flip-flops are delayed level-sensitive. These inputs can be used to select among branches of state changes caused by the clock input. For example, the input *YADDR* in Fig. 6-19 selects between alternate next states. The actual state transition is caused by *YASTB*, but *YADDR* selects the state to which the transition will occur. This is easily accomplished by connecting *YADDR* to the *D* input of the state flip-flop.

Most flip-flops have only one clock input. Often, the most straightforward circuit will require that a state flip-flop be changed by transitions on more than one input. The most straightforward edge-detector ASM chart is shown in Fig. 6-20. A positive edge on input *YINP* is detected by the circuit, and *HEDGE* is asserted. The circuit is reset to look for another edge by a positive transition on input *YACK*. Since only two

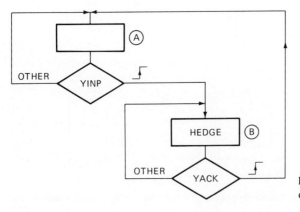

Figure 6-20 Straightforward edge detector.

states are needed, one flip-flop would be required, but that flip-flop would have to respond to transitions on two edge-sensitive inputs. Since such a flip-flop is not readily available, the ASM chart in Fig. 6-18 was devised as an alternative to Fig. 6-20. The *immediate level-sensitive* preset input of the flip-flop was used to set the circuit to look for another input edge. Although this eliminated the need for a flip-flop with two edge-sensitive inputs, using this immediate acting input had an undesirable effect as well. An additional decision diamond appeared after state *A*. As long as input *NACK* is low, the circuit is prevented from changing to state *B*, even though *YINP* may make a 0-to-1 transition. Immediate-acting inputs, like clear and preset, override the action of the clock input. An alternative to using direct-acting inputs is switching the clock source with gates among as many inputs as required. This can be a dangerous practice, and such circuits should be carefully designed. Hazards and races could erroneously clock the flip-flop.

The design of asynchronous ASMs using time-oriented design and edge-triggered flip-flops may be summarized as follows.

1. Draw a timing diagram showing the order in which inputs will occur and outputs should occur. Draw multiple timing diagrams if alternate sequences are possible.
2. Draw an ASM chart from the timing diagram, including edge-sensitive transitions. Use as *few* edge-sensitive transitions as possible to minimize the possibility of needing flip-flops with more than one edge-sensitive input.
3. Try to implement the ASM chart with edge-sensitive D or JK flip-flops. Use clock inputs to change states caused by input transitions. Select among next states with *D*, *J*, and *K* inputs and appropriate gating. Use clear and preset inputs to change states when clock inputs are exhausted. Check your use of immediate-acting inputs against the timing diagram to ensure that these inputs do not override state changes to be caused by the clock input. Go back and change the ASM chart to reflect the override action of the immediate-acting inputs.
4. If no circuit can be found because of insufficient edge-sensitive inputs and timing incompatibilities of immediate-acting inputs, return to step 2 and try to redraw the ASM chart to eliminate these problems.
5. If you still can't find a solution, try switching clock inputs, classical asynchronous design,[1] or a synchronous circuit.

Monostables

A logic circuit often seen in asynchronous designs is a *monostable multivibrator* or simply a *monostable*. Shown in Fig. 6-21, a monostable has one or more edge-sensitive inputs which cause this circuit's output to set ($Q = 1$, $\overline{Q} = 0$). The monostable resets itself after a fixed time delay. This delay is proportional to the product of the values of the resistor and capacitor connected to the monostable. Unfortunately, even if the resistor and capacitor were ideal, this "fixed" time delay would change with the mono-stable's power supply voltage and temperature. Also, actual capacitors and resistors

---

[1] Hill and Peterson, *Switching Theory and Logical Design*, chaps. 11, 13.

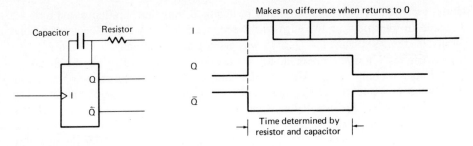

Figure 6-21 Monostable.

may have large initial tolerances and may change value considerably with time, temperature, and humidity. For these reasons, monostable timing can seldom be regarded as accurate. Monostable circuits must be designed and adjusted to account for wide variations in delay times. Monostables also "magnify" noise. If a monostable is accidentally started by a short electric noise pulse, the monostable's output will provide a normal-length pulse, which will easily operate other circuitry connected to it.

Nevertheless, monostables sometimes prove useful, especially in asynchronous circuits. In Fig. 6-19, address and data information may have traveled a long distance

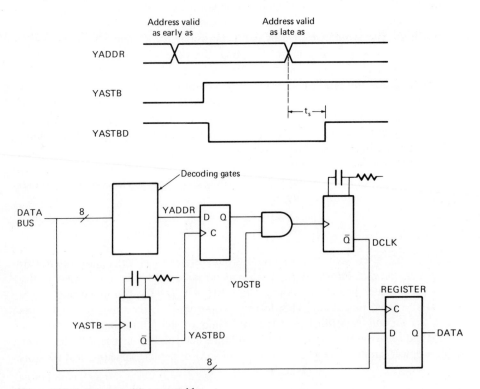

Figure 6-22 Deskewing with monostables.

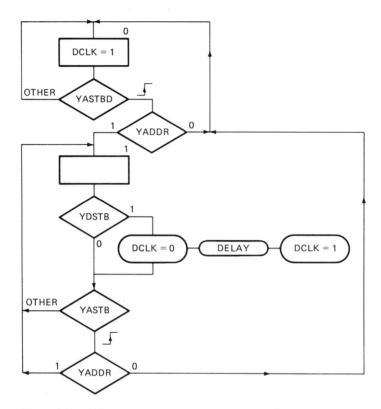

Figure 6-23 ASM with monostable delay.

over various wires and through various gates. In fact, not only will the bits of the address arrive at different times, but the address strobe may arrive before or after different address bits. This variation in arrival times is called data skew and is analogous to clock skew. The address and data strobe must take place only after data have arrived and the setup time of the flip-flops has been satisfied. Monostables are used in Fig. 6-22 to delay the strobes by a time at least equal to the worst time skew expected for signals traveling down the bus from the computer. The timing diagram in Fig. 6-22 shows the address monostable is adjusted so that it will clock the state flip-flop after its setup time, even if the address arrives as late as could be caused by other circuitry. Monostable operation may be indicated in an ASM chart by a DELAY box, as shown in Fig. 6-23. This ASM chart is carefully drawn to make it clear that the *DCLK* monostable affects only the output *DCLK* and will not delay a state transition.

Switch Debouncing

When a mechanical switch closes, its metallic contacts bounce against each other hundreds of times before coming to rest. Several tens of milliseconds may elapse before the contacts come to rest, as shown in Fig. 6-24. The resistor connected to logic "0"

Figure 6-24 Switch bounce.

assures that the signal *HSWTCH* will be a 0 when the switch is open, while the mechanical switch connected to logic 1 causes *HSWTCH* to become 1 when the switch is closed. Obviously, the signal *HSWTCH* is not a suitable input for an ASM. A single operation of the mechanical switch may look like hundreds of transitions to the ASM. Logic circuits used to rectify this problem are called switch debouncers. The oldest and simplest debouncing circuit is shown in Fig. 6-25. The first closure of the switch after it is operated causes the SR flip-flop to set. Additional bounces of the switch are of no consequence because the SR flip-flop simply remembers the first bounce. When the switch is operated back to its original position, the reset input performs the same function. Although this circuit is the simplest logic circuit for debouncing, it does require a switch with two contacts, rather than one, and one additional interconnection wire to the switch. Since the switch and the interconnection wiring may be much more expensive than the logic circuitry, we'd like to find a circuit that will debounce a single contact switch.

The circuit of Fig. 6-26 uses two monostables to debounce a single contact switch. One or the other monostable will set first, depending on the direction the switch is thrown. (Both should set eventually as the bouncing logic signal will be changing in both directions.) The monostables reset after a time delay designed to be greater than the time required for the switch contacts to stabilize. At that time the correct stable state of the switch is clocked into the D flip-flop. Some monostables have both negative and positive edge-triggered inputs, so that only one monostable would be needed. Besides the disadvantage of additional circuitry, the monostable circuit introduces a delay between switch operation and recognition. Unlike the SR flip-flop circuit which operates on the first switch closure, the monostable circuit must wait until bouncing has stopped. This delay is usually not significant but may be if, for example, the switch and logic circuit must precisely control the position of a moving object.

The monostables of Fig. 6-26 provide a time delay. A clock and counter also provide a time delay. You should expect that a synchronous ASM could be built to

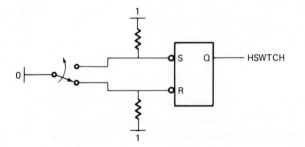

Figure 6-25 Switch debouncing with SR flip-flop.

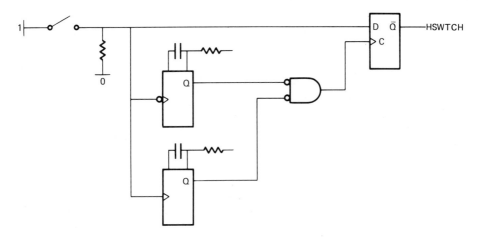

Figure 6-26 Switch debouncing with monostables.

perform the same debouncing function. In fact, four such ASMs are available as a preengineered single integrated circuit just for the purpose of switch debouncing.

PROBLEMS

6-1 (*a*) Assign states to the ASM of Fig. P6-1 so that transition races cannot occur. *All* inputs are asynchronous.

(*b*) Compare the complexity of part (*a*) with the complexity of a circuit using a synchronizing register instead of state assignment.

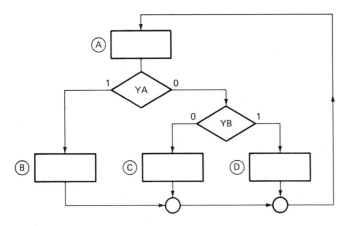

Figure P6-1 ASM chart for Prob. 6-1.

6-2 (*a*) Find the minimal gating for the output function in Fig. P6-2.

(*b*) Find the minimal hazard-free output gating for the output function in Fig. P6-2.

(*c*) Compare the complexity of part (*b*) with a circuit, using the result of part (*a*) and an

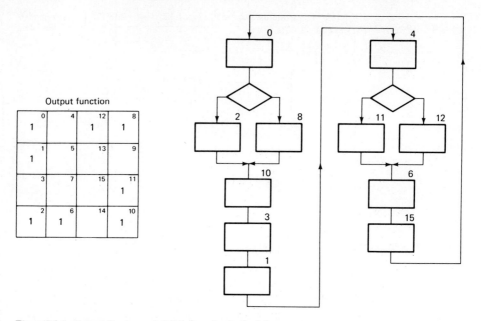

Output function

0	4	12	8
1		1	1
1	5	13	9
1			
3	7	15	11
			1
2	6	14	10
1	1		1

Figure P6-2 Output K map and ASM chart for Prob. 6-2.

output synchronizing register. Assume that delaying this output one clock period is of no consequence.

6-3 (*a*) The circuit in Fig. P6-3 uses 7474 flip-flops. All gates have propagation delays identical to the 7400. The specifications of these parts were given in the problems for Chap. 5. Draw a timing diagram showing the longest time during which output glitches could appear. Include the clock and the state variables on your timing diagram.

(*b*) Add a synchronizing register of 7474s to the outputs of Fig. P6-3. Use a 7404 to provide an inverted clock for this register to halve the output delay. The delay in the resynchronized outputs must be less than one half clock period. Draw the asymmetric clock signal needed to reduce the delay through the output register as much as possible. Use the results of part (*a*) and a 200-ns clock period.

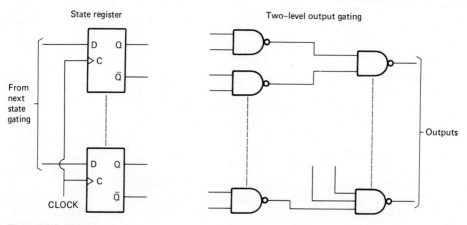

Figure P6-3 Output races.

6-4 The ASM chart of Fig. P6-4 has one asynchronous input YX. Complete the timing diagram in Fig. P6-4. Fill in the states and outputs.

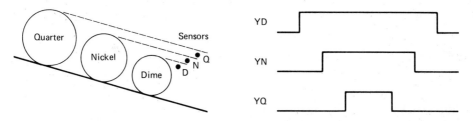

Figure P6-4 Synchronous ASM.

6-5 Implement an SR flip-flop using NAND gates. Describe its operation with a timing diagram.

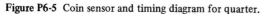

Figure P6-5 Coin sensor and timing diagram for quarter.

6-6 (*a*) The coin sensor in Fig. P6-5 is part of a vending machine. As each coin rolls down a chute, it covers one or more optical sensors, breaking a light beam and causing that sensor's outputs to become a 1. The timing diagram for a quarter is shown. Draw the timing diagrams for a nickel and a dime. Design an *asynchronous* ASM that has three outputs corresponding to the three coins and three inputs corresponding to the three sensors. The ASM's outputs should change to 1 to indicate the coin that rolled past the sensor. The output corresponding to the coin detected should remain asserted until another coin rolls past the sensor. The output may be momentarily incorrect while the coin is rolling past the sensors.

(*b*) Modify the circuit of part (*a*) so that incorrect outputs do not appear even while the coin is rolling past the sensor.

6-7 Design an *asynchronous* controller for the tram of Prob. 1-5. Use a monostable for the 10-s stop delay.

SEVEN

SYSTEMS AND SYSTEM COMPONENTS

When we looked at the traffic light controller, the bank teller, and the tram controller examples in previous chapters, we were concerned with describing an algorithm for operation of a small system—the algorithm, in fact, that described the *systematic behavior* of the example in each case.

Systems are all about us today—some quite simple and many very complex. Many (e.g., a bank teller) were designed by one or a few people. Such a simple system is relatively easy to describe. Proper operation of such a system is easily tested. Other systems are "designed" by a much broader "team" over a longer time period. It is often very difficult to tell whether the system is operating well, and if not, what to do about it (e.g., the Federal Government or the petroleum industry).

Systems are aggregate collections of components arranged in a precise, or at least particular, order to perform a specific function. Systems may be improved by improving the performance of any component area, by rearranging component blocks, or by the addition or deletion of component blocks.

Good systems are nearly always designed by thinking about the problem requirements, organizing several alternative block diagrams of system component arrangements which may solve the problem, and then selecting the most promising block diagram.

Fundamental changes in system arrangement as well as component block selection and realization are occurring (e.g., compare a slide rule with an electronic calculator or an analog watch with a digital watch). These changes are a result of dramatic performance increases in integrated-circuit components. The performance of integrated circuits will continue to improve; so we can expect continuing changes in system design.

MODELS AND BLOCK DIAGRAMS

One important concept is the use of *models* to represent real behavior. Models are valuable for several reasons:

1. Models allow simplification of the system behavior from many variables to just a relevant few.
2. Models permit analogy to other more readily understood systems.
3. Models are changeable if found to be in error or insufficiently illustrative.

We use models to provide insight into complex situations and to simplify and idealize problems so that we can describe them in mathematical form or by a graphical plot. It is important to keep this modeling activity firmly in mind—to be constantly aware that models are, at best, shallow imitations of reality—and not to delude ourselves into equating the two.

Models can be developed in several forms. The Bohr model of the atom is a *physical model.* Newton's laws are *mathematical models.* Other models may be *graphical.* For many engineering problems, *block diagrams* are common models representing the component parts of a system. Block diagrams hide most of the details of a system, so that fundamental functions are clear.

Designing with Block Diagrams

Much effective design is carried out at the system block-diagram level. Engineers are often concerned with reducing cost or increasing performance. Therefore, system improvements are often conceptualized as a reduction in the cost/performance ratio. Usually, changes in the block diagram will cause more dramatic improvements in the cost/performance ratio than changes within a subsystem. Considerable effort should be spent optimizing the system block diagram before concentrating on the subsystems. In fact, a wrong solution may be obtained by focusing on subsystem improvement too early.

The arrangement and function of subsystems is often called the system's *architecture.* The architecture of a system is often hierarchical, as shown in Fig. 7-1. A very generalized system block diagram is shown in Fig. 7-1*a*. This block diagram may not seem very useful, and, indeed, it is seldom drawn. However, the first step of any system's design is *represented* by this diagram. That first step is the description of the inputs and outputs of the system and the general algorithm to be implemented. Many questions must be accurately answered before continuing with the system's design. Are additional outputs required? Are there sufficient inputs to calculate the required outputs? How will the outputs be calculated? Are there too many inputs? Some inputs may be redundant or completely irrelevant. Once you're satisfied that inputs, outputs, and overall system operation are correctly defined, divide the block in Fig. 7-1*a* into appropriate subsystems. For many instrumentation systems, this subdivision would look like Fig. 7-1*b*. The arrangement of this simple block diagram may also have

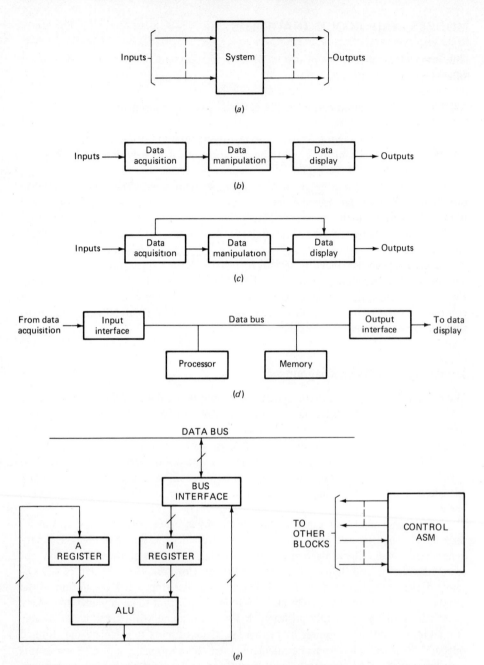

Figure 7-1 (a) Generalized system. (b) Typical instrumentation system. (c) Modified instrumentation system. (d) Data manipulation block. (e) Processor block.

important consequences. For example, suppose that a large amount of data needs only to be displayed and not manipulated. As drawn, the block diagram of Fig. 7-1*b* would require *all* data to travel through the data manipulation block. The data manipulation block must transfer many data that do not need manipulation from input to output subsystem. The manipulation block may have to be much higher-performance than really necessary in order to transfer all this data. Optimization of the manipulation block will not improve this situation. A change in the block diagram is necessary. If many data were not manipulated, we'd want to modify the block diagram to Fig. 7-1*c*. An additional data path has been added to allow data that does not need manipulation to be transferred directly from input to output subsystem.

Next, each of the blocks of Fig. 7-1*c* must be implemented. Often blocks are sufficiently complex to require further subdivision. The data manipulation block is subdivided in Fig. 7-1*d*. This block consists of a processing unit and memory as well as connections called *interfaces* to other blocks. An important decision we made in drawing Fig. 7-1*d* was to use a single common data bus. Only one data transfer may take place between two of the four subsystems at any one time. Not allowing simultaneous data transfers limits performance but also reduces cost, as multiple data busses would be expensive.

Finally, the processing unit of Fig. 7-1*d* is sufficiently complex to require subdivision into the subsystems of Fig. 7-1*e*. An ALU performs processing operations under the direction of an ASM. Two registers *A* and *M* allow temporary data storage in the processing unit.

It may seem that the decisions we made in this example were easy to make. In real problems the "best" arrangement of subsystems is not obvious. Considerable study and iteration may be required to develop a suitable solution.

SYSTEM DESIGN

By now, it should be obvious that system design is complex. Widely divergent choices are available to the designer. *Intuition and experience play a far greater role in the process than is generally recognized.* However, there are some steps that are beneficial to study in preparation for effective system design:

1. It is valuable to be able to describe desired functions in terms of flowcharts. These are implementation-independent algorithms.
2. It is equally valuable to be able to develop algorithm solutions and to realize them in operational circuitry. We have done this in simple ways in previous chapters.
3. It is important to be familiar with alternative architectures. The remainder of this book will give some examples of microprocessor architectures. Experience is important here. Familiarity with alternatives chosen by other designers is the first step to creativity.
4. It is important to understand major component blocks that are generally used (e.g., transducers, *A*-to-*D* converters, and arithmetic processors). These are discussed throughout this book.

5. It is important to realize that block diagrams are only models of reality. Attention must be paid to differences between idealized blocks and real circuitry. We have already discussed some realities such as fan out, delay, races, hazards, and noise.

LARGE DIGITAL SYSTEMS

As digital integrated circuits become less costly and more complex, more and more functions are added to formerly simple systems. The block diagram technique described previously will allow system architecture to be planned. The classical ASM technique, by itself, will be insufficient to implement these systems. The processing unit in Fig. 7-1d could have been implemented as a ROM and flip-flop ASM. Dozens of flip-flops and millions of bits of ROM would have been required. A distinguishing characteristic of this processing unit (and many others) is that it processes several bits grouped together as a *word* simultaneously. This data word might contain 4, 8, 16, or more bits of data. The implementation we postulated in Fig. 7-1e was oriented toward this data word. Data paths guided data words among bus interface, registers, and arithmetic logic unit. Because data and control were separated, the ASM controlling the flow of these data words was a reasonable size. This controlling ASM did not have to have all the data bus bits as inputs because the internal data paths and the ALU actually moved and manipulated the data. This controlling ASM did not need additional state flip-flops to remember data states because the A and M registers stored data states. As you might guess, the generality and performance of this processing unit were reduced by using a specific arrangement of ALU, registers, and data paths, rather than a very large classical ASM. Only those operations allowed by the configuration of data paths chosen and by the limited ALU functions available can be performed. Dozens of clock cycles may be required to perform an operation requiring one clock cycle in a classical ASM. Yet, the economic saving is so great that division of data flow and processing circuits from the controlling ASM is almost universal. Data flow and processing components are mass-produced and inexpensive. More importantly, engineers easily familiarize themselves with the limited and standardized functions of these components. This familiarity reduces the cost of designing complex systems.

The system blocks associated with data flow and processing fall into three general categories:

Processor. Processors manipulate and move data. They often contain a small amount of memory (even if only a register or two) to hold intermediate results of their manipulations. Traditionally, the control ASM has been considered part of the processing unit. The controller has more interaction with the processor than with other subsystems.

Memory. Data memory holds operands and intermediate and final results. Operands are variables used by the processor to calculate the results stored in memory.

Input-Output. A digital system must input operands from outside sources and out-

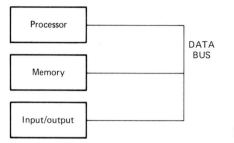

Figure 7-2 A generalized architecture.

put results of its calculations to be useful. Input-output subsystems provide connections, or *interfaces*, with people or machines not part of the digital system.

These three subsystems are so common that we shall want to connect them together in a generalized architecture. They could be interconnected in a large variety of ways. One simple and common technique is shown in Fig. 7-2. A single common data bus allows data to move among the three subsystems. Although limited to one data transfer at a time, the economics of this configuration make it widely used for many applications for which its performance is sufficient.

The task of specifying or *programming* the ROM in the controlling ASM (part of the processor in Fig. 7-2) is time-consuming, prone to error, and expensive. An alternative is the stored-program technique.

Stored-Program Control

The ASM in the processor of Fig. 7-2 controls the operation of the entire system via a control program stored in its ROM. Since Fig. 7-2 is supposed to be a generalized architecture, it is essential to be able to change the ROM program to perform different functions for different applications. Programming the ASM's ROM is expensive and time-consuming. The *programmer* must be intimately familiar with the circuitry of this digital system. Each line of ROM contents must specify the control signals of the system in gruesome detail. A hierarchical approach called *stored-program control* has been developed to remove the necessity for intimate familiarity with the circuitry and reduce the detailed specifications required.

In a stored-program system, the ROM in the controlling ASM contains a standardized program used for all applications. The ASM ROM guides the system to read and interpret instructions from the programmer. The programmer's instructions are stored, not in the ASM's ROM, but in the memory subsystem of Fig. 7-2. Furthermore, each of these instructions initiates a complex sequence of actions in the control ASM. Now, a single instruction stored in the memory subsystem may cause a complex sequence of actions to be performed by the controlling ASM. For example, stored-program instructions specify entire data manipulations to be performed, rather than control signals to be activated. The standard program in the controlling ASM's ROM sequences all the control signals to perform the specified data manipulation. Commonly implemented instructions are data movement, arithmetic, boolean functions, and data shifting.

Again, performance has suffered for economy. The programmer is limited to a small specific set of data manipulations that are understood and interpreted by the controlling ASM. However, the digital system of Fig. 7-2 is now completely standardized with the exception of the application-dependent instructions to be stored in the memory subsystem. Because this system can be applied to solve many problems by changing the instruction sequence, it can be and is mass-produced very inexpensively. Such a system is called a *microcomputer*, and the application of microcomputers is the topic of the remainder of this book. Microcomputers are advantageous, not only because they are mass-produced and inexpensive, but also because they reduce the development cost of complex digital systems.

Microcomputer Operation

Let's examine the operation of a very simple microcomputer. Part of the microcomputer is shown in Fig. 7-3. A memory subsystem contains both a ROM for storing instructions and an RWM for storing data. The subsystems are interconnected with a single bus. This bus consists of two subbusses: the data and the address bus. Addresses are sent to the memory from the processor. Data may be sent from the processor to the memory or from the memory to the processor. Instructions are also transferred on the data bus from the memory to the processor.

This simple processor system consists of two major parts. The *A* register and the arithmetic logic unit (ALU) manipulate data transferred between processor and memory via the data bus. The rest of the processor sequences the operation of the instructions stored in the memory system's ROM. The *PC* or program counter register provides the address of the instruction to be performed. The *IR* or instruction register holds the instruction after it is extracted from memory. The control ASM sequences all the control signals needed to perform these operations and those signals needed to perform the data operations specified by the instruction in the *IR*. The control ASM also provides memory control signals. An I/O subsystem, if it had been shown, would have been connected similarly to memory with I/O control signals from the processor's control ASM.

Let's trace the operation of this microcomputer by using the partial ASM chart of Fig. 7-4. When power is first applied, initialization circuitry starts the ASM in state *INIT*. State *INIT* has output *HCLPC*, which clears the program counter to 000H. We have stored the first instruction to be performed at address 000H in the ROM. The ASM sequences to state *FETCH*. The *PC* is sent to the memory via the address bus (*IHPCON*). A 16-bit instruction, located at address 000H, is put on the data bus (*ILRD*), and this instruction is stored in the instruction register (*HIRLD*). The instruction fetch cycle simply retrieves the instruction specified by the program counter from memory.

Instructions in our simple computer look like Fig. 7-5. The most significant 4 bits of the instruction are called the operation code or opcode and specify 1 of 16 possible operations to be performed. The least significant 12 bits contain the address of

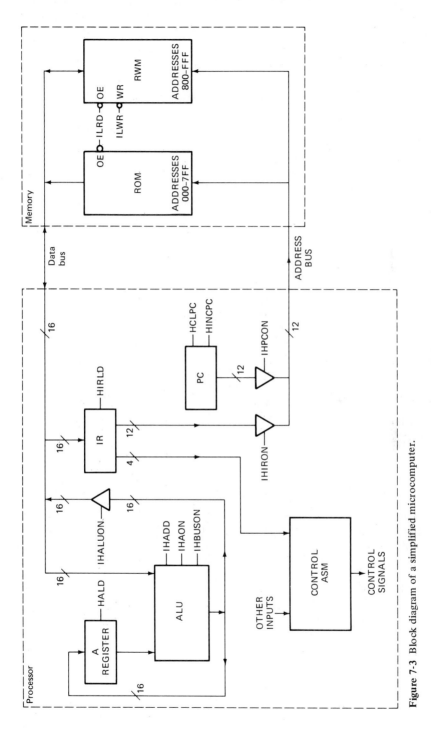

Figure 7-3 Block diagram of a simplified microcomputer.

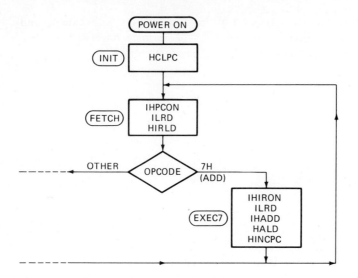

Figure 7-4 Part of the ASM chart for the computer of Fig. 7-3.

a data operand in memory. In this example we've fetched the instruction 79FAH from memory. Operation code 7H means add the contents of a memory location to the *A* register. The address of the datum to be added is 9FAH.

Return to the ASM chart and block diagram to notice that the most significant 4 bits of the *IR* are inputs to the ASM. Since, in our example, these bits are 7H, the ASM chart takes the branch to state *EXEC7*. This state executes the required data operation. The least significant 12 bits of the *IR* are sent to the address bus (*IHIRON*). The datum stored in RWM at address 9FAH is put on the data bus (*ILRD*). This datum becomes one input to the ALU. The memory datum and the *A* register are summed (*IHADD*) and the result stored in the *A* register (*HALD*). Independently, the program counter is incremented (*HINCPC*). After each instruction is executed, another is fetched from memory. Now, when the ASM returns to the *FETCH* state, the *PC* contains 001H; so the next instruction, stored in memory at address 001H, is fetched to be executed. You can see that a fairly complex ASM sequence is necessary, even in this simple computer, to fetch and execute instructions.

Fortunately, the programmer need know nothing about the details of this internal ASM sequence. The designer of the instruction sequence need only remember the overall characteristics of each instruction. For example, he or she must know that opcode 7H means add a memory datum to the *A* register. Even the engineer designing the memory and I/O systems for this computer must only know enough of the computer's internal operation to understand the sequencing of the external memory and

4	12
OPCODE	OPERAND ADDRESS

Figure 7-5 Instruction format for the computer of Fig. 7-3.

I/O control signals. Our interest in the rest of this book will be in the external and macroscopic description of microcomputers. We will be more interested in using microcomputers than in designing the individual processor circuits.

PROBLEMS

7-1 Because of its low cost, engineers often try to use the microcomputer of Fig. 7-2 in systems in which its performance would ordinarily be insufficient. Changes are made in its architecture to increase its performance. A common change is to allow data transfers between memory and input-output *simultaneously* with transfers between processor and memory. Modify the block diagram of Fig. 7-2 to permit such simultaneous transfers. Make as few changes as possible.

7-2 Figure P7-1 shows a simple but large automated railroad. Trains stop at 200 stations along the line and may pass each other at passing sidings. Two alternative architectures are to be examined: one large single controller and many smaller controllers. Draw block diagrams of each architecture and discuss merits and drawbacks of each.

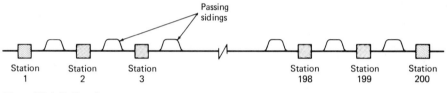

Figure P7-1 Railroad.

7-3 Many times, a single processing unit will not be sufficiently fast for a particular application. An alternative to a single fast processor is several slower processors. One such multiple processor architecture, called a pipeline, is shown in Fig. P7-2. Each processor performs only a part of the data manipulation and transfers the partially processed data to the next processor in the pipe. Assume that a single processor with the same performance as one of the three in the diagram could perform the *entire* data manipulation in time T. Thus, a new input datum could be processed at intervals of T seconds. How should the data manipulation task be divided among the three processors in the pipeline for maximum performance? How often could a new datum be processed by the pipeline processor? How long does it take to process a single datum from input to output? What would happen if the task could not be subdivided among the processors optimally?

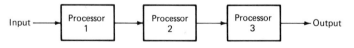

Figure P7-2 Pipeline processor.

7-4 Figure P7-3 is one of many architectures of parallel processors. Each processor implements an entire data manipulation in time T, but each manipulates only every third datum. Thus, processor 1 manipulates data input at times 1, 4, 7, 10, etc.; processor 2 at times 2, 5, 8, 11, etc.; processor 3 at times 3, 6, 9, 12, etc. Compare the performance of this parallel processor with the pipeline

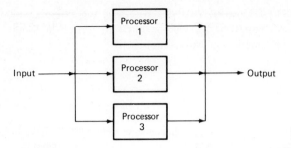

Figure P7-3 Parallel processor.

processor of Fig. P7-2. Are there algorithms for which one or the other architecture may not work? Explain.

7-5 A digital system must be designed to independently control the temperatures of 100 vats of colored dyes. Each vat has a temperature sensor, which will be an input to the digital system, and a heater controlled by an output of the digital system. A single processor has sufficient speed to control the temperature of up to 10 vats. What multiple-processor architecture would you use for this temperature controller and why? You are *not* constrained to use only the architectures previously discussed.

7-6 Consider the microcomputer of Fig. 7-3. Expand the ASM chart of Fig. 7-4 to perform the following functions.

(*a*) Implement a store the *A* register into memory instruction. This instruction has opcode 3H.

(*b*) Change the ASM chart so that even and odd opcodes perform identical functions except for addressing. Opcodes 6H and 7H would both add the contents of a memory location to the *A* register, while opcodes 2H and 3H would both store the datum from the *A* register into memory. The odd opcodes would address memory like the example in the text. The even opcodes assume that the address in the instruction is actually the address of a memory location which contains the address of the operand. Signal *HIRLD* still loads an entire 16-bit instruction into the *IR*. You can use a new signal *HIRALD*, which loads only the 12 address bits into the *IR* without changing the 4 most significant bits.

(*c*) So far, we have no way to implement a decision with our simple microcomputer. Normally, the *PC* is incremented after each instruction. A decision is implemented by changing the *PC* to the address contained in the decision instruction if a condition is true. Implement an instruction that changes the contents of the *PC* to the address contained in the instruction only if the *A* register is not 0. If the *A* register is 0, increment the *PC* as usual. You can use a signal named *YZERO*, which is 1 if the output of the ALU is 0. A signal named *HPCLD* allows you to load the program counter, rather than just incrementing it. Besides designing the ASM chart, show any changes required in the block diagram.

EIGHT

MICROCOMPUTERS AND PROGRAMMING

The word microcomputer implies a very small computer. Computers in which the central processing unit is fabricated as a single integrated circuit are called microcomputers. The first microcomputers were physically small, had little computation ability, had limited amounts of memory, and had few interfaces to external devices. Their scope of application was also limited. Even these early microcomputers were inexpensive compared with other available computers and were widely used.

Advances in technology have drastically changed the microcomputer since the first crude devices were introduced. Computational power has been increased dramatically. Microcomputers now have large amounts of memory and connect to many external devices. Even with this added capability, microcomputers have become much less expensive than they once were.

In the process of being improved, the microcomputer has become much more difficult to identify. Important identifying characteristics are physical size, cost, and type of application. The term microcomputer is almost always reserved for computers in which the main processing unit is fabricated as a single integrated circuit or, occasionally, a few integrated circuits. Being fabricated as ICs, microcomputers are inexpensive. Even more parts of the computer, such as memory, are being added to this single integrated circuit.

Microcomputers are often dedicated to a single problem or a group of related problems. Formerly, expensive computers had to be shared among several users to justify their cost. The microcomputer's low cost makes it possible to dedicate a computer to a single task or small group of tasks that were formerly implemented with specialized ASMs. Thus, we find microcomputers in sewing machines, microwave ovens, and automobiles. More complex tasks, such as control of an industrial plant, have been partitioned into smaller tasks assigned to multiple microcomputers.

Importance of Microcomputers

The scope of the application of microcomputers made possible by their small size and low cost has important implications for the quality of life in the world. Micros help to improve productivity and reduce costs. More importantly, micros often save scarce raw materials and conserve energy that would otherwise be wasted. Microcomputers monitor and control industrial processes to reduce pollution. Microcomputers control automobile timing and fuel injection to maximize gas mileage while minimizing pollutants.

Components of a Microcomputer

The terms microprocessor and microcomputer are often used interchangeably in the literature. Although distinctions can be made, the trend to integrating more of the computer system in a single integrated circuit continually makes it more difficult to differentiate between these terms. The term microprocessor is sometimes used to describe only the processing element, while the term microcomputer describes the entire system of processor, memory, and input-output. For the purpose of this text, the terms microprocessor and microcomputer will be used interchangeably.

A basic microcomputer system is shown in Fig. 8-1. Each block may represent one or more integrated circuits and any additional components needed to make those circuits operational. The microprocessor is the heart of the microcomputer system, controlling the operation of the system.

The memory block contains circuits to remember results of calculations performed by the microprocessors. It also contains the instruction sequence that causes these calculations to be performed. This instruction sequence causes this microcomputer to solve a specific problem. Two kinds of memory are important. The microprocessor can store and retrieve data from RWM. It can also follow instructions contained in RWM. Since RWM forgets all data and instructions that have been stored in it whenever power

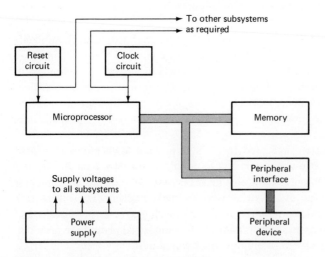

Figure 8-1 Components of a microcomputer.

is turned off, the instructions would have to be restored somehow each time the microcomputer was turned on. The instructions may be restored from a peripheral storage device, such as a cassette tape unit. Program restoration from magnetic tape is often used in traditional computer applications, such as payroll processing and scientific problem solving.

Including a peripheral mechanical storage device in every microcomputer-controlled sewing machine would be cumbersome and expensive. More seriously, it would be almost impossible to include such a device in some environments, such as an automobile. A mechanical storage unit would not be able to cope with the environment in which an automobile operates and would not be sufficiently reliable. For this reason, the instruction sequence for a microcomputer is usually stored in a ROM, just as was done previously in ASM controllers. PROMs or EPROMs are often used instead of ROMs for reasons of cost or convenience. The terms ROM, PROM, and EPROM will be used interchangeably as they perform the same basic function: the permanent storage of data or instructions.

Strictly speaking, the phrase "random access memory" or RAM applies to all the above memories. Any datum stored in the memory may be immediately accessed by the microprocessor. However, for historical reasons, the term RAM is almost universally used to mean RWM.

External devices to be controlled by the microprocessor are connected to the microcomputer system by an interface. These interfaces are often unique to the system being designed. The interface to a computer printer is different from the interface to a brake cylinder of a truck. Most of the customized hardware or circuitry needed for applying a microcomputer are these interfaces. Fortunately, many interfaces have common functions, and microcomputer manufacturers have integrated this common circuitry into a single circuit, usually called a programmable peripheral interface (PPI). Complete single integrated-circuit interfaces are manufactured for commonly interfaced peripheral devices, such as printers, displays, keyboards, and magnetic disks. Peripheral interfaces will be discussed in a later chapter.

A clock circuit provides master timing for the microcomputer system. The reset circuit initializes the processor and starts it running after the power is switched on. Both of these circuits are often included as integral parts of newer microprocessor integrated circuits. A power supply is required to generate the various voltages required by each integrated circuit in the system.

Importance of Programming

Although the advent of the microcomputer has proliferated the application of computers, it is not obvious that the proliferation of computers is of any benefit. The key benefits from the application of computers lie in the computer's ability to be *programmed* to perform a specific task. The sequence of instructions to the central processor that causes it to solve a particular problem is called the *program*. The art of designing this sequence is called *programming*. Programs are often called *software* in order to distinguish them from the logic circuits, which are *hardware*. Programming is important for several reasons. A microcomputer is applied to solve a problem by designing the program and interfaces needed to solve that problem. All the rest of the microcomputer system remains the same regardless of the application. Since these other components (processor, memory, etc.) are common to all applications, they may be mass-produced, with corresponding economies of scale.

Since the function of a microcomputer system may be changed by altering the program stored in the ROM, such modifications are relatively easily done. Changes in function may be needed to customize a system for a particular application or simply to correct an original design error.

Additional functions may be added by additional programming at little increase in the cost of each system manufactured. Even if additional ROM is required, it may be inexpensive compared to the benefit gained from the functions implemented by the programs it contains.

Designing the program is the major part of designing a microcomputer system. Therefore, programming is the first topic we will discuss.

Preengineered Systems

Since a sequence of "instructions" is stored in a ROM when implementing any ASM, you may wonder why a microcomputer is "better" or even different from an ASM designed specifically for the problem to be solved. The design of the microcomputer system is much less expensive than the ASM for two reasons. First, the majority of the microcomputer's hardware is predesigned. The microcomputer manufacturer has spent a great amount of effort in defining and designing processing, memory, and input-output functions. This vast engineering effort is shared by everyone who uses the microcomputer; so this engineering cost is only a very small part of the cost of the microcomputer. Second, the microcomputer's instruction sequence is easier to design and implement than the specialized ASM's ROM sequence for several reasons. First, each microcomputer instruction does more than each ASM instruction. Fewer and more easily comprehended instructions are required for the microcomputer. Second, standardization of instructions, data formats, and hardware allows the system designer to become proficient in a microcomputer's application and to use that proficiency repeatedly in other projects. Third, instruction standardization allows the microcomputer manufacturer to supply standardized automated aids for developing programs and even to supply standardized application software, such as arithmetic computation programs.

Of course, the benefits of standardization also bring inherent inefficiencies. Fortunately, in all but a few cases, these inefficiencies are more than offset by benefits. Even where microcomputers cannot be applied directly to solve a problem, they are often used in conjunction with a specialized ASM. The ASM performs tasks that the microcomputer cannot perform. The microcomputer performs the tasks that it can to reduce the complexity of the ASM.

Program Planning

Since programs are implementations of algorithms, they may be described by any technique used for algorithms. As in the case of the ASM, the most obvious technique is a

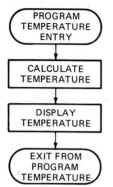

Figure 8-2 Entry/exit ovals.

word description of what the program does. This word description is often the best way to start developing a program. However, word descriptions may get cumbersome when implementing or testing a program; so other techniques are used. Just as in the case of ASMs, we will often use flowcharts to describe a program, although other techniques will and should be used when they are simpler. For example, you might want to use a table of actions required for various conditions. In actual practice, all useful techniques can and should be combined to facilitate development of programs.

The flowcharts we'll use to describe computer programs will be similar to those flowcharts used to describe ASMs. Action boxes and decision diamonds will have the same meaning as before. Figure 8-2 shows an oval that will be used to designate entry and exit points of parts of flowcharts. This notation will greatly simplify our drawings by allowing us to draw flowcharts on multiple sheets of paper. Each sheet may describe a single program, and the ovals show how the programs are interconnected.

Decision diamonds may have more than two exit paths, as shown in Figure 8-3. Here the temperature is tested to determine whether it is in one of three temperature ranges. Figure 8-4 shows two ways of drawing a multiway branch. The structure of Figure 8-4*a* implies that the branch decisions are sequential. Thus, the variable *KEY* is

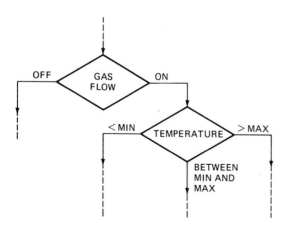

Figure 8-3 Decision diamonds.

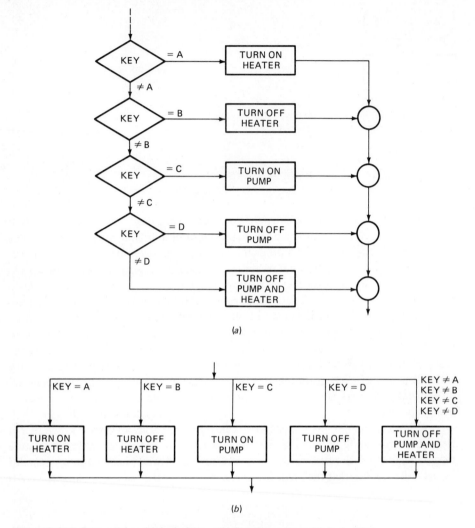

Figure 8-4(*a*) Sequential multiple decisions. (*b*) Simultaneous multiple decisions.

compared with *A* first, *B* second, etc. Figure 8-4*b* implies simultaneous testing of all branch conditions. It is important that all possible conditions are represented. It is easy to draw simultaneous decision figures that are ambiguous and do not precisely describe the action to be performed for all possible input conditions. Microcomputers can perform both sequential and simultaneous testing. It is best to use the flowchart form for the actual action desired.

The variety of possible flowcharts is unlimited. In order to minimize the chance of error, only a few different flowchart forms should be used. We will use one action box followed by another to show sequence of action. Once we start making decisions, we'll have to limit the forms the flowcharts take. Flowchart figures with decisions can

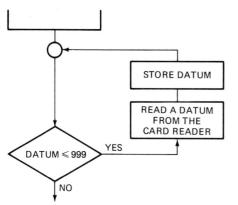

Figure 8-5 Do while flowchart.

be divided into two categories. These are alternate action and repetition. Figure 8-4 shows alternate-action flowcharts. Actions are or are not performed depending on the condition of input variables.

Figure 8-5 shows one common repetition flowchart. All repetition flowcharts are commonly called *loops*. In Figure 8-5, data are read from a card reader until a datum greater than 999 is encountered. This flowchart is called a *do while* figure because an action is repeated while some condition remains true. *Do while* constructions are often used for indefinite iteration, like this example. The loop of Fig. 8-5 can read one or many data.

A *do until* construction is shown in Fig. 8-6. This flowchart starts exactly six pumps. The action of starting a pump is repeated until some condition is true. In this example the condition is that pump number 6 has been started. *Do until* flowcharts are often used for definite iteration, when the number of actions to be performed is fixed and known in advance. Actually, *do until* and *do while* loops can each be used for definite and indefinite iteration. The loop type that most closely or naturally matches the problem statement should be chosen. There is one important difference

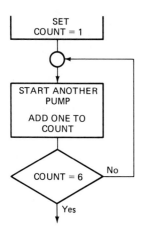

Figure 8-6 Do until flowchart.

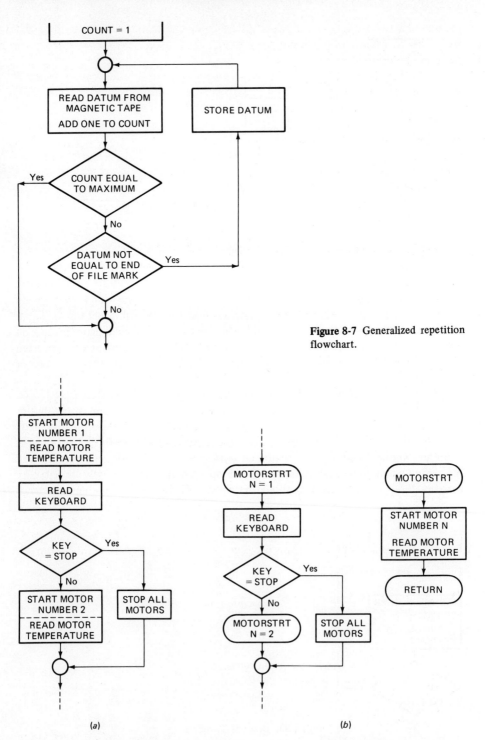

Figure 8-7 Generalized repetition flowchart.

Figure 8-8(a) Flowchart with repeated similar actions. (**b**) Abbreviated flowchart.

between the two loop figures if the loops are entered with the test condition *already true*. The *do while* figure will not perform any action, while the *do until* figure will perform its action once.

Both loop figures can be combined, as shown in Fig. 8-7. Many computer operations involve getting a datum, checking to see if it is the last datum, and processing that datum. This sequence is repeated for all data in a list.

Figure 8-8 shows two flowcharts that represent the same actions. We noticed that two action boxes in Fig. 8-8*a* were very similar. We've abbreviated the flowchart in Fig. 8-8*b* by writing the common action only once and referencing it from the main flowchart when needed. The common action could have been much more complex and have involved many action boxes and decision diamonds. You'll notice that we still must specify which motor we want to start each time we reference the *MOTORSTRT* sequence in Fig. 8-8*b*. The motor number *N* is called an *argument*. In the next chapter, we'll see that these abbreviations are not merely a notational device but may be actually implemented by the microcomputer as *subroutine* programs.

Data Types

Most instructions performed by the microprocessor cause an operation to be performed on data. Microcomputers use a few standard data types to simplify program development. Of course, the basic unit of data is still the bit, which may have a value of either 0 or 1. Eight bits concatenated are still a *byte*. Bytes are the most-often-used unit of data in microcomputers. Sometimes 8 or more bits concatenated are called a *word*. Sixteen bits is the most common size for a word.

A group of bits may be used to represent many kinds of data. The simple microcomputer we'll use as an example recognizes only a few representations. An unsigned binary integer is shown in Fig. 8-9. As was discussed in a previous chapter, each bit represents the value of a power of 2. If a bit is a 1, that power of 2 is present in the number being represented. An 8-bit positive binary integer can represent numbers from 0 to 255. The binary point need not be located at the extreme right, but can be anywhere desired, as shown in Fig. 8-10. Although we can no longer represent as large a number, we can now represent some fractional values. The location of the binary point is not automatically stored with the data; the location of the point usually exists only in the mind of the programmer and in the significance he attaches to each of the bits.

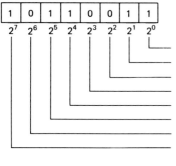

| 1 | 0 | 1 | 1 | 0 | 0 | 1 | 1 | Unsigned binary integer |

2^7 2^6 2^5 2^4 2^3 2^2 2^1 2^0 Weights of each bit

$1 \times 2^0 = 1$
$1 \times 2^1 = 2$
$0 \times 2^2 = 0$
$0 \times 2^3 = 0$
$1 \times 2^4 = 16$
$1 \times 2^5 = 32$
$0 \times 2^6 = 0$
$1 \times 2^7 = 128$
Total $= 179$

Figure 8-9 Unsigned binary integer equivalent to decimal 179.

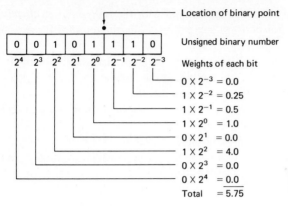

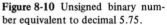

Figure 8-10 Unsigned binary number equivalent to decimal 5.75.

As was explained in a previous chapter, two's-complement notation is most commonly used to represent signed binary numbers. Figure 8-11 shows the weights attached to each binary bit in an 8-bit two's-complement number. The most significant (largest-weight) bit has a negative value. The consequences of this negative weighting are shown in the number line of Fig. 8-12. This number line represents the possible values of an 8-bit two's-complement integer. These values range from -128 to $+127$. Whenever the first bit is a 1, the number will be negative. A 0 first bit indicates a positive number. You should become familiar with the pattern of two's-complement numbers. A microcomputer negates a number in two's-complement form by first changing all bits to their opposites (called complementing or one's complementing) and then adding 1.

Binary representations, as described above, are the most efficient way to store numbers and compute results. However, binary numbers are not easy to convert from or to decimal numbers to be input by, or displayed to, a human operator. If efficiency of storage and speed of computation are not critical, *binary-coded decimal* (BCD) number representations may be preferable because BCD numbers are easier to convert to a human-compatible format. An 8-bit BCD number is shown in Fig. 8-13. A BCD number is divided into 4-bit groups. The bits within each group are binary-weighted but may take on the values from only 0 to 9. Each group or *BCD digit* has a weight corresponding to a power of 10. Note that an 8-bit BCD number may represent integers from 0 to 99, while an 8-bit binary number may represent values from 0 to 255.

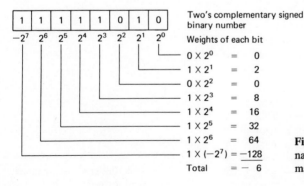

Figure 8-11 Two's-complement binary-number equivalent to decimal -6.

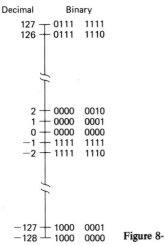

Figure 8-12 Two's-complement 8-bit numbers.

Very often a single bit may be sufficient to represent the required datum. A motor may be either on or off, a door open or closed. In these cases, a single bit will suffice to represent the condition. If the bit is 1, the motor is on. If the bit is 0, the motor is off. Since there are 8 bits in a byte, this most commonly used microprocessor datum may be used to represent eight such on/off conditions, as shown in Fig. 8-14. These bits are naturally called *boolean* variables.

Data Storage

Data may be stored and retrieved from registers and memory locations. Physically, the registers are in the microprocessor block of Fig. 8-1, while the memory locations are in the memory block. Each register or memory location will hold a single byte of data. From the programmer's point of view, the primary difference between memory locations and registers is that there are fewer registers than memory locations. Also, operations performed on data in registers are often faster than the same operations on data

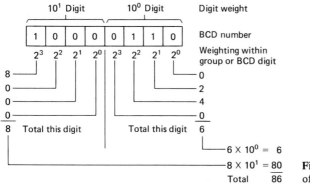

Figure 8-13 BCD representation of decimal 86.

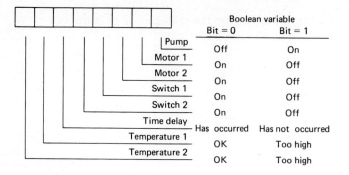

	Boolean variable	
	Bit = 0	Bit = 1
Pump	Off	On
Motor 1	On	Off
Motor 2	On	Off
Switch 1	On	Off
Switch 2	On	Off
Time delay	Has occurred	Has not occurred
Temperature 1	OK	Too high
Temperature 2	OK	Too high

Figure 8-14 Boolean variables.

in memory locations. Registers are usually used as temporary storage for calculations currently in progress, while memory locations are long-term storage for the results of calculations. A microcomputer with eight registers will use 3 bits to specify which register is to be used in a data operation. It is not unusual to find tens of thousands of memory locations available. Sixteen bits will hold a positive binary integer representing values from 0 to 65,535. Each possible integer specifies a memory location, and these 16 bits are called a *memory address*. Each memory location has a unique memory address, which enables the microprocessor to specify that the 8 bits of data stored in that memory location are to be used in a computation.

While they are not strictly used for data storage, data may be stored into, or retrieved from, peripheral interface registers. These registers are used to transfer data in and out of the microprocessor system. Each peripheral interface register has a unique *peripheral address* to allow the microprocessor to specify which peripheral device is to supply or receive data.

Instructions

The instructions that guide the operation of the microprocessor must be stored in memory locations. Therefore, instructions are groups of bits representing the operation to be performed. Instruction bits are often divided into fields that specify different attributes of the instructions, as shown in Fig. 8-15. The operation code or opcode field specifies the operation to be performed, such as add, subtract, move, complement, etc. Each operation is represented by a unique combination of bits. The register field specifies the register containing the datum to be used in the operation, while the memory address field specifies the memory location containing the datum to be used in the computation.

Instructions are placed in memory in the sequence in which they are to be performed or *executed*. The next instruction to be executed is specified by the contents

OPERATION CODE	REGISTER	MEMORY ADDRESS

Figure 8-15 Instruction divided into fields.

of a register called the *program counter*. After the execution of an instruction, one is added to the program counter; so it specifies the memory location of the next instruction to be executed. The microprocessor uses the contents of the program counter to retrieve this instruction from its memory location. The instruction is stored temporarily in the microprocessor's *instruction register* while it is being executed.

The representation of some instructions may require more bits than other instructions. For example, some instructions require memory addresses and some do not. Rather than waste bits in some instructions by making all instructions use the largest number of bits required, most microcomputers use variable-length instructions. Some instructions may be 1 byte long, some 2 bytes, and some 3 bytes. Now, to find the next instruction, the microprocessor must add 1, 2, or 3 to the program counter, depending on the length of the last instructions executed.

8080/8085 MICROCOMPUTER ORGANIZATION

The 8080 and 8085 are very similar 8-bit microcomputers that will be studied in this book. To the programmer these microcomputers consist of:

1. Seven working registers, each containing 8 bits
2. 65,536 memory locations, each containing 8 bits
3. A 16-bit program-counter register
4. A 16-bit stack-pointer register, used to facilitate subroutines and other functions
5. A flag register, containing status flags
6. An input-output interface containing up to 256 input and 256 output bytes

Each register may be referenced by a number or letter as follows:

Name	Number	Letter
Accumulator	7	*A*
Register	0	*B*
Register	1	*C*
Register	2	*D*
Register	3	*E*
Register	4	*H*
Register	5	*L*

Registers are sometimes used in pairs in order to handle 16-bit operands or addresses. Commonly used pairs may be referenced by a single number or letter as follows:

Name	Number	Letter	Registers referenced
Register pair	0	*B*	*B* and *C*
Register pair	1	*D*	*D* and *E*
Register pair	2	*H*	*H* and *L*
Program status word	3	*PSW*	*A* and flags
Stack pointer	3	*SP*	Stack pointer

Flag Register

The flag register contains five boolean variables, called status or condition flags as shown below:

Bit number	Letter	Name
7	S	Sign
6	Z	Zero
4	A	Auxiliary carry
2	P	Parity
0	C	Carry

These flags are changed by certain instructions, as will be described later. For convenience, each flag bit has a common interpretation, to which the actions of most instructions adhere.

The Z or zero bit is set (1) if the result of an instruction operation is zero. Otherwise, it is reset (0).

The S or sign bit is set (1) if the result of an instruction operation has a most significant bit which is 1. Otherwise, it is reset.

The P or parity bit is set if the result has even parity; that is, the result has an even number of 1s in it.

The C or carry bit is set if a carry or borrow occurs after an arithmetic operation. The significance of this bit in arithmetic operations will be discussed later. The C bit is also used for other purposes in nonarithmetic operations.

The A or auxiliary carry bit is the carry out of bit 3 into bit 4 from an arithmetic operation. The A bit is used for implementing decimal arithmetic, and its significance will be discussed later.

Addressing Modes

The performance of any computer is very dependent on the convenience with which it can retrieve and store data from memory. The 8085 microcomputer must generate 16-bit memory addresses to specify the memory location in which the desired data is located. The 8085 constructs memory addresses in four ways, called *addressing modes*. These are called direct, register-pair, stack-pointer, and immediate addressing.

Direct Addressing

Direct addressing, shown in Fig. 8-16, is the simplest addressing mode. Each instruction using direct addressing simply contains the complete memory address of the memory location containing the datum to be used. Three bytes are required to hold a direct address instruction. The first byte contains the opcode. The second byte contains the least significant byte of the address, while the third byte contains the most significant byte.

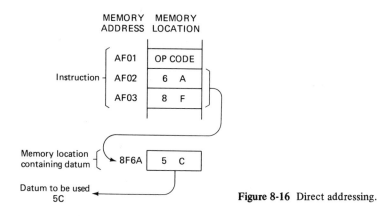

Figure 8-16 Direct addressing.

Register-Pair Addressing

A memory address may be specified by the 16-bit contents of a register pair. The contents of this register pair are used as the memory address of the memory location containing the datum to be used, as shown in Fig. 8-17. By holding an address that is used repeatedly in a register pair, each instruction using that address need not contain the extra 2 bytes needed to specify a memory address. Memory size required for instruction storage is reduced. Execution speed is increased because extra address bytes need not be retrieved from memory. A common use of this addressing mode is to manipulate data lists in memory. List manipulation is especially easy because the microprocessor has instructions that will increment or decrement register pairs, so that the address contained in the register pair can be made to point to the next datum in a sequential list.

Usually the *H* register pair is used for register-pair addressing. A few instructions allow the *B* or *D* register pairs to be used for addresses.

Stack-Pointer Addressing

Stack-pointer addressing allows the programmer to automatically add or remove a 16-bit datum from a list. This list is called a *stack* and is contained in **RWM**. Two stack operations are possible and are called *push* and *pop*. In a stack push, the 16-bit contents of a register pair are transferred to the stack by storing 8 bits at the location

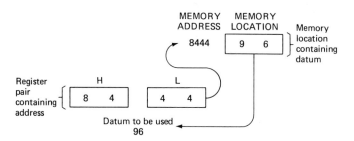

Figure 8-17 Register pair addressing.

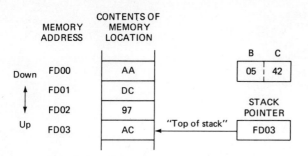

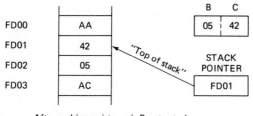

Before pushing register pair B onto stack

After pushing register pair B onto stack

Figure 8-18 Stack PUSH operation.

specified by 1 less than the contents of the *SP* register and storing an additional 8 bits at 2 less than the contents of the *SP*. The *SP* register is then set to its original value minus 2, in order to prepare it to store another 16 bits of data below the data just stored, as shown in Fig. 8-18. The stack pointer is always left pointing to the last byte pushed onto the stack. This location is called the *top of the stack*.

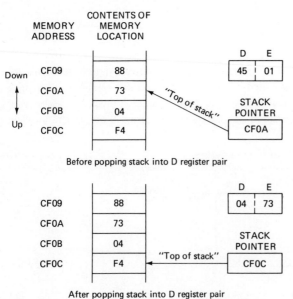

Before popping stack into D register pair

After popping stack into D register pair

Figure 8-19 Stack POP operation.

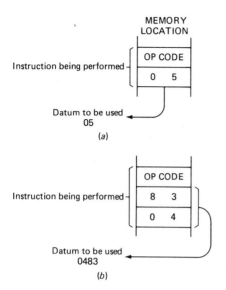

Figure 8-20(*a*) Immediate addressing with 1-byte datum. (*b*) Immediate addressing with 2-byte operand.

A stack pop operation retrieves 16 bits from the stack. Eight bits of data located at the location specified by the contents of the *SP* are read first. An additional 8 bits located at the contents of *SP* plus 1 are then retrieved, as shown in Fig. 8-19. Then 2 is added to the original contents of the *SP*, in order to leave it pointing to the next datum on the stack. In this way the *SP* is prepared for an additional pop operation to remove another 16 bits or for a push operation to add 16 bits to the list.

The stack is a variable-length list that expands downward in memory as more data are added to it (pushed) and contracts upward as data are removed (popped). More importantly, the stack is used for implementing subroutines, as will be discussed later.

Immediate Addressing

When using immediate addressing, the actual datum to be used is contained within the instruction, as shown in Fig. 8-20. Immediate instructions exist for both 8- and 16-bit data. In the first case, a 2-byte instruction is required; the additional byte is required to contain the 8-bit datum to be used. If a 16-bit datum is needed, a 3-byte instruction is required; 2 bytes are needed to hold the 16-bit datum to be used. Immediate addressing is used to enter constants into a calculation. Sixteen-bit immediate operands may be memory addresses to be put in the H register pair for use as register-pair addresses.

ASSEMBLY LANGUAGE

Instructions to the microprocessor are actually groups of 1s and 0s representing the desired operation to be performed. We have seen how hex notation can be used to abbreviate binary notation. Hex notation can obviously be used to abbreviate instruction representations, but hex programs are still difficult to understand. In order to make programs easily understandable, they are usually written in *assembly language*. In assembly language, combinations of bits are represented by names or mnemonics that correspond to the action of the instruction. For example, the 8085 instruction that moves an 8-bit data byte from the A register to the D register is represented by

0101 0111   or   57H

This representation is called machine language because it is the representation actually used by the microprocessor (machine). This instruction has three distinct fields. These fields are the operation, the destination register, and the source register, as shown in Fig. 8-21. Each of these fields is given a mnemonic that makes sense to the programmer. Since the operation field represents the move data instruction, we will call it *MOV*. Similarly, we will call the destination-field contents D and the source-field contents A for the registers named D and A, respectively. Written in assembly language, this instruction would be:

> MOV   D,A

This is much easier to understand than machine language. Programming is often done in assembly language. After the program has been written in assembly language, it can be converted to machine language manually (called hand assembly) or automatically by a computer program (called an assembler).

We would also like to refer to memory locations by names representing their memory addresses, rather than cumbersome hexadecimal numbers. The memory location containing the temperature of motor number 1 could be referenced by its address, *TEMP1*; or the first location in a program could be called *START*.

> START: MOV   D,A
>   MOV   B,C
>   ⋮   ⋮

Not all memory locations need be given names. Only those locations which must be referenced by instructions are given names corresponding to their memory addresses. Unnamed locations are assumed to follow named instructions in numerical order in memory. The instruction *MOV B,C* above would be contained in location 3C11H if *START* represented the address 3C10H.

If the assembly language program is to be automatically *assembled* (translated to machine language) by a computer, it is necessary to indicate to the assembler what

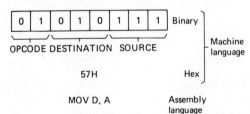

Figure 8-21 Machine and assembly language.

memory location the *first* memory address name is to represent or the addresses of memory locations that are not in numerical order. We could specify *START* to be memory location 3C10H as follows:

```
         ORG    3C10H
START:   MOV    D, A
         MOV    B, C
```

The letters *ORG* stand for the word origin. The next memory location after the *ORG pseudoinstruction* is given the address specified by the *ORG*. In this case, the next location is called *START* and will represent memory address 3C10H. The next location after *ORG* need not have an explicit name like *START* in order to be assigned the memory address specified in the *ORG* pseudoinstruction. Pseudoinstructions do not appear in the machine language program. They are only instructions to the assembler program or hand assembler, telling something about *how* the program should be assembled (e.g., what the first address should be).

In addition to making a program more understandable, symbolic names for memory addresses have other advantages. Very often, correcting a programming error or adding a new function requires that additional instructions be inserted between existing instructions. All instructions following the newly inserted instruction must be moved in memory to make room for these new instructions. The hexadecimal addresses of *all* following instructions will be changed so that all *references* to these following instructions must be changed to correspond to their new hex addresses. The machine language program must be altered. However, since the *names* of these memory locations do not change, the assembly language program will not have to be changed. The assembler will take care of reassigning names to memory addresses, to make room for the new instructions. For example, assume we started with the program shown in Fig. 8-22a. You do not need to know what each instruction means, only that two instructions reference other instructions by the names of their memory locations, *START* and *NEXT*. If we find that we need to add an instruction, as shown in Fig. 8-22b, none of the *names* by which these instructions are referenced need be changed. However, the assembler *has* assigned new memory addresses to these names to make room for the added instruction. The assembler has also automatically changed all references to changed memory locations to correspond to their new assignments. The assembler eliminates the tremendous burden of keeping track of all references that need to be changed when altering a program.

An assembly language program is divided into fields for convenience as shown below.

Label	Code	Operand	Comment
HERE:	MVI	C, 56H	; LOAD C WITH 56H
THERE:	JMP	NEXT	; JUMP TO NEXT
MAYBE:	XRA	D	; EXCLUSIVE OR A WITH D
	CMA		; COMPLEMENT A

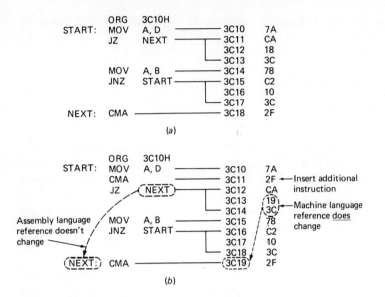

Figure 8-22(a) Original program. (b) Modified program.

The *label field* contains any symbolic name given to that memory location which will be assigned a memory address. Each name in this field is followed by a colon (:). The *code field* contains the name of the operation to be performed. The source or destination of data is specified in the *operand field*. This can be a register letter designation, an immediate datum, or a symbolic memory address. If two operands need to be specified, they are both put in the operand field, separated by a comma (,). An additional and very important field is the comment field, separated from the other fields by a semicolon (;). The programmer describes the program in the comment field. The assembler fields we've described are for a particular assembler. Other assembler programs may interpret fields differently, although all assemblers are very similar. Common variations include not using a colon after the label and using different characters to start the comment field.

DATA MOVEMENT INSTRUCTIONS

We shall study the 8085 instructions grouped by the function that they perform. The first instructions we'll examine are instructions that simply move data. Data may be moved among memory locations and registers. In following sections, each instruction or group of similar instructions will be presented in a standardized format. Each section will begin by listing the instruction's binary representation. The assembly language format will be listed, followed by a list of flag-register bits affected by the instruction.

To simplify our descriptions of instructions, we shall use the following abbreviations:

ADDR. | The mnemonic or name of a memory location
MSPA. | The most significant byte of a memory address
LSPA. | The least significant byte of a memory address
(LABEL:). | An optional address name

DATA. | The name or hex representation of a datum
MSPD. | The most significant byte of a 16-bit datum
LSPD. | The least significant byte of a 16-bit datum
DATA 8. | An 8-bit datum

DST. | The name of a destination for data
DDD. | The bits specifying a data destination
SRC. | The name of a source of data
SSS. | The bits specifying a data source
RP. | The bits specifying a register pair
M. | The memory named as a data source or destination

Comments will be added to the instruction presentations to clarify these abbreviations as necessary.

LDA and STA Instructions

Binary instruction format

	LDA	STA
First byte	0 0 1 1 1 0 1 0	0 0 1 1 0 0 1 0
Second byte	LSPA	LSPA
Third byte	MSPA	MSPA

Assembly language format

(LABEL:)	LDA	ADDR
(LABEL:)	STA	ADDR

Flag register
Not affected.

As you will see when you study more 8085 instructions, most operations on data require that one operand be located in the A register. For this reason, it is important that data can be moved into, or out of, the A register in an efficient manner. The load A register (LDA) and store A register (STA) instructions allow data to be transferred between the A register and memory by explicitly specifying the memory address (direct addressing) of the datum. The *LDA* instruction is used to retrieve a datum from memory and put it into a register where the datum may be manipulated by other instructions. The *LDA* instruction does not alter the datum in the memory location. The *STA* instruction is used to store the result of a calculation contained in the *A* register into a memory location. One of the simplest uses of these instructions is the transfer of data from one memory location to another.

```
START:    LDA    LOG
          STA    CON
```

The *LDA* instruction copies the data contained in the memory location with address *LOG* into the *A* register. The *STA* instruction copies the data contained in the *A* register into the memory location with the address *CON*. The original contents of *CON* are lost, as are the original contents of the *A* register. The contents of memory location *LOG* are not changed. After this portion of a program is executed, the contents of memory location *LOG* are transferred to memory location *CON*.

LDAX and STAX Instructions

Binary instruction format

	LDAX	STAX
First byte	0 0 R P 1 0 1 0	0 0 R P 0 0 1 0

RP = 00 for *B* register pair and RP = 01 for *D* register pair.

Assembly language format

```
(LABEL:)    LDAX    B
(LABEL:)    LDAX    D
(LABEL:)    STAX    B
(LABEL:)    STAX    D
```

Flag register
Not affected.

The load the *A* register indexed (*LDAX*) and store the *A* register indexed (*STAX*) instructions are similar to the *LDA* and *STA* instructions except *LDAX* and *STAX* use register-pair addressing, rather than direct addressing. Either the contents of the *B* or *D* register pair may be used as an address to reference the datum to be accessed. The *LDAX* and *STAX* instructions are often used to retrieve data from a list stored sequentially in memory and to put that data list in a different list.

```
LDAX    B
STAX    D
```

If the register pair *B*, *C* contains 0200 and register pair *D*, *E* contains 0300, this short program will copy the contents of memory location 0200 into memory location 0300.

Later, you'll learn instructions that can increment and decrement register pairs *B* and *D*. These instructions will allow you to change the addresses in *B* and *D* to sequence through a list contained in memory.

MOV Instruction

Binary instruction format

MOV
First byte   0 1 D D D S S S

DDD or SSS may be 000 for *B*, 001 for *C*, 010 for *D*, 011 for *E*, 100 for *H*, 101 for *L*, 111 for *A*, or 110 for *M*.

Assembly language format

(LABEL:)   MOV   DST, SRC

where DST and SRC may not both be *M* simultaneously..

Flag register
Not affected.

The move (*MOV*) instruction will move the contents of any data register to any other data register. The *MOV* instruction allows the other registers to be used for storage of intermediate operands in a calculation. Since *MOV* instructions occupy one-third the space in memory and execute 3 times faster than *LDA* and *STA* instructions, it is often better to use registers, rather than memory locations, for temporary storage. No equivalent of the *LDA* and *STA* instructions exists for any other register. The *MOV* instruction, in concert with the *LDA* or *STA* instructions, allows any data register to be loaded from, or stored into, a memory location by direct addressing in two steps.

An important special case of the *MOV* instruction occurs if 110 is specified as either a source or destination register address (110 cannot be specified as both). You will remember that there is no register designated by the number 110. However, whenever the microprocessor detects the number 110 in a register field, the processor assumes the operand to be used is contained in a memory location specified by the memory address contained in the *H* register pair. This technique is used by many kinds of instructions to make use of the *H* and *L* registers for register-pair addressing. Instructions using register address 110 to specify data in memory use the symbol *M* to indicate register-pair addressing using the *H* and *L* registers.

MOV   B, M

This instruction moves the datum in the memory location, whose address is in registers *H* and *L*, into the *B* register.

MVI Instruction

Binary instruction format

	MVI
First byte	0 0 D D D 1 1 0
Second byte	DATA 8

DDD is 000 for *B*, 001 for *C*, 010 for *D*, 011 for *E*, 100 for *H*, 101 for *L*, 111 for *A*, or 110 for *M*.

Assembly language format

(LABEL:)   MVI   DST, DATA

Flag register
Not affected.

The move immediate (*MVI*) instruction moves a single byte into a register. The datum is the second byte of the *MVI* instruction. This instruction is often used for entering constants into calculations. Like the *MOV* instruction, the *MVI* instruction allows register-pair addressing using register pair *H*.

MVI   M, 00H

This instruction puts an all-0 byte into the memory location whose address is in the *H* register pair.

LXI Instruction

Binary instruction format

	LXI
First byte	0 0 R P 0 0 0 1
Second byte	LSPD
Third byte	MSPD

RP may be 00 for *B*, 01 for *D*, 10 for *H*, or 11 for *SP*.

Assembly language format

(LABEL:)	LXI	B, DATA
(LABEL:)	LXI	D, DATA
(LABEL:)	LXI	H, DATA
(LABEL:)	LXI	SP, DATA

Flag register
Not affected.

The load index register immediate (*LXI*) instruction will place a 16-bit datum into any one of the register pairs: *B*, *D*, *H*, or *SP*. The 16-bit datum is contained in the second and third bytes of the *LXI* instruction. The *LXI* instruction is commonly used to place addresses into register pairs in preparation for either register-pair or stack addressing. The *LXI* instruction can also be used to place a 16-bit constant or two 8-bit constants into registers to be used in calculations.

LXI   B, 1122H

This instruction places the hex constant 11 into register *B* and the hex constant 22 into register *C*.

LXI   H, TEMP1
MOV   M, B

This portion of a program stores the datum in the *B* register into a memory location whose address is *TEMP1*. First, address *TEMP1* is placed in the *H* register pair. Next, the datum in the *B* register is stored into memory location *TEMP1* using register-pair addressing.

LHLD and SHLD Instructions

Binary instruction format

	LHLD	SHLD
First byte	0 0 1 0 1 0 1 0	0 0 1 0 0 0 1 0
Second byte	LSPA	LSPA
Third byte	MSPA	MSPA

Assembly language format

(LABEL:)   LHLD   ADDR
(LABEL:)   SHLD   ADDR

Flag register
Not affected.

The load *H* and *L* direct (*LHLD*) and store *H* and *L* direct (*SHLD*) instructions are similar to the *LDA* and *STA* instructions. The *LHLD* and *SHLD* instructions move a 16-bit datum between the *H* register pair and two memory locations. The memory address of the least significant part of the 16-bit datum is contained in the second and third bytes of the *LHLD* and *SHLD* instructions. The most significant part of the

16-bit datum is assumed to be in a memory location whose address is 1 greater than the address of the least significant part. The datum in the first memory location is moved to the *L* register. The datum in the second location is moved to the *H* register. These instructions can be used for temporarily saving a register-pair address in a memory location and restoring it at a later time. The *LHLD* and *SHLD* instructions also are commonly used for moving 16-bit operands. The 8085 has a subset of instructions that use the *H* register pair to simplify 16-bit calculations. Sixteen-bit calculations are common not only for manipulating 16-bit data, but also for manipulating memory addresses.

```
SHLD    SAVE
LHLD    NEW
```

This portion of a program saves the contents of the *H* and *L* registers in two consecutive memory locations, starting at memory address *SAVE*. A new 16-bit datum from two memory locations at address *NEW* is placed in the *H* register pair.

PUSH and POP Instructions

Binary instruction format

	PUSH	POP
First byte	1 1 R P 0 1 0 1	1 1 R P 0 0 0 1

RP may be 00 for *B*, 01 for *D*, 10 for *H*, or 11 for *PSW*.

Assembly language format

(LABEL:)	PUSH	B
(LABEL:)	PUSH	D
(LABEL:)	PUSH	H
(LABEL:)	PUSH	PSW
(LABEL:)	POP	B
(LABEL:)	POP	D
(LABEL:)	POP	H
(LABEL:)	POP	PSW

Flag register
Not affected.

The *PUSH* and *POP* instructions add or delete data from the stack, respectively. A 16-bit datum is added to the stack whenever a *PUSH* is executed. A 16-bit datum is removed from the stack whenever a *POP* is executed. The *PUSH* or *POP* instructions specify a register pair as the origin or destination of these 16 bits of data. The stack-pointer register pair *may not* be specified as an operand. The most significant half of the 16-bit operand is pushed onto the stack first (at the highest memory address) and popped off the stack last. Thus, a *PUSH B* operation first places the data in register *B* on the stack and then places the data in register *C* on the stack in the next-lower memory address (remember the stack builds downward in memory). A *POP D* instruction first pops a byte from the stack's lowest address into the *E* register. It then pops the data in the next-higher memory address into the *D* register. The symbol *PSW* stands for program status word. When the *PSW* is specified as the register pair, the *A* and flag registers are the 16-bit datum to be used.

```
PUSH   H
PUSH   PSW
   .
   .
   .
POP    PSW
POP    H
```

This portion of a program first saves the *H*, *L*, *A*, and flag registers on the stack. The program is then free to use these registers for any purpose. Later, the program restores the original contents of the flag, *A*, *H*, and *L* registers by retrieving them from the stack. Notice that the data must be popped off the stack in reverse order. The last datum pushed onto the stack is the first datum popped off.

Before you use the stack, you must initialize the *SP* register to the first (highest) address to be used by the stack. An *LXI SP, ADDR* instruction is most often used to initialize the stack-pointer register.

The Flag Register

None of the data movement instructions affect the flags. We will often want to preserve the flags from the last calculation, even while storing the data from that calculation and retrieving new operands for the next calculation.

BOOLEAN MANIPULATION INSTRUCTIONS

Boolean instructions are most often used to manipulate data bytes in which each bit is an individual boolean variable. Boolean manipulation instructions perform bit-by-bit operations on data. That is, each bit in a byte is only combined with the bit in that same position in another byte. The result of the manipulation is then stored in that same bit position. However, the data manipulation is performed simultaneously on all eight bit locations in a register or memory location.

The flag register is affected by the boolean manipulation instructions. The carry and auxiliary carry bits are always reset by these instructions, while the sign, zero, and parity bits have their usual meaning. That is, the sign bit is set to 1 if the result of the boolean operation has a 1 as its most significant bit. The zero bit is set if the result is 0, and the parity bit is set if the result has even parity.

One operand of a boolean manipulation is always in the *A* register. The other operand can be in any register, or in a memory location through register-pair addressing, or it can be an immediate operand. The result is always stored in the *A* register.

ANA and ANI Instructions

Binary instruction format

	ANA	ANI
First byte	1 0 1 0 0 S S S	1 1 1 0 0 1 1 0
Second byte	None	DATA 8

SSS can be 000 for B, 001 for C, 010 for D, 011 for E, 100 for H, 101 for L, 111 for A, or 110 for M.

Assembly language format

(LABEL:)	ANA	SRC
(LABEL:)	ANI	DATA

Flag register

C, AC	Reset to 0.
Z, S, P	Set to 1 if result is zero, negative, or even parity, respectively. Otherwise these bits are reset to 0.

The AND accumulator (ANA) instruction computes the boolean AND function of the A register and a second operand. The result is stored in the A register. In the case of the AND immediate (ANI) instruction, the second operand is contained in the second byte of the instruction.

Each bit of the result of the AND operation is set to 1 only if both corresponding bits of the operands are 1. The AND function has two common uses. The AND function can selectively reset 1 or more bits in a byte, while leaving other bits unchanged. Thus, the AND function can be used to reset an individual boolean variable to 0. The byte containing the variable to be set to 0 is ANDed with a *mask* byte. The mask contains 0 bits in those positions corresponding to the boolean variables that are to be reset. All other mask bits are 1. After the AND function is performed, those boolean variables in bit positions corresponding to 0 mask bits will be 0. Boolean variables corresponding to 1 mask bits will be unchanged.

        ANI   FEH

This instruction resets bit 0 of the A register. All other bits of the A register are unchanged.

The second use of the AND function is to select 1 or more bits from a byte so that these bits can be manipulated independently of the other bits in that byte. For example:

        MVI   A,0FH
        ANA   B

This portion of a program selects bits 0 to 3 of the datum in the B register and leaves those bits in the corresponding bit positions of the A register. Bits 4 to 7 of the A register will all be 0, regardless of bits 4 to 7 of the B register.

ORA and ORI Instructions

Binary instruction format

	ORA	ORI
First byte	1 0 1 1 0 S S S	1 1 1 1 0 1 1 0
Second byte	None	DATA 8

SSS can be 000 for *B*, 001 for *C*, 010 for *D*, 011 for *E*, 100 for *H*, 101 for *L*, 111 for *A*, or 110 for *M*.

Assembly language format

(LABEL:)	ORA	SRC
(LABEL:)	ORI	DATA

Flag register

C, AC Reset to 0.

Z, S, P Set to 1 if result is zero, negative, or even parity, respectively. Otherwise these bits are reset to 0.

The OR function of two boolean variables is 1 if either or both of the variables are 1. In other words, the OR function is 0 only if both of its operands are 0. While the AND function could selectively reset a bit to 0, the OR function can selectively *set* a bit to one. The byte containing the boolean variable to be set to 1 is ORed with a mask byte. The mask byte contains a 1 in those bit positions corresponding to boolean variables to be set to 1. All other mask bits are 0.

    ORI   81H

This instruction sets bits 0 and 7 in the *A* register to 1. All other *A* register bits are unchanged.

XRA and XRI Instructions

Binary instruction format

	XRA	XRI
First byte	1 0 1 0 1 S S S	1 1 1 0 1 1 1 0
Second byte	None	DATA 8

SSS can be 000 for *B*, 001 for *C*, 010 for *D*, 011 for *E*, 100 for *H*, 101 for *L*, 111 for *A*, or 110 for *M*.

Assembly language format

(LABEL:)	XRA	SRC
(LABEL:)	XRI	DATA

Flag register

C, AC Reset to 0.

Z, S, P Set to 1 if result is zero, negative, or even parity, respectively. Otherwise these bits are reset to 0.

The exclusive OR (XOR) function is a 1 only if the bits of its operands differ. The exculsive OR function is 0 if both of its operands are the same. Again, a more appropriate definition can be made for the purposes of programming. An exclusive OR is used to selectively toggle (complement) boolean variables. That is, a bit is made the opposite of what it originally was: a 1 becomes a 0 and a 0 becomes a 1. The byte containing the variable to be complemented is XORed with a mask byte. The mask byte contains a 1 in those bit positions corresponding to boolean variables to be toggled. All other mask bits are 0.

     XRI   25H

This instruction complements boolean variables in bits 0, 2, and 5 of the A register. All other A register bits are unchanged.

CMA Instruction

Binary instruction format

CMA
First byte   0 0 1 0 1 1 1 1

Assembly language format

     (LABEL:)   CMA

Flag register
     Not affected.

The complement the A register (CMA) instruction simply toggles or complements all the bits in the accumulator simultaneously. The CMA instruction does *not* affect *any* flag register bits. This instruction can be used as part of the operation of negating a two's-complement number (complement and add 1) or can be used to invert all the bits in a byte. Common reasons for inverting an entire byte include preparing for one of the boolean operations described previously or preparing data coming from, or going to, a peripheral device that supplies inverted data for electrical reasons.

ROTATE INSTRUCTIONS

Rotate instructions are used to change the position of bits in a byte, usually to align a boolean variable in one byte with a variable in another byte in preparation for a boolean operation. In addition, a left shift is equivalent to multiplying by 2 and a right shift to dividing by 2 when the byte shifted represents an unsigned binary number.

Rotate instructions *only* affect the carry bit in the flag register.

RLC and RRC Instructions

Binary instruction format

	RLC	RRC
First byte	0 0 0 0 0 1 1 1	0 0 0 0 1 1 1 1

Assembly language format

(LABEL:)	RLC
(LABEL:)	RRC

Flag register

AC, Z, S, P	Not affected.
C	Changed as described in instruction description.

The rotate left with carry (*RLC*) and rotate right with carry (*RRC*) instructions shift the *A* register's bits to the left or right, respectively. The bit that is shifted out the end of the *A* register is routed back around to the opposite side of the *A* register in order to become the bit shifted in to that side. The bit that is shifted out the end of the *A* register is also stored in the carry bit of the flag register. No bit is ever lost, and the operand can be restored to its original condition if desired. Also, any bit may be stored in the carry bit by an appropriate number of rotate instructions.

The operations of the *RLC* and *RRC* instructions are shown in Fig. 8-23.

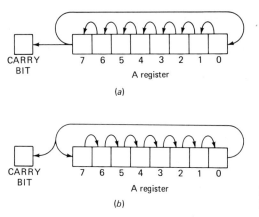

Figure 8-23(*a*) RLC instruction. (*b*) RRC instruction.

RAL and RAR Instructions

Binary instruction format

	RAL	RAR
First byte	0 0 0 1 0 1 1 1	0 0 0 1 1 1 1 1

Assembly language format

(LABEL:)	RAL
(LABEL:)	RAR

Flag register

AC, Z, S, P	Not affected.
C	Changed as described in instruction description.

The rotate A register left (RAL) and rotate A register right (RAR) instructions are similar to the RLC and RRC instructions with the exception of the *source* of the bit that is shifted *into* the A register. The operations of the RAL and RAR instructions are shown in Fig. 8-24.

The bit that is shifted into the A register is now the carry bit. The programmer can specify whether a 1 or 0 will be shifted into the vacated bit position by setting or resetting the carry bit before performing a RAL or a RAR. The bit shifted out during one rotate instruction becomes the bit shifted in during the next instruction. These instructions can be used to implement multiple-byte shifts. To shift a 24-bit operand 1 bit to the left, start with the least significant byte.

```
LDA    LSB    ; GET LEAST SIG. BYTE
RAL           ; ASSUME CARRY IS ZERO AT START
STA    LSB    ; SAVE RESULT
```

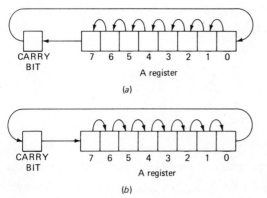

(a)

(b)

Figure 8-24(a) RAL instruction. **(b)** RAR instruction.

```
LDA    SSB    ; GET SECOND SIG. BYTE
RAL           ; LAST BIT SHIFTED OUT FOR BIT TO BE SHIFTED IN
STA    SSB    ; SAVE RESULT
LDA    MSB    ; GET MOST SIG. BYTE
RAL           ; LAST BIT SHIFTED OUT IS BIT TO BE SHIFTED IN
STA    MSB    ; SAVE RESULT
```

A similar sequence can be used to right-shift multiple bytes, starting with the most significant byte.

STC and CMC Instructions

Binary instruction format

	STC	CMC
First byte	0 0 1 1 0 1 1 1	0 0 1 1 1 1 1 1

Assembly language format

```
(LABEL:)    STC
(LABEL:)    CMC
```

Flag register

AC, Z, S, P Not affected.
C Set to 1 for STC instruction. Complemented for CMC instruction.

The set the carry (STC) and complement carry (CMC) instructions give the programmer direct control over the carry bit. Control of the carry bit is important for many operations where the initial state of the carry bit is important, such as the RAL and RAR instructions just described. The set the carry instruction sets the carry bit to a 1. The complement the carry instruction toggles or complements the carry bit to its opposite state. Although there is no clear the carry instruction, there are several ways to clear the carry bit.

```
STC
CMC
```

This sequence of two instructions resets the carry bit to 0.

```
ORA    A
ANA    A
```

Either of the instructions above will clear the carry and auxiliary carry bits. The contents of the A register will be unchanged. However, the Z, P, and S flag-register bits will be changed to reflect the contents of the A register.

BRANCHING INSTRUCTIONS

Branch instructions allow changing the sequential order in which a program is normally executed by explicitly changing the program counter. Each branch instruction occupies 3 bytes in memory. The last 2 bytes hold the new contents of the program counter. This is called the branch address and is the address of the next instruction that will be executed if and when the branch is performed. The processor simply places the branch address in the *PC* register to perform a branch.

JMP Instruction

Binary instruction format

	JMP
First byte	1 1 0 0 0 0 1 1
Second byte	LSPA
Third byte	MSPA

Assembly language format

   (LABEL:)   JMP   ADDR

Flag register
   Not affected.

The jump (*JMP*) instruction simply causes the microprocessor to start executing instructions at the address specified by the instruction's branch address. It is used to jump around program segments that are not to be executed at this time. The *JMP* instruction is sometimes called an *unconditional jump* instruction because it always causes a branch whenever it is executed.

JC, JNC, JZ, JNZ, JP, JM, JPE, and JPO Instructions

Binary instruction format

	Jxx
First byte	1 1 C C C 0 1 0
Second byte	LSPA
Third byte	MSPA

CCC is 000 for JNZ, 001 for JZ, 010 for JNC, 011 for JC, 100 for JPO, 101 for JPE, 110 for JP, or 111 for JM.

Assembly language format

(LABEL:)	JNZ	ADDR
(LABEL:)	JZ	ADDR
(LABEL:)	JNC	ADDR
(LABEL:)	JC	ADDR
(LABEL:)	JPO	ADDR
(LABEL:)	JPE	ADDR
(LABEL:)	JP	ADDR
(LABEL:)	JM	ADDR

Flag register
Not affected.

This set of eight instructions allows branching only if the condition specified by the instruction is true. If the branch condition is not satisfied, the microprocessor simply executes the next instruction in sequence. The conditions tested are the states of the flag-register bits. Since the flag-register bits are altered by many different instructions, the conditional branch instructions can test the result of many kinds of operations. The eight conditional branch instructions are

JNZ	Jump if result was not zero	(Z bit is 0)
JZ	Jump if result was zero	(Z bit is 1)
JNC	Jump if no carry	(C bit is 0)
JC	Jump if carry	(C bit is 1)
JPO	Jump if parity odd	(P bit is 0)
JPE	Jump if parity even	(P bit is 1)
JP	Jump if result was positive	(S bit is 0)
JM	Jump if result was minus	(S bit is 1)

PCHL Instruction

Binary instruction format

PCHL	
First byte	1 1 1 0 1 0 0 1

Assembly language format

(LABEL:)   PCHL

Flag register
Not affected.

The transfer H and L to program counter (*PCHL*) instruction simply replaces the contents of the *PC* with the contents of the *H* register pair. The *PCHL* instruction might be called an unconditional jump using register-pair addressing. The branch address is contained in register H and L. Multiway branches can be implemented by forming an address in the H register pair using arithmetic or boolean manipulation and branching to that address with the *PCHL* instruction. One of many techniques for forming such an address is shown below. A table of unconditional jumps is used so that the programs referenced by this multiway jump could be anywhere in memory. The branch address for the *PCHL* is formed by combining the table starting address with the branch number. Since the *JMP* instructions are located every four memory addresses, we multiplied the program branch number by 4. Since the least significant byte of the table address was 00H, we need only move the quadrupled program number to the L register to form the address.

```
          ORG    3C10H
START:    LXI    H, TABL    ; SET UP TABLE STARTING ADDRESS
          LDA    PGMNO      ; GET PROGRAM NUMBER
          RLC
          RLC               ; MULTIPLY BY FOUR
          MOV    L, A       ; PUT MODIFIED ADDRESS INTO L
          PCHL              ; TRANSFER ADDRESS TO PC
          ORG    3D00H
TABL:     JMP    PGM0       ; JUMP TO PROGRAM 0
          0                 ; PLACE HOLDER SO JUMPS OCCUR
                            ;    EVERY 4 BYTES
          JMP    PGM1       ; JUMP TO PROGRAM 1
          0                 ; PLACE HOLDER
          JMP    PGM2       ; JUMP TO PROGRAM 2
          0
          JMP    PGM3
          0
          JMP    PGM4
          0
          JMP    PGM5
          0
          JMP    PGM6
          0
          JMP    PGM7
```

An example might help you understand the operation of this program.

Table 8-1   Multiway branch

	H				L				
			0 0 0 0	0 N N N					Contents of PGMNO
0 0 1 1	1 1 0 1		0 0 0 0	0 0 0 0					Original address = TABL
0 0 1 1	1 1 0 1		0 0 0 N	N N 0 0					Modified address for branch

If *PGMNO* contains 5, the two rotates will multiply by 4. Thus, the *L* register will contain 20 decimal or 14H. The *PCHL* instruction will cause the *JMP PGM5* instruction to be executed next at memory address 3D14H. Table 8-1 shows how the program number is shifted and how it becomes part of the table address.

INPUT AND OUTPUT INSTRUCTIONS

IN and OUT Instructions

Binary instruction format

	IN	OUT
First byte	1 1 0 1 1 0 1	1 1 0 1 0 0 1 1
Second byte	I/O Register No.	I/O Register No.

Assembly language format

(LABEL:)	IN	IORN
(LABEL:)	OUT	IORN

Flag register
Not affected.

Data must be input from, and output to, external devices. The *IN* instruction transfers data from a peripheral or I/O register to the *A* register. The *OUT* instruction transfers data from the *A* register to a peripheral or I/O register. The 8085 allows up to 256 input ports or registers and up to 256 output ports or registers to be connected to peripherals. The second byte of these instructions contains the address of the I/O port from which the data are to come or to which the data are to go.

INCREMENT AND DECREMENT INSTRUCTIONS

INR and DCR Instructions

Binary instruction format

	INR	DCR
First byte	0 0 D D D 1 0 0	0 0 D D D 1 0 1

DDD can be 000 for *B*, 001 for *C*, 010 for *D*, 011 for *E*, 100 for *H*, 101 for *L*, 111 for *A*, or 110 for *M*.

Assembly language

(LABEL:)	INR	DST
(LABEL:)	DCR	DST

Flag register

C	Not affected.
AC	Set to 1 if there is a carry out of bit 3. Reset to 0 otherwise.
Z, P, S	Set to 1 if the result is zero, even parity, or negative, respectively. Set to 0 otherwise.

The increment register (INR) and decrement register (DCR) instructions add or subtract 1, respectively, from the quantity contained in any register. In addition, by specifying register 110, register-pair addressing may be used to increment or decrement the data contained in memory locations. The INR and DCR instructions affect all the flag-register bits *except the carry bit.*

Besides being used to add or subtract 1 from data, the INR and DCR instructions are often used to modify binary numbers used as counters in loops. Counters are used to control the number of iterations through a program loop, as has been previously described. For example, multiple passes through a program loop are often used to implement time delays. Each pass through the loop requires a fixed amount of time. Multiple passes through a loop generate longer times.

```
              ⋮
           MVI    B, 100D
LOOP:      · · ·
              ⋮
           DCR    B
           JNZ    LOOP
```

This simple program loop repeats 100 times. The B register is initialized to 100 (the D tells the assembler that 100 is a decimal number). After each execution of the instructions following $LOOP$, the B register is decremented. As long as the B register is not 0, the $LOOP$ instructions will be repeated. After 100 passes through the loop, the B register will be decremented to 0 and the instruction after the JNZ will be executed.

INX and DCX Instructions

Binary instruction format

	INX	DCX
First byte	0 0 R P 0 0 1 1	0 0 R P 1 0 1 1

RP can be 00 for B, 01 for D, 10 for H, or 11 for SP.

Assembly language format

(LABEL:)	INX	B
(LABEL:)	INX	D
(LABEL:)	INX	H
(LABEL:)	INX	SP

(LABEL:)	DCX	B
(LABEL:)	DCX	D
(LABEL:)	DCX	H
(LABEL:)	DCX	SP

Flag register

Not affected.

The increment index (*INX*) and decrement index (*DCX*) instructions add or subtract 1 from a 16-bit quantity contained in any *register pair*. These instructions are used to modify addresses contained in register pairs. Because these instructions are meant to operate on addresses, they do not affect any of the bits in the flag register. Usually, we want to maintain the flags from the last operation on data in the flag register, even while modifying addresses to prepare to retrieve new data. The result of a previous data operation may be needed for the next data operation. For example, the carry bit must be saved when doing multiple-byte shifts. The following program searches through a table in memory looking for a memory location that is all 0. After this program is done, the number of nonzero table entries is contained in the *D* register pair.

```
            LXI     D, 000H     ; SET D, E to 0
            LXI     H, TBL      ; STARTING ADDRESS OF TABLE
LOOP:       MOV     A, M        ; GET BYTE FROM TBL
            ORA     A           ; SET Z BIT IF A IS ZERO
            JZ      DONE        ; DONE IF BYTE IS ALL ZERO
            INX     D           ; D, E COUNTS NONZERO BYTES
            INX     H           ; INCREMENT ADDRESS TO NEXT
                                ;    TABLE LOCATION
            JMP     LOOP        ; GET NEXT BYTE FROM TABLE
DONE:       · · ·
```

A LOGIC CONTROLLER EXAMPLE

A common requirement in an industrial plant is the control of motors and other devices by switches, pressure sensors, etc. The control output is often a simple boolean function of inputs. This control can be accomplished by relay logic, semiconductor gates (a simple ASM), or by a microcomputer with an appropriate program. The functions needed are usually quite simple. For example, a motor should be on only if its switch is on and a heater is also turned on.

It may seem like gross overdesign to use a microcomputer to implement these simple functions, but it is often done for these reasons:

1. The microcomputer is more reliable than relay logic.
2. The microcomputer may be easily reprogrammed to change the functions easily and quickly.

3. Although each function is usually quite simple, hundreds of functions may be required to operate pumps, fans, etc. A single microcomputer may replace hundreds of relays.
4. Additional functions such as time delays or counters are easy to add to the microcomputer system.

Let's program a microcomputer to be a simple logic controller. It will compute four boolean functions of four input variables. The four input variables are called IA, IB, IC, and ID. The four output variables are called OA, OB, OC, and OD. The relationships between the input and output variables are simple boolean functions.

$$OA = (IA) \cdot (IB) \cdot (IC) \cdot (ID)$$

$$OB = IA + IB + IC + ID$$

$$OC = (IA \cdot IB) + (IC \cdot ID)$$

$$OD = (IA + IB) \cdot (IC \cdot ID)$$

One input and one output register will be sufficient for external signals. The input and output signals will be connected to these ports as follows:

Function	I/O port	Bits							
		7	6	5	4	3	2	1	0
INPUT	02H	0	0	0	0	ID	IC	IB	IA
OUTPUT	F2H	0	0	0	0	OD	OC	OB	OA

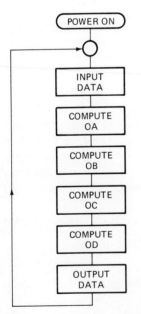

Figure 8-25 Logic controller flowchart.

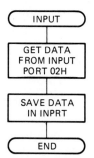

Figure 8-26 Logic controller input program.

The first step in developing the program to implement these functions is the flow-chart of Fig. 8-25. We must expand each of the blocks of this diagram into more detailed flowcharts until the flowcharts are sufficiently elementary to allow the program's instruction sequence to be written. Some blocks will be quite simple. The *INPUT DATA* block has been expanded in Fig. 8-26. The flowchart of Fig. 8-26 be-comes the portion of the program starting at memory location *DIN*.

DIN:	IN	02H	; READ INPUT PORT
	STA	INPUT	; SAVE DATA

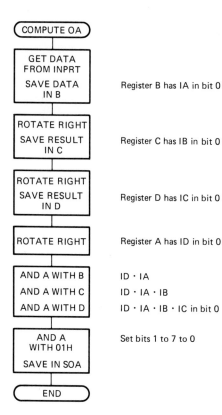

Figure 8-27 Logic controller function *A*.

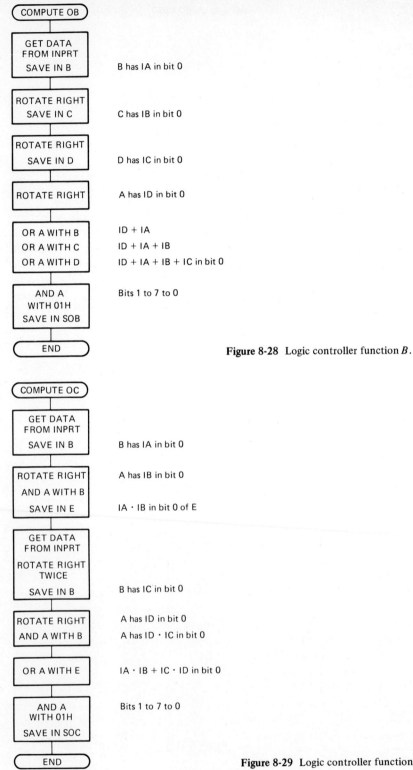

Figure 8-28 Logic controller function B.

Figure 8-29 Logic controller function C.

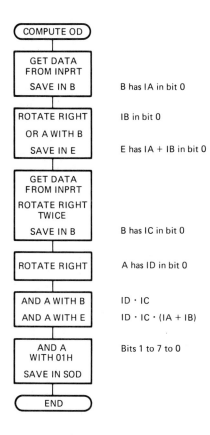

B has IA in bit 0

IB in bit 0

E has IA + IB in bit 0

B has IC in bit 0

A has ID in bit 0

ID · IC

ID · IC · (IA + IB)

Bits 1 to 7 to 0

Figure 8-30 Logic controller function *D*.

The complete program is listed at the end of this section, and we shall reference memory locations in this listing in our discussion.

The programs to compute functions *OA* and *OB* are flowcharted in Figs. 8-27 and 8-28, respectively. Rotate instructions are used to align the boolean variables for ANDing or ORing. Notice that we have planned ahead and standardized a format for storing the output functions. The output boolean function is always stored in bit 0 of its memory location, and all other bits are reset to 0.

The programs to compute functions *OC* and *OD* are flowcharted in Figs. 8-29 and 8-30, respectively. These functions are slightly more complex and require the temporary storage of intermediate values in other registers. For example, the program of Fig. 8-29 stores the function $IA \cdot IB$ temporarily in the *E* register while computing the function $IC \cdot ID$. The programs that compute functions *OA*, *OB*, *OC*, and *OD* start at memory locations *POA*, *POB*, *POC*, and *POD*, respectively.

The output data program is shown in Fig. 8-31. A loop is arranged to align the four output bits to their correct locations. By placing all the output functions in the same bit position and placing the four memory locations containing these bits together in proper sequence, a simple loop will retrieve each bit from memory and align it to its correct position. The output program starts at memory location *DOUT*.

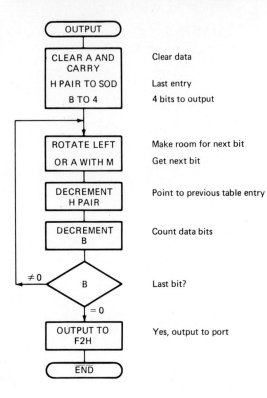

OUTPUT	
CLEAR A AND CARRY	Clear data
H PAIR TO SOD	Last entry
B TO 4	4 bits to output
ROTATE LEFT	Make room for next bit
OR A WITH M	Get next bit
DECREMENT H PAIR	Point to previous table entry
DECREMENT B	Count data bits
B ≠0 / =0	Last bit?
OUTPUT TO F2H	Yes, output to port
END	

Figure 8-31 Logic controller output program.

The complete program is listed next.

```
DIN:    IN      02H         ; READ INPUT PORT
        STA     INPRT       ; SAVE DATA

POA:    LDA     INPRT       ; GET INPUT DATA
        MOV     B, A        ; SAVE IN B
        RRC                 ; ROTATE RIGHT, ALIGN IB
        MOV     C, A        ; SAVE IN C
        RRC                 ; ROTATE RIGHT, ALIGN IC
        MOV     D, A        ; SAVE IN D
        RRC                 ; ROTATE RIGHT, ALIGN ID
        ANA     B           ; ID AND IA
        ANA     C           ; AND IB
        ANA     D           ; AND IC
        ANI     01H         ; RESET BITS 1 TO 7
        STA     SOA         ; SAVE RESULT

POB:    LDA     INPRT       ; GET INPUT DATA
        MOV     B, A        ; SAVE IN B
        RRC                 ; ROTATE RIGHT, ALIGN IB
        MOV     C, A        ; SAVE IN C
        RRC                 ; ROTATE RIGHT, ALIGN IC
```

```
            MOV    D, A        ; SAVE IN D
            RRC                ; ROTATE RIGHT, ALIGN ID
            ORA    B           ; ID OR IA
            ORA    C           ; OR IB
            ORA    D           ; OR IC
            ANI    01H         ; RESET BITS 1 TO 7
            STA    SOB         ; SAVE RESULT
POC:        LDA    INPRT       ; GET INPUT DATA
            MOV    B, A        ; SAVE IN B
            RRC                ; ROTATE RIGHT, ALIGN IB
            ANA    B           ; IA AND IB
            MOV    E, A        ; SAVE IN E
            LDA    INPRT       ; GET INPUT DATA
            RRC                ; ROTATE RIGHT
            RRC                ; ROTATE RIGHT, ALIGN IC
            MOV    B, A        ; SAVE IN B
            RRC                ; ROTATE RIGHT, ALIGN ID
            ANA    B           ; IC AND ID
            ORA    E           ; (IC AND ID) OR (IA AND IB)
            ANI    01H         ; SET BITS 1 TO 7 to ZERO
            STA    SOC         ; SAVE RESULT
POD:        LDA    INPRT       ; GET INPUT DATA
            MOV    B, A        ; SAVE IN B
            RRC                ; ALIGN IB
            ORA    B           ; IA OR IB
            MOV    E, A        ; SAVE IN E
            LDA    INPRT       ; GET INPUT DATA
            RRC
            RRC                ; ALIGN IC
            MOV    B, A        ; SAVE IN B
            RRC                ; ALIGN ID
            ANA    B           ; ID AND IC
            ANA    E           ; ID AND IC AND (IA OR IB)
            ANI    01H         ; SET BITS 1 TO 7 TO ZERO
            STA    SOD         ; SAVE RESULT
DOUT:       XRA    A           ; CLEAR REG A AND CARRY
            LXI    H, SOD      ; SET REG TO LAST FUNCTION
            MVI    B, 4H       ; SET ITERATION COUNTER TO 4
LOOP:       RLC                ; MAKE ROOM FOR NEXT BIT
            ORA    M           ; ENTER NEXT OUTPUT FUNCTION
            DCX    H           ; POINT TO PREVIOUS ENTRY
            DCR    B           ; DECREMENT ITERATION COUNTER
            JNZ    LOOP        ; LOOP UNTIL COUNTER IS 0
            OUT    F2H         ; OUTPUT 4 FUNCTIONS
            JMP    DIN         ; GO BACK AND DO AGAIN
```

INPRT:	0	; STORAGE FOR INPUT DATA
SOA:	0	; BIT 0 IS FUNCTION OA
SOB:	0	; BIT 0 IS FUNCTION OB
SOC:	0	; BIT 0 IS FUNCTION OC
SOD:	0	; BIT 0 IS FUNCTION OD

ANOTHER APPROACH TO THE LOGIC CONTROLLER

Although the above program is perfectly satisfactory, it is difficult to change if one or more functions need to be changed. Figure 8-32 shows the flowchart of a program that behaves identically to the previous program but simply *looks up* the functional values in a table, rather than computing them. Since the functions are stored in a table, changes in those functions are easily made by changing entries in that table to cor-

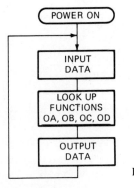

Figure 8-32 Logic controller with look-up table.

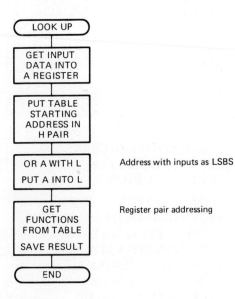

Figure 8-33 Data look-up program.

Table 8-2 Look-up table

Address	Least significant bits of address				Functions				Hex data
	ID	IC	IB	IA	OD	OC	OB	OA	
3D50	0	0	0	0	0	0	0	0	00
3D51	0	0	0	1	0	0	1	0	02
3D52	0	0	1	0	0	0	1	0	02
3D53	0	0	1	1	0	1	1	0	06
3D54	0	1	0	0	0	0	1	0	02
3D55	0	1	0	1	0	0	1	0	02
3D56	0	1	1	0	0	0	1	0	02
3D57	0	1	1	1	0	1	1	0	06
3D58	1	0	0	0	0	0	1	0	02
3D59	1	0	0	1	0	0	1	0	02
3D5A	1	0	1	0	0	0	1	0	02
3D5B	1	0	1	1	0	1	1	0	06
3D5C	1	1	0	0	0	1	1	0	06
3D5D	1	1	0	1	1	1	1	0	0E
3D5E	1	1	1	0	1	1	1	0	0E
3D5F	1	1	1	1	1	1	1	1	0F

respond to the new function desired. The flowchart for the table-look-up program is shown in Fig. 8-33. The table starting address is combined with the input port data. The resulting address has 4 least significant bits, which *are* the input variables. Thus, each of 16 possible table addresses corresponds to a combination of these four input variables. Each of these memory locations has 4 bits corresponding to the value of each of the four functions for that combination of input variables. The programmer calculates the proper values of the four functions and constructs Table 8-2. The microcomputer never computes a function but merely looks up a value that has been precomputed by the programmer.

The entire program is listed below. Because the least significant bits of the table address are 0, the 4 input data bits may be just ORed into these four bit positions.

```
        ORG     3C10H
STRT:   IN      02H         ; GET DATA
        LXI     H, TABL     ; TABLE STARTING ADDRESS
        ORA     L           ; INSERT DATA AS LSBS
        MOV     L, A        ; MODIFY ADDRESS IN H, L
        MOV     A, M        ; GET THE TABLE ENTRY
        OUT     F2H         ; OUTPUT THE FUNCTIONS
        JMP     STRT        ; DO IT AGAIN

        ORG     3D50H
TABL:   00H                 ; TABLE OF FUNCTION VALUES
        02H
        02H
```

06H
02H
02H
02H
06H
02H
02H
02H
06H
06H
0EH
0EH
0FH

You will notice that not only are the functions much easier to change in this program, but the program is much shorter and simpler. Short and simple programs save design effort and memory, increase the speed of execution, and minimize the chance for programmer error. We seem to have found a much better way of generating functions with a microcomputer. It is generally true that the use of tables for either data look-up or multiway branching will provide the above mentioned benefits. Table-oriented (sometimes called table-driven) programming is highly recommended.

Since there are 4 unused bits in each table entry, we could easily add four more functions to this system. Thus, eight functions of four variables could be represented by the example table. If the input data were shifted left one place before being inserted in the table starting address, as shown in Fig. 8-34, each input combination would specify a 2-byte table entry, in which up to 16 functions could be specified. On the other hand, if we desire to double the number of input variables, 256 bytes would be necessary to specify up to eight functions of eight variables. The size of the table doubles when we double the number of outputs, but the table size doubles for each

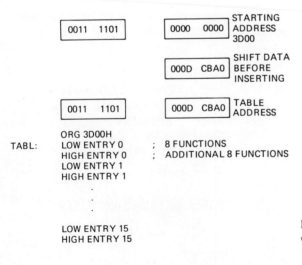

Figure 8-34 Increasing the size of each table entry.

single input variable added. Often, table-driven programming will require large amounts of memory to hold the tables. Remember, though, that the cost of memory is dramatically declining, while the cost of designing systems using that memory is increasing. It pays to use memory to save design effort.

Very often the size of a table can be reduced by clever programming. Divide tables into smaller tables when possible. For example, a table of eight functions of eight variables requires 256 bytes. If we examine the functions, we might discover that two outputs are functions of five variables requiring 32 bytes. The other six outputs are functions of three variables requiring 8 bytes. By separating the functions into two tables, we require only 40 bytes of memory for the tables.

PROBLEMS

8-1 Write a program to move 10 bytes of data from a list starting at memory location *HERE* to a list starting at memory location *THERE*.

8-2 Write a program to test bit 0 of the *A* register. If bit 0 is a 1, set bit 3 of a memory location called *FLAG1*. If bit 0 is a 0, set bit 4 of a memory location called *FLAG2*.

8-3 What single instruction will clear the *A* register, auxiliary carry flag, and carry flag?

8-4 Write a program to input data from port 0. If the datum input from port 0 is odd-valued, output this same datum to port 1. If the input datum is even, output it to port 2.

8-5 Write a program that first outputs FFH to output port 2 and then outputs 00H to output port 2. The program should repeat this pattern of outputs 450 decimal times.

8-6 Write a program that examines the datum in the *A* register. If the contents of the *A* register are nonzero, even-valued, positive and has even parity, continue processing at memory location *CONT*. Otherwise, continue execution at memory location *DSCARD*.

8-7 Write a program to shift a 16-bit datum contained in two consecutive memory locations to the right.

8-8 What is the datum in memory location *BDR* after the following program is executed?

```
          MVI    A, FFH
          ORA    A
          LDA    ADR
          JM     NXT
          INR    A
NXT:      STA    BDR

ADR:      03H
BDR:      00H
```

8-9 Write a program that implements a time delay of 0.1 s. Use instruction times contained in the MCS-85 manual.

8-10 Design a system that implements a simple traffic light controller. The controller simply alternates traffic on two streets. Two 8-bit binary numbers read through input ports specify the time the light will spend in a state. Each binary number represents the number of 0.1-s intervals the light is to spend in a state. One number specifies the length of the green indications, while the other number specifies the length of the yellow indications.
Include the following material in your design:

(*a*) Specifications of all input and output ports (e.g., what external signals are connected to which bits?)

(*b*) Flowcharts

(*c*) Commented program listing

NINE

SUBROUTINES, INTERRUPTS, AND ARITHMETIC

SUBROUTINES

Subroutines are subprograms that, although stored in only one place in memory, may be used more than once in the solution algorithm. Commonly used sequences of instructions are implemented as subroutines and occupy much less memory than would otherwise be required. Subroutines also allow commonly used functions to be designed, programmed, and debugged independently of any other program. These subroutines then form a library of common functions that may be inserted into a wide variety of programs.

A subroutine is executed as part of a sequence of programming steps by *calling* the subroutine from the algorithm step that uses the subroutine. The subroutine completes its function and *returns* to the program step after the step that called it, as shown in Fig. 9-1. The subroutine may be called many times from different program steps. A subroutine must remember the place in the program from which it was called so that it can return there. One 16-bit storage location is required to save the address to which the subroutine should return.

Subroutines also call other subroutines, as shown in Fig. 9-2. When the second subroutine is called, a second return address must be saved. When the second subroutine returns to the first, the processor must know which return address to use. Keeping track of return addresses may seem hopeless, with the possibility of the second subroutine calling a third and the third calling a fourth, etc.

We must find a place to store the return address, whether there is one or ten. We also need to retrieve the return addresses in the correct order. The last return address stored should be the first retrieved; the second from the last saved should be the second retrieved; etc. We have already studied a technique for creating a variable-length list that stores and retrieves data in a last-in, first-out fashion. A last-in, first-out list is a stack, and the 8085 uses its stack to store the return addresses for its subroutines.

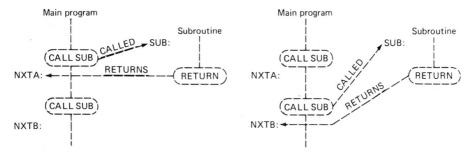

Figure 9-1 Subroutine calls and returns.

Figure 9-3 shows the operation of the stack for the subroutines of Fig. 9-2. When subroutine *SUBA* is called, the address *NXTA* of the instruction after the subroutine call is pushed onto the stack. If subroutine *SUBB* is called by subroutine *SUBA*, the second return address *NXTB* is also pushed onto the stack. When the subroutine *SUBB* returns to *SUBA*, the correct return address *NXTB* is popped off the stack. Finally, subroutine *SUBA* returns to the main program by popping the next return address *NXTA* off the stack. Subroutines may call other subroutines as required. The number of subroutines called is limited only by the amount of RWM available for expansion of the stack.

CALL, CC, CNC, CZ, CNZ, CP, CM, CPE, and CPO Instructions

Binary instruction format

	CALL	Cxx
First byte	1 1 0 0 1 1 0 1	1 1 C C C 1 0 0
Second byte	LSPA	LSPA
Third byte	MSPA	MSPA

CCC is 000 for CNZ, 001 for CZ, 010 for CNC, 011 for CC, 100 for CPO, 101 for CPE, 110 for CP, or 111 for CM.

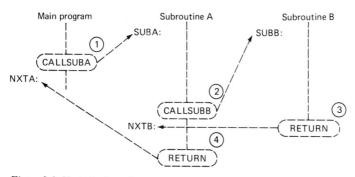

Figure 9-2 Nested subroutines.

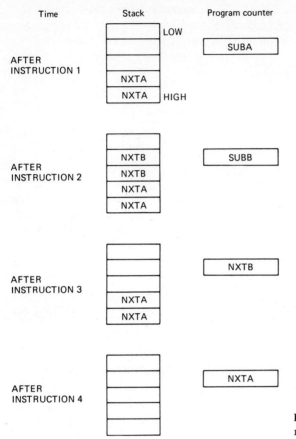

Figure 9-3 Using the stack for subroutine returns.

Assembly language format

(LABEL:)	CALL	ADDR
(LABEL:)	CNZ	ADDR
(LABEL:)	CZ	ADDR
(LABEL:)	CNC	ADDR
(LABEL:)	CC	ADDR
(LABEL:)	CPO	ADDR
(LABEL:)	CPE	ADDR
(LABEL:)	CP	ADDR
(LABEL:)	CM	ADDR

Flag register

Not affected.

Each of these instructions calls a subroutine by storing the contents of the program counter on the stack. This address is the location of the instruction following the

CALL instruction. The subroutine address in the second and third bytes of the *CALL* instruction is placed in the program counter. Eight conditional subroutine call instructions will call a subroutine only if the specified condition is satisfied. These conditions are identical to those of the conditional jump instructions described in the previous chapter.

RET, RC, RNC, RZ, RNZ, RP, RM, RPE, and RPO Instructions

Binary instruction format

	RET	Rxx
First byte	1 1 0 0 1 0 0 1	1 1 C C C 0 0 0

CCC is 000 for RNZ, 001 for RZ, 010 for RNC, 011 for RC, 100 for RPO, 101 for RPE, 110 for RP, or 111 for RM.

Assembly language format

(LABEL:)	RET
(LABEL:)	RNZ
(LABEL:)	RZ
(LABEL:)	RNC
(LABEL:)	RC
(LABEL:)	RPO
(LABEL:)	RPE
(LABEL:)	RP
(LABEL:)	RM

Flag register
Not affected.

The return instructions pop a 16-bit subroutine return address from the stack to the program counter.

Data for Subroutines

Some subroutines use data stored in the same memory locations each time they are called. Usually at least some of the data will be different at each place the subroutine is called. These variable data are called *arguments* of the subroutine and are said to be *passed* to the subroutine. Data may be passed to the subroutine in many ways.

If only a small amount of data is to be passed to a subroutine, that data could be stored in registers before the subroutine is called and retrieved from those registers by the subroutine. A single byte is usually passed to the subroutine in the *A* register. Of course, results may be passed back to the main program in the same way. If one or more lists of data or arrays must be passed to the subroutine, the starting addresses of

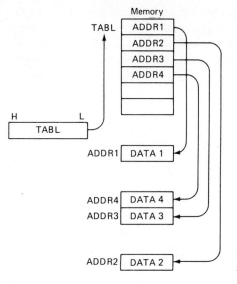

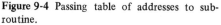

Figure 9-4 Passing table of addresses to subroutine.

these *arrays* are passed to the subroutine in register pairs in order to allow the subroutine to access the entire list through register-pair addressing.

Another technique, shown in Fig. 9-4, is used when many data need to be passed to a subroutine but these data are scattered throughout memory rather than contained in a sequential list. A list of addresses of each of the data is compiled by the main program and placed somewhere in memory. The starting address of this list of addresses is then passed to the subroutine in a register pair. Two *MOV* instructions using register-pair addressing can transfer the addresses in the table to another register pair where, finally, a *STAX* or *LDAX* instruction can be used to access the data. This is a cumbersome technique but may be the only possible solution on occasion.

Any datum passed via a register could also be pushed onto the stack. The subroutine must pop and save its return address before popping data off the stack. The return address must be pushed back on the stack before returning from the subroutine.

Register Usage

A programmer would specify which registers a subroutine uses. A main program using this subroutine would assume that these registers would not hold the same data after the subroutine returns as they held before the subroutine was called. Unless the subroutine is extremely simple, at least the *A* register usually must be used by the subroutine.

If the programmer desires that the original contents of registers remain inviolate after returning from the subroutine, the subroutine must save these registers before destroying the data in them. The original contents of the registers are restored before returning to the main program. Although these registers may be saved in any fashion, they are most easily saved in pairs on the stack.

Subroutine Example

The following example shows a main program calling a subroutine *SUBR* in two different places. The second *CALL* instruction is imbedded in a loop. The loop may use the *A* register as a counter only because the subroutine saves and restores the *A* register.

```
            .
            .
            .
        CALL  SUBR        ; GO TO SUBROUTINE
            .
            .
            .
        MVI   A, 10D
LOOP:   CALL  SUBR        ; GO TO SUBROUTINE 10 MORE TIMES
        DCR   A
        JNZ   LOOP
SUBR:   PUSH  PSW         ; SAVE A AND FLAGS
            .
            .
            .
        POP   PSW         ; RESTORE A AND FLAGS
        RET               ; RETURN TO MAIN PROGRAM
```

All data pushed onto the stack *must* be popped off the stack before returning to the main program. The stack pointer will point to the correct return address when the return instruction is executed. This example subroutine could even have called another subroutine. The second return address would then be pushed on the stack after the *PSW* register contents. This second return address will be popped off when the second subroutine returns to the first. The stack pointer will again point to the saved *PSW* register so that it can be popped off the stack.

INTERRUPTS

An external signal can be used to signal the processor to stop what it is doing and take some other action. This signal is called an *interrupt*. Interrupts are necessary because an external peripheral device may require an immediate action by the microcomputer that cannot wait for the completion of other computations.

The interrupt signal causes the processor to execute a subprogram in much the same way a subroutine is called. The interrupt signal causes the processor to stop after the execution of the instruction in progress. The interrupt system is now disabled; so other interrupts will be disabled. The program counter contains the location of the next instruction to be executed after the interrupt subroutine is finished. This return address is pushed on the stack. The address of the interrupt subroutine is put in the program counter. The processor is now able to execute the interrupt routine to service the peripheral that caused the interrupt. This subroutine will return to the main program by executing an ordinary *RET* instruction to pop the return address from the stack to the program counter.

Table 9-1   8085 interrupts

Priority	Name	Address	Comments
Highest	TRAP	24H	Can't be disabled
	RST7.5	3CH	Internal edge-sensitive flip-flop
	RST6.5	34H	
	RST5.5	2CH	
Lowest	INTR	See below	Only interrupt on 8080
	RST0	00H	All these have same priority but different addresses
	RST1	08H	
	RST2	10H	
	RST3	18H	
	RST4	20H	
	RST5	28H	
	RST6	30H	
	RST7	38H	

Each interrupt input on the processor has a fixed memory location that is the address of the subroutine to be executed for that interrupt. These addresses are shown in Table 9-1. Ordinarily, each of these addresses would contain a *JMP* instruction to the interrupt subroutine. The five interrupt inputs are assigned priorities, as shown in Table 9-1. The processor services the highest priority interrupt first if more than one interrupt occurs simultaneously. The next-highest-priority interrupt is serviced after the first interrupt serviced has returned to the main program.

Initialization

The 8085 also uses location 0 for initialization. The first instruction executed when power is first applied to the microcomputer is in location 0. This instruction is usually a *JMP* to the start of the main program.

EI and DI Instructions

Binary instruction format

	EI	DI
First byte	1 1 1 1 1 0 1 1	1 1 1 1 0 0 1 1

Assembly language format

    (LABEL:)   EI
    (LABEL:)   DI

Flag register
    Not affected.

When an interrupt is acknowledged by the processor, the interrupt system is automatically disabled for two reasons. First, the cause of the interrupt must be removed (usually by resetting a flip-flop in the peripheral) before enabling the interrupt system. Otherwise, the peripheral would interrupt its own interrupt subroutine. The processor would be completely disabled, caught in a continuous interrupt response. Second, it is usually not desirable to allow one peripheral device to interrupt the service routine of another peripheral. When one device must interrupt another's service routine, special provision must be made to assure proper operation.

The interrupt system must be enabled when leaving the interrupt service routine in order to allow any additional interrupts to be serviced. The *EI* or enable interrupt instruction enables the interrupt system. The enable interrupt instruction is always the last instruction executed before the return (*RET*) instruction. The enable interrupt instruction does not enable the interrupt system until after the execution of the *next* instruction. By putting the enable interrupt just before the return, we can be sure that the interrupt will not be enabled until after the return address is popped off the stack into the program counter and the microprocessor returned to the main program. At least one main program instruction will be executed before another interrupt is serviced. The return address will always be a correct main-program address.

A *DI* or disable interrupt instruction allows the interrupt to be disabled explicitly by the main program if desired. The main program may be involved in a critical timing loop or computation that cannot be interrupted, or it may simply want to ignore peripherals when it does not need to service them. The main program and interrupt routine may exchange arguments by passing them through memory locations. The main program and interrupt routine may share more than one argument. The interrupt will have to be disabled while the main program is reading or changing related arguments. For example, suppose the interrupt has not been disabled and the main program has changed two of three related arguments. An interrupt occurs. The interrupt routine will use the new value of the first two arguments and the old value of the third!

Finally, the *TRAP* interrupt is not disabled by the *DI* instruction. The *TRAP* interrupt is commonly used for catastrophic events that require immediate service regardless of any other interrupts. For example, a common use of TRAP is to signal the processor that the microcomputer's power source has been disconnected. Enough energy remains in the power supply to allow the microcomputer to operate for a few milliseconds. During this time, the microcomputer may disable peripherals and otherwise set the system to a safe state before power is lost.

RIM and SIM Instructions

Binary instruction format

	RIM	SIM
First byte	0 0 1 0 0 0 0 0	0 0 1 1 0 0 0 0

Assembly language format

    (LABEL:)   RIM

    (LABEL:)   SIM

Flag register

Not affected.

The RIM or *read interrupt mask* instruction transfers the internal processor status bit in Table 9-2 to the A register. The SIM or *set interrupt mask* instruction transfers the A register to the processor status bits in Table 9-2.

The interrupt mask bits M7.5, M6.5, and M5.5 can be read by RIM and changed by SIM. These mask bits allow their corresponding interrupt inputs to be selectively disabled. Service requests from a particular peripheral might be ignored while some other peripheral is being serviced. The SIM instruction will change the mask bits only if the MSE bit is a 1. Because SIM is used for three diverse functions, it wouldn't be convenient to have it change all three functions each time it was executed.

Bit *IE* of the *RIM* instruction indicates that the interrupt system is enabled or disabled. This *IE* bit is set and reset by the *EI* and *DI* instructions. The *EI* and *DI* instructions enable or disable interrupts *RST7.5*, *RST6.5*, *RST5.5*, and *INTR* together. *SIM* can be used to selectively enable or disable *RST7.5*, *RST6.5*, and *RST5.5*. Of course, *TRAP* can't be disabled.

If the interrupts have been disabled, it is sometimes useful to determine if any require service but *not* to service them via the interrupt. The *I7.5*, *I6.5*, and *I5.5* bits of the RIM data format indicate the status of their corresponding interrupts. For example, if *I6.5* is a 1, an interrupt is pending on input *RST6.5*.

Table 9-2   RIM and SIM data formats

Bit	Name	RIM data format
7	SID	Serial input data
6	I7.5	Interrupt 7.5 pending if 1
5	I6.5	Interrupt 6.5 pending if 1
4	I5.5	Interrupt 5.5 pending if 1
3	IE	Interrupts Enabled if 1
2	M7.5	Interrupt 7.5 disabled if 1
1	M6.5	Interrupt 6.5 disabled if 1
0	M5.5	Interrupt 5.5 disabled if 1

Bit	Name	SIM data format
7	SOD	Serial output data
6	SOE	Serial output enable if 1
5	X	
4	R7.5	Reset the 7.5 interrupt flop if 1
3	MSE	Mask set enable if 1
2	M7.5	Mask (disable) interrupt 7.5 if 1
1	M6.5	Mask (disable) interrupt 6.5 if 1
0	M5.5	Mask (disable) interrupt 5.5 if 1

The *RST7.5* input is edge-sensitive. A positive transition of the logic signal on this input sets an internal flip-flop that remembers the interrupt, even if the *RST7.5* signal disappears. This internal flip-flop is automatically reset by the *RET* instruction after the *RST7.5* interrupt is serviced. The *R7.5* bit of the *SIM* data format will also reset the internal 7.5 flip-flop.

Finally, these two instructions control a 1-bit input port *SID* and a 1-bit output port *SOD* that are built into the processor. The *RIM* instruction reads the input port into the *SID* bit of its data format. The *SIM* instruction changes the output port to the state of its *SOD* bit. The *SOD* bit will be changed only if the *SOE* bit is 1. This allows *SIM* to set the interrupt masks without affecting the *SOD* output port. The bits *SID* and *SOD* are called serial data bits. Neither bit is intrinsically serial in any way. Each bit is simply a 1-bit port. They are called serial ports because they can be, and often are, *programmed* to input and output data serially.

Register Usage with Interrupts

Since an interrupt could occur between any two instructions in a program (except where the interrupt is explicitly disabled), the interrupt routine will almost always have to save the *PSW* and the *A* register on the stack and restore them before returning to the main program. In addition, all other registers will usually have to be saved and restored.

An Interrupt Example

The following example program waits for 10 interrupts to occur on *INTR* at *RST* 3.

```
        ORG    0H
        JMP    STRT          ; POWER UP HERE
        ORG    18H
        JMP    INTR          ; INTERRUPT COMES HERE
        ORG    400H
STRT:   MVI    A, 10D        ; INITIALIZE TO COUNT 10
        STA    COUNT
        LXI    SP, TOP       ; INITIALIZE STACK
        EI                   ; TURN ON INTERRUPTS
WAIT:   LDA    COUNT         ; WAIT FOR 10 INTERRUPTS
        ORA    A             ; CHECK COUNT
        JNZ    WAIT
        DI                   ; DISABLE INTERRUPTS IF
        :                    ;    NO LONGER NEEDED
        :                    ; REST OF PROGRAM
        :
INTR:   PUSH   PSW           ; SAVE A AND FLAGS
        LDA    COUNT         ; INTERRUPT COUNT
        DCR    A             ; DECREMENT COUNT
        STA    COUNT
        POP    PSW           ; RESTORE A AND FLAGS
        EI                   ; ENABLE INTERRUPTS
        RET                  ; RETURN
```

HLT and NOP Instructions

Binary instruction format

	HLT	NOP
First byte	0 1 1 1 0 1 1 0	0 0 0 0 0 0 0 0

Assembly language format

(LABEL:)	HLT
(LABEL:)	NOP

Flag register
Not affected.

The halt instruction might better be called a wait for interrupt instruction. *HLT* simply stops the processor until the next interrupt occurs. Upon returning from the interrupt service routine, the processor executes the instruction following the halt instruction.

The *NOP* or no operation instruction does nothing except increment the program counter. It can be used as a time delay.

ADDITIONAL PSEUDOINSTRUCTIONS

As was discussed for the *ORG* pseudoinstruction, pseudoinstructions are instructions to the assembler program. The *ORG* pseudoinstruction allows the programmer to tell the assembler where to start assigning memory locations. Pseudoinstructions and their formats will vary from assembler to assembler, but, besides *ORG*, there are two more pseudoinstructions that all assemblers will have.

The first of these pseudoinstructions is *EQU*. These *equate* pseudoinstructions allow the programmer to define new symbols to be used in the program. They have the following format:

NAME   EQU   EXPRESSION

Note that *NAME* has no colon, even though it is in the label field. *NAME* is not the label of an actual memory location. The assembler will substitute the expression listed to the right of *EQU* every time *NAME* appears in the program. For example, in the logic controller example, we could have put the following pseudoinstruction at the beginning of the program:

IRN	EQU	02H	; INPUT REG. NUMBER
ORN	EQU	F2H	; OUTPUT REG. NUMBER
LBM	EQU	01H	; LEAST SIG. BIT MASK

Then, we could have written the following instruction in the program:

```
IN    IRN      ; READ INPUT DATA
OUT   ORN      ; OUTPUT DATA
ANI   LBM      ; SAVE ONLY LSB
```

This extra cross reference may seem like a useless additional step but is actually a very useful technique. The *EQU* pseudoinstructions are normally written together at the beginning of a program. If the output register number in the previous example needed to be changed to C3H, a *single* change in the *EQU* pseudoinstruction would cause the assembler to change the value of *ORN everywhere* in the program. Making changes is easier, and the possibility of missing a program line to be changed is eliminated.

By using symbolic names rather than hex constants, the program becomes more easily understood. More importantly, symbolic names allow the programmer to start designing the program even while the microcomputer hardware is being designed and before addresses are known. After the hardware design is finalized, the *EQU* statements can be completed, specifying the memory and peripheral addresses to be used. The use of symbolic names will speed development of the software.

The second pseudoinstruction is *END*, which simply tells the assembler that the physical end of the program has been reached and there are no more instructions to be assembled. It is simply written in the code field:

```
END                  ; END OF THIS PROGRAM
```

MANUAL-MODE LOGIC CONTROLLER EXAMPLE

The logic controller example in Chap. 8 could also include a manual operation mode. In the manual mode, a set of input switches will change the outputs directly, bypassing the algorithms otherwise used to determine the outputs. A pushbutton switch connected to the interrupt will cause the mode to alternate between normal and manual each time it is depressed.

The flowchart for the manual-mode logic controller is shown in Fig. 9-5. The flowchart is similar to the example in the last chapter in normal mode. After data are input, a variable called *MODE* is checked. If the *MODE* is manual, inputs from the manual switches are simply output to the controlled devices.

Each time the pushbutton causes an interrupt, the mode is toggled to its opposite state.

The actual program is listed below. Notice that the main program is almost identical to the last chapter's example except that the *MODE* variable is tested. If the mode is manual, the state of switches connected to port 04H is sent to the output port. The interrupt routine simply toggles all 8 bits in *MODE* each time this routine is executed by pushing the interrupt button.

```
ORG    0
JMP    INIT           ; START HERE WHEN POWER
                      ;   APPLIED
```

```
                ORG     3CH
                JMP     INTR            ; INTERRUPT VECTOR

                ORG     400H
INIT:           MVI     A, 0
                STA     MODE            ; SET MODE TO NORMAL
                LXI     SP, 3FFH        ; INITIALIZE STACK POINTER
                EI                      ; ENABLE INTERRUPTS
START:          IN      02H             ; READ INPUT
                MOV     B, A            ; SAVE INPUT
                LDA     MODE            ; CHECK MODE
                ORA     A               ; SET FLAGS
                JNZ     MAN             ; NOT ZERO = MANUAL
                LXI     H, TABL         ; TABLE START ADDRESS
                                        ; CREATE ADDRESS OF ENTRY
                MOV     L, B
                MOV     A, M            ; GET OUTPUT VALUE
                JMP     OUTPUT
MAN:            IN      04H             ; GET MANUAL SWITCH DATA
OUTPUT:         OUT     F2H
                JMP     START           ; REPEAT PROCESS
INTR:           PUSH    PSW             ; SAVE A & PSW
                LDA     MODE
```

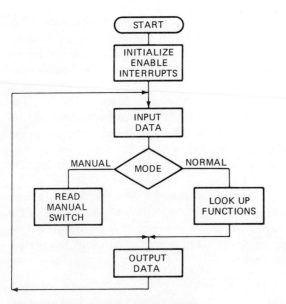

Figure 9-5 Manual mode logic controller.

```
            XRI     FFH          ; REVERSE MODE
            STA     MODE
            POP     PSW          ; RESTORE A & PSW
            EI                   ; ENABLE INTERRUPT
            RET                  ; RETURN
            ORG     500H
TABL:       00H                  ; TABLE OF FUNCTION VALUES
            02H
            02H
            06H
            02H
            02H
            02H
            06H
            02H
            02H
            02H
            06H
            06H
            0EH
            0EH
            0FH
MODE:       00                   ; 0 IS NORMAL MODE, ≠ 0 IS
                                   MANUAL MODE
```

ARITHMETIC

Binary Addition

The binary addition table is very simple.

0	0	1	1
+0	+1	+0	+1
00	01	01	10

Multidigit binary numbers are summed least significant digit first, just as in decimal arithmetic. If a carry occurs, it is added to the next most significant bit. Let's add two 8-bit numbers.

```
    0   0   1   1   1   0   0   1        Carry
        0   0   1   0   1   1   0   1    Operand
+   1   0   1   1   1   0   0   1        Operand
    1   1   1   0   0   1   1   0        Sum
```

In the 8085, as in most computers, the carry out of the most significant bit is stored in the carry bit of the flag register.

When adding unsigned binary numbers, a 1 carry bit out of the most significant bit (the carry stored in the flag register) indicates that the result of the addition was too large to be represented by the number of bits in the register. This is called overflow. The flag-register carry bit may be used to test for arithmetic overflow. Of course, the carry stored in the flag register could be added to the next most significant bit of the result if the result is to be contained in more than one byte.

The same addition table will work correctly for two's-complement numbers. The flag register's carry bit may still be added to the next most significant bit if the result is contained in more than 1 byte. However, the carry bit can no longer be tested for overflow. Adding two numbers of opposite sign will never cause an arithmetic overflow. That is, the register holding the result will always have enough bits to represent the answer properly.

	0 1 1 1 1 1 1 1	(127, largest positive number)
	1 1 1 1 1 1 1 1	(-1, smallest negative number)
Carry = 1	0 1 1 1 1 1 1 0	(126, correct answer)

This is the largest positive result from adding opposite-signed operands. Overflow has not occurred.

	1 0 0 0 0 0 0 0	(-128, most-negative number)
	0 0 0 0 0 0 0 0	(0, smallest "positive" number)
Carry = 0	1 0 0 0 0 0 0 0	(-128, correct answer)

This is the most negative result from adding opposite-signed operands. Overflow did not occur.

However, when two's-complement numbers of the same sign are added, an arithmetic overflow can occur. An attempt to represent a number greater than +127 or less than -128 will cause the result to seem to change sign. Since the sum of two positive numbers should always be positive and the sum of two negative numbers should be negative, a sign change indicates arithmetic overflow. If both operands have the same sign, the result must also have that same sign or arithmetic overflow has occurred.

	1 0 0 0 0 0 0 0	(-128)
	1 1 1 1 1 1 1 1	(-1)
Carry = 1	0 1 1 1 1 1 1 1	(+127, wrong answer)

This addition of negative operands gives a positive result. Arithmetic overflow has occurred.

	0 1 1 1 1 1 1 1	(+127)
	0 0 0 0 0 0 0 1	(+1)
Carry = 0	1 0 0 0 0 0 0 0	(-128, wrong answer)

This addition of positive operands gives a negative result. Arithmetic overflow has occurred.

ADD and ADI Instructions

Binary instruction format

	ADD	ADI
First byte	1 0 0 0 0 S S S	1 1 0 0 0 1 1 0
Second byte	NONE	DATA 8

SSS is 000 for *B*, 001 for *C*, 010 for *D*, 011 for *E*, 100 for *H*, 101 for *L*, 111 for *A* or 110 for *M*.

Assembly language format

(LABEL:)	ADD	SRC
(LABEL:)	ADI	DATA

Flag register

All flag-register bits are affected and have their standard interpretation.

The *ADD* and *ADI* instructions both add an operand to the *A* register and leave the result in the *A* register. The *ADD* instruction will add the contents of any register to the *A* register. The *ADD* instruction will add the contents of any memory location using register-pair addressing to the *A* register. The *ADI* or *add immediate* instruction will add an 8-bit immediate operand to the *A* register. All flag-register bits are affected. The carry bit contains the carry out of bit 7, the most significant bit. The auxiliary carry bit contains a copy of the carry out of bit 3 into bit 4. The zero, sign, and parity bits are set according to the result of the addition.

```
STRT:   MVI   A,10D       ; SET A TO 10
        MVI   E,5D        ; SET D TO 5
        LXI   H,DATA      ; H,L POINT TO DATA
        ADD   E           ; ADD E TO A
        ADI   2           ; ADD 2 TO A
        ADD   M           ; ADD CONTENTS OF DATA
        STA   RESLT       ; STORE RESULT
          .
          .
          .
DATA:   4D                ; VALUE OF 4
RESLT:  0                 ; CONTAINS RESULTS
```

After this program is executed, memory location *RESLT* will contain 21D.

ADC and ACI Instructions

Binary instruction format

	ADC	ACI
First byte	1 0 0 0 1 S S S	1 1 0 0 1 1 1 0
Second byte	NONE	DATA 8

SSS is 000 for *B*, 001 for *C*, 010 for *D*, 011 for *E*, 100 for *H*, 101 for *L*, 111 for *A*, or 110 for *M*.

Assembly language format

(LABEL:)	ADC	SRC
(LABEL:)	ACI	DATA

Flag register

All flag-register bits are affected and have their standard interpretation.

The *ADC* or *add with carry* instruction and the *ACI* or *add with carry immediate* instruction are similar to the *ADD* and *ADI* instructions. The *ADC* and *ACI* instructions add the initial value of the carry bit to the least significant bit of the result. The result of the addition is incremented by 1 if the carry bit is 1. If the carry bit is 1 because of a previous *ADD* instruction, the *ADC* instruction can add the carry out of the MSB of that previous addition into the least significant bit of the current result. The carry can be propagated from 1 byte to another for multiple-byte additions. The operands and result may be 16, 24, 32, or more bits long. An example of a 16-bit addition is shown below.

```
STRT:   LDA   LSG     ; LEAST SIG. PART OF ONE OPERAND
        MOV   B,A     ; SAVE IT
        LDA   LSH     ; LEAST SIG. PART OF OTHER
                      ;   OPERAND
        ADD   B       ; ADD LSP, CARRY OUT IN FLAG REG
        STA   LSA     ; SAVE IN LSP OF ANSWER
        LDA   MSG     ; GET MSP OF ONE OPERAND
        MOV   B,A     ; SAVE IT
        LDA   MSH     ; GET MSP OF OTHER OPERAND
        ADC   B       ; ADD MSP WITH CARRY OUT OF LSP
        STA   MSA     ; SAVE IN MSP OF ANSWER
```

Binary Subtraction

The binary subtract table is also simple.

1	1	0	0	Minuend
−0	−1	−0	−1	Subtrahend
1	0	0	1	Difference
0	0	0	1	Borrow

Multiple-bit binary numbers are subtracted like multiple-digit decimal numbers. Start with the least significant bit.

Whenever 1 must be subtracted from 0, a borrow is made from the next most significant bit position. That is, the borrow is subtracted from the minuend.

	0	1	1	0	1	0	0	0	Borrow
	1	1	0	1	0	1	1	0	Minuend
−	0	1	1	0	1	0	1	0	Subtrahend
	0	1	1	0	1	1	0	0	Difference

In bit position 3, 1 is subtracted from 0. A borrow from bit 4 changes this subtraction to 10 minus 1, which is 1. Thus, bit 3 of the difference is 1. The borrow is subtracted from bit 4 of the minuend and leaves 0 minus 0, which is 0. Thus, bit 4 of the result is 0.

If the register's *most*-significant-bit subtraction needs to borrow from the *next* most significant bit, the flag-register carry bit will be 1, indicating a borrow occurred that could not be satisfied. Even though the flag register's carry bit is set to the borrow out of the most significant bit of a subtraction, don't assume that a carry is identical to a borrow. For example, a subtract instruction will cause the carry bit (really a borrow) to be set to the opposite state than the carry bit set by the same arithmetic operation performed by the addition of the two's complement of the subtrahend. The following addition performs the previous example subtraction by adding the two's complement of the subtrahend. The carry out of the MSB is opposite the borrow obtained by subtraction.

		0	1	1	0	1	0	1	0	Subtrahend
		1	0	0	1	0	1	0	1	One's complement
		1	0	0	1	0	1	1	0	Two's complement
+		1	1	0	1	0	1	1	0	Minuend
		0	1	1	0	1	1	0	0	Difference
1		0	0	1	0	1	1	0		Carry

When subtracting unsigned binary numbers, a borrow out of the most significant bit indicates the subtrahend was larger than the minuend. The result would have been negative and cannot be represented as an unsigned number. A flag-register carry bit of 1 indicates arithmetic overflow for unsigned subtraction.

When subtracting two's-complement numbers of the *same* sign, arithmetic overflow will never occur.

		0	1	1	1	1	1	1	1	(127, most-positive number)
	−	0	0	0	0	0	0	0	0	(0, smallest positive number)
Borrow = 0		0	1	1	1	1	1	1	1	(127, correct answer)

This is the most positive result possible from subtracting same-signed operands. No overflow has occurred.

		1	0	0	0	0	0	0	0	(−128, most-negative number)
	−	1	1	1	1	1	1	1	1	(−1, smallest negative number)
Borrow = 1		1	0	0	0	0	0	0	1	(−127, correct answer)

This is the most-negative result possible from subtracting same-signed operands. No overflow has occurred.

Subtracting two's-complement numbers of opposite sign can cause overflow to occur. When subtracting two's-complement numbers of opposite sign, the result should always have the same sign as the minuend; otherwise arithmetic overflow has occurred.

$$
\begin{array}{r}
0\ \ 1\ \ 1\ \ 1\ \ 1\ \ 1\ \ 1\ \ 1 \quad (+127) \\
-\ \ 1\ \ 1\ \ 1\ \ 1\ \ 1\ \ 1\ \ 1\ \ 1 \quad (-1) \\
\hline
\text{Borrow} = 1 \qquad 1\ \ 0\ \ 0\ \ 0\ \ 0\ \ 0\ \ 0\ \ 0 \quad (-128, \text{wrong answer})
\end{array}
$$

The correct answer is +128. The result appears negative because +128 can't be represented by 8 bits. Overflow has occurred.

$$
\begin{array}{r}
1\ \ 0\ \ 0\ \ 0\ \ 0\ \ 0\ \ 0\ \ 0 \quad (-128) \\
-\ \ 0\ \ 0\ \ 0\ \ 0\ \ 0\ \ 0\ \ 0\ \ 1 \quad (+1) \\
\hline
\text{Borrow} = 0 \qquad 0\ \ 1\ \ 1\ \ 1\ \ 1\ \ 1\ \ 1\ \ 1 \quad (+127, \text{wrong answer})
\end{array}
$$

The correct answer is -129. The answer appears positive because -129 can't be represented by 8 bits. Overflow has occurred.

SUB and SUI Instructions

Binary instruction format

	SUB	SUI
First byte	1 0 0 1 0 S S S	1 1 0 1 0 1 1 0
Second byte		DATA 8

SSS can be 000 for B, 001 for C, 010 for D, 011 for E, 100 for H, 101 for L, 111 for A, or 110 for M.

Assembly language format

(LABEL:)   SUB   SRC
(LABEL:)   SUI   DATA

Flag register

All flag-register bits are affected, and all but C have their standard interpretation. The C bit contains the borrow out of the subtraction.

The subtract or *SUB* and subtract immediate or *SUI* instructions subtract the specified data byte from the A register and leave the result in the A register. For the *SUB* instruction, the specified data byte can be the contents of any register or the contents of any memory location specified by register-pair addressing. The *SUI* instruction subtracts the 8 bits of immediate data carried with the instruction. The *borrow* out of bit 7 is stored in the flag-register carry bit. However, the auxiliary carry or *AC* bit is set to the *carry* out of bit 3 into bit 4 and *not* the borrow out of bit 3.

SBB and SBI Instructions

Binary instruction format

	SBB	SBI
First byte	1 0 0 1 1 S S S	1 1 0 1 1 1 1 0
Second byte		DATA 8

SSS can be 000 for *B*, 001 for *C*, 010 for *D*, 011 for *E*, 100 for *H*, 101 for *L*, 111 for *A*, or 110 for *M*.

Assembly language format

(LABEL:)	SBB	SRC
(LABEL:)	SBI	DATA

Flag register

All flag-register bits are affected, and all but *C* have their standard interpretation. The *C* bit contains the borrow out of the subtraction.

The subtract with borrow or *SBB* and the subtract with borrow immediate or *SBI* instructions are similar to the *SUB* and *SUI* instructions. If the flag register's carry bit is 1 before the instruction is executed, that 1 will be subtracted from the result of the subtraction. The flag register's carry bit is set by a borrow out of a previous subtraction. Thus, these instructions can be used for multiple-byte subtraction. The following program subtracts *G* from *H*. Both *G* and *H* are 16-bit binary numbers.

```
STRT:   LDA   LSG     ; LSP OF SUBTRAHEND
        MOV   B,A     ; SAVE IT
        LDA   LSH     ; LSP OF MINUEND
        SUB   B       ; SUBTRACT LSPS, SAVE BORROW
        STA   LSA     ; SAVE LSP OF ANSWER
        LDA   MSG     ; MSP OF SUBTRAHEND
        MOV   B,A     ; SAVE IT
        LDA   MSH     ; MSP OF MINUEND
        SBB   B       ; SUBTRACT WITH BORROW FROM LSP
        STA   MSA     ; SAVE MSP OF ANSWER
```

DAD Instruction

Binary instruction format

	DAD
First byte	0 0 R P 1 0 0 1

RP can be 00 for *B*, 01 for *D*, 10 for *H*, or 11 for *SP*.

Assembly language format

(LABEL:)	DAD	B
(LABEL:)	DAD	D
(LABEL:)	DAD	H
(LABEL:)	DAD	SP

Flag register

The C bit is set to the carry out of the most significant bit of the most significant byte of the addition. No other flag-register bits are affected.

Sixteen-bit additions are very commonly performed for both address arithmetic and data calculations. The *DAD* or double add instruction performs 16-bit additions conveniently. The *DAD* instruction adds the contents of any register pair to the 16-bit number in the H register pair. The result of the addition remains in the H register pair. *Only the carry bit* in the flag register is affected. The C bit is set to the carry out of the most significant bit of the 16-bit addition.

Besides serving as a convenient 16-bit addition instruction, the *DAD* instruction has two other important uses. The instruction *DAD H* adds the H register pair to itself. Since *DAD H* doubles the number in H and L, it is equivalent to a one-place left shift of 16 bits. The *DAD H* instruction is a left shift of the H register pair.

The *DAD SP* instruction is the *only* instruction that will allow the program to retrieve the contents of the stack pointer. A program might need to check the contents of the *SP* to determine if the stack still has room to expand. The following sample program will check the *SP* against a limit address stored in memory.

STRT:	LDA	LIMIT	; LSP OF LIMIT ADDRESS
	CMA		; COMPLEMENT IT
	MOV	L,A	; SAVE IN LSP OF H PAIR
	LDA	LIMIT+1	; MSP OF LIMIT ADDRESS
	CMA		; COMPLEMENT IT
	MOV	H,A	; SAVE IN MSP OF H PAIR
	INX	H	; INCREMENT TO FORM 2's
			; COMPLEMENT
	DAD	SP	; ADD CONTENTS OF STACK
			; POINTER
	JNC	OFLW	; JUMP IF (SP) IS BELOW LIMIT
			; ADDRESS
	NOP		; OK TO PUSH ONTO STACK

This short program adds the two's complement of the *LIMIT* address to the *SP*. Since the stack expands downward in memory, stack overflow occurs whenever the *SP* is below the *LIMIT*. The result of the calculation *SP-LIMIT* will be positive whenever the *SP* is equal to or above the *LIMIT*. If we were using a subtract instruction, we'd expect a 0 borrow bit. Since we are adding the two's complement, the carry bit will be opposite the borrow. Thus, *C* will be 1 whenever the *SP* is equal to or above the *LIMIT*. *C* will be 0 when the stack has overflowed the *LIMIT*.

CMP and CPI Instructions

Binary instruction format

	CMP	CPI
First byte	1 0 1 1 1 S S S	1 1 1 1 1 1 1 0
Secnod byte	NONE	DATA 8

SSS can be 000 for *B*, 001 for *C*, 010 for *D*, 011 for *E*, 100 for *H*, 101 for *L*, 111 for *A*, or 110 for *M*.

Assembly language format

| (LABEL:) | CMP | SRC |
| (LABEL:) | CPI | DATA |

Flag register

All flag register bits are affected, and all but *C* have their standard interpretation. The *C* bit contains the borrow out of the subtraction.

The *CMP* or compare and *CPI* or compare immediate instructions compare the contents of the specified byte with the accumulator. The datum to be compared can be the contents of any register or of any memory location specified by register-pair addressing. The *CPI* instruction allows the specified byte to be an immediate datum carried with the instruction.

The comparison is performed by subtracting the specified data byte from the contents of the *A* register. All flag-register bits are set as if a *SUB* instruction had been executed. The result of the subtraction is not stored anywhere. The specified data byte and the contents of the *A* register remain unchanged. After performing a compare, the program may conditionally branch on the flag-register bits.

If the zero bit is 1, the two operands were equal; otherwise they were unequal. The sign bit could be used to compare the relative sizes of the two operands *if no arithmetic overflow occurred*. If the sign bit is 1, indicating a negative result, the data byte was larger than the *A* register. If the sign bit is 0, the *A* register is larger than or equal to the data byte. Since we would have to verify that no overflow occurred to believe our comparison and since we may still want to compare the data *even if* overflow occurred, another test must be devised. We can test the state of the carry bit in the flag register to determine relative size. The carry bit of the flag register will contain the borrow bit out of the most significant bit of the subtraction.

If both operands have the same sign and the *A* register is larger than or equal to the data byte, no borrow will occur and the carry bit will be 0. If the carry bit is set to

1, indicating a borrow, the data byte is greater than the contents of the A register. If the signs of the operands are different, the sense of the carry bit will be reversed. We can summarize the compare operation as follows:

Signs of operands	Flag register	Meaning
Any	$Z = 1$	$(A) =$ Data
Any	$Z = 0$	$(A) \neq$ Data
Same	$C = 1$	$(A) <$ Data
Same	$C = 0$	$(A) \geqslant$ Data
Different	$C = 1$	$(A) \geqslant$ Data
Different	$C = 0$	$(A) <$ Data

If you are comparing numbers known to be small, it is still easiest to test the sign bit for comparison. Often, numbers to be compared are limited to a range known not to cause overflow.

DAA Instruction

Binary instruction format

DAA
First byte   0 0 1 0 0 1 1 1

Assembly language format

(LABEL:)   DAA

Flag register

All flag register bits are affected and have their standard interpretation.

The *DAA* or decimal adjust A register instruction is used in conjunction with other arithmetic instructions to perform BCD arithmetic. If two valid BCD digits, each having a range of 0 to 9 are added using a binary arithmetic instruction, the result is not necessarily a valid BCD digit. For example:

Case 1	0001	(1)	
	+0011	(3)	
	0100	(4)	Valid BCD digit
Case 2	0001	(1)	
	+1001	(9)	
	1010	(A)	Not a valid BCD digit

```
Case 3          0111    (7)
              +1001    (9)
Carry = 1       0000    (0)     Valid BCD digit but incorrect result
```

These three examples represent the only three possible cases. The result could be a valid BCD digit and correct. The result could be a hex digit between A and F. The result could be a valid BCD digit between 0 and 8 but not correct (a carry out of the digit is always generated in this case).

The *DAA* instruction corrects the last two cases to valid BCD numbers representing the correct result. After an *ADD* instruction is executed to add two BCD numbers, a *DAA* instruction is executed to correct the result in two steps.

1. If the least significant digit is greater than 9 (case 2 above) or if the auxiliary carry bit is set (case 3 above), the *entire A* register is incremented by 6. For the case 2 example above, the least significant digit would be 0000 and the most significant digit would be incremented by 1. For the case 3 example above, the least significant digit would be 6. In case 2, when the BCD digit A is corrected to 0, a carry is propagated to the most significant digit to add ten to the entire number. In case 3, the original binary addition propagated a carry to the most significant digit so that, when the digit 0 is corrected to 6, no additional carry need be propagated.

2. Finally, the *DAA* instruction corrects the most significant digit. If the most significant digit is greater than 9 (case 2) or if the normal carry bit is set (case 3), the *most significant* digit is incremented by 6. Any carry out of bit 7 from this operation is stored in the normal carry bit of the flag register. The other flag-register bits are set according to the final result.

After the *DAA* instruction is executed, the contents of the *A* register are valid BCD digits representing the correct sum of the two BCD operands. If the sum should have been greater than 99, the carry bit will be set, which will indicate an overflow or a carry into the next most significant digit. An *ADC* instruction can be used to continue the sum if operands with more than two BCD digits must be summed. The *DAA* instruction will not work after a subtract instruction. Decimal subtraction must be performed by adding the *ten's-complement* representation of the BCD subtrahend. Ten's complement is a representation for negative BCD numbers analogous to two's complement for binary numbers. This example program subtracts the subtrahend by finding its ten's complement and adding it to the minuend.

```
STRT:   LXI     D,MIN       ; ADDRESS OF MINUEND
        LXI     H,SBTR      ; ADDRESS OF SUBTRAHEND
        MVI     C,2         ; 4 DIGITS OR 2 BYTES
        STC                 ; NO BORROW

LOOP:   MVI     99H         ; 99 BCD
        ACI     0           ; ADD CARRY
        SUB     M           ; COMPLEMENT OF SUBTRAHEND
```

```
        XCHG                ; GET ADDRESS OF MINUEND
        ADD     M           ; ADD MINUEND
        DAA                 ; DECIMAL ADJUST RESULT
        MOV     M,A         ; STORE RESULT
        XCHG                ; GET ADDRESS OF SUBTRAHEND
        DCR     C           ; CHECK FOR LAST BYTE
        JZ      DONE        ; YES, WE ARE DONE
        INX     D           ; NO, ADDRESS NEXT BYTE
        INX     H           ; NEXT BYTE
        JMP     LOOP        ; GET NEXT TWO DECIMAL DIGITS
```

SOME ADDITIONAL DATA MOVEMENT INSTRUCTIONS

XCHG and XTHL Instructions

Binary instruction format

	XCHG	XTHL
First byte	1 1 1 0 1 0 1 1	1 1 1 0 0 0 1 1

Assembly language format

```
    (LABEL:)    XCHG
    (LABEL:)    XTHL
```

Flag register

Not affected.

The *XCHG* or exchange instruction exchanges the contents of the D register pair with those of the H register pair. Register-pair addressing must often be used to specify the operand of a logical or arithmetic operation. Only the H register pair can be used for register-pair addressing for arithmetic and logical operations. A second address can be placed in the D register pair and exchanged with the H pair when a different operand is to be addressed. For example, the following program adds a constant to an array, subtracts the corresponding locations of another array from the result, and places the result in the first array.

```
STRT:   LXI     D,AR2       ; ARRAY 2
        LXI     H,AR1       ; ARRAY 1
        MVI     B,SIZE      ; SIZE OF ARRAYS
LOOP:   MVI     A,CONST     ; CONSTANT TO ADD
        ADD     M           ; ADD ARRAY 1
        XCHG                ; EXCHANGE ADDRESSES
        SUB     M           ; SUBTRACT ARRAY 2
```

```
XCHG                    ; RESTORE AR1 ADDRESS
MOV      M,A            ; STORE RESULT IN ARRAY 1
INX      D              ; NEXT ARRAY 2 LOCATION
INX      H              ; NEXT ARRAY 1 LOCATION
DCR      B              ; DECREMENT COUNTER
JNZ      LOOP           ; CONTINUE IF NOT DONE
```

The *XTHL* or exchange *HL* with top of stack instruction allows the current return address to be changed and the original return address to be saved.

SPHL Instruction

Binary instruction format

SPHL

First byte	1 1 1 1 1 0 0 1

Assembly language format

(LABEL:)   SPHL

Flag register

Not affected.

The *SPHL* or *HL* to *SP* instruction puts the contents of the *H* register pair into the stack pointer. Like the *LXI SP,DATA* instruction, *SPHL* can be used to initialize the stack pointer. The *LXI* instruction will only initialize the SP to a predetermined constant, while the *SPHL* will allow the microcomputer to set the stack pointer to any value calculated in the *H* register pair.

PROGRAMMED ARITHMETIC OPERATIONS

Multiplication

Some microcomputers, including the 8085, do not have multiply or divide instructions. These arithmetic operations are performed by subroutines written by the programmer. First, we'll consider the multiplication of unsigned binary numbers. Let's examine the multiplication of two decimal numbers:

483	Multiplicand
X 24	Multiplier
1932	Partial product
966	Partial product
11592	Product

Start with the rightmost multiplier digit to form the first partial product (by using the decimal multiplication table and propagating carries). The next multiplier digit to the left forms another parital product that is shifted one digit to the left because it represents a number 10 times as large as the first partial product. Continue generating partial products for all multiplier digits. The partial products are summed to obtain the product.

The first thing we need to perform a binary multiplication is the binary multiplication table:

```
  0        0        1        1
 ×0       ×1       ×0       ×1
 ──       ──       ──       ──
  0        0        0        1
```

Let's multiply two 4-bit unsigned binary numbers:

$$
\begin{array}{ll}
1011 & (11) \\
\times 0101 & (5) \\
\hline
1011 & \\
0000 & \\
1011 & \\
0000 & \\
\hline
0110111 & (55)
\end{array}
$$

Because of the simplicity of the binary multiplication table, a multiplier bit of 1 causes the associated partial to be equal to the multiplicand. If a multiplier bit is 0, the corresponding partial product is 0. In the microcomputer, we will test each multiplier bit and either add or not add the multiplicand. We will not store each partial product, but add the next partial product immediately to form an accumulated partial product.

Let's examine the same multiplication used previously as an example:

0000	1011	Multiplicand
	0101	Multiplier
0000	0000	Accumulated partial product

Since the least significant bit of the multiplier is one, we will add the multiplicand to the partial product. At the same time, we will shift the multiplier right to prepare to check the next bit and the multiplicand left to prepare for the next partial product.

0001	0110	Multiplicand
	0010	Multiplier
0000	1011	Partial product

Since the next multiplier bit is 0, we shall simply shift the multiplicand and multiplier without adding the multiplicand.

0010	1100	Multiplicand
	0001	Multiplier
0000	1011	Partial product

The next multiplier bit is a 1; so we shall add the multiplicand.

0101	1000	Multiplicand
	0000	Multiplier
0011	0111	Partial product

The next and last multiplier bit is 0; so we do not need to add the multiplicand.

1011	0000	Multiplicand
	0000	Multiplier
0011	0111	Product

Although this algorithm could be programmed as shown, it usually is not used for several reasons. First, an 8-bit register is needed for the 4-bit multiplicand, and, second, an 8-bit addition was required, even though we are using only 4-bit operands. We shift the partial product to the right, rather than shift the multiplicand left.

START	1011			Multiplicand	
	0101			Multiplier	
	0000	0000		Product	
1. ADD	1011		2. SHIFT	1011	
	0101			0010	
	1011	0000		0101	1000
3. NO ADD	1011		4. SHIFT	1011	
	0010			0001	
	0101	1000		0010	1100
5. ADD	1011		6. SHIFT	1011	
	0001			0000	
	1101	1100		0110	1110
7. NO ADD	1011		8. SHIFT	1011	
	0000			0000	
	0110	1110		0011	0111

Notice that we shift the multiplier right each time we shift the accumulated partial product right. We could have stored the multiplier in the least significant byte of the product. Each time we shifted right we would set up the next multiplier bit to be tested and simultaneously make room for the next product bit.

A multiplication algorithm is flowcharted in Fig. 9-6 for the 8085. The 8085 cannot test the least significant bit of a register without an extra masking step. We will first shift the product/multiplier right, so the least significant bit will be stored in the carry bit of the flag register. The carry bit is easily tested with a conditional jump instruction. A multiplication program may be written from this flowchart.

```
; SINGLE PRECISION MULTIPLY
; MULTIPLIER IN B
; MULTIPLICAND IN C
; RESULT IN A,B (16 BITS)
; BIT COUNTER IN D
```

```
MPY:    XRA    A        ; INITIALIZE PARTIAL PRODUCT
        MVI    D,8      ; TEST 8 MULTIPLIER BITS
LOOP:   ORA    A        ; CLEAR CARRY
        RAR             ; SHIFT PRODUCT RIGHT
        MOV    E,A      ; SAVE PARTIAL PRODUCT
        MOV    A,B      ; GET MULTIPLIER
        RAR             ; ROTATE
        MOV    B,A      ; RESTORE MULTIPLIER
        MOV    A,E      ; RESTORE PARTIAL PRODUCT
        JNC    NOADD    ; CHECK MULTIPLIER BIT
        ADD    C        ; MULT. BIT = 1, ADD MULTIPLICAND
```

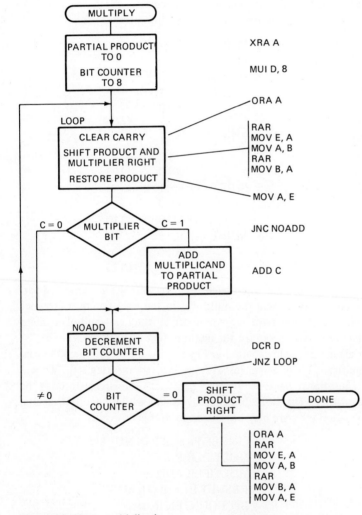

Figure 9-6 Binary multiplication.

```
NOADD:    DCR    D          ; DECREMENT BIT COUNTER
          JNZ    LOOP       ; NOT DONE. NEXT PARTIAL PRODUCT
          ORA    A          ; CLEAR CARRY
          RAR               ; PRODUCT SHIFTED ONCE MORE
          MOV    E,A
          MOV    A,B
          RAR
          MOV    B,A
          MOV    A,E
```

Division

Binary division is performed similarly to decimal division. Let's examine a decimal division:

$$
\begin{array}{r}
021 \quad \text{Quotient} \\
22\,\overline{)478} \quad \text{Dividend} \\
\underline{44} \\
38 \\
\underline{22} \\
16 \quad \text{Remainder}
\end{array}
$$

Divisor

First, we try to divide the first digit of the dividend by the entire divisor. This division cannot be done, and we enter 0 as the first quotient digit. Next, we try to divide the first two digits of the dividend by the divisor and continue until a division can be performed. We calculate the remainder from that division, bring down the next dividend digit, and attempt to divide again by the divisor. If division cannot be accomplished, we enter 0 in the quotient, bring down the next dividend digit, and try to divide again. If division is possible, we enter the appropriate digit in the quotient and calculate a new remainder.

A binary division will proceed similarly.

$$
\begin{array}{r}
0001\ 1011 \quad (27) \\
(6) \quad 0000\ 0110\,\overline{)1010\ 0111} \quad (167) \\
\underline{0110} \\
0100\ 0 \\
\underline{011\ 0} \\
001\ 011 \\
\underline{0\ 110} \\
0\ 1011 \\
\underline{0110} \\
0101 \quad (5)
\end{array}
$$

As in multiplication, division is simplified in binary. The divisor is either subtracted or not subtracted from the remainder depending on whether the quotient bit is 1 or 0. In fact, the divisor can be subtracted from the dividend to *determine* whether the quotient bit should be 0 or 1. Consider the same division example:

Remainder   *Dividend and quotient*
0000 0000   1010 0111

Shift the remainder and dividend left and try to subtract the divisor:

1. 0000 0001   0100 1110
    -0000 0110

The result would be negative. Shift left and try again. Enter 0 in the quotient. Since we are shifting the dividend left at each step, we'll use the bits vacated on the right to hold the quotient.

2. 0000 0010   1001 1100
    -0000 0110

The result would be negative. Enter 0 in the quotient.

3. 0000 0101   0011 1000
    -0000 0110

The result would be negative. Enter 0 in the quotient.

4. 0000 1010   0111 0000
    -0000 0110
     0000 0100

The subtraction was successful. Enter 1 in the quotient.

5. 0000 1000   1110 0001
    -0000 0110
     0000 0010

The subtraction was successful. Enter 1 in the quotient.

6. 0000 0101   1100 0011
    -0000 0110

The result would be negative. Enter 0 in the quotient.

7. 0000 1011   1000 0110
    -0000 0110
     0000 0101

The subtraction was successful. Enter 1 in the quotient.

8. 0000 1011   0000 1101
    -0000 0110
     0000 0101

The subtraction was successful. Enter 1 in the quotient.

9. 0000 1010   0001 1011

We have run out of dividend bits and have calculated the quotient. In order to enter the last quotient bit, we had to shift the remainder one more place than necessary. We must shift the remainder one to the right to correct it.

Just as in multiplication, where the multiplier and product shared the same register, the dividend and quotient share the same register in division. Every time a new quotient bit is ready, another dividend bit may be shifted into the partial product. Since we are using unsigned binary arithmetic, a negative result is indicated by a borrow bit of 1 (stored in the flag register's carry bit). Since we need a 1 quotient bit if we have a positive result and a 0 quotient bit if we have a negative result, we can just

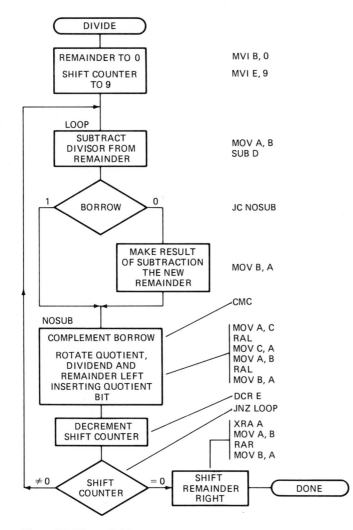

Figure 9-7 Binary division.

complement the carry bit and use it as the new quotient bit. The first shift can be accomplished by allowing an extra division step to be performed. Subtracting the divisor from the original 0 remainder will cause a 0 quotient bit and a left shift. This extra division step will be exactly equivalent to the first of the nine shifts in the above example.

This division algorithm is flowcharted in Fig. 9-7. A division program may be written from this flowchart.

```
                                      ; SINGLE PRECISION DIVISION
                                      ; REMAINDER IN B
                                      ; DIVIDEND/QUOTIENT IN C
                                      ; DIVISOR IN D
                                      ; BIT COUNTER IN E
DIV:        MVI     E,9               ; 9 SHIFTS
            MVI     B,0               ; ZERO REMAINDER
LOOP:       MOV     A,B               ; GET REMAINDER
            SUB     D                 ; SUBTRACT DIVISOR
            JC      NOSUB             ; NEGATIVE RESULT, DON'T SAVE
                                      ;   RESULT
            MOV     B,A               ; POSITIVE RESULT, SAVE NEW
                                      ;   REMAINDER
NOSUB:      CMC                       ; FOR NEW QUOTIENT BIT
            MOV     A,C               ; GET QUOTIENT/DIVIDEND
            RAL                       ; ROTATE LEFT
            MOV     C,A               ; RESTORE
            MOV     A,B               ; GET REMAINDER
            RAL                       ; INSERT NEW DIVIDEND BIT
            MOV     B,A               ; RESTORE
            DCR     E                 ; BUMP COUNTER
            JNZ     LOOP              ; DO 9 TIMES
            XRA     A                 ; CLEAR CARRY
            MOV     A,B               ; GET REMAINDER
            RAR                       ; CORRECT IT
            MOV     B,A               ; RESTORE
```

Signed Multiplication and Division

One way to perform two's-complement multiplication and division would be to calculate the sign of the result separately and take the absolute value of the operands. Use unsigned multiplication or division and correct the result to the previously calculated sign. When the signs of the operands are different, the sign of the result will be negative. When the signs of the operands are identical, the sign of the result will be positive. A single subroutine can be used to compute the correct sign for multiplication or division.

The unsigned multiplication algorithm previously described will give a correct result for a negative multiplicand. In this case, only the absolute value of the multiplier need be calculated. The sign of the result is then reversed if the original sign of the multiplier was negative.

Many other techniques exist for performing two's-complement signed multiplication and division but usually offer little or no advantage when programmed for a microcomputer.

Multiplication by Small Constants

It is often necessary to multiply by small constants. For example, a table entry number must be multiplied by 3 for a ROM table that has 3 bytes per entry. In a previous example, we showed how a 3-byte-per-entry table could be padded with do-nothing bytes to make it a 4-byte-per-entry table. We could use two left shifts to multiply by 4 to access the table. If the table had many entries, we would not want to waste a large amount of memory space by inserting do-nothing bytes. On the other hand, it seems that a complete multiplication program is slow and cumbersome if all we need to do is multiply by 3 or 5. Multiplication by a small constant can be performed by only performing the multiplication steps that correspond to each 1 bit in the multiplier. If the multiplier has only a few 1 bits (like the numbers 3 and 5), the multiplication will proceed much faster than a complete multiplication program. The following program uses this technique to access a 3-byte-per-entry jump table.

```
STRT:   LDA    RTNUM      ; NUMBER OF ROUTINE TO EXECUTE
        MOV    B,A        ; SAVE ORIGINAL NUMBER
        ADD    A          ; MULTIPLY BY 2
        ADD    B          ; 2*RTNUM + RTNUM = 3*RTNUM
        LXI    H,JTBL     ; STARTING ADDRESS OF JUMP
                          ;   TABLE
        MVI    B,0        ; MSP OF OFFSET
        MOV    C,A        ; LSP OF OFFSET
        DAD    B          ; ADD STARTING ADDRESS AND
                          ;   OFFSET
        PCHL              ; JUMP TO THIS ADDRESS
JTBL:   JMP    RT0        ; 3 BYTE TABLE ENTRY
        JMP    RT1
        JMP    RT2
                .
                .
                .
        JMP    RT84       ; MAXIMUM OF 84 DECIMAL
                          ;   ROUTINES
```

If more than 84 entries were needed, the multiplication by 3 would have to accumulate a 16-bit result to accommodate offsets greater than 255.

Moving the Binary Point

The position of the binary point must often be moved when performing arithmetic operations on numbers representing fractional values. The binary points must be aligned in both operands when adding or subtracting. The binary point of the result is in the same position as the point in the operands.

$$
\begin{array}{r}
00101.001 \\
+01010.110 \\
\hline
01111.111
\end{array}
$$

If the binary points are not aligned, one or the other operand must be shifted to align the point. If the operand with the leftmost point is shifted right, the least significant bits will be lost. You can also be certain that the register will be able to represent the shifted operand properly.

$$
\begin{array}{ll}
\text{Original operand} & 101.00101 \\
\text{Shift right} & 00101.001 \\
& +01010.110 \\
\hline
& 01111.111
\end{array}
$$

Shifting an operand to the left to align the binary point will prevent least significant bits from being lost. However, you must be sure that most significant bits are not lost, which would render the result invalid.

When multiplying two binary numbers, the binary point of the result is displaced to the left by the sum of the displacements of the points of the two operands.

$$
\begin{array}{ll}
00101.000 & \text{Point is displaced 3 places to the left} \\
\times000011.00 & \text{Point is displaced 2 places to the left} \\
\hline
00000001111.00000 & \text{Point is displaced 5 places to the left}
\end{array}
$$

When dividing binary numbers, the binary point of the result is displaced to the left by the displacement of the dividend's point minus the displacement of the divisor's point.

Shifting Two's-Complement Numbers

We have previously discussed use of a left shift to multiply by 2 and a right shift to divide by 2 for unsigned binary numbers. Signed binary numbers can also be shifted. A two's-complement number may be multiplied by 2 by shifting it left and filling the least significant bit with a 0. If you are not sure of the initial magnitude of the number, you must check for overflow of the result by looking for a change in sign. The old sign bit is stored in the carry bit after the left shift.

```
DOBL:   ADD     A           ; SHIFT LEFT, INSERT ZERO,
                            ;   SET ALL FLAGS
        JP      POS         ; CHECK NEW SIGN BIT
```

```
            JNC     OFLW       ; OLD SIGN WAS 0, NEW SIGN IS 1
            JMP     CONT       ; OLD SIGN WAS 1, NEW SIGN IS 1
   POS:     JC      OFLW       ; OLD SIGN WAS 1, NEW SIGN IS 0
   CONT:    NOP                ; NO OVERFLOW, CONTINUE
```

A two's-complement number may be halved by shifting it right. Rather than shifting a 0 into the most significant bit, the sign bit must be replicated to preserve the sign and value of the number.

```
   HALF:    ORA     A          ; SET SIGN FLAG, CLEAR CARRY
                               ;   FLAG
            JP      ROT        ; POSITIVE NUMBER, CARRY IS 0
            CMC                ; NEGATIVE NUMBER, SET CARRY
                               ;   TO 1
   ROT:     RAR                ; HALVE NUMBER, INSERT CORRECT
                               ;   SIGN
```

Floating-Point Numbers

The kinds of numbers we have been using are called fixed-point numbers. To represent a larger fixed-point number than the number of bits allows, we must use additional bits to the left of the binary point. If we must represent very small numbers, we use additional bits to the right of the binary point. Fixed-point numbers can be cumbersome. The programmer must know the range of the numbers expected at all stages of the computation. The original data for the program usually comes from an external device (terminal, temperature sensor, etc.). The range of input data may be very large, and the range of intermediate computational results may be even larger. An excessively large number of bits would be required to represent variables in the computation.

A number representation that does not have the above problems is called floating point. Floating-point binary numbers are analogous to decimal numbers in scientific notation. Each floating-point number is represented by two fixed-point binary numbers, a mantissa and an exponent. The floating-point number represented by these two fixed-point numbers is:

$$(\text{MANTISSA}) \times 2^{(\text{EXPONENT})}$$

In floating-point representation, all numbers have the same precision regardless of their magnitude. Extremely large and small numbers may be represented in a relatively small number of bits. A microcomputer typically uses an 8- to 32-bit mantissa and a 6- to 16-bit exponent. Since the size of the exponent and mantissa are determined by the programmer who writes the floating-point arithmetic subroutine, the mantissa and exponent may be sized to fit the requirements of the problem. However, writing these arithmetic routines is a substantial job; so most programmers try to find standard floating-point arithmetic subroutines that meet their requirements.

PROBLEMS

9-1 Should the interrupt be explicitly disabled in the following program? If the interrupt should be disabled, add *EI* and *DI* instructions where they are required.

```
S1:       EI
          ⋮
          LDA    COUNT1      ; INCREMENT COUNT1
          ADI    1
          STA    COUNT1
          CALL   SUBR
          LDA    COUNT2      ; INCREMENT COUNT2
          SUI    1
          STA    COUNT2
          ⋮

INTR:     PUSH   PSW         ; INTERRUPT HANDLER
          LDA    COUNT2      ; ADD 1 TO COUNT2
          ADI    1
          STA    COUNT2
          POP    PSW
          RET
```

9-2 Write a program that checks the datum in the *A* register. The program should call subroutines according to the following table.

A register datum	Subroutine called
Zero	SZERO
Negative	SMINUS

Each subroutine will save and restore the *A* register.

9-3 Use other 8085 instructions, such as *PUSH, POP, PCHL*, etc., to perform subroutine calls and returns. Write an example subroutine call and return.

9-4 Perform the following binary additions. List the carry out of the most significant bit.

(*a*)
```
  0010 1101
+ 1011 1001
```

(*b*)
```
  1100 1001
+ 1000 1110
```

(*c*)
```
  0101 1100
+ 1110 0001
```

9-5 Perform the following binary subtractions. What is the borrow out of the MSB of each result?

(*a*)
```
  1101 0110
- 0110 1010
```

(*b*)
```
  0111 1011
- 1001 1000
```

(*c*)
```
  1001 1000
- 1100 1001
```

9-6 What is the content of the A register after this program is executed?

```
        LDA     DNUM
        ADI     99H
        DAA
        HLT
DNUM:   82H
```

9-7 Perform the following binary multiplication. Be sure to position the binary point properly.

$$0.101$$
$$\underline{\times 01.01}$$

9-8 Perform the following binary division. Be sure to position the binary point properly.

$$1.01\overline{)1.1001}$$

9-9 A regular periodic interrupt is called a real-time clock. Write a clock interrupt routine that keeps track of seconds in memory location *SEC* and minutes in *MIN*. Both minutes and seconds should be *BCD* numbers. The clock interrupt occurs every 5.0 ms.

9-10 Write a program to compare two 8-bit two's-complement numbers R and S. Branch to subroutines *GT*, *EQ*, or *LT* if R is greater than S, R is equal to S, or R is less than S, respectively.

9-11 Write a program that works like the program of Prob. 9-10 except compares 16-bit numbers.

9-12 Write signed multiplication and division programs. Use subroutine calls to the unsigned multiplication and division subroutines given in the text as part of your program.

9-13 Counting can be used to perform arithmetic. Write flowcharts and programs that perform the following operations on 8-bit operands, using counting:
  (*a*) BCD to binary conversion
  (*b*) Binary to BCD conversion
  (*c*) Multiplication
  (*d*) Division

9-14 Write a program that multiplies by the constant 13, using the method described in the text for multiplying by small constants.

9-15 Write the programs that do the following for 16-bit two's-complement operands:
  (*a*) Double and check for overflow.
  (*b*) Halve.

CHAPTER TEN

NUTS AND BOLTS

Up to now, we have only been discussing microcomputer programming. The 8080 and 8085 are programmed almost identically. The instructions of the newer 8085 were made as identical to the 8080 instructions as possible. These nearly identical instructions reduce the cost of developing new 8085 systems. A designer, already experienced in 8080 programming, will only have to learn the few new 8085 instructions. In most cases, programs previously developed for the 8080 will also run on the 8085.

However, the implementation of this nearly identical instruction set in the newer 8085 is very different from that in the 8080. In this chapter, we will examine the 8085's hardware and contrast it with the 8080. We will also discuss interface circuits used with both microcomputers and the peripherals with which they interface.

Although much factual information will be presented in this chapter, more information is needed to use the 8085 and its peripheral and memory circuits. This information is contained in the MCS-85 User's Manual.[1] This manual does not use the notation we've been using for logic signals. This chapter follows the MCS-85 Manual's notation; so you can compare diagrams and explanations to the MCS-85 Manual if desired. When we have previously prefixed a signal name with H or Y, this chapter will use no prefix. When we had previously prefixed a signal name with L or N, this chapter will overscore the signal name. Thus, $HALE$ will be ALE and LRD will be $\overline{RD}$.

THE 8085 MICROPROCESSOR

A block diagram of the internal structure of the 8085 integrated circuit is shown in Fig. 10-1. There are several major sections on this drawing. Data are transmitted on an

---

[1] $MCS\text{-}85^{TM}$ User's Manual, Intel Corporation, Santa Clara, Calif., 1977.

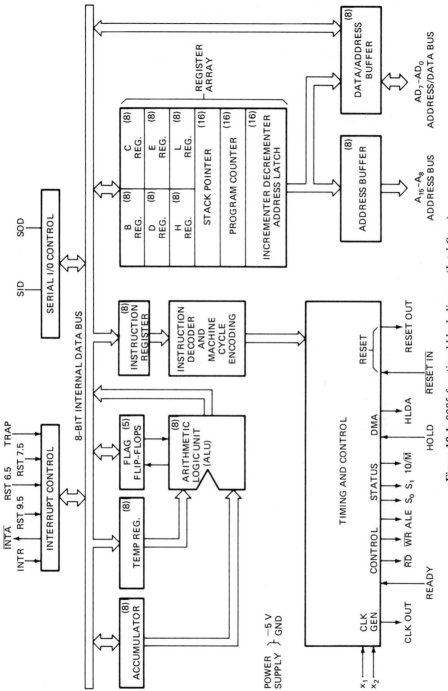

Figure 10-1 8085 functional block diagram (*Intel Corp.*).

293

8-bit internal data bus. This data bus is used to transfer data between the *register array* and the *arithmetic unit*. The arithmetic unit consists of the *A*, temporary, and flag registers and the arithmetic logic unit. An instruction register and decoder supply information to a timing and control ASM. The control ASM generates both internal control signals for the arithmetic unit, register file, and other internal components and external control signals for memory and peripheral devices. Interrupts are routed to an interrupt control unit. A data and address multiplexer allows either the 8-bit internal data bus or the least significant 8 bits of the address to be output to the external *AD* bus. This multiplexer is bidirectional and allows the external bus to be routed to the internal bus when external data must be read into the processor. The 8 most significant address bits are routed to an external address bus. Single-bit input and output ports are part of the serial I/O control unit.

Address and Data Busses

The external connections to the 8085 may be divided into two general categories, support and data transmission. The support connections simply allow the processor to operate. Support connections include clock, power, and reset signals. The data transmission connections allow the movement of data among the processor and external memories and peripherals. These data transmission interconnections may be divided into three categories: address, data, and control. Sixteen address signals specify the individual peripheral or memory location to be accessed. Eight data signals transmit data between the processor and the data location specified by the address lines. Control signals are used to initiate and control data transfers.

The cost of an integrated circuit and the expense of assembling that circuit into a system are proportional to the physical size and number of pins on the IC's package. At the time the 8085 was designed, a 40-pin package was considered the largest practical size. The 8085 would have required more than 40 pins on its integrated-circuit package. Some change had to be made to the 8085 to reduce the number of interconnections required. The 8 least significant address bits *share* the same interconnection pins with the data bus. Obviously, the data and address bits cannot appear on one bus simultaneously. The address bits appear first and must be saved in an external register, as shown in Fig. 10-2. The most significant address bits simply appear on a separate

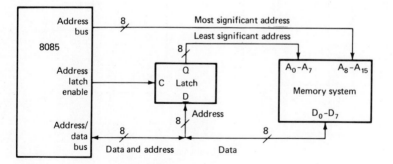

Figure 10-2 Demultiplexing 8085 addresses.

8-bit address bus. After the least significant address bits have been saved in the register, the data bus may be used for data transfers.

SUPPORT CIRCUITRY

The 8085 operates from a single power supply of 5 V, as shown in Fig. 10-3. Two inputs labeled X may be connected to a frequency-determining element, such as a crystal or RC circuit, in lieu of an external clock circuit. A *CLK* output allows the clock signal generated in the 8085 to be used by other parts of the system.

The crystal's frequency should be double the desired clock rate. The 8085, like many complex integrated circuits, is available in several versions. These versions differ in the maximum speed at which they will operate. For example, the 8085A will operate at a clock rate of 3.125 MHz with a 6.25-MHz crystal. The 8085A-2 will operate at a clock rate of 5 MHz with a 10-MHz crystal. A *RESET IN* input may be connected to an RC delay circuit to initialize or reset the processor when power is first applied. A *RESET OUT* output makes this internally generated signal available to other parts of the system. The condition of the processor after being reset is shown in Table 10-1.

TIMING

The states of the 8085 are grouped hierarchically, as shown in Fig. 10-4. An *instruction cycle* contains all those states needed to perform a single instruction. An instruction cycle is divided into from one to five *machine cycles*. A machine cycle corre-

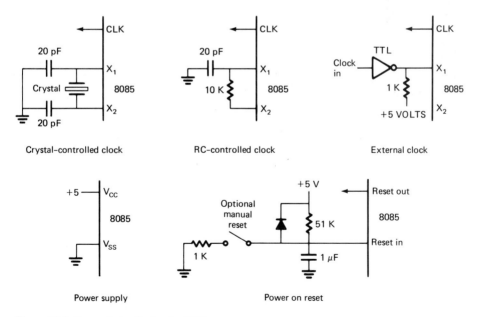

Figure 10-3 Support circuits for the 8085.

Table 10-1 Condition of processor after reset

Bit affected	Function
EI = 0	Disables interrupt system
M5.5 = 1	Disable RST5.5 interrupt
M6.5 = 1	Disable RST6.5 interrupt
M7.5 = 1	Disable RST7.5 interrupt
RST7.5 = 0	Reset internal interrupt flip-flop, so no interrupt is pending on RST7.5
PC = 0	Reset program counter, so first instruction executed is at location 0
SOD = 0	Serial output data flip-flop

Also internal flip-flops related to *HLDA, TRAP, HOLD, INTR, READY*, the instruction register, machine cycles, and *T* states are all reset. Resetting these flip-flops ensures that the 8085 will start correctly.

sponds to a single data transfer on the external bus, for example, a memory read. Each machine cycle is divided into from three to six *states* or *T states*. The diagram of Fig. 10-4 shows the execution of an STA instruction. In machine cycle *M1*, the *opcode fetch*, the incremented program counter specifies a memory address from which the *STA* opcode is extracted. The opcode is stored in the processor's instruction register. The processor decodes this opcode and realizes that this instruction is actually 3 bytes long. Two more machine cycles *M2* and *M3* are generated to read the second and third bytes, containing the direct address. Finally, this direct address is used in machine cycle *M4* to specify the memory location into which data from the *A* register are to be stored.

The operation of each instruction will be different, but common characteristics exist. Each instruction must have an opcode fetch machine cycle, which has either four or six *T* states. All other machine cycles will always have three *T* states. Each instruction requires from one to five machine cycles. Each machine cycle will be one of the seven types of machine cycles listed in Table 10-2. Each of these machine cycles causes specific control bus outputs to be activated.

Each machine cycle is composed of from three to six *T* states. A *T* state is one clock cycle long. Each *T* state may be one of ten possible *T* states shown in the partial ASM chart of Fig. 10-5. Each machine cycle starts in *T1*. State *T2* is a delay state to give the memory or peripheral time to access the data requested. Data are output in *T2* if the machine cycle is to write data. If the memory is very slow, the processor will

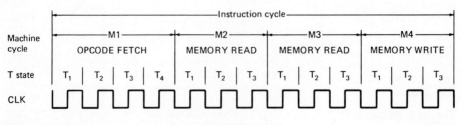

Figure 10-4 Instruction cycle, machine cycles, and *T* states.

Table 10-2 Machine cycles

Machine cycle	Control signals				Status signals	
	$\overline{RD}$	$\overline{WR}$	$IO/\overline{M}$	$\overline{INTA}$	S1	S0
Opcode fetch	0	1	0	1	1	1
Memory read	0	1	0	1	1	0
Memory write	1	0	0	1	0	1
I/O read	0	1	1	1	1	0
I/O write	1	0	1	1	0	1
Intr acknowledge	1	1	0	0	1	1
Bus idle	1	1	0	1	1	X

wait indefinitely in state *TWAIT* until the memory datum is ready. State *T3* is the last state of most machine cycles. Data are read into the processor in state *T3*. An opcode fetch cycle will include state *T4*, used for processing the opcode. Some opcode fetch cycles will also include states *T5* and *T6*. States *T5* and *T6* perform the instruction's operation when an additional machine cycle is not required to access memory. The processor waits in state *THALT* if an *HLT* instruction is executed. An interrupt starts the execution of another instruction after an *HLT*. State *THOLD* is used when another processor or peripheral wants to use the system's bus without intervention of the 8085. The 8085 disconnects itself from the bus in *THOLD*, so that another processor can share the bus.

DATA TRANSFERS

Four signals are available for control of simple data transfers on the external bus. The signal *ALE* (*address latch enable*) is used to load the least significant bits of the address into a holding register. The signals $\overline{RD}$ and $\overline{WR}$ are used to specify read and write operations, respectively. Direction of transfer is always specified *relative to the processor*. A read operation means that data are *read into the processor*. The $IO/\overline{M}$ signal selects between a peripheral device and a memory location for a particular data transfer. Only these four signals are required to control bus data transfers, as shown in Fig. 10-6. The signal $IO/\overline{M}$ selects either the memory or the peripheral system to respond to the $\overline{RD}$ or $\overline{WR}$ signals. Also, notice that the 8-bit peripheral address (from an *IN* or *OUT* instruction) appears on both the least significant *and* the *most* significant address byte. The least significant address bits need not be demultiplexed from the data bus for peripheral selection.

Bus Timing

The timing diagram in Fig. 10-7 shows an opcode fetch cycle. During state *T1*, the $IO/\overline{M}$ signal becomes a 0 to indicate a *memory* read is to take place. The program

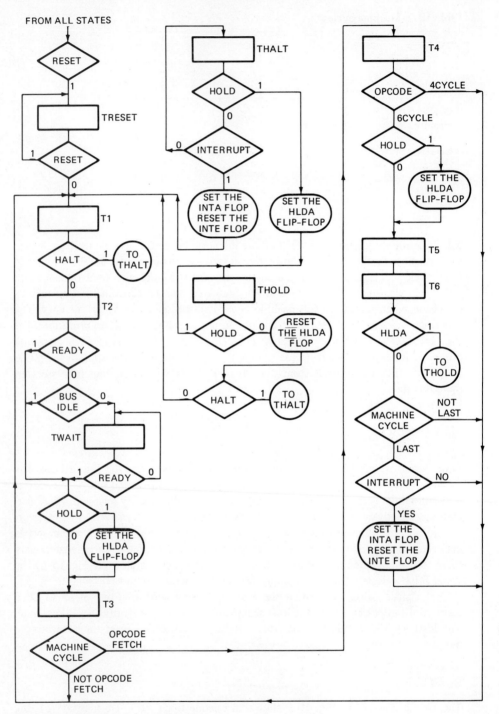

Figure 10-5 Simplified T state ASM chart.

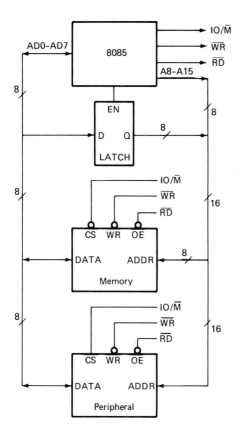

Figure 10-6 8085 interfaces.

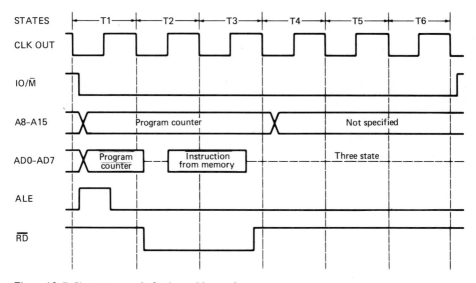

Figure 10-7 Six-state opcode fetch machine cycle.

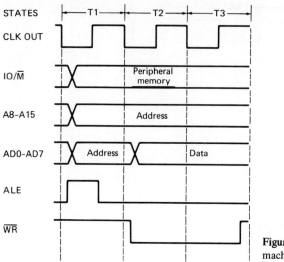

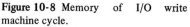

Figure 10-8 Memory of I/O write machine cycle.

counter is output to the address and data busses. The signal *ALE* occurs to save the program counter's least significant address bits, now present on the data bus. During *T2*, $\overline{RD}$ will be output enabling the memory circuit's output to send data to the processor. In this case, the opcode for the *DCX* instruction is placed on the data bus. This datum is actually loaded into the processor's instruction register at the end of state *T3* and decoded during state *T4*. The *DCX* instruction requires six *T* states in its opcode fetch so that the processor will continue through states *T5* and *T6*. These last two states are used for executing the *DCX* instruction. The specified register pair is decremented by the processor's arithmetic unit during states *T5* and *T6*. A memory read or I/O read machine cycle is similar to the first three *T* states of the opcode fetch machine cycle.

A memory or I/O write cycle is shown in Fig. 10-8. Data are output from the processor during states *T2* and *T3*. These data are stored in a memory location or peripheral register by the signal $\overline{WR}$.

Wait State

When in state *T2*, the processor tests the state of the *READY* input from the control bus, as was shown in Fig. 10-5. If the *READY* input is low, the processor enters state *TWAIT* instead of *T3*, as shown in Fig. 10-9. Completion of a read or write operation can be delayed one or more clock cycles. Memory circuits that have access times longer than required to operate the 8085 at maximum speed use the *READY* line to slow the processor's read and write operations.

Direct Memory Access and the Hold State

The 8085 periodically tests the *HOLD* input. If this input is a 1, the processor will generate an *HLDA* or hold acknowledge signal and disconnect itself from the data,

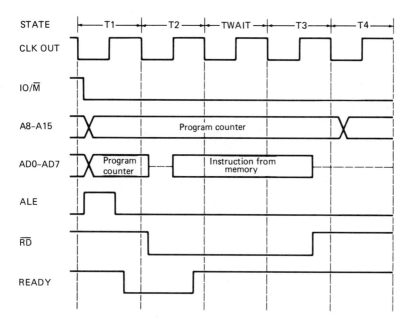

Figure 10-9 Opcode fetch machine cycle with wait state.

address, and part of the control bus. The data and address bus outputs as well as $\overline{RD}$, $\overline{WR}$, ALE, and $IO/\overline{M}$ have three state outputs. When the processor is disconnected, any peripheral or even another processor can connect itself to the bus and transfer data to and from memory directly! This data transfer method is called *direct memory access* or *DMA*. Since data do not have to travel through the processor to get to memory, significantly higher data transfer rates can be attained by DMA. A DMA peripheral must perform many data transfer functions, formerly performed by the microprocessor. A DMA peripheral will often contain a specialized peripheral processor in addition to more complex bus interface circuitry.

Single integrated-circuit DMA controllers are manufactured to reduce the cost of a DMA interface. The 8257-5 DMA controller is designed to work with the 8085 or 8080 microcomputers. This DMA controller accepts data transfer requests from up to four peripheral devices. Each of the four peripherals is given a priority. The 8257-5 grants simultaneous requests for data transfers in order of priority. The 8257-5 asserts the *HOLD* signal input of the 8085 and takes control of the system bus. The DMA controller also keeps track of the number of bytes to be transferred and the memory addresses into which the data are to be transferred for each peripheral.

Parametric Timing

Small 8085 systems may not be much more complex than Fig. 10-6. As we'll see later in this chapter, manufacturers publish complete circuits of small systems. The manufacturer has verified the operation of such sample circuits. Often, more complex systems are needed. The design of larger systems must include calculations for both fan out and timing. Fortunately, microcomputer manufacturers often publish application information explaining these calculations. For example, Intel Corporation publishes an application note for the 8085 bus.[1]

A general approach exists that should help analyze any microcomputer bus. First, perform the fan-out calculation. For all but small systems, you'll probably have to add buffer circuits to increase fan out. In very large systems, every printed circuit card may have to be buffered. None of the processor, memory, or peripheral circuits actually connect directly to the bus.

In any case, now you'll have the circuit configuration that will allow you to calculate circuit timing. Each signal output by the processor causes a response by a memory or peripheral circuit. These responses must arrive back at the processor in time to be read correctly. A timing analysis consists of examining each signal to see that the response to that signal arrives at the processor at the right time. For example, an 8085 outputs a new address during a memory read cycle. The processor expects the datum at that address to appear at the processor's data bus pins no later than 575 ns after the address appeared. Thus, the total of the propagation delays of any address buffers, memory circuits, and data buffers must be less than 575 ns.

For the 8085, you'll want to check timing, as described above for $\overline{RD}$, ALE, and the address bus. The analysis for $\overline{WR}$ is a little different. The signal $\overline{WR}$ must be long enough to guarantee that the memory or peripheral circuit will remember the data correctly. Also, the data from the processor must arrive soon enough to meet the setup time of the memory or peripheral. The data must stay long enough to meet the hold time of the memory or peripheral. Finally, the propagation delays controlling three-state outputs must be fast enough to guarantee that only one three-state output is enabled at one time.

INTERRUPTS

The operation of the interrupt system was described in a previous chapter and will not be again here. We'll only describe the hardware operations not previously described. The most complex interrupt is *INTR;* so we'll describe it first. An *INTR* signal from a peripheral will be recognized at the end of the current instruction cycle if the interrupt system is enabled, as shown in Fig. 10-10. The 8085 freezes the program counter, disables the interrupt, and starts another instruction fetch. Instead of generating $\overline{RD}$, the 8085 processor will generate $\overline{INTA}$ of interrupt acknowledge. The signal $\overline{INTA}$ disables memory data and enables the interrupting peripheral to supply the instruction to be fetched. Although the peripheral can supply any instruction desired, a set of eight instructions are included in the 8085's instruction set for interrupts.

[1] Bruce McCormick, *Application Techniques for the Intel 8085A Bus, AP-38*, Intel Corporation, Santa Clara, Calif., 1978.

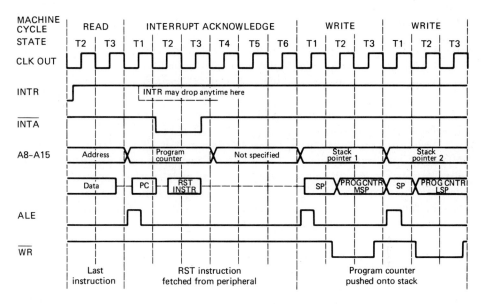

Figure 10-10 Interrupt acknowledge cycle.

RST Instructions

Binary instruction format

	RST
First byte	1 1 N N N 1 1 1

NNN is 000 for RST0, 001 for RST1, 010 for RST2, 011 for RST3, 100 for RST4, 101 for RST5, 110 for RST6, or 111 for RST7.

Assembly language format

(LABEL:)   RST N

Flag register

Not affected

The *Restart* or *RST* instruction acts as a single-byte *CALL* instruction and pushes the return address on the stack before starting the interrupt service routine. The interrupt routine's address is simply 3 times N, where N is the restart number in the instruction.

An Interrupt Controller

An interrupt controller circuit, the 8259-5, simplifies peripheral interfaces to the *INTR* and $\overline{INTA}$ signals, while adding additional capability. The 8259 accepts interrupt requests from up to eight peripherals. Each peripheral is given a priority, and the controller decides which of several simultaneous interrupt requests to service first. The controller issues an *INTR* signal to the 8085 and responds to $\overline{INTA}$ with a *CALL*, rather than an *RST*, instruction.

Each of the eight peripheral request inputs is edge-triggered (like *RST7.5* on the 8085) and may be individually masked. Priority among the eight peripherals may be fixed or rotating. Rotating priority ensures that all peripherals will be serviced; so one high priority peripheral can't monopolize the interrupt system. Up to eight controllers may be connected together to allow up to 64 interrupt inputs from peripherals. Each peripheral will have its own interrupt routine address.

Other Interrupts

You will remember that the 8085 has four additional interrupt inputs, *TRAP*, *RST7.5*, *RST6.5*, and *RST5.5*. These inputs do not require an external *RST* instruction; so a bus idle machine cycle occurs in response to them, rather than an interrupt acknowledge cycle. During the bus idle cycle the processor generates an *RST* instruction *internally*, corresponding to the interrupt input that is being serviced.

THE 8080 MICROPROCESSOR

The older 8080 processor is similar to the 8085. The 8080 requires three power supply voltages, compared with one required by the 8085. The 8080 does not multiplex address signals onto the data bus. Since the 8080 is also in a 40-pin package, other signals must have been multiplexed (or deleted) on the 8080. We have already mentioned that the 8085 has four additional interrupt inputs not found in the 8080. These four inputs are also the easiest to use, requiring no external circuitry to send an *RST* or *CALL* instruction to the processor. More importantly, the 8080 multiplexes part of its *control* bus onto the data bus, rather than multiplexing part of its addresses, as does the 8085. These control signals may be demultiplexed, as shown in Fig. 10-11. These demultiplexed control signals must still be gated with two nonmultiplexed control signals in order to provide useful signals to memories and peripherals, as shown in Fig. 10-11. The 8080 does not have an internal clock or reset generator like the 8085, and a very complex external-clock generator circuit must be used. The demultiplexing, gating, clock, and reset circuitry was integrated in two support circuits as an interim design before the 8085.

Execution and bus timing for the 8080 is different from 8085 timing. We will not detail 8080 timing here except to say the 8080 is somewhat slower and more cumbersome to interface.

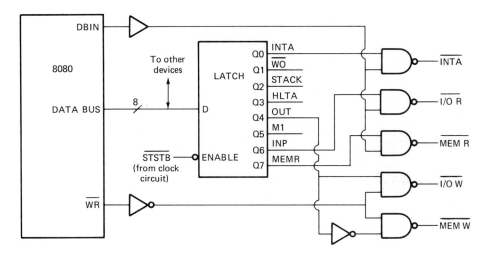

Figure 10-11 Decoding 8080 control signals.

The primary differences between the 8080 and 8085 may be summarized as follows:

8080	8085
Multiplexes control signals	Multiplexes address signals
External support circuitry	Internal support circuitry
One interrupt input	Five interrupt inputs: four have built-in *RST* instructions, one is edge-sensitive, all have priority, three are maskable, one can't be disabled
Three power supplies	One power supply

Why is the 8085 "better" than the 8080? The 8085 is faster than the 8080 and has greater raw processing capability than the 8080. An 8085 system is less expensive to implement than an equivalent 8080 system, because fewer external circuits are required. Most importantly, the simpler 8085 system is less expensive to design than an 8080 system! Unfortunately, software development costs are likely to be identical for both processors. The primary advantage of the 8085 is reduced hardware design and implementation costs.

PERIPHERAL AND MEMORY CIRCUITS

In previous chapters we used both ROMs and RWMs. All these memory circuits can be used with any microcomputer, subject to timing and fan-out restrictions. In this chapter, we'll discuss some memory circuits that are specially designed to be used with the 8085.

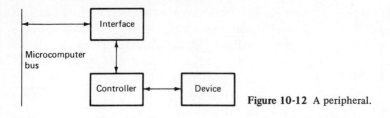

Figure 10-12 A peripheral.

Figure 10-12 shows the organization of any peripheral. Let's use an example to explain this diagram. A printer is a typewriter-like mechanism that allows a computer to output text on paper. The printer mechanism would be the *device* of Fig. 10-12. A digital *controller* must time the printing function, move the carriage one space after each character, check to see if paper is present, and perform many other functions. This controller must communicate with the microcomputer. An *interface* is a digital circuit designed to connect the controller to the microcomputer bus.

Actually, these definitions are usually blurred. If the interface and controller are built in the same box, they are often collectively called an interface. Terminology is not standardized. For example, Intel Corporation's interfaces are called general-purpose peripherals. Controllers and interfaces, fabricated as one circuit, are called dedicated-function peripherals. Fortunately, the description of a circuit clearly delineates its function, regardless of the name given that circuit. Keep in mind that the functions shown in Fig. 10-12 are present in a peripheral, regardless of the names given them.

COMBINATION ROM AND INTERFACE CIRCUIT

The 8355 and 8755 are ROM and interface circuits that are directly compatible with the 8085's multiplexed bus. Signal *ALE* stores the least significant address bits sent via the data bus into an internal address register. This address register is contained in the *bus interface* block of Fig. 10-13. The 8355 contains a 2KB ROM, while the 8755 contains a 2KB EPROM. Two 8-bit I/O ports are included in each circuit. Each

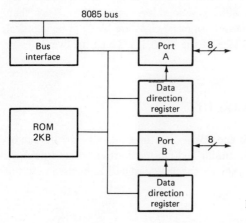

Figure 10-13 ROM and interface circuit.

of these 16 bits may be independently specified as input or output. Two data direction registers, corresponding to the two I/O ports, specify the direction of each bit. An I/O port bit will be an input if the corresponding bit in the data direction register is 0. An I/O port bit will be an output if the corresponding bit in the data direction register is 1. If a data bit is an output bit, its state may also be read by an *IN* instruction.

The port *A* and *B* registers and the port *A* and *B* data direction registers are each assigned one of four I/O port addresses. The data direction register's contents may *not* be read into the processor.

COMBINATION RWM, INTERFACE, AND TIMER CIRCUIT

The 8155 is an RWM, interface, and timer circuit. Like the ROM and interface circuit, the 8355 has a bus interface that demultiplexes the 8085 bus. The block diagram of Fig. 10-14 is similar to the ROM circuit. The RWM has 256 bytes. The RWM circuit has more complex I/O functions and a timer. The interface and timer functions respond to six I/O port addresses. Seven registers are shown in Fig. 10-14. The command and status registers share the same port address. Writing into that address changes the command register. Reading from that address reads the status register.

Interface Functions

I/O ports *A*, *B*, and *C* may be designated as input or output ports by the command register bits, shown in Table 10-3. An entire port must be designated as input or output. Port *A* alone or both ports *A* and *B* may be designated as handshake ports. In

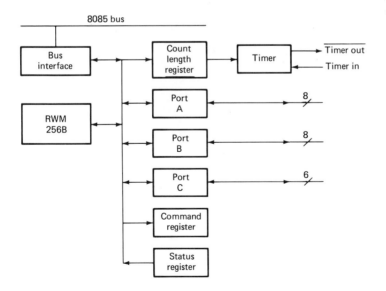

Figure 10-14 RWM, timer and interface circuit.

Table 10-3 Command register of 8155

Bit	Name	Function		
0	PA	Port A direction, 0 is input		
1	PB	Port B direction, 0 is input		
2	PC1	Port C Mode	PC2	PC1
3	PC2	Input	0	0
		Output	1	1
		Port A handshake	0	1
		Port A & B handshake	1	0
4	IEA	1 is enable port A interrupt		
5	IEB	1 is enable port B interrupt		
6	TM1	Timer Command	TM2	TM1
7	TM2	No operation	0	0
		Stop counter	0	1
		Stop after counter reaches 0	1	0
		Start counter	1	1

handshake modes, the pins that were port C bits are used as handshake control signals. Three control signals are needed for each handshake port. If both ports A and B are handshake ports, no port C bits are left for use as general-purpose I/O bits.

Not only does the 8155 implement a handshake with the port C control signals, but it also relays that handshake to the 8085. Figure 10-15 shows the handshake operation of a port in input mode. Data to be sent to the processor are placed on the data port pins. A $\overline{STROBE}$ signal tells the 8155 to save these data in its own internal register. The 8155 raises the buffer full or BF signal to prevent another data byte from being put in the 8155 until the current byte is read by the processor. The 8155 also interrupts the 8085. The 8085 enters an interrupt service routine, and the data byte is read from the 8155 resetting BF so that another transfer can take place.

Output mode is shown in Fig. 10-16. In output mode, the 8155 initially sends an interrupt to the 8085. The 8085 program responds by writing the first datum into the

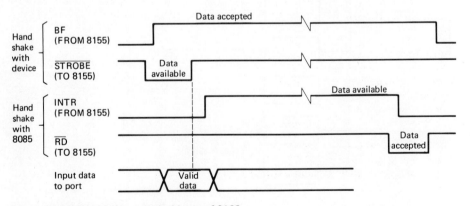

Figure 10-15 Handshake or strobed input of 8155.

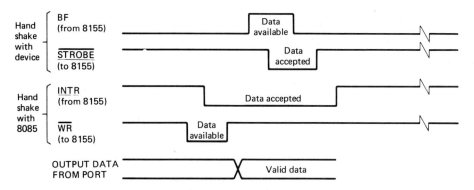

Figure 10-16 Handshake or strobed output of 8155.

8155, which sets *BF*. After the datum is read, a $\overline{STROBE}$ signals the 8155 that this datum has been accepted. The 8155 requests another interrupt to transfer the second datum.

If both ports *A* and *B* are in handshake mode, two interrupts may be generated. These interrupts may be individually masked by bits in the command register of Table 10-3. Also, the state of buffer full (*BF*), the interrupt request, and the interrupt mask for either port may be read through the status register of Table 10-4.

Timer Functions

The timer is a 14-bit counter that is decremented at each positive transition of input *TIMER IN*. These transitions may be a constant clock, like the 8085's clock out signal. The timer may now be used to interrupt the 8085 at regular time intervals. An interrupt at regular intervals is called a *clock interrupt*, and many computer systems keep track of time with clock interrupts. The *TIMER IN* signal may be connected to a peripheral device. The counter could be used to count blocks of data on a magnetic tape or beer cans on a conveyor in a brewery.

The initial 14-bit value to be loaded into the timer and a 2-bit mode is put into the count length register. The counter is started by setting bits in the command regis-

Table 10-4 Status register of 8155

Bit	Name	Function
0	INTR A	Port A interrupt
1	A BF	Port A buffer full
2	INTE A	Port A interrupt enable
3	INTR B	Port B interrupt
4	B BF	Port B buffer full
5	INTE B	Port B interrupt enable
6	TIMER	Timer interrupt
7	X	Not used

Table 10-5 Count length register of 8155

		Most significant count length register
Bit	Name	Function
0–5		Most significant 6 bits of timer constant
6	M1	0, stop when counter reaches 0
		1, reload counter from count length register after reaching 0 and continue counting
7	M2	0, $\overline{\text{TIMER OUT}}$ is low during second half of count
		1, TIMER OUT is low for one TIMER IN period when counter reaches 0

		Least significant count length register
Bit	Name	Function
0–7		Least significant 8 bits of timer constant

ter of Table 10-3. There are two ways to stop the counter listed in Table 10-3. The counter may be stopped immediately or after it next reaches 0.

One mode bit in the count length register in Table 10-5 specifies that the counter will stop after reaching 0 or will reload from the count length register and start again. Repetitive counting is needed for a clock interrupt. The other mode bit specifies the output $\overline{\text{TIMER OUT}}$. This output can be low during the entire second half of the count; so the output looks like a square wave. Alternately, this output could be a one-clock-cycle-long pulse when the timer reaches 0. Square-wave outputs are useful if the timer output is to be a clock signal for another circuit. For example, the timer could be used to generate a clock for a serial interface, as will be described later. A short pulse is used to interrupt the 8085 each time the counter reaches 0. Since this output is only a pulse, it must be saved by a flip-flop. The $\overline{\text{TIMER OUT}}$ signal may be connected to the edge-sensitive *RST7.5* input of the 8085 or any of the edge-sensitive inputs of the 8259-5 interrupt controller. The $\overline{\text{TIMER OUT}}$ signal must be saved in an external flip-flop if used as an input for *RST5.5*, *RST6.5*, or *INTR*.

COMBINATION CIRCUITS

You may wonder why memory and interface functions would be combined in the same circuit. The incremental cost of adding an I/O circuit to a memory circuit is small. Additionally, the application of such a circuit is less expensive. Only one bus interface must be considered rather than two. Only one circuit must be assembled rather than two. Combination circuits are especially attractive in small microcomputer systems. Here, the number of circuits saved may be a significant fraction of the total number of circuits.

The small 8085 system shown in Fig. 10-17 uses only three circuits yet has con-

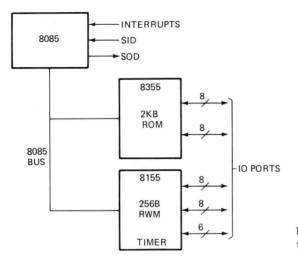

Figure 10-17 Minimum 8085 system configuration.

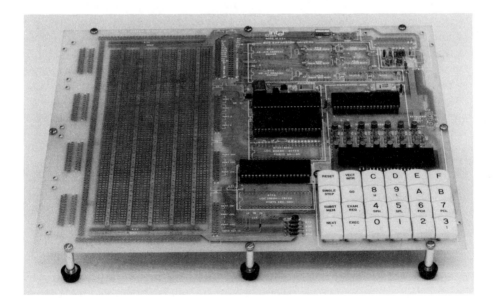

An 8085 system. The three integrated circuits in the center are, from top to bottom, an 8085 processor, 8355 ROM, and 8155 RWM. The IC at upper right is an 8279 keyboard and display interface. The large PC board allows expansion. (*Intel Corporation.*)

siderable capability. This circuit has 2KB of ROM, 256B of RWM, 38 I/O bits, and a programmable clock interrupt. In addition, three processor interrupt inputs and the processor *SID* and *SOD* ports are also available. This entire microcomputer system can be fabricated on a 3.25-in. by 4.25-in. printed circuit board.

SERIAL DATA TRANSMISSION

The I/O instructions we have been using simply output or input 8 bits at a time from a peripheral interface. Since these 8 bits appear simultaneously on 8 wires connecting the peripheral to its interface, this type of I/O is called parallel I/O.

Data must often be sent over telephone lines or other communication links. Usually, only a 1-bit path is available to send and receive data. Sending data 1 bit at a time is called serial data transmission. Computer terminals (teleprinters, CRTs, etc.) are commonly connected to a computer via a phone line. Most terminals have a serial data interface. Most other peripherals that *might* be connected to a phone line are often available with an optional serial interface. Printers, card readers, and many other peripherals may be purchased with a serial interface. Most importantly, standards specify data formats, codes, speeds, and electric levels for serial transmission systems. Other books cover serial interfacing more completely than we will in this book.[1]

Because serial interfacing is so common, special serial-interface integrated circuits are available for microcomputers. A microprocessor could control the sequencing of output bits and the assembling of sequential input bits. This technique of letting the microprocessor itself create and receive serial data is sometimes used if cost is more important than speed of computation. Programmed serial transmission is time-consuming. The 8085's *SOD* and *SID* signals may be used for this purpose. Usually, a special serial interface circuit is used to convert parallel data from the microprocessor to serial form and serial data to parallel form in order to send them to the microprocessor. Before we discuss an actual interface circuit, we'll explain the operation of one type of serial data transmission.

Asynchronous Serial Data Transmission

Asynchronous transmission is the most common serial transmission technique. Serial data are often divided into groups of bits called *characters*. In asynchronous serial transmission, characters may occur one after another at the maximum transmission rate or may be separated by long pauses. Asynchronous transmission is natural for use by computer terminals. The operator will not always be typing at the maximum rate and long pauses may occur between keystrokes. Figure 10-18 shows the transmission of a single asynchronous character. The serial data line rests at 1 between characters. Every character begins with a single 0 bit, called a *start bit*. This start bit is needed so that the receiving station can tell that a new character is about to begin. After the

[1] John McNamara, *Technical Aspects of Data Communication*, Digital Equipment Corporation, Bedford, Mass., 1978.

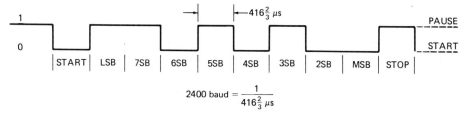

$$2400 \text{ baud} = \frac{1}{416\frac{2}{3}\ \mu s}$$

Figure 10-18 Asychronous serial character.

start bit, 8 data bits are transmitted. The bits are interpreted as if the least significant bit is transmitted first. Finally, a single 1 bit, called a *stop bit*, is transmitted. The stop bit marks the end of the character. Another start bit may occur immediately after the stop bit. Otherwise, the serial data line may remain at 1 for a longer time until another character is to be transmitted.

The *baud rate* is a measure of speed of transmission and is equal to the reciprocal of the time any single bit is transmitted. The baud rate for the system sending the character of Fig. 10-18 is 2400 baud. In this example, each character has 10 bits: a start bit, 8 data bits, and a stop bit. The character rate is the baud rate divided by the number of bits in a character. For this example, the character rate is 240 characters per second. Some mostly mechanical printers require 2 stop bits rather than 1. These teleprinters most often operate at 110 baud and 10 characters per second.

You might wonder how the receiving interface can find each bit since no clock signal is transmitted to locate the bits. The receiving interface must know the baud rate of the transmitting circuit. The receiving interface is an ASM that looks for the 1-to-0 transition of the start bit. After a 1-to-0 transition is located, the ASM waits for one half the bit time to locate the center of the start bit, as shown in Fig. 10-19. The ASM checks to make sure the data wire is still 0. The interface could have been started by a noise pulse, rather than a start bit. If the data line is still 0 at the half bit time, the receiving interface waits one whole bit time to find the center of the next bit. The receiving interface samples each data bit at the center of its bit time. Sampling data at the center of each bit minimizes the chance for error due to distortions of the bits caused by the transmission link. The data rates of the receiver and transmitter must match very closely. Any errors in timing will accumulate over the bits following the start bit since the receiving ASM is resynchronized only at each start bit. The last

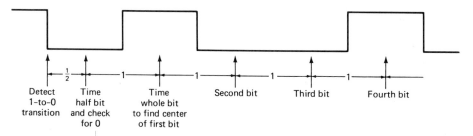

Figure 10-19 Receiving asynchronous data.

bits may be sampled at a position far from their center. Since the sampling circuitry of the receiver is a synchronous ASM, this ASM is only able to locate the exact time of the start bit's center to one of its own clock cycles. The receiver clock must be a large multiple of the baud rate if the receiver is to accurately locate the center of the start bit. One clever implementation of the receiver ASM uses both the rising *and* falling edges of a symmetrical clock signal to sample the serial data. Now, the center of the start bit can be located to one half of the ASM's clock cycle. Most commonly, the receiver ASM is designed so its clock rate is either 16 or 64 times the baud rate.

Data Codes

Since serial I/O is most often used with terminals and other devices using alphanumeric characters, a correspondence must be made between combinations of data bits and alphanumeric characters. This correspondence is called a code, and the alphanumeric data are said to be encoded in each of the serial characters. The most common code for microcomputers is the American Standard Code for Information Interchange or *ASCII* (pronounced as-key), as shown in Table 10-6. The first two columns of this table are *control characters*. Control characters specify nonprinting functions, like carriage return and line feed. The last six columns are called *printing characters* and are the actual alphanumeric data to be transmitted via the serial link.

These codes were not chosen randomly but were assigned very carefully. For example, you can test a single bit to differentiate between control and printing characters. A single bit distinguishes a lower-case letter from its upper-case equivalent. Very importantly, the BCD equivalent of the corresponding numeric character appears in the least significant 4 bits of the codes for the characters 0 through 9. As you can see from the code chart, only 7 data bits are required for any ASCII character. The eighth bit (most significant) in the asynchronous character is used for parity. No standard for the parity bit exists, although even parity is recommended (there should be an even number of 1s in all 8 data bits). In many simple applications, the parity bit is not used. Error-checking and-correcting schemes more complex than parity are often needed where errors can't be tolerated.

Modems

Serial systems are often used to send data over long distances. Data are most often sent via the telephone system. Most long-distance transmission systems, including the telephone system, will not accept digital signals directly. A *modulator* converts a digital signal to a form suitable for the transmission system. A *demodulator* converts the signal from the transmission system back to normal digital form. The combination of modulator and demodulator is called a *modem*. Modems are very common and are found wherever a computer terminal or computer must be connected to a phone line. There are many different kinds of modems. One of the simplest kinds converts the digital signals to tones. A 1 bit is converted to one tone, while a 0 bit is converted to a different tone. These tones are easily transmitted over a phone line. This transmission technique is called *frequency shift keying* or *FSK*.

Table 10-6 ASCII code table

Control characters		Printing characters					
00 NUL	10 DLE	20 SP	30 0	40 @	50 P	60 '	70 p
01 SOH	11 DC1	21 !	31 1	41 A	51 Q	61 a	71 q
02 STX	12 DC2	22 "	32 2	42 B	52 R	62 b	72 r
03 ETX	13 DC3	23 #	33 3	43 C	53 S	63 c	73 s
04 EOT	14 DC4	24 $	34 4	44 D	54 T	64 d	74 t
05 ENG	15 NAK	25 %	35 5	45 E	55 U	65 e	75 u
06 ACK	16 SYN	26 &	36 6	46 F	56 V	66 f	76 v
07 BEL	17 ETC	27 '	37 7	47 G	57 W	67 g	77 w
08 BS	18 CAN	28 (	38 8	48 H	58 X	68 h	78 x
09 HT	19 EM	29)	39 9	49 I	59 Y	69 i	79 y
0A LF	1A SUB	2A *	3A :	4A J	5A Z	6A j	7A z
0B VT	1B ESC	2B +	3B ;	4B K	5B [	6B k	7B {
0C FF	1C FS	2C ,	3C <	4C L	5C \	6C l	7C |
0D CR	1D GS	2D –	3D =	4D M	5D]	6D m	7D }
0E SO	1E RS	2E .	3E >	4E N	5E ^	6E n	7E ~
0F SI	1F US	2F /	3F ?	4F O	5F –	6F o	7F DEL

Most modems are *half-duplex* or *full-duplex*. A half-duplex modem may only transmit or receive data, but not transmit and receive simultaneously. The phone line or *channel* is not capable of simultaneous two-way transmission at the data rates desired. Both ends of such a transmission system must change transmission direction simultaneously. A *message* sent from one end of the system to the other signals the change of direction. Modems have control signals that allow the serial digital system to control their transmission direction. Full-duplex modems allow simultaneous two-way transmission. The channel might be better or the data rate slower so that simultaneous two-way transmission is possible.

SERIAL INTERFACE CIRCUIT

The serial interface circuit we'll use an an example is the 8251A. This circuit is called a *universal synchronous/asynchronous receiver/transmitter* or *USART*. The USART is very complex. Rather than list pages of facts about the USART's operation here, we'll refer you to the 8251's data sheet.[1] The USART can transmit or receive serial data asynchronously, without a data-synchronizing clock, or synchronously, with a data-synchronizing clock. We'll only discuss asynchronous operation.

Figure 10-20 is the block diagram of the USART. A bus interface communicates with the 8085 bus. This bus interface *does not* have address latching or decoding capability. A status register allows the microcomputer to read the condition of the other USART subsystems. Command and mode registers allow the microcomputer to control and initialize the USART. The command and status registers share the same address. The microcomputer outputs to the command register and inputs from the status register at the same address. The mode register also shares the same address!

---

[1]*MCS-85*[TM] *User's Manual. Peripheral Design Handbook*, Intel Corporation, Santa Clara, Calif., 1978.

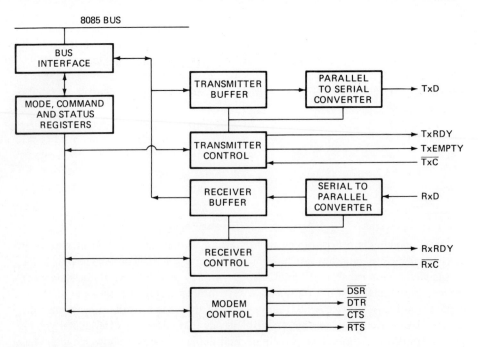

Figure 10-20 USART.

After a RESET signal from the microcomputer bus, the USART allows the micro-computer to output to the mode register once. After the mode register has been set, the USART allows the microcomputer to output only to the command register. The mode register is used to initialize USART parameters that will probably not change. Normally, the mode register need only be initialized once each time power is applied. In case the mode register must be reinitialized, a bit in the command register causes the USART to be reset internally so that the mode register may be changed again.

The mode register specifies that the USART will operate in either asynchronous or synchronous mode. In asynchronous mode, the baud-rate clocks (RxC and TxC) may be specified as being either 16 or 64 times the baud rate. The number of data bits in a character may be specified as 5, 6, 7, or 8. These data bits *do not* include the parity bit. The parity bit is separately enabled by a mode-register bit. If enabled, the parity bit is added to the data bits. The parity bit may be specified as even or odd. Finally, the number of stop bits may be specified as 1, $1\frac{1}{2}$, or 2. One stop bit is most common. Older systems have used $1\frac{1}{2}$ and 2 stop bits.

Three important subsystems are shown in Fig. 10-20. The *transmitter* converts parallel to serial data to be sent from the microcomputer system. Serial data received by the microcomputer system is converted to parallel data by the *receiver*. The *modem control* sends and receives digital signals from a modem. We will not discuss modem control signals. You may learn about these signals elsewhere.[1]

If the transmitter enable bit is sent to the command register, the signal *TxRDY* will become a 1, as shown in Fig. 10-21. The signal *TxRDY* or transmitter ready is usually connected to an interrupt and signals the microcomputer that the USART needs a new character. The microcomputer's interrupt routine outputs a character to the transmitter buffer. Signal *TxRDY* becomes a 0, indicating a character has been received. This data character will be transferred to the parallel-to-serial converter. Signal *TxRDY* will again become a 1 to interrupt the microcomputer to supply an-other character. If one character is to follow the next at the maximum data rate, the microcomputer must send another character to the transmitter buffer before the parallel-to-serial converter is finished with the character it is transmitting. The trans-mitter buffer simplifies data transfers by allowing the microcomputer to send a new character at any time during a one-serial-character time period. Without the buffer,

---

[1] McNamara, *Technical Aspects of Data Communication.*

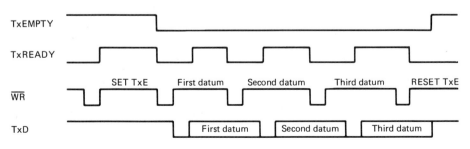

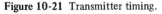

Figure 10-21 Transmitter timing.

the microcomputer would have to send the new character exactly when it was needed —not too soon and not too late.

The parallel-to-serial converter adds start, parity, and stop bits to the data bits from the transmitter buffer. These data are transmitted serially on the *TxD* or transmitter data output. Each bit is transmitted for either 16 or 64 times the clock period of input $\overline{TxC}$ or transmitter clock. Signal *TxE* or transmitter empty is a 1 only if *both* the transmitter buffer *and* parallel-to-serial converter are empty. The microcomputer must be able to tell when the parallel-to-serial converter is finished with the last character in a half-duplex system. The microcomputer must wait until this last character has been completely transmitted before changing the modem's transmission direction.

The microcomputer may disable the transmitter through the command register as soon as the last character has been sent to the transmitter buffer. The USART will not actually be disabled until the parallel-to-serial converter has finished with the last character. Unlike signal *TxRDY*, signal *TXE* is *not* disabled by the transmitter disable bit sent to the command register. If TxE is connected to the interrupt system, you'll probably want to be able to independently mask this interrupt. You can connect *TxE* to *RST5.5*, *RST6.5*, or *RST7.5*, or you can add external masking hardware. Both *TxRDY* and *TxE* may also be read through the status register. The *TxRDY status register bit* is not masked by the transmitter enable signal to the command register. Remember that the *TxRDY signal* is masked by disabling the transmitter. Finally, $\overline{CTS}$ must be a 0 to enable the transmitter. The signal $\overline{CTS}$ is the only modem control signal that directly affects USART operation. The other modem control signals are simply independent I/O bits that may be programmed for any desired function.

The receiver is enabled by sending the appropriate bit to the command register. The receiver looks for the beginning and middle of a start bit on input *RxD* or receiver data and assembles a character from the serial data, as has been described previously. This character is sent to the receiver buffer, and *RxRDY* or receiver ready becomes a 1, as shown in Fig. 10-22. The serial-to-parallel converter may now start assembling the next character. The signal *RxRDY* interrupts the microprocessor. The interrupt routine of the microcomputer reads the datum from the receiver buffer, automatically resetting *RxRDY* to 0. The microcomputer must read the datum in the receiver buffer before one-serial-character time period. Otherwise, the newly received character will

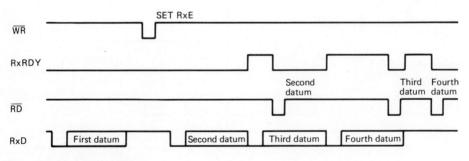

Figure 10-22 Receiver timing.

be transferred to the receiver buffer, and the first character will be lost. If a character is lost because the microcomputer didn't read it in time, the *overrun error* bit will be set in the status register.

Two other receiver errors can occur. These errors also appear in the status register. A *parity error* occurs if the received parity bit is not the correct parity specified by the mode register. A *framing error* occurs if a stop bit did not occur when expected. The receiver may have been enabled while a character was being prematurely transmitted. The receiver could have misinterpreted a 0 data bit for a start bit. Also, the channel (e.g., the phone line) could distort the serial signal so badly that character synchronization would be lost and the receiver could no longer find start or stop bits correctly. All 3 error bits are cumulative. After receiving an entire message, the microcomputer may check the status register to see if an error occurred anywhere in that message. The error bits are reset by sending an error reset bit to the command register. Finally, the signal *RxRDY* can be read through the status register. The *RxRDY status register bit* is *not* masked by the receiver disable bit of the command register. The *signal RxRDY* is masked when the receiver is disabled. The signal *RxRDY*, like the signal *TxRDY*, is ordinarily connected to the interrupt system.

PROGRAMMED SERIAL TRANSMISSION

Finally, remember that the USART could be replaced by programming the USART's functions for the 8085. The *SID* and *SOD* ports can be used for serial input and output, respectively. At slow data rates, a timer can be used for a regular clock interrupt to sample the serial data input at 16 times the input frequency. Alternately, the processor can use a time delay loop to sample the input. Of course, the processor may not do anything else in this latter case. At faster data rates, the processor must use time delay loops. The processor will spend most of its time processing serial data and have no time left for other functions. Even so, programmed serial I/O may be a useful and cost-effective technique in some applications. In fact, it is even possible to program the operation of the modem into the microcomputer.[1] The microcomputer can produce and sense the tones required.

PERIPHERALS

All digital systems must have peripherals to be useful. The system must do *something* to its environment and not just compute to itself. Microcomputers control traffic lights, solve scientific problems, write paychecks, etc. An unlimited variety of peripheral devices may be connected to a digital system; so we can only discuss some of the most commonly used peripherals here. Some common peripheral categories are mass-storage, human-language, and real-time peripherals.

[1]John Whorton, *Using the Intel 8085 Serial I/O Lines, AP-29*, Intel Corporation, Santa Clara, Calif., 1977.

MASS-STORAGE PERIPHERALS

Sometimes, the memory requirements of a microcomputer system are very large. Since millions or even hundreds of millions of bytes of RWM would be prohibitively expensive, mass-storage peripherals have been developed that store large amounts of data inexpensively. Mass-storage peripherals are usually much slower than RWM.

The memory of a complex digital system is often represented as a hierarchy. The normal RWM is called primary memory. The data in primary memory are most easily accessed. Additional data are stored in secondary memory, such as a magnetic disk. These data are not as easily accessible as the data in RWM. Data in secondary memory are transferred to primary memory, and vice-versa, as required. Other data may only be needed once in a great while. Such *archival* data may only be accessed once each week, month, or year! Other data may have to be exchanged among other computers. These data are stored in tertiary memory, such as magnetic tape or removable magnetic disks.

Magnetic Disk and Tape

One common mass-storage technique stores data as a magnetic pattern. This pattern is impressed into a disk covered with a metallic oxide or into a flexible tape, much like home recording tape. The pattern is written onto the recording media or read from it by an array of electric coils called a head. The magnetic recording media are physically moved past the head by electric motors. As the media move past, the *write head* generates a magnetic field, which represents the sequence of data bits sent to it. The data are recorded serially on the magnetic media. The *read head* generates an electric signal, which varies according to the magnetic pattern on the recording media. The output of the read head is the serial data recorded on the disk. Data must be encoded in such a way that they will be compatible with the magnetic characteristics of the media. Read and write electronics encode and decode the data as well as provide proper electric levels for the magnetic heads. Several ways are commonly used to encode the data. Common encoding methods are *NRZI* or *NonReturn to Zero Inverted* and *PE* or *Phase Encoding*. The encoding method will affect the cost of the system, the amount of data that can be put on the media (data density), and the probability of an error when reading the data (error rate).

Since mechanical motion is involved in reading and writing data, you probably have guessed that data rates can be relatively slow. More importantly, the time to find or access a datum will be slow. A magnetic disk may require a full revolution (about 16 ms) if the data to be accessed have just passed the heads.

Data are recorded as concentric tracks on the disk's surface. Each track could have its own read and write heads. These disks are called *fixed-head disks*. It is less expensive to use only one head that moves back and forth across the disk's surface to access the desired track. These disks are called *moving-head disks*. One of the lowest-performance and least-expensive disk systems is the *floppy disk*, shown in Fig. 10-23. The medium is actually a flexible magnetic disk that looks like a small phonograph record. The floppy disk is removable. A floppy disk system is very slow. As much as 1 s may be needed to position the head over the desired data.

A floppy disk drive. The disk is inserted in the slot at the right. Disk drive and head positioning motors are at the left. (*Memorex Corporation.*)

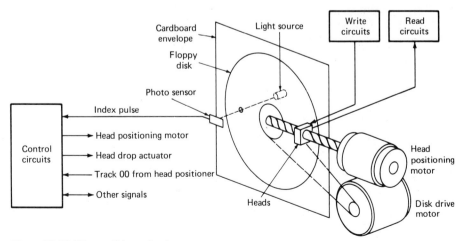

Figure 10-23 Floppy disk mechanism.

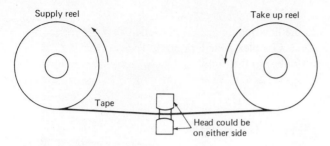

Figure 10-24 Tape mechanism.

All magnetic tape systems move tape past a read or write head, as shown in Fig. 10-24. The tape may be packaged in various ways. Figure 10-25 shows three common tape packages. The reel of $\frac{1}{2}$-in.-wide tape is the most-expensive and highest-performance system. The tape cassette is the least-expensive and lowest-performance system. The tape cartridge is an intermediate-performance system. Magnetic tape systems may require very long times to access data. Many seconds or even minutes may be required to access data on a 2400-ft reel of tape.

Figure 10-25(*a*) Half-inch computer tape on reel. (*b*) Cassette computer tape. (*c*) Cartridge computer tape. (*3M Company.*)

Data must be moved efficiently to and from the microcomputer system. A long time may be needed to access the data required. It is important that the microcomputer not have to wait for data. Complex programs are written to facilitate these data transfers. No program can look into the future to determine the data that will be required. The programmer must design the system so that advance notice of data needed is given to the disk or tape peripheral. The required data will then be available when needed.

Once the head is positioned over the required data, data transfers occur rapidly. Data transfers are often so rapid that the interrupt system can't be used to request the microcomputer's help in transferring data. Magnetic tapes and disks usually move data to and from memory without the help of the processor. Direct data movements between a peripheral and memory is called *DMA* or *direct memory access.* Since DMA transfers don't require the microprocessor, it is free to perform other functions. The tape or disk subsystem can be instructed to search for the required data and transfer those data to memory while the microcomputer system is performing other functions. Tape and disk controllers are very complex, often containing microcomputers themselves. Single IC controllers (e.g., the 8271) are available for floppy disks.

CCDs and Magnetic Bubbles

Mechanical storage systems, such as tapes and disks, suffer from several problems. Mechanical subsystems are usually not as reliable as electronic subsystems. Wear, vibration, dust, temperature, and humidity adversely affect the operation of mechanical devices. Mechanical subsystems weigh more and consume more power than electronic systems. You might expect that all electronic systems should be less expensive. The manufacturing process for electronic components is more efficient than the manufacturing process for mechanical components. In fact, electronic replacements for mechanical memories exist. In the past, these electronic mass-storage systems have been more expensive than their mechanical counterparts. Electronic mass memories were only considered where environmental factors precluded the use of mechanical memories. The cost of electronic mass storage is declining. Small disk systems are more likely to be replaced first by electronic mass storage. The cost of read-write electronics, motors, and other mechanical components is a larger percentage of the cost of a smaller disk system. The cost per bit of small disk systems is higher than the cost per bit of large disk systems. The cost per bit of electronic mass storage is almost constant as system size changes.

The first commercial use of large semiconductor memories was in computer terminals. Long semiconductor shift registers were used to remember the characters being displayed on the computer terminal's screen. These shift-register memories used the same technology (MOS) as is now used for microcomputers, ROMs, and RWMs. Thus, RWMs soon replaced shift registers in computer terminals.

The shift register is well-suited for implementing large memories for two reasons. First, since no address inputs are required, many bits may be enclosed in a small IC package with few pins for interconnections. Second, the shift register's structure is more easily fabricated than an addressable memory. Two new technologies are

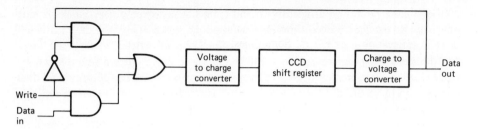

Figure 10-26 CCD shift register.

especially suited to fabricating large shift-register memories. Both *charge-coupled devices* or *CCDs* and *magnetic bubbles* can be used to fabricate large shift registers.

Charge-coupled devices store bits of information as packets of electric charge. These packets of charge are moved by an alternating electric field. This charge would eventually dissipate owing to small unavoidable losses. The shift register of Fig. 10-26 keeps data recirculating so that the voltage-to-charge converter on the shift register's input continually generates fresh charge packets. This shift register must be designed so that enough charge is left at the shift register's output to allow the charge-to-voltage converter to tell the difference between a 0 and 1.

Magnetic-bubble memories use small magnetized areas, called bubbles, to represent data bits. An alternating electric field causes the bubbles to shift down the register. A constant magnetic field must also be supplied by an external magnet. Magnetic bubble memories are nonvolatile. That is, the magnetic bubbles do not disappear when power is turned off. CCD memory systems must include a battery if data must be retained after power is turned off. Most magnetic-bubble memories require an external magnet. The CCDs are completely monolithic and can be manufactured without the additional mechanical fabrication of a magnet assembly.

HUMAN-LANGUAGE PERIPHERALS

Peripherals that input and output data via English or some other human language have existed for a long time. In fact, one of the first large-scale uses of digital signals was reporting stock market transactions on printed tape.

A *computer terminal* is the most common human-language peripheral. A terminal ordinarily consists of both an input and an output device. The input device is almost always a keyboard. The output device may be either a *hard-* or *soft-copy* device. Hard-copy devices produce a permanant physical record of the output data. This physical medium is most often paper but can also be photographic film. Soft-copy devices display data as lighted characters, and no permanent record is produced. A hard-copy terminal without a keyboard is also called a printer. We will examine some of the most common types of terminals. Many other types exist.

Hard-Copy Terminals

The first hard-copy terminals were similar to typewriters. The impact of a formed character on an inked ribbon created an image on paper. One character is printed at a time as the *carriage* moves across the paper. Many variations of this technique exist today. Instead of individual fabricated characters, whole *character sets* are fabricated as balls, wheels, and cylinders. Sometimes, the character set is removable so that it may be changed. Typewriter-like printers produce high-quality images but at low speed. Printing an entire line simultaneously without a moving carriage will increase printing speed. A cylinder or *drum* has formed images for every character at *each position* on the paper. This drum rotates at high speed, making one revolution for each line to be printed. Print hammers at each print position form the correct image. The hammers impact the paper when the proper character is positioned over the hammer. An entire line may be printed simultaneously (in one drum revolution). This mechanism is called a *line printer*. Characters may also be fabricated as a chain or belt. The quality of the images formed by a line printer is not as good as that of the images formed by a character printer.

An impact *matrix printer* is faster than a typewriter-like printer yet slower than a line printer. Each character is formed by imprinting a pattern of inked dots on the paper. As shown in Fig. 10-27, a carriage transports an array of solenoids and metal

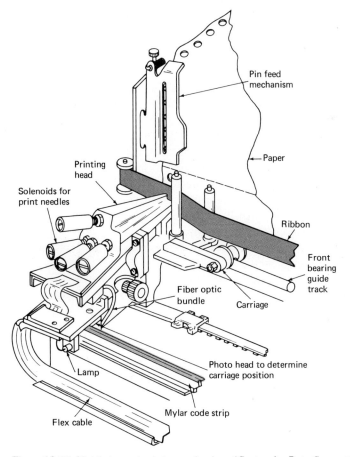

Figure 10-27 Matrix impact printer mechanism. (*Centronics Data Computer Corp.*)

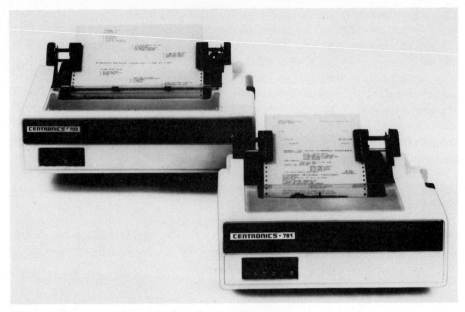

Impact matrix printers. (*Centronics Data Computer Corp.*)

needles (print hammers) across the page. The solenoids are activated by a microcomputer controlling the printer. Each solenoid causes a needle to strike the inked ribbon and make a dot on the paper. Any character may be formed by activating the solenoids in the correct order. The character patterns are stored in a ROM. Changing this ROM will change the character set used by the printer. A single printer can print in a number of different alphabets. The quality of the printed character can be varied by increasing the number of dots used to form the character. Upper-case English-language characters require a minimum of 35 dots in a matrix that is 5 dots wide and 7 dots high, as shown in Fig. 10-28. A 7 × 9 matrix forms better-looking characters and can also form lower-case characters. A few matrix printers have so many dots that different type styles may be selected. Matrix impact printers are often the most reliable and cost-effective of all types of impact printers.

Hard copy may be obtained without an impact in several ways. Nonimpact printers are quieter than impact printers. Since a nonimpact printer has fewer moving

Figure 10-28 5 × 7 character matrix.

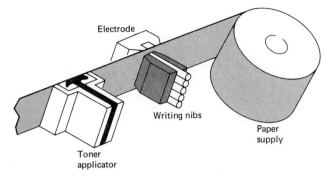

Electrode

Writing nibs

Paper
supply

Toner
applicator

Figure 10-29 Electrostatic printer mechanism. (*Versatec, A Xerox Company.*)

parts, it can be expected to be more reliable. In addition, nonimpact printers can be built that are faster than impact printers. Nonimpact printers almost always form characters by the matrix method. Many image-forming techniques are used. We will discuss only two common techniques used for generating an image on paper. A thermal printer uses electrically controlled heaters to form each character on heat-sensitive paper. The paper darkens when exposed to heat. Thermal printers are inexpensive. Image quality is not as good as other methods. The image may degrade after being printed, especially if the paper is exposed to high temperatures.

An electrostatic printer, shown in Fig. 10-29, uses a linear array of needles or *nibs* extending the width of the paper. Each needle may deposit a small dot of electrical

An electrostatic printer and plotter. (*Versatec, A Xerox Company.*)

charge on the specially treated paper. The charged paper is run past a *toner* applicator. The toner chemical adheres to the charged areas of the paper to form the image. Electrostatic printers can be very fast and relatively inexpensive. A wide variety of models is available, handling paper widths from inches to 6 ft! Almost all nonimpact image-forming techniques share a common problem. Special paper is required for operation of the printer. Special papers are still more expensive than ordinary paper, even though their cost has been declining.

Graphics

Matrix printers are easily adapted to graphics since any dot in the matrix may be printed or not. Some impact and electrostatic matrix printers have such a fine matrix that they can print solid-black block characters and even reproduce half-tone photographs. Graphics may be output with pen and ink plotters. Plotters actually draw the graph by moving a motor-driven pen across the paper. Plotters are very slow and expensive but do generate high-quality drawings. If both high-speed and good-quality output is required, photographic imaging techniques may be used. A very fine matrix of lighted dots is recorded on photographic film.

SOFT-COPY TERMINALS

A *CRT terminal* or *cathode-ray-tube terminal* forms characters as glowing phosphor dots on the face of a television-like tube. Most CRT terminals use the matrix technique

A CRT terminal with graphics capability. A cartridge tape drive is located on the right of the screen. This terminal also contains an integral microcomputer. (*Tektronix, Inc.*)

for forming characters. CRT terminals can display graphics. Some terminals can display more than one color simultaneously. Color can be very useful. For example, emergency messages can be flashed on and off in red characters. CRT terminals are inexpensive and reliable and are often used as computer input-output devices.

If higher-quality images are required, CRT terminals can actually draw continuous lines, rather than use a matrix of dots. The television tube in a CRT terminal is bulky, heavy, unreliable, subject to breakage, power-consuming, and interfaced with difficulty. Some alternatives have been developed, although none has yet achieved the popularity of the CRT. Plasma, light-emitting diode, and liquid-crystal displays may all be arranged to form a dot matrix and used to form characters and graphs under computer control.

REAL-TIME INTERFACE ELEMENTS

Control Panels

Very often, a traditional computer terminal is not the best solution to operator communication in a microcomputer system. In a simple system, an application-specific control panel may be the best solution. Only a few switches and indicators may be required. A control panel will be less expensive than a computer terminal. Unskilled operators will find the control panel easier to operate. A simple control panel will be more reliable than a terminal since the control panel has fewer parts (assuming equal quality). Microcomputer-controlled sewing machines, microwave ovens, and digital voltmeters use simple control panels.

Application-specific control panels are also useful in very complex systems. A skilled operator would not be able to efficiently operate the system without a specialized control panel. Such a control panel may be very sophisticated. This control panel could include one or more CRT displays, indicator lights, keyboards, switches, and even a touch-sensitive interface to sense where the operator's finger touches the CRT display. Such a complex control panel is difficult to design. The electric interface is easily solved, but the human interface is not easily defined. Complex application-specific control panels are used in process control (oil refineries, etc.) and in sophisticated instrumentation, like logic analyzers.

It may be necessary to interface a microcomputer to a wide variety of electrical, mechanical, hydraulic, pneumatic, or other type of equipment. Fortunately, most such interfaces required may be divided into four categories: discrete output (*DO*), discrete input (*DI*), analog output (*AO*), and analog input (*AI*). The terms *discrete* input and output refer to on/off signals to and from the microcomputer. These are simple boolean variables, but we prefer to call them *discrete* rather than *digital* to avoid any confusion with the myriad of internal digital signals. The terms *analog* input and output are commonly used to describe continuous signals. These analog signals are proportional to the value that is to be represented. Although other techniques are possible, an analog signal is usually a voltage or current whose value is proportional to a physical variable, like temperature, flow or voltage.

Transducers convert one form of energy into another. A *sensor* may convert heat energy to electric energy. A voltage proportional to temperature allows the microcomputer to know the temperature of a chemical process. An *actuator* may convert electric to mechanical energy. A voltage may open a valve and allow the microcomputer to direct cooling water to an overheated chemical reaction. A large variety of transducers are available.

Discrete Outputs

The individual bits of an output port are discrete outputs. Most of the time, these bits will not have sufficient voltage or current for the application desired. Many discrete-output interfaces are transistors that boost current or voltage to the required level. Even transistors have voltage and current limitations; so other techniques are necessary. Also, *alternating-current* or *ac* signals must often be controlled from the *dc* or *direct-current* outputs of the microcomputer's ports.

The earliest method of switching large voltages or currents, both ac and dc, was the *electromechanical relay*. A small dc voltage is applied to an electromagnet. The resulting magnetic field attracts a metal contact arm. The contact arm physically moves to touch another contact and close the circuit to be controlled. Mechanical relays are expensive and subject to wear and failure.

A *solid-state relay* or *SSR* has been developed to replace the mechanical relay. Most SSRs use a semiconductor component called a *Triac* to control only ac signals.

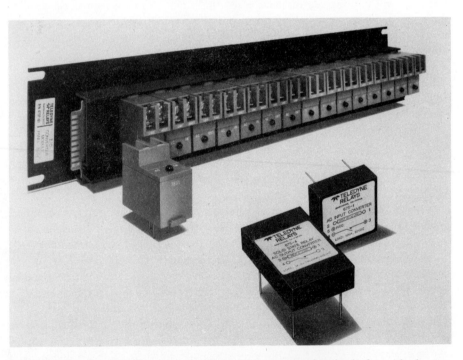

Solid state relays for controlling large ac voltages and input conversion circuits for sensing large ac voltages. The circuits at right are soldered to a PC board; the circuits at left mount in the rack shown. (*Teledyne Relays.*)

Some SSRs will control large dc signals, but these are not very common. As is the case with many interface subsystems, you may purchase complete SSRs, as well as design and construct them yourself. Standard SSRs will control a few hundred volts at a few tens of amperes. You must design your own SSR or use a mechanical relay if you must control higher voltages or currents. Designing reliable and safe circuits for high voltages and currents is difficult.

Discrete Inputs

The individual bits of an input port are discrete inputs. As before, the voltage levels of these inputs may not be compatible with the discrete input to be sensed. Electronic conversion circuits for inputs are simpler than output conversion circuits. Discrete-input conversion circuitry is less often purchased as a complete subsystem.

Input conversion circuitry may perform a variety of functions: reduce voltage levels, convert ac to dc signals, eliminate large transient voltages, and debounce mechanical contacts.

Electric Isolation

Microcomputers often measure or control lethal voltages and currents. The mechanical relay is an electrically isolated system. Its output contacts have no electric connection to its input signal, applied to the electromagnet. Any dangerous voltages are isolated from the microcomputer system. The magnetic field in a relay transmits the datum through the relay without an electric connection.

Special provisions must be made in all electronic devices like SSRs and discrete-input conversion circuits in order to provide electric isolation. Electronic devices are often isolated with optical couplers, which use light as the isolating medium. Transformers, which use a magnetic field, are also used for electric isolation.

Electric isolation is often used even where safety is not a concern. Electric noise from external sources may be prevented from entering the microcomputer system by isolating its inputs and outputs. Analog signals may be electrically isolated. Electric isolation of analog signals requires much more complex circuits than isolation of discrete signals.

Analog Output

Often, a voltage that is proportional to a binary number calculated by the microcomputer must be generated. This voltage is used to control an actuator that requires proportional control (e.g., a valve), rather than simple on/off control. Although some actuators require a pulse whose period or frequency is proportional to the binary value, we will limit our discussion to voltage analogs, rather than time analogs.

Digital-to-analog converters are components that generate an analog output voltage proportional to a digital code. Digital-to-analog converters are also called *DACs* and D/A converters. Most DACs are purchased as complete subsystems. Many DACs are fabricated as single monolithic integrated circuits. Very-high-performance

DACs may be *hybrid integrated circuits*, consisting of many individual ICs wired together in a single IC package. A 3-bit DAC may have the following output voltages.

Input	Output
000	0
001	1.25
010	2.5
011	3.75
100	5.0
101	6.25
110	7.5
111	8.75

This converter would be specified as having a 0- to 10-V output, even though its maximum output falls one LSB short of 10 V. *Resolution* is the measure of the fineness of division of the analog voltage. For this converter, resolution could be specified as 3 bits or as 1 part in 8 or as 1.25 out of 10 V. This converter is unipolar because it has only positive outputs proportional to a *straight* or *unsigned binary* code. Bipolar converters' outputs can be positive or negative and are proportional to a two's-complement code. We haven't specified the *accuracy* of this converter. Accuracy is a measure of how close the actual voltages are to the ideal voltages in the above table. Many other parameters must be specified for a digital-to-analog converter, including several types of *linearity*, *drift* with time and temperature, *power supply sensitivity*, and *speed*.

Common output ranges are 0 to 10 V for unipolar converters and −10 to +10 V for bipolar converters. Ranges of 5 and 2.5 V are sometimes used. Resolutions of 8, 10, and 12 bits are most common. Converters of 16 or more bits are rare. Sometimes, the output of a converter will be a current, rather than a voltage. A popular industrial control standard uses a current signal of 4 to 20 mA.

Don't forget that you must change all the DACs inputs simultaneously if you require a smooth transition of the output voltage. In Fig. 10-30, the least significant 8

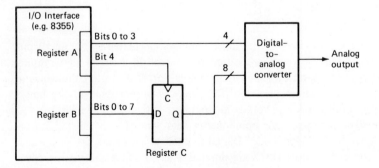

Figure 10-30 Interfacing a 12-bit D/A converter.

bits of a 12-bit value are first put into port register *B*. Next, the most significant 4 bits are put into port register *A*. Simultaneously, bit 4 of register *A* is set to 1. Bit 4 loads register *C* with the least significant 8 bits. The DAC sees all 12 bits change simultaneously.

Analog Input

Even more common than the need for a proportional output is the requirement for a proportional input. A large number of transducers have voltage outputs proportional to the value of the variable they are measuring. The electric output characteristics of transducers vary greatly, but circuitry can be designed or purchased to convert transducer outputs to a voltage in the range of -10 to $+10$ V or a current of 4 to 20 mA.

Analog-to-digital converters, also called ADCs or A/D converters, convert a voltage to its digital equivalent. Most analog-to-digital converters compare a known to an unknown voltage to determine the unknown. The most common technique is *successive approximation.*

Figure 10-31 is a simplified successive-approximation A/D converter. This converter compares an unknown voltage with the known voltage from a D/A converter. The comparison is done by a *comparator*. The comparator's digital output changes from 0 to 1 when the voltage on its plus input becomes more positive than the voltage on its minus input. Successive approximation is a technique that speeds this comparison by specifying in what order known voltages should be compared with the unknown. The microcomputer first sets the MSB of the D/A to a 1. All other bits are 0. The comparator will be 1 if the analog input is greater than half scale and 0 if the input is less than half scale. If the analog voltage is greater than half scale, we'll leave the MSB set to 1; otherwise, we'll reset the MSB to 0. After trying this first voltage, half the range of the D/A converter's output has been eliminated from consideration. Next, the microcomputer sets the 2SB of the D/A to split the remaining range in half again. The 2SB will remain set to 1 if the comparator output is 1; otherwise, the 2SB is reset to 0. Now, we know in which quarter of the D/A's range the unknown lies. Continue trying each bit in turn, successively dividing smaller ranges in 2. Finally, when the smallest range corresponding to the LSB has been tested, the microcomputer has determined the digital value corresponding to the unknown analog input. This

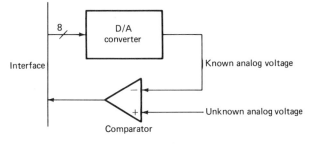

Figure 10-31 Software successive approximation A/D converter.

An analog to digital converter is at right center. Two digital to analog converters are above and slightly to the left of the A/D converter. Digital and analog interface circuits occupy the rest of the printed circuit. (*Burr-Brown Research Corp.*)

process requires one comparison step for each bit. An 8-bit converter always requires 8 steps, no more and no less, regardless of the value of the unknown.

A programmed successive-approximation converter is inexpensive but slow and wasteful of the processor's time. An IC ASM is manufactured that implements successive approximation, as shown in Fig. 10-32. This successive-approximation converter is available as a single component. We have assumed throughout our discussion that the unknown voltage does not change appreciably while it is being converted to digital form. In many applications, the unknown voltage could change while being converted. An additional circuit called a sample and hold (S/H) is shown in Fig. 10-32. A sample-hold circuit samples an analog voltage on its input and holds that voltage constant on its output for the time required for the conversion. After the conversion is complete, the S/H control signal from the microcomputer allows the S/H to retrieve a new sample for conversion. Analog-to-digital converters are complex devices and are often purchased as tested subassemblies.

Several other types of A/D converters are sometimes used. The *integrating converter* is very common, and several implementations have been developed. Integrating converters convert an unknown voltage to a proportional time period. The time period is measured by a clock and counter. Although much slower than successive-approxi-

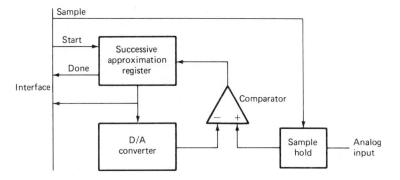

Figure 10-32 Hardware successive approximation register with sample/hold.

mation converters, integrating converters can be built with much higher resolutions. Integrating converters actually measure the average value of a voltage over a time period. Any noise voltage with a zero average value will not affect the output of the integrating converter.

Analog-to-digital converters are often used with other circuits, as shown in Fig. 10-33. *Filters* eliminate unwanted signals. An *analog multiplexer* switches several analog inputs into one A/D converter. An *amplifier* boosts the signals to a proper level before entering the S/H and A/D. A real-time clock starts the A/D converter at regular intervals. The A/D converter interrupts the processor after each conversion is complete. Designing an analog input system is a complex task. Fortunately, at least one good reference exists.[1]

[1] Patrick Garrett, *Analog Systems for Microprocessors and Minicomputers*, Reston Publishing Co., Reston, Va, 1978.

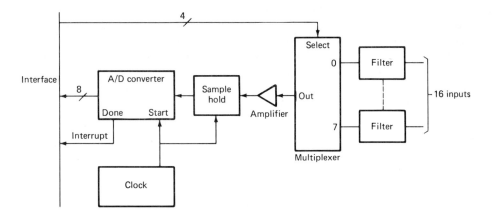

Figure 10-33 Typical A/D subsystem.

PERIPHERAL SOFTWARE

You may wonder how anything general can be said about peripheral software, considering the diversity of peripherals. Fortunately, peripheral data transfers can be divided into three categories. These categories are program-controlled, interrupt-initiated, and direct-memory-access data transfers. The program that controls the peripheral is called a *peripheral* or *device handler*. Most device handlers must perform four main functions:

1. Device initialization
2. Data transfer initiation
3. Data transfers
4. Data transfer termination

Device initialization usually occurs only once, when power is first applied. The interface, controller, and peripheral device may be completely initialized by the RESET signal. Usually, however, some options must be initialized by the microcomputer. The direction of I/O ports must be specified. Rates, formats, modes, and codes may be specified during device initialization. For the USART previously described, device initialization would consist of setting the mode register. For example, we would select asynchronous operation at a baud rate factor of 64, 1 stop bit, 7 data bits, and an even-parity bit.

Program-Controlled Transfers

The nature of the last three handler functions will depend on the type data transfer used. These three functions are shown in the flowchart of Fig. 10-34 for a program-controlled transfer. All three functions are combined in a single subroutine. The transfer-initiation section of this program initializes a counter that specifies the length of the array or *buffer* in memory into which data are to be transferred. The program also initializes the first address into which data are to be stored and starts the peripheral. The data-transfer segment of this subroutine repeatedly transfers data by waiting for the peripheral's *ready flag* bit. Data transfers are terminated in three ways. An error will terminate a data transfer. A separate error exit allows the main program to include an error recovery routine. An *end of message* signal from the peripheral indicates no more data are available. If the buffer fills up, the data transfer is also terminated. The termination segment of this subroutine passes the actual number of data transferred back to the main program and stops the peripheral.

Although some steps will depend on the peripherals, all program-controlled peripheral transfers proceed similarly. Program-controlled transfers are inefficient when the data transfer rate is slow. Most of the processor's time is spent waiting for the *ready flag* of the peripheral. We use interrupt-controlled transfers to make use of this waiting time.

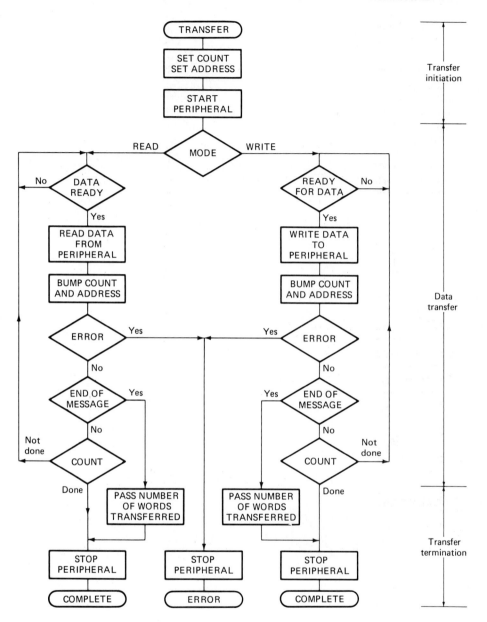

Figure 10-34 Program-controlled data transfer.

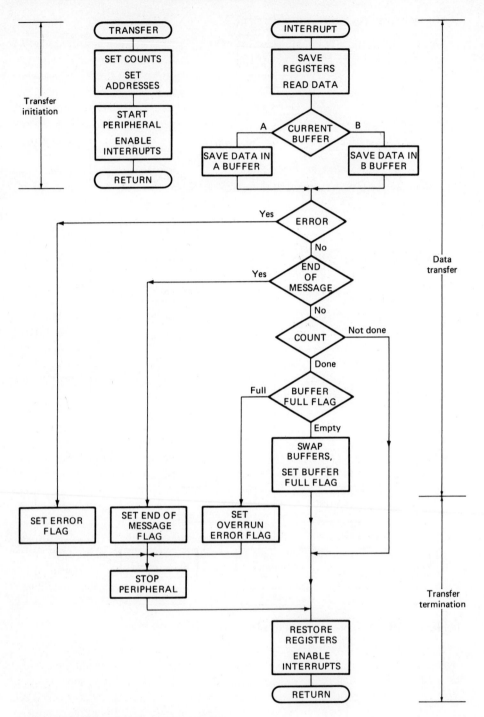

Figure 10-35 Interrupt-initiated data transfer.

Interrupt-Initiated Data Transfers

In Fig. 10-35, the transfer initiation section of an interrupt handler is a subroutine that initializes buffer lengths and addresses. This initiation subroutine also starts the peripheral and enables the peripheral's interrupt. Usually, the main program is given the responsibility of enabling the processor's interrupt system. The processor is now free to perform other operations. When the peripheral requires a data transfer, it will interrupt the processor. The transfer and termination segments work like the equivalent program-controlled segments. Now, these segments are called by the interrupt, rather than a processor loop.

Often so many data are to be transferred that the microcomputer doesn't have sufficient RWM to hold all data simultaneously. Also, it would be wasteful for the processor to wait for all data to be received before starting to process some of it. If the processor is sending data, it should be able to prepare a new group of data to be sent even while the last group of data is being sent. The solution to all these problems is called *double buffering* and is also shown in Fig. 10-35. Two buffers are specified for data transfers. When one buffer is full, the buffers are swapped so that transfers can continue. A buffer full flag is set to signal the main program that another buffer of data must be processed. The main program must test the buffer full flag, process the data in the full buffer, and reset the buffer full flag before the buffer is needed again. If the buffer is needed before it has been processed, the termination segment sets an overrun flag. The overrun error flag indicates that data were arriving too quickly for the processor to handle. An end of message signal terminates the data transfer after all data have been transferred. Figure 10-35 is drawn to read data from a peripheral but could easily be changed to write data to a peripheral.

Direct-Memory-Access Transfers

DMA software is the simplest of all three methods because the entire data transfer function is performed by the DMA hardware. The transfer initiation subroutine of Fig. 10-36 sends the buffer address and length to the DMA interface. After the peripheral has been started, the DMA interface transfers data directly into memory without intervention of the processor. These periodic data transfers continue until the buffer is finished and an end of message signal or an error occurs. The DMA interface interrupts the processor when transfers stop. This interrupt causes the termination routine to be executed. The termination routine determines the reason the data transfers were terminated and passes that information to the main program via flags in memory locations.

Interface Method and Peripheral-Dependent Functions

Program-controlled transfers are usually used when cost is paramount and performance can be sacrificed. Sometimes, program-controlled transfers are used to transfer data from a device that is too fast for interrupt transfers. By writing a small efficient data transfer loop, program-controlled transfers may work, saving the cost of a DMA interface. Data rates of around 50,000 bytes/s are possible with the 8085. Maximum

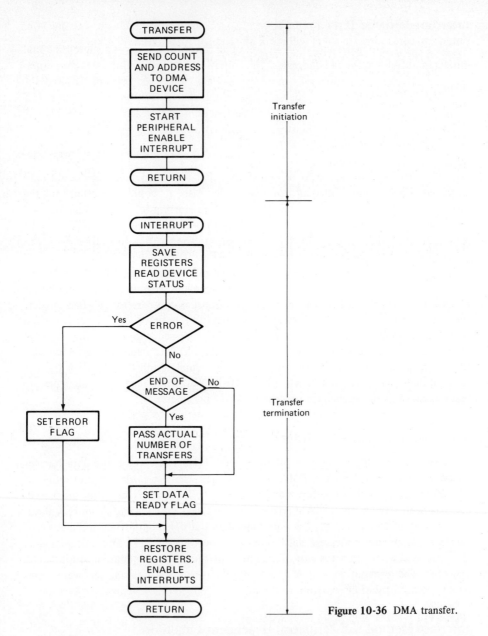

Figure 10-36 DMA transfer.

data rate is very much dependent on the design of both program and interface. Finally, program-controlled transfers are used when waiting times are known to be small. For example, a fast A/D converter requires only a few microseconds to supply data.

Interrupt-initiated transfers are the most common data transfer method. Interrupt transfers free the processor for other computation between data transfers. Interrupt transfers are also inexpensive to implement in peripheral hardware. On the 8085, interrupt-controlled transfers will work at rates up to 10,000 to 20,000 bytes/s. Data rates above these require program-controlled transfers or DMA transfers.

DMA transfers are used when fastest data rates are required. Magnetic disks and high-speed tape drives often use DMA interfaces. Data rates into the millions of bytes per second range are possible. DMA interfaces are sometimes used with slower peripherals to reduce software requirements. Interfacing a slow serial interface or an A/D converter sampling each millisecond by DMA is not necessary but may be desirable for two reasons. First, although a DMA interface must be designed, less software must be written. Second, the DMA transfers do not require processor intervention, and the processor will perform other tasks faster.

All peripherals have device-dependent functions. Disks must be sent track addresses. Tapes must be rewound. Analog-to-digital systems must be sent channel numbers. Printers must be checked to see if paper is present. These device-dependent functions are included in the peripheral's handler program. The handler should operate the peripheral as automatically as possible, relieving the main program of as many tasks as possible.

PROBLEMS

10-1 Figure P10-1 shows a partial timing diagram for the 8085's read cycle. We could consider three types of address registers: positive edge-triggered, negative edge-triggered, and positive level-enabled (i.e., a gated latch).

(*a*) Will all three registers work? If not, which ones won't work and why not?

(*b*) Of the types that will work, will one type let you operate the processor at full speed with a slower memory? Explain.

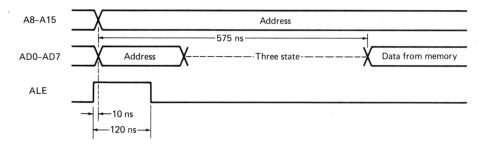

Figure P10-1 Partial timing diagram of 8085 read cycle.

10-2 Design an interface to the *INTR* input of the 8085. Use eight tristate buffers to put the *RST* instruction on the *AD* bus. Your interface should have an edge-triggered interrupt request input. Have the interrupt automatically cleared so the program *doesn't* have to clear the interrupt flip-flop explicitly with an I/O instruction. Don't forget power-on initialization.

10-3 Design an interface like the one in Prob. 10-2 except use the *RST6.5* input. Of course, you won't need the *RST* instruction. Is it possible to automatically clear this interrupt flop?

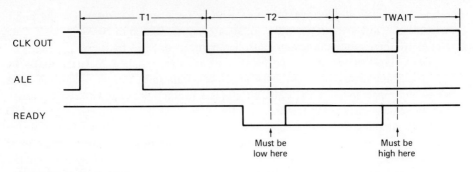

Figure P10-2 Ready input.

10-4 Figure P10-2 shows a partial timing diagram for the 8085's *READY* input.

(*a*) Design a circuit that will cause the 8085 to add one wait state to each of its machine cycles. The *READY* input is sensed on the rising edge of *CLK OUT* during states *T2* and *TWAIT*. The setup time for the *READY* input is 110 ns. The hold time is 0 ns. The clock period is 320 ns.

(*b*) What is the easiest way to change this circuit so that you may easily select some machine cycles to have a wait state and some not to have a wait state? Some peripherals and memory circuits may require a wait state while others will not.

10-5 A microcomputer system requires an A/D converter with a multiplexer and 10 inputs. The A/D must convert a new input every 200 μs. Thus, each input is converted every 2000 μs or 2 ms. Sketch the interface required and flowchart the software for the following cases:

(*a*) The ADC is interfaced via interrupt-initiated transfers.

(*b*) The ADC is interfaced via DMA. Don't forget that you need to time the conversions at 200-μs intervals. You must keep track of the channel numbers so that the analog multiplexer is sequenced through all 10 channels and data from these channels are put in the correct memory locations.

10-6 Draw the flowchart for an interrupt-initiated transfer that writes data to a peripheral. The transfer routine should be double-buffered.

10-7 Draw the flowchart for the software of a DMA interface that reads data from a peripheral. The transfer should be double-buffered.

ELEVEN

ADDITIONAL MICROCOMPUTERS

The 8085 is a medium-performance microcomputer for use in medium-size systems. Many other 8-bit microcomputers are similar to the 8085. These "average" 8-bit microcomputers evolved similarly to match the requirements of the most prevalent applications. As the scope of applications widened and the microcomputer industry became more sophisticated, new microcomputers evolved in new directions. In the first part of this chapter, we'll examine two microcomputers that represent the two major trends in microcomputer architecture. One of these trends is simply bigger and faster microcomputers. We'll examine the 8086 microcomputer. The 8086 is a very high performance 16-bit microcomputer for medium to very large size systems. Another equally important trend exists toward smaller microcomputers. The microcomputer we'll examine first in this chapter is the 8048. The 8048 is a completely integrated computer system. The processor, memory, I/O, and support functions are contained in a single integrated circuit. The 8048's performance is comparable to the performance of the 8085. Unlike the 8085, the 8048 is more suitable for very-small-size systems.

THE 8048 MICROCOMPUTER

The 8048 is a single integrated-circuit microcomputer system. The 8048 circuit includes the following subsystems:

An 8-bit processor
A 1024-byte ROM
A 64-byte RWM
Three 8-bit I/O ports

Two 1-bit input ports
One interrupt input
A timer/counter peripheral

We'll examine the 8048 in some detail, but you should read this processor's reference manual if you plan to use the processor.[1]

The 8048's memory is divided into two parts. The ROM is called program memory. The RWM is called data memory. Each memory has its own set of addresses. The program memory is shown in Fig. 11-1. Of the 1024 bytes available for instruction storage, 3 bytes have special functions. When the processor is first reset, it starts at location 0. An external interrupt causes the instruction at location 3 to be executed. A timer interrupt causes the instruction at location 7 to be executed. Program memory is divided into four pages of 256 bytes. Page 0 starts at location 0, while page 3 ends at location 3FFH.

The organization of data memory in Fig. 11-2 is much more unusual than program memory. With the exception of the single *A* register, all data registers are actually contained in RWM. Thus, eight registers, *R0* through *R7*, occupy the bottom eight

---

[1] MCS-48™ *Microcomputer User's Manual*, Intel Corporation, Santa Clara, Calif., 1976.

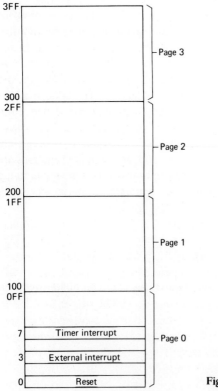

Figure 11-1 8048 program memory.

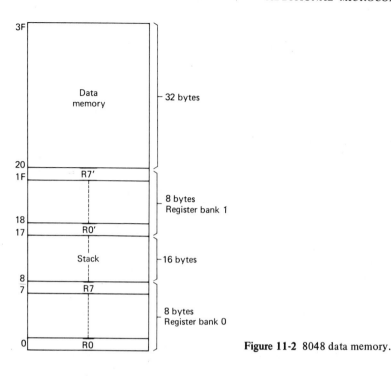

Figure 11-2 8048 data memory.

locations of RWM. An additional bank of eight registers, $R0'$ through $R7'$, occupies memory locations 18H through 1FH. The processor may use either bank of registers by executing a register-bank select instruction. The second register bank is often used by the interrupt program; so the primary registers will not have to be saved in RWM. The stack occupies RWM locations 8H through 17H. The stack is used only for the return addresses of subroutines and interrupts. Two bytes are required to store the 12-bit return address and four status flags. Thus, the 16-byte stack will store up to eight return addresses. No warning is given if too many return addresses are pushed on the stack. The stack pointer "wraps around"; so the first return address stored is destroyed by the ninth, etc. Finally, the top 32 bytes of RWM may be used for general data storage. Instructions that address RWM can access *all* of RWM. Any register or part of the stack that isn't needed may be used for general data storage.

Besides the A register and two sets of R registers, the 8048 has two user flag bits and a program status register. The user flags are called $F0$ and $F1$. These flags are single boolean variables that may be set, reset, and tested by the program. $F0$ and $F1$ simplify decision structures by allowing the program to control and test boolean flags with single instructions. The program status word is shown in Fig. 11-3. The *PSW* may be read and changed by explicit instructions, as will be seen later. The 4 most significant bits of the *PSW* are stored on the stack with the return address at every subroutine call or interrupt. These 4 bits may or may not be restored from the stack when the computer returns to the main program. The *carry* (*CY*) and *auxiliary carry* (*AC*) bits are like the corresponding bits of the 8085's flag register. User flag $F0$ is included in the status word. Because $F0$ is saved on the stack, it may be used by an interrupt

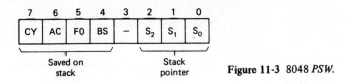

Figure 11-3 8048 *PSW*.

routine or subroutine. The original state of *F0* is restored when the computer returns to the main program. The *bank select (BS)* bit is 0 if the processor is using register bank 0 and is 1 if the processor is using register bank 1. If the main program uses both register banks, the correct bank must be restored after an interrupt routine.

The 8048 has two addressing modes. Immediate addressing is indicated by a # sign.

MOV   A,#F3H

This instruction moves the datum F3 in the second byte of the instruction to the *A* register. Register addressing is indicated by an @ sign. Only registers 0 and 1 may be used for register addressing.

MOV   A,@R1

This instruction moves a datum in RWM into the *A* register. The RWM address of the datum is contained in register *R1*.

Data Movement Instructions

Data may be moved between any register and the *A* register.

MOV   A,R3   Move R3 to A
MOV   R7,A   Move A to R7

Data may be moved between any RWM location and the *A* register.

MOV   A,@R0   Move RWM at R0 to A
MOV   @R1,A   Move A to RWM at R1

Immediate data may be put in the *A* register or any RWM location.

MOV   A,#C4H   Move C4H to A
MOV   @R1,#00H   Move 00H to RWM at R1

The program status word may be read into or changed from the *A* register.

MOV   A,PSW   Move PSW to A
MOV   PSW,A   Move A to PSW

Notice that you can't move data directly from one *R* register to another.

We must be able to retrieve data from the program memory ROM. Permanent data tables must be stored in ROM and not in RWM. Register addressing using the *A* register accesses program memory. Since an 8-bit register will address only 256 bytes, the 1024-byte program memory is divided into four pages. One data movement instruction allows data to be accessed on the page on which this instruction is located.

Thus, an instruction on page 0 will access data on page 0. Another data movement instruction always accesses data on page 3. Page 3 of the program memory could be used to store up to 256 bytes of data tables.

206H: MOVP   A,@A   Move current page data to A

This instruction is located on memory page 2. The A register contains D2H before this instruction is executed. This instruction will move the data byte stored at 2D2H in the ROM to the A register.

206H: MOVP3   A,@A   Move page 3 data to A

Even though this instruction is on page 2, it always accesses page 3 data. The A register contains D2H before this instruction is executed. This instruction will move the data byte stored at 3D2H in the ROM to the A register.

The 8048 has instructions that will exchange data between the A register and any other register or between the A register and any RWM location.

XCH   A,R2   Exchange A and R2
XCH   A,@R0   Exchange A and RWM at R0

One instruction exchanges only the least significant 4 bits of the A register and the least significant 4 bits of an RWM location. The most significant bits are not affected.

XCHD   A,@R1   Exchange the LSBs of A and RWM at R1

The letter D stands for *digit*, as this instruction is often used to move BCD digits. A 4-bit group is also called a *nibble*. This instruction might also be called an exchange-nibbles instruction.

Two instructions select the register bank to be used.

SEL   RB0   Select register bank 0
SEL   RB1   Select register bank 1

Of course, these instructions affect the bank-select (*BS*) bit in the *PSW*. None of the data movement instructions affect the *PSW*.

Boolean Instructions

The 8048 has all three common boolean functions: AND, OR, and exclusive OR. One operand of any boolean function is always in the A register. The result of the boolean operation is always placed in the A register.

ANL   A,R2   AND A with R2
ANL   A,@R1   AND A with RWM at R1
ANL   A,#83H   AND A with 83H
ORL   A,R5   OR A with R5
ORL   A,@R1   OR A with RWM at R1
ORL   A,#87H   OR A with 87H
XRL   A,R6   Exclusive OR A with R6
XRL   A,@R0   Exclusive OR A with RWM at R0
XRL   A,#84H   Exclusive OR A with 84H

The letter *L* in these mnemonics stands for *logical.* A logical AND is the same as a boolean AND. These instructions *do not* affect the *PSW*.

Instructions can clear or complement the *A* register, the carry bit, and the user flags.

CLR	A	Clear the A register
CPL	A	Complement the A register
CLR	C	Clear the carry bit
CPL	C	Complement the carry bit
CLR	F0	Clear user flag 0
CPL	F0	Complement user flag 0
CLR	F1	Clear user flag 1
CPL	F1	Complement user flag 1

The *CLR A* and *CPL A* instructions do not affect the *PSW*.

Rotate Instructions

Two instructions rotate the *A* register without affecting the carry bit.

RL	A	Rotate A left
RR	A	Rotate A right

These two instructions are similar to the *RLC* and *RRC* instructions of the 8085. Unlike the 8085's instructions, these instructions do not affect the carry bit at all! The *A* register is rotated one bit position. The bit rotated out one end of the *A* register is rotated in the other end. Two additional instructions rotate the *A* register with the carry bit.

RLC	A	Rotate A left through carry
RRC	A	Rotate A right through carry

These two instructions are identical to the *RAL* and *RAR* instructions of the 8085. The carry bit is shifted into the emptied bit position of the *A* register. The bit shifted out of the *A* register is stored in the carry bit.

One more 8048 instruction rearranges the bits in the *A* register.

SWAP	A	Swap nibbles of A

This instruction exchanges the least significant 4 bits of *A* with the most significant 4 bits of *A*. It can be used with *XCHD* for BCD manipulations. *SWAP* is equivalent to four rotates and can save time and instructions if long rotates are required. *SWAP* does not affect the *PSW*.

Branching Instructions

The 8048 has two unconditional branch instructions.

JMP	ADDR	Jump to ADDR
JMPP	@A	Jump indirect within page

The *JMPP @A* instruction is similar to the 8085's *PCHL* instruction. The 8 bits in the *A* register are loaded into the least significant 8 bits of the program counter. The most significant bits of the program counter are unchanged. We can calculate an address in the *A* register and use that address to access a branch table.

Four conditional branch instructions are similar to the 8085's instructions.

JC	ADDR	Jump if carry = 1
JNC	ADDR	Jump if carry = 0
JZ	ADDR	Jump if A register is 0
JNZ	ADDR	Jump if A register is not 0

Two conditional branch instructions allow the user flags to be tested.

JF0	ADDR	Jump if F0 is 1
JF1	ADDR	Jump if F1 is 1

Unlike the *JMP* instruction, these six instructions carry only 8-bit addresses. These 8 bits replace the 8 LSBs of the program counter. The MSBs are unchanged; so a branch occurs within the current page. Note that the *JZ* and *JNZ* instructions branch on the current contents of the *A* register since no *Z* bit exists in the *PSW*.

Testing boolean flags stored in a byte is often unwieldly and time consuming. A single 8048 instruction will test any of the 8 bits in the *A* register.

JB4	ADDR	Jump if bit 4 of A is a 1
JB7	ADDR	Jump if bit 7 of A is a 1

Only one instruction is required to test any bit. The original contents of the *A* register are unchanged since we didn't need a masking step to pick the bit we wanted to test.

You may have noticed that many program loops decrement a counter in a register and jump back if the register hasn't yet reached 0. The 8048 combines the decrement and jump if not zero functions into a single loop control instruction *DJNZ*. Simple repetition is easily implemented.

```
            MOV     A,#9          Put 9 in R2 to use as a loop counter
            MOV     R2,A
LOOP:        .
             .
             .
            DJNZ    R2,LOOP       Decrement R2 and jump back to
                                  LOOP if R2 isn't 0
```

Like the other conditional jump instructions, *DJNZ* branches only within the current page. The *DJNZ* instruction does not affect the *PSW*.

Input-Output Instructions

The 8048 has three 8-bit I/O ports called port 1, port 2, and *BUS* port. Ports 1 and 2 are bidirectional and may be transferred to and from the *A* register

IN	A,P2	Move port 2 data to A
OUTL	P1,A	Move A data to port 1

Input and output bits may be mixed in a single port. A 1 is output to any bit position to be used as an input. The output registers of ports 1 and 2 are wire-ANDable. A 1 output to a port will be ANDed with the external input to that port bit. The result of this AND is just the state of the external input which may be sensed by the *IN* instruction. To facilitate using input and output bits in the same port, the 8048 includes boolean I/O operations. One operand is the original contents of the I/O port. The other operand is an immediate datum. The result is always deposited in the I/O port.

ANL	P2,#FEH	AND P2 with FEH
ORL	P1,#80H	OR P1 with 80H

These instructions are especially powerful when single I/O bits must be manipulated. The above *ANL* instruction will reset bit 0 of port 2 without affecting the other bits. The above *ORL* instruction will set bit 7 of port 1 without affecting the other bits. Any output port bit may be independently set or reset!

As you might guess, the *BUS* port is special. The *BUS* port is used in expanded-mode operation that we'll discuss later. If you are not using expanded mode, you may use the *BUS* port similarly to ports 1 and 2. All the *BUS* port bits must be input or output. You cannot combine input and output bits on the *BUS* port!

INS	A,BUS	Move BUS data to A
OUTL	BUS,A	Move A data to BUS

The *INS* and *OUTL* instructions also output pulses on the $\overline{RD}$ and $\overline{WR}$ signals, respectively. Normally, these signals are not needed for simple I/O but are available if required. You may also perform boolean operations on the *BUS* port.

ANL	BUS,#73H	AND BUS with 73H
ORL	BUS,#78H	OR BUS with 78H

Unlike ports 1 and 2, you must perform at least one *OUTL BUS,A* instruction before using the *ANL* and *ORL* instructions on the *BUS* port.

The 8048 has two single-bit input ports called *test inputs*. Four conditional jump instructions make branching on these two inputs easy.

JT0	ADDR	Jump if test input 0 is 1
JNT0	ADDR	Jump if test input 0 is 0
JT1	ADDR	Jump if test input 1 is 1
JNT1	ADDR	Jump if test input 1 is 0

Like the other conditional branch instructions, these instructions have an 8-bit address and branch only on the current page.

Increment and Decrement Instructions

You may increment and decrement the *A* register and the *R* registers. You can also increment the contents of any memory location.

INC	A	Increment A
DEC	A	Decrement A

INC	R4	Increment R4
DEC	R7	Decrement R7
INC	@R1	Increment RWM at R1

The increment and decrement instructions do not affect the *PSW*.

Subroutine Instructions

As was previously explained, the 8048 has an eight-level stack for storing return addresses. A subroutine call pushes the return address and *PSW* bits 4 through 7 on the stack.

CALL	ADDR	Call subroutine at ADDR

The return instruction simply pops the return address off the stack into the program counter.

RET		Return from subroutine

The status bits previously saved on the stack are ignored. The *RET* instruction is used when the subroutine must communicate with the main program via the status bits. For example, the subroutine might set the carry bit if an error occurred. The main program could sense the carry bit to determine if an error occurred. Another return instruction pops the return address *and the status bits* off the stack into the program counter and *PSW*.

RETR	Return and restore status

The original status bits that existed before the subroutine call are restored to the *PSW*. This instruction is always used to return from interrupt routines, as will be explained later.

Arithmetic Instructions

One operand of all arithmetic operations is always in the *A* register. The result is always deposited in the *A* register.

ADD	A,R2	Add R2 to A
ADD	A,@R1	Add RWM at R1 to A
ADD	A,#40H	Add 40H to A
ADDC	A,R7	Add R7 and carry to A
ADDC	A,@R0	Add RWM at R0 and carry to A
ADDC	A,#44H	Add 44H and carry to A

The *ADD* and *ADDC* instructions of the 8048 operate identically to the *ADD* and *ADC* instructions of the 8085. These instructions affect the carry and auxiliary carry bits of the *PSW*. The 8048 does not have a subtract instruction. Subtraction is performed by two's complementing the subtrahend and adding it to the minuend. The 8048 will perform decimal addition.

DA	A	Decimal adjust A

The 8048's *DA A* instruction is identical to the *DAA* instruction of the 8085. The 8048 also has a *NOP* instruction.

Interrupt Instructions

Interrupts can be caused by applying a 0 to an external input pin or by an overflow of an internal timer. Both of these interrupts will disable the interrupt system and start execution of the interrupt routine. The external interrupt starts at location 3, while the timer interrupt starts at location 7. One way to assign registers is to dedicate register bank 0 to the main program and register bank 1 to the interrupt routine. Only the common *A* register must be saved by the interrupt routine. The interrupt system must be reenabled after the interrupt routine is done. The *RETR* instruction automatically enables the interrupt *if executed in an interrupt routine.* A typical interrupt routine might appear as follows.

INTR:	SEL	RB1	Use register bank 1
	MOV	@R0,A	Save the A register in RWM
	:		Interrupt processing includes an instruction that cancels the interrupt signal
	MOV	R0,#SAV	Restore the RWM address
	MOV	A,@R0	Restore the A register
	RETR		Return, restore PSW, and enable the interrupts

Three other interrupt system instructions exist.

EN	I	Enable external interrupt
DIS	I	Disable external interrupt
JNI	ADDR	Jump if $\overline{INT} = 0$

The *EN* and *DIS* instructions explicitly enable and disable the *external* interrupt. The *JNI* instruction tests the status of the external interrupt input $\overline{INT}$. The *JNI* instruction can test for a pending interrupt before enabling the external interrupt. If the interrupt system isn't being used, the $\overline{INT}$ input can be used as a third test input, along with *T0* and *T1*.

Clock Circuits

Before explaining the timer operation, it will be helpful to examine the clock circuits shown in Fig. 11-4. A frequency determining circuit may be a crystal and capacitors or an RC circuit. In one model of the 8048, the crystal frequency may be as high as 6 MHz. The RC circuit provides an approximate frequency of 3 MHz. A machine cycle consists of 15 clock cycles (2.5 µs at 6 MHz). All instructions have either one or two machine cycles. A signal called address latch enable (*ALE*) is output each machine cycle. The signal *ALE* is used in the expanded mode of operation, as will be discussed later. This same 2.5-µs signal is sent to the timer circuit of Fig. 11-5.

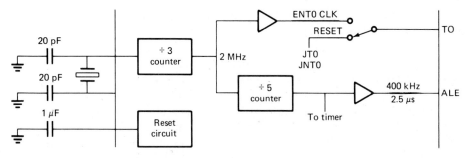

Figure 11-4 8048 clock circuits.

The 8048 has one clock control instruction.

ENT0   CLK

This instruction changes test input *T0* to a clock output. The clock frequency is the crystal frequency divided by 3. This output may be used to operate other circuitry. *T0* is restored as a test input when the processor is reset.

The reset circuit of the 8048 is simply a 1-μF capacitor connected to the $\overline{RESET}$ pin of the processor. There is no reset output.

Timer-Counter Instructions

The timer-counter circuit is shown in Fig. 11-5. Two instructions start this circuit.

STRT   T   Start timer
STRT   CNT   Start counter

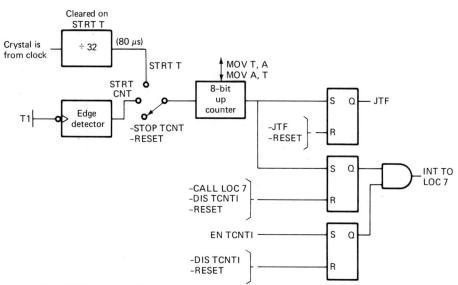

Figure 11-5 8048 timer circuit.

The *STRT CNT* instruction connects the 8-bit counter's input to input *T1* through an edge detector. The counter will count 1-to-0 transitions on the *T1* input. If the *STRT T* instruction is executed, the counter will count at a constant rate equal to the crystal frequency divided by 480 (80 μs for a 6-MHz crystal). The *STRT T* instruction also clears the 5-bit counter used to reduce the crystal frequency. This divide-by-32 counter is called a *prescaler*. Without the prescaler, an uncertainty of up to 80 μs could exist in the first timing interval. The instruction that starts the timer could be executed anywhere in an 80-μs timer clock interval. As much as 80 μs could elapse before the first count or as little as 0 μs. The prescaler is reset to 0 so that exactly 32 machine cycles (80 μs) will elapse after the timer is started before the first count.

The remaining timer-counter instructions are not affected by the clock source of the up counter.

STOP	TCNT	Stop timer-counter
MOV	A,T	Move timer to A
MOV	T,A	Move A to timer

The stop instruction simply stops the up counter from counting. The two *MOV* instructions allow you to retrieve or change the up counter's contents. Regardless of what signal is being counted, the up counter will eventually reach FFH. When the counter overflows to 00H, two flip-flops are set. One flip-flop can be tested and then reset by a branch instruction.

JTF	ADDR	Jump if timer flag = 1

This instruction carries an 8-bit address and will branch only to the current page. You would use this instruction if you did not use the timer interrupt. A second flip-flop, an interrupt flip-flop, is also set by the up-counter overflow. This flip-flop causes an interrupt to location 7. The timer interrupt is automatically canceled when the interrupt call to location 7 occurs. The timer interrupt may be enabled and disabled.

EN	TCNTI	Enable timer-counter interrupt
DIS	TCNTI	Disable timer-counter interrupt

The *DIS* instruction also resets the interrupt flip-flop, canceling any pending timer interrupt. If an external interrupt occurs simultaneously with a timer interrupt, the external interrupt will be serviced first. The timer interrupt will remain pending and will be serviced after the external interrupt routine is done.

With a 6-MHz crystal, the timer can provide delays of 80 μs to 20.48 ms. Longer delays can be generated by accumulating counter overflows in a register or memory location at each timer interrupt. Finer resolution is possible by using the counter mode and connecting *T1* to a higher-frequency external clock. The frequency of the signal connected to *T1* must be less than one-third the *ALE* frequency. Thus, you may connect a clock no faster than 7.5 μs per cycle to *T1* if you are using a 6-MHz clock.

The counter has other uses. You can preset the counter to the two's complement of a desired count. For example, we'll connect *T1* to an output from a magnetic-tape controller that pulses each time a new record is reached on the tape. If we want to search for the eighth record on the tape, we'll set the counter to −8 and wait for an overflow. The 8048 can perform other processing until interrupted when the eighth record is reached.

We can use the counter to accumulate totals. We'll connect *T1* to a photoelectric sensor counting beer cans at a brewery. Since we'd expect many more than 256 cans, we'll write a program that increments a large accumulator in RWM each time a counter interrupt occurs. The 8048 could simply display the total number of cans. The microcomputer could also stop the can conveyor after a preset number of cans had been counted.

Hardware

A single component 8048 system is shown in Fig. 11-6. We've already discussed most of the circuitry on this diagram. An 8048 system could be difficult to test since all its memory busses are internal and we can't monitor its operation. Several signals are shown in Fig. 11-6 that help test an 8048 system. The input *external access (EA)* forces the 8048 to fetch all its instructions from an external ROM via the *BUS* port. Program addresses and data are now available to external instrumentation. We have sacrificed the use of some I/O bits. The *single-step ($\overline{SS}$)* input may be used with *ALE* to execute one instruction at a time. Each time a button is pushed, the 8048 executes one instruction. In between instructions, the operator monitors and changes I/O lines to test program operation.

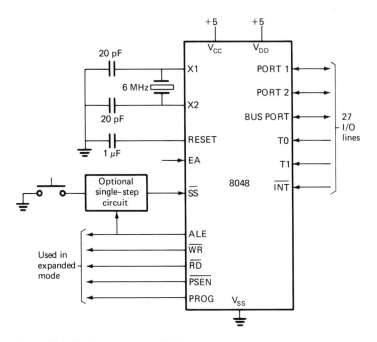

Figure 11-6 Single component 8048 systems.

You'll notice that the 8048 has two power supply inputs. The input marked *VDD* only supplies the RWM. If used correctly, this input can be connected to a battery to keep the RWM from forgetting even when power is lost. An interrupt from the power supply would make the 8048 store its *PSW*, *A* register, and any I/O data desired in RWM. As the main power supply voltage dropped to 0, a battery would allow the RWM to remember the correct status for restarting when main power was reapplied.

Since the 8048 has a ROM, expensive tooling operations and large orders are required to justify production. To aid in evaluation of prototypes and make possible small quantity production, an EPROM version of the 8048 is called the 8748. The 8748 works almost identically to the 8048 with a few exceptions. The 8748 uses the program (*PROG*) and *VDD* pins to program the EPROM. *PROG* is shared with another function yet to be described. Power input *VDD* can't be shared with the battery backup system. The 8748 does not have the RWM battery backup capability of the 8048.

Expanded 8048 System

Program memory, data memory, and I/O may all be expanded on the 8048. Expansion of each of these resources requires both suitable hardware and instructions to access the expanded system. All three resources may be expanded simultaneously. Take care to consider fan out and timing parameters in an expanded system. Consult the 8048 manual before undertaking a design, either single component or expanded.[1]

The 8048 contains a 12-bit program counter. A program could have a *CALL* or *JMP* instruction that changes the program counter to an address greater than 3FFH. The processor will automatically try to fetch instructions externally when the program counter exceeds 3FF. The 8048 puts the most significant 4 address bits on the least significant 4 bits of port 2. The least significant 8 address bits are put on the *BUS* port and latched externally by an *ALE* pulse. The signal *program store enable* (*PSEN*) is issued to enable the external ROM's three state outputs, as shown in Fig. 11-7. The most significant bit of the 12-bit program counter does not count with the least signifi-

[1]MCS-48^{TM} *Microcomputer User's Manual*, Intel Corporation, Santa Clara, Calif., 1978.

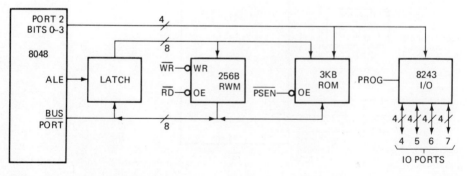

Figure 11-7 Expanded 8048 system.

cant 11 bits. Two memory-bank select instructions set and reset this most significant bit.

SEL	MB0	Select memory bank 0
SEL	MB1	Select memory bank 1

Memory bank 0 includes addresses 000 to 7FF. Memory bank 1 includes addresses 800 to FFF. These instructions don't set the MSB of the *PC* immediately. They simply set or reset an address buffer flip-flop. The contents of the address buffer flop are loaded into the MSB of the *PC* when the next *CALL* or *JMP* instruction is executed. All 12 bits of the *PC* are changed simultaneously.

Additional RWM may be added to the 8048, as shown in Fig. 11-7. An 8-bit address is multiplexed onto the *BUS* port and is latched by *ALE*. One of 256 RWM bytes selected is read or changed via the *BUS* port. Conventional $\overline{WR}$ and $\overline{RD}$ signals are used to determine transfer direction. The address space of external RWM is *not* the same as that of internal RWM. Two additional *MOV* instructions access external memory, using register addressing.

MOVX	A,@R1	Move external RWM at R1 to A
MOVX	@R0,A	Move A to external RWM at R0

These are the only two instructions that affect external RWM. Peripheral registers can be substituted for RWM registers. These two instructions will then access peripherals, such as the 8251 USART we discussed previously.

Another I/O expansion method is to use the 8243 I/O expander, shown in Fig. 11-7. A 4-bit "address" selects the desired expander port and determines the method of transfer. Expander ports are numbered 4 through 7. A 4-bit datum is sent to, or received from, an expander port. Both address and data are sent via the least significant 4 bits of port 2. A signal from the *PROG* pin times the transfers. The leading edge of this signal (1 to 0) strobes the address, while the trailing edge (0 to 1) strobes the data. The four methods of transfer encoded in the port address correspond to the four instructions used for the expander ports.

MOVD	A,P5	Move nibble from P5 to A
MOVD	P4,A	Move nibble from A to P4
ANLD	P6,A	AND A to P6
ORLD	P7,A	OR A to P7

The first instruction moves a 4-bit nibble to the 4 least significant bits of the *A* register. The most significant 4 bits are set to 0. The other three instructions use the least significant 4 bits of the *A* register as an operand but don't affect the most significant 4 bits of *A*. We can independently set and reset each bit of the expander ports. The masks for the boolean operations are contained in the *A* register, rather than in an immediate datum, as they were for ports *BUS*, 1, and 2.

Why is the I/O expander interfaced via port 2 bits? Only 4 I/O bits have been sacrificed in port 2 to gain 16 on the expander. A small system consisting of an 8048 and an 8243 will have 39 I/O lines. A more grandiose interface to the 8243 wouldn't have been as efficient in a small system.

Why Use the 8048?

You can continue expanding the 8048. You can interface multiple 8243s by connecting their chip select inputs to additional port 2 outputs. You can use 8085 parts, such as the 8155 RWM and 8355 ROM, to expand memory and I/O. You can add USARTs, disk interfaces, etc. You can even expand program memory beyond 4K by adding external bank-select flip-flops. Let's examine one example of such expansion, shown in Fig. 11-8. The 8155 RWM and 8355 ROM contain an address holding register that can be connected directly to *ALE* to demultiplex the 8048's addresses. We'd expect Fig. 11-8 to be a pretty efficient three-IC system. Compare this with a system using a larger 8-bit microcomputer. An 8085 system using the 8155 and 8355 would require the *same number of components!* The 8085 is a substantially more powerful processor. The 8048 system does have 15 more I/O lines, but the 8085 system has other potential advantages. The 8085 has four more interrupt lines and can handle direct-memory-access transfers. Our choice of processors is not very clear since the application impacts our decision heavily. We may need those extra I/O lines or the RWM battery backup of the 8048. We may need the interrupt or processing capability of the 8085. The point is that even for such a small system consisting of three LSI circuits, the 8048 seems to be of questionable usefulness. The cost of the parts themselves must be taken into account, but the costs of printed circuit, assembly, testing, power supplies, etc., will probably greatly overshadow any cost difference between the 8048 and 8085.

Why use the 8048? Although one can certainly find contrary examples, the 8048 is best used in very small systems. At most, one additional LSI circuit or a couple of MSI support circuits should be necessary to implement the system. The 8048 is attractive for very-high-volume products. The low cost of a single IC system makes it ideal for children's games, microwave ovens, and other consumer items. Industrial systems manufactured in large quantities also benefit from a single IC system. The 8748 allows the economies of a single IC computer to be applied to systems whose volume could not justify the tooling costs or quantities required of an 8048. Since the 8048 and

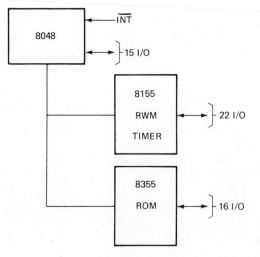

Figure 11-8 Possible 8048 system.

8748 plug into the same socket, a manufacturer could start with the 8748 to get into production quickly and later switch to the 8048. If market response failed to justify the costly 8048 tooling, the 8748 could be retained in the product. The system's manufacturer has deferred a large financial risk until the market has been tested.

A Family of Single-Circuit Computers

The 8048 is only one member of a large family of single-IC microcomputers, shown in Table 11-1. As we saw previously, these computers are most attractive when used by themselves, without expansion circuits. In order to make these single-circuit microcomputers more generally useful, a variety of configurations are available. Hopefully, one of these configurations will match the requirements of most applications without extra circuits. Table 11-1 lists the processors in this microcomputer family, as well as the speed and memory size of these processors. The processors without any on-chip memory must use the bus port to access external memory. Processors without memory may be useful in prototype development and other special applications. All these processors execute almost identical instructions. The 8041, 8022, and 8021 have slightly different instructions than the other processors. You'll notice some blank spaces in Table 11-1. Manufacturers may or may not develop future processors that fit these gaps in the table. Other family processors, not allocated space in our table, may also be developed. Table 11-2 lists the I/O capability of each of the existing processor families.

The 8049 family is simply a faster, larger-memory version of the 8048 family. The 8041 is designed to be programmed as a peripheral controller. The 8041's slave port can be interfaced to another microcomputer's bus. The 8041 is programmed to act like an interface and controller for a peripheral for which no standard IC controller exists. The 8022 and 8021 are both low-performance, low-cost processors to be incorporated in high-volume products, like automobiles and other consumer items. Neither processor has an interrupt system. The 8021 is contained in a 28-pin package. This processor's small package and limited capability make the 8021 inexpensive enough to be considered for children's toys and other very-low-cost products.

The 8022 has twice the ROM and more I/O capability than the 8021. The 8022 has an integral 8-bit analog-to-digital converter! One of the 8-bit ports may be configured as a touch-panel interface. Touch panels are the glass control panels seen in

Table 11-1 Speed and memory capacity of single-chip computers

Instruction cycle	ROM	RWM	No memory	ROM	EPROM
—	4K	256	—	—	—
1.36 μs	2K	128	8039	8049	—
2.5 μs	1K	64	8035	8048	8748
2.5 μs	1K	64	—	8041	8741
10 μs	2K	64	—	8022	—
10 μs	1K	64	—	8021	—

Table 11-2 I/O capacity of single-chip computers

Family	Bus port	Bidirectional port	Slave port	External interrupt	Test input	Analog to digital	Touch panel	Zero crossing
8049	8	16	—	1	2	—	—	—
8048	8	16	—	1	2	—	—	—
8041	0	16	8	1	2	—	—	—
8022	0	24	—	0	2	Yes	Yes	Yes
8021	0	20	—	0	1	—	—	—

modern consumer appliances. Switches are formed by silk-screened patterns on the surface of the glass. These switches have no moving parts. For example, the 8022 would be right at home in a microwave oven. The touch-panel port would connect to the oven's control panel, while the analog-to-digital converter would be connected to a temperature sensor probe. The 8022 also has a test input that will work as a zero-crossing detector. A zero-crossing detector can sense the zero points of an ac voltage. A zero-crossing detector could be used to count cycles of the ac line voltage. The ac line frequency is very stable and the zero crossings could be used to keep track of time. Thyristors are electronic components which control large amounts of ac power. The 8022 could also control thyristors, using the zero-crossing feature.

The 8022 and, especially, the 8021 could be considered as an alternative to even very small ASMs. Development of an 8021 system will almost surely be less expensive than the development of an ASM. Of course, the quantity of systems to be manufactured must be sufficient to justify the 8021's tooling expense. The product cost of the 8021-based system will probably be less than the cost of a special ASM.

Products must get more complex to justify inclusion of the 8048 or 8049. Even so, the cost of the 8048/49 is liable to be less than the cost of all but the simplest ASM. You can see that single-chip microcomputers can potentially replace most low-performance ASMs advantageously. At the other end of the microcomputer spectrum, very fast and large microcomputer systems can be used to implement products that, otherwise, would be impossible to implement. A small desk-top instrument can now contain a computer system that used to require several cubic meters of space and be prohibitively expensive. The next computer we'll discuss is a high-performance microcomputer called the 8086.

THE 8086 MICROCOMPUTER

The 8086 is a high-performance, 16-bit microcomputer. Sixteen-bit data are manipulated using 16-bit registers and busses. The 8086 will address up to 1,048,576 bytes (1MB) of memory and up to 65,536 bytes of I/O registers. In order to simplify programming such a complex microcomputer, the 8086's instruction set was purposely designed to be easy to understand. For example, only one *MOV* instruction mnemonic is used to move 8- or 16-bit data from any source to any destination. The *MOV* instruction can move the contents of any general, pointer, index, or segment register. The *MOV* instruction can move immediate and memory data, using many addressing modes. To accommodate all these alternatives, the *MOV* instruction mnemonic is assembled into one of seven machine language formats. The seven formats occupy from 2 to 4 bytes of memory. We will omit most of the implementation details and some of the operational details of the 8086. You'll be able to understand the important features of the 8086 without obscuring detail. If you intend to use the 8086 you should read the 8086 user's manual and other supportive literature.[1]

From the programmer's point of view, the 8086 contains 14 registers of 16 bits each, as shown in Fig. 11-9. Most instructions can specify any of the *general, pointer*, and *index registers* as operands. Normally, the general registers would be used for data. The pointer and index registers are usually used for addresses. Each of the general

[1] MCS-86^{TM} *User's Manual*, Intel Corporation, Santa Clara, Calif., 1978.

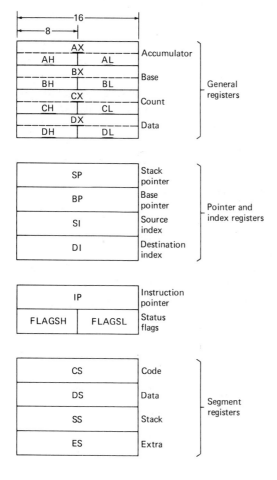

Figure 11-9 8086 registers.

Table 11-3 8086 status flags

Bit	Mnemonic	Name
0	CF	Carry flag
2	PF	Parity flag
4	AF	Auxiliary carry flag
6	ZF	Zero flag
7	SF	Sign flag
8	TF	Trap flag
9	IF	Interrupt flag
10	DF	Direction flag
11	OF	Overflow flag

registers is divided into two 8-bit registers. Most instructions can access these eight 8-bit registers. Even though the 8086 is a 16-bit computer, many data are still 8 bits. For example, ASCII character codes are 8-bit data. The 8-bit form of most instructions makes handling byte data easy and efficient. Most instructions can use all the general, pointer, and index registers. The general registers are dedicated to specific functions in a few cases. To help remember these functions, the general registers are given the names *accumulator*, *base*, *count*, and *data*.

The *instruction pointer* is the 16-bit program counter of the 8086. The processor's flags are contained in a 16-bit *status register*, which may also be accessed as two 8-bit registers. So far, we have no way of generating the 20-bit address we'll need for 1MB of memory. The four segment registers provide the additional information required to convert a 16-bit address into a 20-bit address.

The *FLAGSL* register contains 5 flag bits identical to the 8085's flags, as shown in Table 11-3. The *FLAGSH* register contains four flags. The *TF* bit aids in program debugging. Setting the *TF* bit causes an interrupt after the *next* instruction is executed. An interrupt routine allows the programmer to examine registers and memory locations via a terminal. The programmer instructs the debugging routine to return to the main program with the *TF* bit set. Exactly one main program instruction will be executed before an interrupt to the debugging routine. The programmer may now use the debugging routine to examine changes caused by that one main-program instruction. The programmer may *single-step* through a program while observing the effect of each instruction.

The *IF* bit is the interrupt enable bit. Certain 8086 instructions modify operand addresses to scan through an array automatically. If the *DF* bit is 0, these addresses are incremented. If the *DF* bit is 1, these addresses are decremented. Instructions can scan through an array in either direction, using the *DF* bit. The *OF* bit is set if overflow occurs when performing arithmetic on signed numbers. Arithmetic overflow of signed numbers is easily detected by testing a single flag bit.

Addressing Memory

Memory addresses are formed by two separate steps in the 8086. The first step calculates a 16-bit effective address (*EA*). The second step converts that 16-bit *EA* to a

20-bit physical address (*PA*). The *PA* is the address that actually appears on the 8086's address bus.

The effective addresses of memory operands may be computed in several ways. The effective address may be a 16-bit *direct address* carried with the instruction. The effective address may be *indirect*, through a base or index register. This indirect-addressing mode is like register-pair addressing of the 8085. An 8086 instruction using indirect addressing may also contain an 8- or 16-bit displacement, which is added to the contents of the base or index register to form the *EA*. The content of the register is not changed. Often, the displacement is the starting address of an array. The index register contains the number of the array element to be accessed. Since different in-structions can have different displacements, the same index value could access corre-sponding elements in different arrays. You could easily write a loop that adds one array to another and deposits the sum in a third array. The loop's instructions would carry displacements corresponding to the three arrays' starting addresses. An index register would be initialized to 0 to access the first elements of all three arrays. The index register is incremented on each pass through the loop to access consecutive ele-ments of the three arrays. Finally, an *EA* may be indirect through the sum of a base and an index register. As before, the instruction using this kind of indirect address may also add an 8- or 16-bit displacement to the *EA*. One possible use of indirect addressing using two registers is accessing two dimensional arrays. The base registers we've been using are the *BX* and *BP* registers, while the index registers are the *SI* and *DI* registers. The 8086 has *immediate addressing* with 8- or 16-bit data. The 8086 also has *stack addressing*. A full 16-bit register is pushed or popped on the stack. The stack address is contained in the *SP* register. The stack builds downward in memory like the 8085's stack.

The 16-bit *EA* or *SP* or *IP* will only access 65,536 memory bytes. Every 16-bit memory address must be converted to a 20-bit physical address to access the 1MB memory. The 8086's memory is divided into *segments*, each of which is 65,536 bytes long. Segments begin on 16-byte increments. That is, the least significant 4 bits of the 20-bit segment starting addresses are always 0. Segments can overlap or can be separate areas of memory. Any 16-bit address is converted to a physical address by adding the 20-bit segment address, as shown in Fig. 11-10. A 16-bit 8086 address is really an offset from the beginning of a memory segment.

The most significant 16 bits of the segment starting address are stored in a seg-ment register. Four segment registers allow access to four 64KB segments simulta-

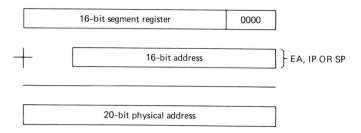

Figure 11-10 8086 physical address calculation.

neously. These segments could be identical, representing only 64KB of physical memory. These segments could be mutually exclusive, representing 256KB of physical memory, or could have any amount of overlap. Each segment is used for a specific purpose. The *code segment (CS)* is the segment in which instructions are stored. The *CS* register is added to the 16-bit *IP* address to form a physical address. Instructions are always fetched from the code segment. The *stack segment (SS)* contains the 8086's stack. Any stack instruction causes the *SS* register to be added to the 16-bit address from the *SP* to form a physical address. Data are always pushed and popped in the stack segment. The *data segment (DS)* contains the operands to be used in a calculation. The *DS* register is always added to a direct or indirect *EA* to form a physical address. Data are fetched and stored in the data segment. There is one exception to the segment used for data. Both pointers *BP* and *SP* use the stack segment. Any *EA* calculation using the base pointer will use the stack segment, rather than the data segment. Sometimes, data must be manipulated on the stack in ways other than a simple *PUSH* or *POP*. The stack segment may be accessed by any 8086 instruction when the base pointer is specified as part of the effective address.

The segment-register operations are summarized in Table 11-4. A 1-byte segment override may be prefixed to any instruction calculating an effective address. As shown in Table 11-4, any data address may be directed to any segment. The *extra segment (ES)* is usually used as an additional data segment.

Segment registers may be used in several ways. The application program may manipulate the segment registers to gain access to large amounts of memory. Very large programs with very large data storage requirements may be accommodated. Alternately, the 8086 may need to execute several different programs. Each program is scheduled at a certain time signaled by a real-time clock or by an external event signaled by an interrupt. An *operating system* program decides which program is to execute next. The operating system also resolves conflicts among programs for memory and peripherals. If a program does not manipulate segment registers, that program is *dynamically relocatable*. The operating system may move any segment of that program to another place in physical memory. The operating system will change the corresponding segment registers so that the same data are still correctly addressed. In the extreme case, the operating system may actually remove a program from memory by storing that program on a disk. More memory is made available to run another program which may be read from the disk. Later, the original program may be retrieved and restarted. The original program may then be placed anywhere there is room in memory. The operating system changes the segment registers to allow the program to operate at its new physical memory location.

Table 11-4 Segment-register usage

Operation	Registers	Override
Instruction fetch	IP + CS	None
Stack	SP + SS	None
Data	BP + SS	DS, ES, CS
Data	EA + DS	ES, SS, CS

Data Movement Instructions

The 8086's *MOV* instruction will transfer data among any general, pointer, index, or segment register and memory. The *MOV* instruction can move a byte or a word. Unlike the 8085, the 8086's *MOV* instruction can use any addressing mode: direct, several indirect, and immediate modes. You can see that allowing the *MOV* instruction to transfer data from any source to any destination simplifies learning to program the 8086. The *PUSH* and *POP* instructions add or delete a 16-bit datum from the stack, respectively. Any 16-bit register may be the source or destination operand. Only the *MOV*, *PUSH*, and *POP* instructions can access the segment registers. When we say "any register" in further discussion, we will implicitly exclude the segment registers.

The *XCHG* instruction can exchange two operands. The operands can be any register (except the segment registers) or memory. The *XCHG* instruction can use any addressing mode except immediate addressing. The *XLAT* or translate instruction is a table look-up instruction. The starting address of a 256-byte table is placed in the *BX* register. The table index is placed in the *AL* register. The *XLAT* instruction adds *AL* and *BX* to find a data byte in the table. This data byte is placed in *AL*.

Three 8086 instructions are used specifically for address operands. All three instructions must specify a register as a destination and memory as a source. Immediate-mode addressing may not be used with any of these address manipulation instructions. The *LEA* or *load effective address* instruction allows an *EA*, rather than an operand, to be transferred to a register. The *EA* is computed normally. Instead of accessing the operand at the effective address, the *EA* itself is transferred to any register.

Two more address manipulation instructions allow 32 bits of address to be transferred simultaneously. Two 16-bit registers must be set to completely specify a location anywhere in memory. The *LDS* or *load DS* instruction transfers a word from memory to any register. *LDS* also transfers the next word in memory (*EA* + 2) to the data segment register. You can use the *LDS* instruction to simultaneously load an index or base register and the *DS* register. These 32 bits specify a memory location anywhere in 1MB of memory, which may now be accessed by indirect addressing. The *LES* or *load ES* instruction works like the LDS instruction except *LES* loads the extra segment register.

Four instructions allow byte and word manipulation of the flag register. The *LAHF* or load *AH* with flags and the *SAHF* or store *AH* into flags instructions allow exchange of data between *AH* and *FLAGSL*. Notice that the *most* significant byte of *A* and the *least* significant byte of the flag register are used by these instructions. An equivalent instruction is *not* available to access *FLAGSH*. These instructions are specifically designed to make the *AX* register of the 8086 look like the *PSW* (*A* register and flags) of the 8085. A later section will describe the relationship of the 8086 to the 8085. Finally, the *PUSHF* and *POPF* instructions add or delete the entire contents of the 16-bit flag register to the stack.

Boolean Instructions

The 8086 has *AND*, *OR*, and *XOR* instructions. These instructions have all the addressing modes of the *MOV* instruction. A memory or register operand may be ANDed with a register. The result could be deposited in the register or the memory location. An immediate operand could be ANDed to a register. An immediate operand could be ANDed to a memory location. Of course, either byte or word operands could be specified. Compare the flexibility of the 8086's boolean (and arithmetic) operations with the 8085's instruction. The 8085 used only 8-bit operands. One operand had to be in the *A* register, as was the result. Only register-pair and immediate addressing were possible.

The 8086's *TEST* instruction operates exactly like its *AND* instruction except that the result is not stored anywhere. Both operands remain unchanged. Only the flag register is changed to reflect the result of the *AND* operation. The *TEST* instruction can select and test a single bit in a boolean byte or word without destroying the operands. The *NOT* instruction complements all the bits in a byte or word. The operand can be in a register or memory location. All addressing modes are possible except immediate addressing.

Individual bits of the flag register may be controlled by certain instructions. The carry flag may be cleared, complemented, and set by the *CLC*, *CMC*, and *STC* instructions. The direction flag may be cleared and set by the *CLD* and *STD* instructions. The interrupt flag may be cleared and set by the *CLI* and *STI* instructions.

Rotate and Shift Instructions

Just as with all single-operand instructions, the rotate and shift instructions have all addressing modes except immediate addressing. Thus, a byte or word in any register or memory location may be rotated or shifted. Every shift and rotate instruction has two forms. In one form, the bits are shifted only once. In the second form, the bits are shifted any number of times. The number of shifts is specified by a constant in the *CL* register. The *CF* bit *always* contains the last bit shifted out. The *OF* bit is set if the original and new sign bit differ in *single*-bit rotates on shifts. Flag bits *PF*, *SF*, and *ZF* are affected normally.

The *ROL* and *ROR* instructions circularly rotate a byte or word like the 8085's *RLC* and *RRC* instructions. The bit shifted out of one side of the register is shifted in the other side. The *RCL* and *RCR* instructions circularly rotate a byte or word, like the 8085's *RAL* and *RAR* instructions. The bit shifted into one side of the register is the carry flag bit. As always, the bit shifted out the other side is put in the carry flag.

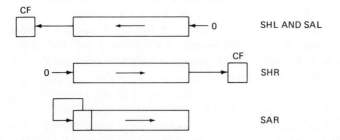

Figure 11-11 8086 shift instructions.

The shift instructions are *not* circular, as shown in Fig. 11-11. An *SHL* or *shift left* instruction simply shifts all bits left, while inserting 0s in the vacated bits. An *SHR* or *shift right* instruction simply shifts all bits right, while inserting 0s in the vacated bits. You'll remember that shifting is equivalent to multiplying or dividing by 2. Two instructions simplify signed arithmetic shifts. The *SAR* or *shift arithmetically right* instruction shifts all bits right and replicates the sign bit at each shift. You'll remember that we halve two's-complement numbers by leaving the sign bit the same after every right shift. The *SAL* or *shift arithmetically left* instruction is actually the same as the *SHL* instruction. This instruction has two names. Simply shifting a number left, while shifting 0s into vacated bits, will correctly double a two's-complement number.

Branching Instructions

The unconditional *JMP* instruction has several forms. Direct-addressing instructions compute the new *IP* address by adding a displacement carried with the *JMP* instruction to the current contents of the *IP*. Displacements may be 8 or 16 bits. Thus, direct addressing is *relative* to the location of the instruction. A section of program containing relative *JMP*s can be moved in memory and will still work correctly as long as all instructions are moved by the same amount. A program using relative addressing is called *position-independent code*. In addition to relative addressing, a *JMP* may specify any indirect-addressing mode. Indirect addressing is *not* relative. Finally, a single *JMP* instruction will transfer control to any of the 1M locations of memory. This *JMP* instruction specifies a new 16-bit value for the *CS* register, as well as a 16-bit value for the *IP* register.

The 8086's conditional branch instructions use relative addressing with an 8-bit displacement. The 8-bit displacement is interpreted as a signed number; so both forward and backward branches can occur (the 8086 always extends the sign of an 8-bit datum used in place of a 16-bit datum). The conditional branch instructions are shown in Table 11-5. The branch conditions are flag-register bits or combinations of flag-register bits. Branching on combinations of bits allows implementation of any arithmetic inequality as a single instruction. Separate sets of instructions are provided for signed and unsigned numbers. For signed comparisons, a single 8086 instruction replaces a small 8085 program! In Table 11-5, the instruction mnemonics in parentheses are synonyms. Thus, the *JL* (jump if less) mnemonic and the *JNGE* (jump if not greater or equal) mnemonic both assemble to the same machine instruction.

A few other conditional branch instructions simplify implementation of loops. The *JCXZ* or *jump if CX zero* instruction branches if *CX* is 0. The *CX* register is often used as a counter. The *LOOP* instruction decrements the *CX* register and branches if *CX* is not zero. The *LOOP* instruction is like the 8048's *DJNZ* instruction. Often a loop must be repeated while some condition is true or until a certain number of passes have been completed. Two 8086 instructions facilitate such loops. The *LOOPZ* or *loop while zero* instruction decrements *CX* and branches if *CX* is not 0 *and* ZF is 1. This instruction is also called *LOOPE* or *loop while equal*. The *LOOPNZ* or *loop while not zero* instruction decrements *CX* and branches if *CX* is not 0 *and* ZF is 0. This instruction is also called *LOOPNE* or *loop while not equal*.

Table 11-5 8086 conditional branch instructions

Signed numbers

Mnemonic	Jump if	Condition
JL (JNGE)	Less	SF $\oplus$ OF = 1
JLE (JNG)	Less or equal	(SF $\oplus$ OF) + ZF = 1
JE	Equal	ZF = 1
JNE	Not equal	ZF = 0
JGE (JNL)	Greater or equal	SF $\oplus$ OF = 0
JG (JNLE)	Greater	(SF $\oplus$ OF) + ZF = 0

Unsigned numbers

Mnemonic	Jump if	Condition
JB (JNAE)	Below	CF = 1
JBE (JNA)	Below or equal	CF + ZF = 1
JE	Equal	ZF = 1
JNE	Not equal	ZF = 0
JAE (JNB)	Above or equal	CF = 0
JA (JNBE)	Above	CF + ZF = 0

Single-bit tests

Jump if bit	= 0	= 1
ZF	JNZ	JZ
PF	JPO (JNP)	JPE (JP)
OF	JNO	JO
SF	JNS	JS

Input-Output Instructions

The *IN* and *OUT* instructions transfer 8-bit data into or out of the *AL* register. An 8-bit peripheral address contained in the instruction selects 1 of up to 256 I/O ports. The *INW* and *OUTW* instructions move 16-bit data between the *AX* register and peripherals. All four of these I/O instructions may also address a peripheral indirectly through the *DX* register. By using the 16-bit contents of the *DX* register as an address, up to 65,536 I/O bytes may be addressed.

The *WAIT* instruction causes the processor to stop executing instructions until an external *TEST* input is asserted. The *WAIT* instruction can be used to synchronize the processor to a peripheral or another processor. The *ESC* or *escape* instruction computes an *EA* and accesses the operand at that *EA*. The 8086 doesn't supply or receive the operand. An auxiliary processor can supply or receive the operand. The *ESC* instruction used with a separate IC processor can expand the 8086's instruction set. For example, the auxiliary processor could implement floating-point arithmetic operations or complex I/O operations. A 1-byte instruction prefix called *LOCK* causes the 8086 to assert an external lock signal for the duration of the prefixed instruction. The *LOCK* signal is used to disable bus access by any other processor sharing the bus. *LOCK* is often used with *XCHG* to ensure that another processor does not change or read memory data while those data are being exchanged. *LOCK* prevents possible ambiguities in the exchange of data among several processors sharing the same memory.

Subroutine Instructions

The 8086's *CALL* instruction pushes the *IP* onto the stack and branches to a 16-bit address in the current code segment. A direct branch address is relative to the original *IP*, exactly like the *JMP* instruction. Alternately, an indirect-addressing *CALL* instruction computes an *EA,* which specifies a memory location containing the branch address. Like the *JMP* instruction, the *CALL* may contain two 16-bit data that will be loaded into the *CS* register as well as the *IP* register. Both the original *IP and CS* registers are pushed onto the stack. An indirect addressing intersegment *CALL* retrieves the 32-bit *IP* and *CS* contents from 4 memory bytes specified by an *EA* computation.

The *RET* or *return* instruction pops the return address off the stack into the *IP*. As you might expect, the *RET* must also have two forms, intersegment and intrasegment. An intrasegment return pops a 16-bit return address off the stack into the *IP*. An intersegment return pops two 16-bit data into both the *IP* and *CS*. You must be sure to use the correct *RET* instruction that corresponds to the *CALL* instruction used.

Both forms of *RET* have an option that adds an immediate 16-bit constant to the *SP* after performing the normal return function. Arguments may be passed to a subroutine by pushing them on the stack before calling the subroutine. These *RET* instructions add the number of arguments on the stack to the *SP* so that these arguments are deleted from the stack.

Arithmetic Instructions

All arithmetic instructions operate on byte and word operands. Most instructions have both direct and indirect addressing. Most two-operand instructions also allow immediate addressing. The *DX* register is used to extend the *AX* register when 32-bit operaands are needed. The 8086's arithmetic instructions are listed in Table 11-6. We'll only comment on new instructions not seen before. The multiply and divide instructions require one operand and the result to be located in the *A* register. The second operand can be in a register or memory location. If a byte multiply is specified, an operand is in *AL* with the 16-bit result in *AX*. In a word multiply, one operand is in *AX,* while the 32-bit result is in *AX* and *DX*. In a byte divide, the 16-bit numerator is in *AX*. The quotient is in *AL*, while the remainder is in *AH*. In a word divide, the 32-bit numerator is in *AX* and *DX*. The quotient is in *AX*, while the remainder is in *DX*.

The *NEG* instruction takes the two's complement of a byte or word operand. The *CBW* or *convert byte to word* instruction converts the signed byte in *AL* to a signed word in *AX*. The sign bit of *AL* is simply replicated in all the *AH* bits. The *CWD* or

Table 11-6 8086 arithmetic instructions

Basic instructions	
ADD	Add
ADC	Add with carry
SUB	Subtract
SBB	Subtract with borrow
MUL	Unsigned multiply
IMUL	Signed multiply
DIV	Unsigned divide
IDIV	Signed divide

Additional instructions	
INC	Increment
DEC	Decrement
NEG	Negate (two's complement)
CMP	Compare (subtract, don't store result)
CBW	Convert byte to word
CWD	Convert word to double word

Packed decimal		Unpacked decimal	
DAA	Decimal adjust addition	AAA	ASCII adjust addition
DAS	Decimal adjust subtraction	AAS	ASCII adjust subtraction
		AAM	ASCII adjust multiplication
		AAD	ASCII adjust division

convert word to double instruction converts the signed word in *AX* to a 32-bit datum in *DX* and *AX*. The sign bit of *AX* is simply replicated in all the *DX* bits.

Two sets of decimal correction instructions are provided. The packed instructions correct 8-bit results in the *AL* register if operands were packed two BCD digits per byte. The unpacked corrections work if only one decimal digit is stored in each byte. The result is represented as two unpacked digits in *AL* and *AH*. These instructions are called *ASCII adjust instructions* because the source of unpacked BCD operands is often the least significant 4 bits of a numeric ASCII character.

String Operations

A string is a sequence of bytes or words. One common string is a sequence of bytes containing ASCII characters representing a line typed on a terminal by an operator. The 8086 has a group of instructions useful for processing strings. These instructions are called *primitive* operations because they are often used with a repeat prefix. The repeat prefix allows one instruction to operate sequentially on all string elements. The *REP* or repeat prefix has two forms, similarly to the *LOOP* instruction. All *REP* prefixes decrement the *CX* register. One *REP* prefix repeats the string primitive while $ZF = 1$ or until $CX = 0$. The other *REP* prefix repeats the string primitive while $ZF = 0$

or until $CX = 0$. Several primitive operations can change *ZF*. *REP* combined with these instructions can search through a string automatically.

Each string primitive uses the *SI* and *DI* registers to address the strings in memory. After each execution, the primitive modifies *SI* and *DI* to point to the next element in the string. The *DF* bit in the flag register specifies whether *SI* and *DI* should be incremented ($DF = 0$) or decremented ($DF = 1$). All primitives have byte and word forms; so the index registers are incremented or decremented by one or two, respectively.

The *MOVB* and *MOVW* primitives can move an entire block of words or bytes from one place in memory to another when combined with *REP*. The *STOB* and *STOW* instructions store the *AL* or *AX* registers into memory addressed by *DI*. Combined with *REP*, these instructions can initialize each element in an entire string to the same value. The *LODB* and *LODW* instructions load the *AL* or *AX* registers from memory addressed by *SI*. These two primitives would ordinarily not be used with *REP*.

The *CMPB* and *CMPW* primitives subtract the operand addressed by *DI* from the operand addressed by *SI*. The result is not saved, but the flag register is changed to match the result. Used with the *ZF* testing capability of *REP*, these primitives allow two strings to be compared. The first nonmatching elements cause *ZF* to be reset and the repetition to terminate. You can also search for the first matching elements. The *SCAB* and *SCAW* or *scan* primitives subtract the operand addressed by *DI* and from the *A* register. These instructions can be used with *REP* to search a string for the first occurrence of, or a departure from, a constant in the *A* register.

Interrupt Instructions

The 8086 has two interrupt inputs *NMI* and *INTR*. The *INTR* signal is the primary interrupt input and is enabled and disabled by the flag register's *IF* bit. The 8086 responds to an *INTR* by pushing the flags on the stack, disabling the interrupt system, and issuing two interrupt acknowledge cycles. An external device (peripheral or interrupt controller) responds to the second interrupt acknowledge cycle by sending an 8-bit *interrupt type code* to the processor via the data bus. The processor multiplies the type code by 4, so that it may be used as an address for an indirect intersegment subroutine call. The lower 1K bytes of memory are a table with 256 entries. Each entry contains the 16-bit address and the 16-bit code segment address of an interrupt routine. An interrupt routine can be located anywhere in the 1MB memory. Five interrupt types are dedicated to specific functions of the 8086, as shown in Table 11-7. The *NMI* or nonmaskable interrupt always uses the type 2 interrupt address. *NMI* cannot be disabled. An *IRET* or interrupt return instruction must be used to return from an interrupt. An ordinary *RET* instruction would not pop the flags off the stack. The *IRET* instruction pops the *IP*, *CS*, and flag register off the stack. No explicit enable interrupt instruction is needed since *IF* will be set when the flag register is popped off the stack.

Two 8086 instructions cause *software interrupts*. Programs as well as peripherals can cause interrupts. Software interrupts often simplify complex operating system programs. The *INT* instruction causes a software interrupt to any one of the 256

Table 11-7 8086 dedicated interrupt types

Type	Location	Function
0	0H–3H	Divide by zero
1	4H–7H	Single step
2	8H–BH	Nonmaskable interrupt
3	CH–FH	Single byte interrupt instruction
4	10H–13H	Interrupt on overflow instruction

interrupt types. A special form of *INT* is only 1 byte long and always causes a type 3 interrupt. The *INTO* or *interrupt on overflow* instruction causes a type 4 interrupt only if the *OF* flag is set. *INTO* simplifies testing for arithmetic overflow. An overflow error or recovery routine can be located at the type 4 interrupt.

Hardware

The 8086's internal architecture is shown in Fig. 11-12. The processor is divided into two distinct processing units: the *EU* or *execution unit* and the *BIU* or *bus interface unit*. The *EU* contains the general, pointer, index, and flag registers. The *EU* executes 8086 instructions sent to it from the *BIU*. Operands and 16-bit addresses are also transferred between *BIU* and *EU*. The *BIU* controls the 8086 bus and handles memory accesses for the *EU*. The *BIU* converts the 16-bit *EU* addresses to 20-bit addresses, using the segment registers in the *BIU*. The *BIU* also contains the *IP* and fetches 8086 instructions from memory for the *EU*. The *BIU* will fetch instruction bytes from memory whenever the bus isn't being used for data transfers. A 6-byte *instruction*

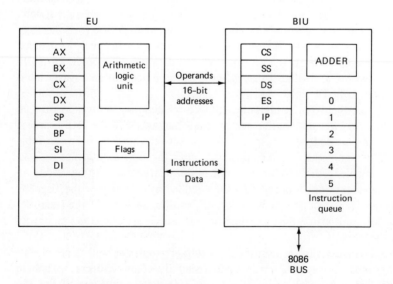

Figure 11-12 8086 internal organization.

queue allows the *BIU* to fetch 6 bytes of instruction in advance of execution. While the *EU* is performing internal computations, the *BIU* is already fetching the next instruction. Most of the time, instruction fetches appear to be instantaneous to the *EU*. Overlapping *EU* and *BIU* operations significantly improve the 8086's performance.

The 8086's 20 address bits and 16-bit data bus make fitting the 8086 into a standard 40-pin IC package difficult. Sixteen address bits are multiplexed on the data bus similar to the 8085's bus. The remaining 4 address bits are multiplexed with status bits; so these address bits must also be latched externally. Even so, not enough pins remain for all 8086 functions. Sometimes an 8086 will be used in simple single processor systems requiring simple memory and peripheral interfaces. Other times, the 8086 will be used in complex multiple processor systems requiring many control signals. An 8086 pin called *MN/MX* can be connected permanently to a 1 or 0 in order to change the functions of the 8086's control pins and match the complexity of the system. In Fig. 11-13, the *MN/MX* pin is connected to 1 in order to cause the 8086 to output minimum mode control signals. Minimum mode control signals *INTA*, *ALE*, *M/IO*, $\overline{RD}$, $\overline{WR}$, *HOLD*, and *HLDA* are similar to 8085 signals with the same name. If an optional bus transceiver circuit is used to buffer large systems, two minimum mode signals are provided to control that transceiver. The signal $\overline{DEN}$ is used to disable and 3 state the external transceiver circuit when that circuit is not engaged in an actual data transfer. The signal $DT/\overline{R}$ specifies the direction of data transfers through the external transceiver circuit.

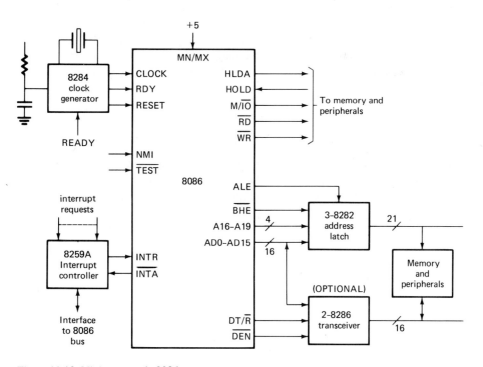

Figure 11-13 Minimum mode 8086 system.

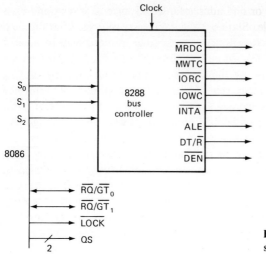

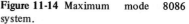

Figure 11-14 Maximum mode 8086 system.

By connecting *MN/MX* to 0, a maximum mode system is implemented. A partial diagram of a maximum mode system is shown in Fig. 11-14. All the minimum mode control signals are generated by an external bus controller circuit (an 8288) from only three status pins. These status pins used to be $\overline{DEN}$, $DT/\overline{R}$, and $M/\overline{IO}$ in the minimum mode system but were redefined when the *MN/MX* pin was tied to a 0. The bus controller provides separate memory and peripheral, read and write signals. The memory and peripheral interfaces don't have to use an $M/\overline{IO}$ signal to gate the read and write signals. Five 8086 pins remain that are no longer needed for bus control in the maximum mode system. These pins are used as multiple processor control signals. Two request/grant ($\overline{RQ/GT}$) pins allow multiple processors to request and be granted control of the bus. The $\overline{LOCK}$ pin is asserted by the *LOCK* instruction prefix, as was previously described. Two status pins (*QS*) allow external instrumentation or an auxiliary processor to track the 8086's internal instruction queue.

Returning to Fig. 11-13, notice that the 8086 bus transfers 16-bit data even though the 20-bit address is the address of a byte in memory. A 21st bit $\overline{BHE}$ is used to control byte addressing, as shown in Table 11-8. The signal $\overline{BHE}$ is multiplexed with a status signal; so $\overline{BHE}$ must also be latched externally. Although the 8086 allows

Table 11-8 8086 byte access control signals

BHE	A0	Data
0	0	Whole word
0	1	Upper byte only
1	0	Lower byte only
1	1	None

16-bit words to be located at even or odd addresses, words located at even addresses can be transferred in one bus cycle. Sixteen-bit data should be located at even addresses for best performance. Instructions are 1 to 5 bytes long and may be located at even or odd addresses with no effect on performance. The instruction queue of the *BIU* allows instruction fetches to be overlapped with other processing anyway! As shown in Table 11-8, odd bus addresses always transfer a single byte. An even bus address can transfer a single byte or an entire word, depending on the state of $\overline{BHE}$.

Like the 8080, the 8086 requires an external clock generator circuit (the 8284). The clock generator also provides the reset function and a synchronizing flip-flop for the *READY* signal (for slow memory or peripherals). The reset function sets *IP* to 0000H and *CS* to FFFFH; so the first instruction is fetched from FFFF0H. The 8259A interrupt controller in Fig. 11-13 is similar to the 8259 interrupt controller mentioned previously for the 8085. The 8259A has an additional operation mode in which an interrupt type number is output to an 8086 bus, rather than a *CALL* instruction to an 8085 bus.

Relationship of the 8085 to the 8086

Software development is very expensive. An easy way to use software already developed for the 8085 has been designed into the 8086. Each 8085 register has an equivalent 8086 register, as shown in Table 11-9. The 8086 instructions do *not* have binary representations or mnemonics that match the 8085's instructions. However, a single 8086 instruction exists that performs the same function as an 8085 instruction. In a few cases, a short sequence of 8086 instructions will be needed to replace a single 8085 instruction. This one-to-one correspondence of 8085 and 8086 instructions allows a simple translator program to convert 8085 programs to 8086 programs. The memory requirements and execution time of the 8086 program will be different from those of the 8085 program. Of course, a simple translated 8085 program will not use the 8086 to best advantage.

Table 11-9 Register equivalence between 8085 and 8086

8085 registers	8086 registers
A	AL
H	BH
L	BL
B	CH
C	CL
D	DH
E	DL
PC	IP
SP	SP
FLAG	FLAGSL

OTHER MICROCOMPUTERS

You have seen some examples of all three main categories of microcomputers. The 8048 family is an example of the single-chip microcomputers, often used in simple dedicated applications. The 8085 is an example of a medium-performance microcomputer, used in a very wide variety of applications. The 8086 is an example of a high-performance microcomputer, used when high-speed computation and large amounts of memory are required. Other processors are available in all three categories. You should investigate all the processors appropriate to your application before selecting one. Your selection will probably not only be based on processor cost and speed, but also on system and development cost. Some processors may require more expensive memory or peripherals or a larger power supply or more cooling fans than other processors. The cost of the entire system may bear little relation to the cost of the processor. Finally, the cost of hardware and software development is very significant. The quality of development aids available for the processor you select influences development costs. The costs of purchasing new development aids, retraining engineers and programmers, developing new software, and introducing a new processor in manufacturing and field service will usually be very substantial. Often, new processors cannot be considered because the cost of changing processors is so large. The improvements attributable to a new processor must outweigh the costs of changing processors. Software- and hardware-compatible families of processors are developed to minimize the costs of switching to a newer and better processor.

PROBLEMS

11-1 Of all the processors in the 8048 family, which are more likely to be worth expanding beyond their single-chip configuration?

11-2 One of the 8086's indirect addressing modes sums a pointer *and* index register to the displacement.
  (a) How might this mode aid in implementing position-independent code?
  (b) How would this mode be used to access a two-dimensional array?

11-3 Write a program to move 10 bytes of data from a list starting at a memory location *HERE* to a list starting at memory location *THERE*.
  (a) Write the program for the 8048.
  (b) Write the program for the 8086, using the *REP* prefix and primitives.
  (c) Compare these programs to the 8085 program you wrote for Prob. 8-1.

11-4 Write a program to shift a 16-bit datum contained in memory to the right.
  (a) Write the program for the 8048.
  (b) Write the program for the 8086.
  (c) Compare these programs with the 8085 program you wrote in Prob. 8-7.
  (d) How would programs for all three processors change if multiple bit shifts were required?

11-5 Write a clock routine for the 8048 that keeps track of seconds and minutes as two-digit BCD numbers. Compare this program to the program you wrote in Prob. 9-9.

11-6 Write a program to compare two 8-bit two's-complement numbers R and S. Branch to subroutines *GT*, *EQ*, or *LT* if R is greater than S, R is equal to S, or R is less than S, respectively.
  (a) Write the program for the 8048.
  (b) Write the program for the 8086.

(c) Compare these programs with the program you wrote for the 8085 in Prob. 9-10.

(d) How would the programs for these processors change if R and S were 16-bit numbers?

11-7 Write unsigned multiplication and division programs for the 8048. How do these programs compare to 8085 and 8086 multiplication and division? How would signed operations affect all three processors?

11-8 We need to multiply by the small constant 13 to access a 13-byte-per-entry table.

(a) Write a program to do this for the 8048.

(b) How would you multiply by 13 on the 8086?

(c) Compare your results with the program you wrote for the 8085 in Prob. 9-14.

TWELVE

TOPICS IN MICROCOMPUTING

The goal of our study of logic circuits and microcomputers is the development of useful systems. Such systems fall into two general categories: products for resale and systems for use *in-house*. In either case, system development is similar. We'll use the terminology associated with products and detail the development process in Fig. 12-1. Figure 12-1 is representative of the major steps in developing a product, although the kind and order of steps vary from one company to another. We won't be able to detail all these steps here. We'll concentrate on those steps in which the *product designer* participates most directly. These steps are product definition, product design, and test-equipment design. Other steps are just as important to the success of a product but aren't as closely related to the topics in this book.

The product definition step is expanded in Fig. 12-2a. Most new product ideas arise from a combination of market knowledge and technical expertise. Ideas for new products are often generated from the interaction between marketing and product design personnel. New product ideas are usually extensions of the company's existing product line so that design, manufacturing, sales, and other existing resources may be utilized in product development. Particularly promising new product ideas that require new resources may be developed if this new product area will further the company's long-term goals. A careful economic analysis is always required to ensure that any new product is at least potentially profitable.

A new product is tentatively defined in detail. For a simple product, a few-page description may be adequate. More complex products may require an entire preliminary user's manual. In any case, the product definition should carefully define the product both from the view of the customer and the manufacturer. Product definitions may be reviewed by product design, test-equipment design, and manufacturing in order to assure that the proposed product can be manufactured at the cost desired. The user's manual and other preliminary specifications may be sent to key customers

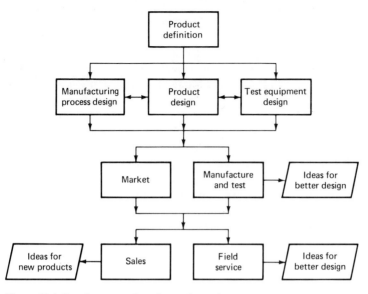

Figure 12-1 Development of an electronic product.

for comment. Questionnaires may be mailed to many potential customers to determine interest in, or problems with, the proposed product. Reviews, comments, and market surveys all contribute to refining the product definition so that the product has the best chance to succeed. As technology develops, product definition becomes more difficult. If one can build almost anything, it is difficult to choose what to build. Previously, limitations of technology often dictated what could be and was built.

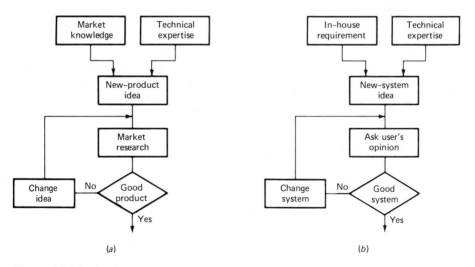

Figure 12-2 Idea development.

Systems to be used in-house go through a similar, but not as elaborate, definition phase. Figure 12-2*b* shows such a definition. Our "customers" are now the in-house group that requires the system. The questions of manufacturability and cost are still important but not as critical as in a product development.

Returning to Fig. 12-1, three design steps follow product definition. Of course, the product itself must be designed. The product must be tested while being manufactured to ensure that it will perform as advertised. Products that fail this test will need to be tested further to be repaired or *reworked*. Some products that work properly when sold will fail after being installed by the customer. Field service personnel must test and repair these products. Three types of test equipment and associated procedures must be designed. In another section of this chapter, we'll discuss product test during manufacture, testing for rework, and field service testing. The economics of testing are complex and important. The cost of testing is always a substantial part of product cost. In some cases, the cost of testing is equal to or greater than the cost of parts and assembly. Finally, if a product requires new manufacturing techniques, these processes must be developed.

As many as three design functions occur simultaneously. These design functions are not independent. The design of test equipment strongly depends on product design, and vice-versa. Part of a product may have to be redesigned to simplify the testing of that product. A proposed manufacturing process may not be possible or economical. The product designer and manufacturing process designer must decide on an alternate course of action that will probably affect both of their designs.

Before we talk about the product design process for microcomputer systems in greater detail, let's finish Fig. 12-1. Product, test-equipment, and process design engineers agree to release the product for production. Usually, a small *pilot run* is manufactured to find problems that would be very costly if not found before a large *production run*. Even before manufacturing has begun, the marketing department has begun preparing manuals and advertising. Key customers, that are most likely to buy many units of the new product, are identified. Seminars are prepared and given to sales representatives. Finally, the product is officially introduced for sale. Advertising appears. Sales representatives visit customers. Seminars are held in cities with large concentrations of potential customers. Sale projections are monitored closely to be sure the product is selling as anticipated. If sales are not sufficient, corrective actions may be taken. Finally, the product must be supported with field service and application assistance. As time goes by, sales will first increase and then decrease as competitors introduce newer products. Marketing personnel project this product *life cycle* and schedule an even newer product to be introduced at the proper time to ensure maximum profitability.

Management of the development of an electronic product is very complex. Many events must be scheduled and made to happen at the right time. Periodic peer reviews assure that mistakes aren't overlooked and that the best possible product is being developed. Complex economic calculations must be made. Often, these economic calculations must be based on questionable data, like estimated sales curves, or insufficient data, like the future costs of field service. Experience and insight are important to a product development.

Product Design

Let's expand the product design function of Fig. 12-1. Figure 12-3 shows one possible product design sequence for a product incorporating a microcomputer. For clarity, the interconnections between product design and test and process design aren't shown. The first and most important step is to design a system that will meet the specifications postulated in the product definition. This system design is a description of the architecture and algorithm of the new system. The system should be completely *detailed* at this time. No step should be left out to be added during implementation. You may as well specify how you really want the system to be built. The system design or even the original product specifications may have to be compromised anyway during implementation, often for economy.

Next, major purchased components are specified. We talked a little about selection of microcomputers in the previous chapter. Major circuits, such as memory ICs, as well as subassemblies, such as a printer, must be chosen and ordered. Performance is certainly important in selection of any component. However, several alternative products will often have adequate performance. Other considerations will decide which component to use. Components with multiple sources will be favored over single-source components. Multiple-source components are likely to be less expensive

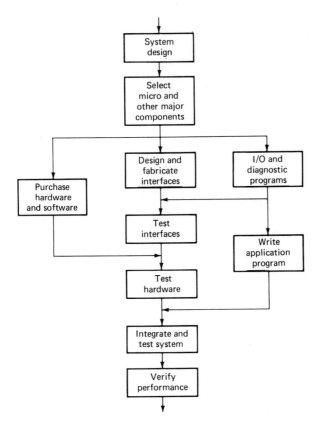

Figure 12-3 Product design.

because very direct competition exists among their manufacturers. In any case, multiple sources reduce the risk of not even being able to obtain the component from a single source. One manufacturer's components may be more reliable than another's. The reputation and financial condition of the component's manufacturer, the terms of extended purchasing agreements, and many other nontechnical factors enter into the selection of major components. Components need not be restricted to hardware, but could also include software. Once components are specified, samples are ordered so that they can be evaluated and incorporated into the *engineering prototype* system.

As mentioned in a previous chapter, interface design is often the major hardware design required in a microcomputer system. For this reason, the interface hardware and software are often designed first. The interface hardware can be tested while the time-consuming task of writing the application program is occurring. The hardware and software are finally integrated, tested together, and debugged if necessary. Finally, a test procedure verifies that the system meets the performance specifications from the original product definition. Of course, test equipment and procedures and manufacturing processes have been simultaneously designed; so our product can be released to manufacturing. Two parts of the design process are so important that we'll expand on our meager descriptions. These important functions are writing the application program and integrating hardware and software.

Writing the Application Program

A small program of 100 lines or less could be written in assembly language, hand assembled into machine language, and programmed into a PROM. Only pencil, paper, and a simple PROM programmer are required. Microcomputer products typically contain thousands or tens of thousands of lines of program. Hand assembly would be out of the question. Usually, at least an automatic assembler and PROM programmer are used to assist the programmer. An automatic assembler is almost always justifiable when compared to the cost of the additional time required of the programmer without such an assembler. Programs larger than 1000 or so lines are usually best written in a high-level language. One *high-level language* is *PASCAL*. High-level languages are independent of any particular computer system. Thus, PASCAL lines of code or *statements* would be identical for the 8048, the 8085, or the 8086. A *compiler* program, written for the specific microcomputer on which the *PASCAL* program is to run, translates the *PASCAL* statements into machine language.

Several high-level languages are commonly available for microcomputers, including *PASCAL*, *PL/M*, *BASIC*, and *FORTRAN*. Two of these languages, *PASCAL* and *PL/M*, are particularly suitable for general software development, including product development. High-level languages simplify programming in two ways. High-level language statements directly correspond to the algorithmic structures desired; so little translation is required. For example, in *PASCAL*, you could write:

```
WHILE     A<B     DO
    BEGIN
    :
    :
```

            other statements
                  .
                  .
                  .

        END

The statements between *BEGIN* and *END* would be repeated as long as *A* was less than *B*. You could repeat a group of statements a fixed number of times by writing:

    FOR   I := 473 TO 483 DO
            BEGIN
                  .
                  .
                  .
            other statements
                  .
                  .
                  .
            END

This program section starts by giving *I* a value of 473. The "other statements" are executed 11 times, once for each value of *I* from 473 to 483. These PASCAL statements directly relate to flowchart figures. We did not need to worry about registers, memory locations, or instruction sets. The compiler translates these statements into the desired machine language. The second way high-level languages simplify programming is simply by shortening programs. We'll use *PASCAL* as an example again.

$$M := A + (B*C)$$

The symbol := means that the value of the expression on the right replaces the original value of *M*. The symbol + means add, while the symbol * means multiply. An arithmetic evaluation that would have required many lines of assembly language is just one line of *PASCAL*.

    High-level languages are a more economical and reliable way of writing programs. High-level languages have potential disadvantages. More machine language instructions are generated by the compiler than would be written by a programmer directly in assembly language. Not only is more memory required, but the program is slower because more instructions must be executed. Memory is becoming less expensive; so storing those additional instructions is less expensive. Often, only very small portions of a large program must execute quickly. Those small portions of the program could

Table 12-1 Costs of programming and memory

	Assembly language	High-level language
Lines of code	10,000	2,000
Bytes of memory needed	20,000	40,000
Cost of programming ($5. per line)	$50,000	$10,000
Cost of memory ($0.005 per byte)	$ 100	$ 200
Cost of other hardware	$ 1,000	$ 1,000

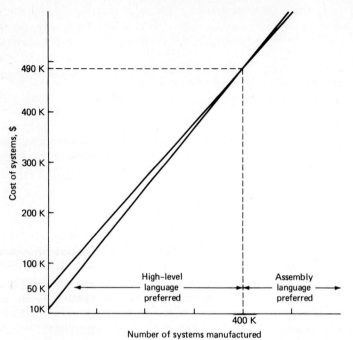

Figure 12-4 Cost of microcomputer system for high-level and assembly language.

be written in assembly language, while the rest of the program is written in a high-level language.

Table 12-1 shows two possible implementations of the same system. Using this data, we've plotted the total cost of a number of systems in Fig. 12-4. In this example, the high-level language approach is less expensive if the total number of systems manufactured is less than 400,000. Of course, this calculation will vary from product to product. Assembly language programming will be less expensive only for very high volume products (e.g., automobiles). Furthermore, the cost of writing one line of a program is going up while the cost of a byte of memory is going down. These two trends combine to increase the number of systems required to make assembly language programming attractive. You should know that our calculations have been simplified. We've disregarded the initial cost of the compiler system. We've disregarded the fact that component costs will vary over the life of the product. The principle we've established is correct. High-level languages are almost always more economical than assembly languages unless expected product volume is very large.

Integration of Hardware and Software

At some point in the product's development, software and hardware must be combined into a working system. Preliminary hardware tests verify gross operation of the circuitry. Software may be tested with the aid of a *simulator*, a program that simulates the microprocessor. You can trace the execution of your program on a simulator. None of these preliminary tests are conclusive. The final test of the integrated system often reveals subtle errors: timing problems, pattern sensitivity, noise susceptibility, etc. One way to proceed would be to build all the hardware, write all the software, and, then, combine hardware and software to see if the system works. Except for the smallest systems, this method is seldom used. Any large system must be debugged in stages. Furthermore, we need a way to test and debug hardware and software that is more powerful than simply turning on the system and seeing if it works.

A *microcomputer development system* is a specialized computer system that aids the development of microcomputer systems. Development systems provide the previously mentioned functions needed to write, assemble, and simulate the operation of programs. Compiler programs provide high-level languages, while a PROM programmer facilitates transferring the program to the product. Most importantly, a development system has two resources, a microprocessor *emulator* and a logic analyzer, that make it unique and powerful. The emulator in Fig. 12-5 is circuitry, terminating in a connector, that acts like a particular microcomputer. The connector is plugged into the microcomputer socket on the product. Operation of the emulator is controlled by the development system's console terminal. The operator can start and stop the emulator, examine and change registers and memory locations, and perform many other functions. Software can be debugged while it is running in the actual product. The emulator is usually coupled to a logic analyzer. The logic analyzer records the state of the emulator's signals. For example, you could set the logic analyzer to stop when a particular memory address occurred. The analyzer would record address, read/write, and other signals until the specified memory address occurred. The operator could now examine the data recorded by the analyzer that led up to the specified address. External inputs to the logic analyzer can also be provided. These external inputs can be connected to signals other than the microprocessor's signals in the product under test.

Now we have a sophisticated way to debug hardware and software in the product. We'd still like some way to debug the microcomputer system in stages. The develop-

A microcomputer development system. From left to right, the system includes a high-performance disk, a printer and the microcomputer with integral CRT, PROM programmer, and cassette tape drive. (*Hewlett-Packard Co.*)

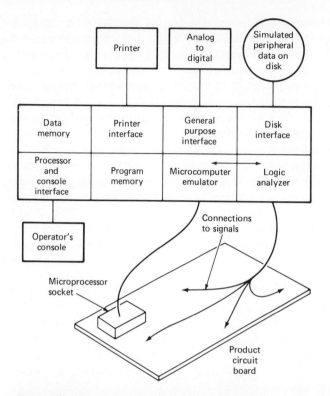

Figure 12-5 Microcomputer development system.

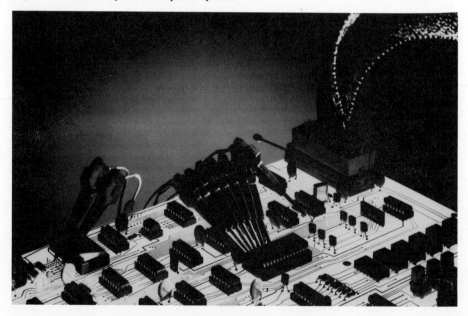

An emulator cable is plugged into the microprocessor socket at right. The individual probes are inputs to a logic analyzer associated with the emulator (*Tektronix, Inc.*).

ment system in Fig. 12-5 contains all common microcomputer resources: program memory, data memory, and I/O. The emulator may direct accesses to these resources either internally to the development system or externally to the product under test. Figure 12-6 shows how this emulator function can be used to debug a microcomputer system in stages. Initially, only the product's support circuitry causes the emulator to function in Fig. 12-6a. After the support circuitry is debugged, the I/O circuits are tested. The emulator accesses the development system for instructions and data memory and accesses the product for peripheral data in Fig. 12-6b. After all the peripherals have been tested, the emulator is set to use the product's RWM, rather than the development system's data memory. By this time, most or all of the application program is also being tested. It might be necessary to backtrack if problems are found. For example, a malfunctioning product peripheral could be replaced with a development system peripheral. Software development could continue while the product's peripheral was debugged. Next, PROMs are programmed and plugged into the product. No development system resources are needed, as shown in Fig. 12-6d. The emulator still

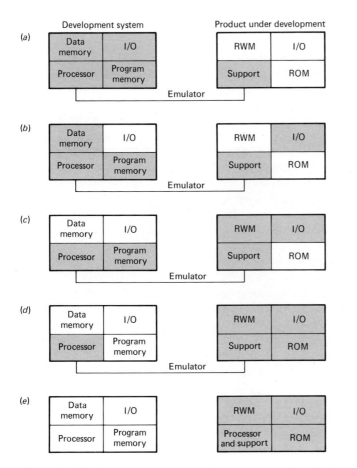

Figure 12-6 Testing and integrating product resources with a development system. (a) Test support circuits. (b) Test I/O. (c) Test RWM. (d) Test ROM. (e) Test processor.

allows us to continue to verify system operation. Finally, the emulator cable is replaced by an actual microcomputer to complete a working prototype of the product.

The actual use of the resource assignment capability of the emulator is often more complex than we've described but follows the sequence and motivation presented. Often I/O resources are difficult resources to emulate in the development system. The development system will have common peripherals, such as a printer, that can be substituted directly for a product's printer. Often, the product's peripherals will be more unusual, such as an analog-to-digital converter. General-purpose interfaces on the development system can be temporarily connected to analog-to-digital converters and other special peripherals to provide an equivalent I/O resource on the development system. Finally, peripherals can be simulated, using a data file stored in RWM or on a disk. A sequence of peripheral input data is prepared and stored in the development system. Each access to a particular peripheral address will actually retrieve the next datum in the stored sequence. Data output to a simulated peripheral are simply stored in RWM or on a disk for later examination.

The Design Team

The design of a microcomputer-based product is usually assigned to a small team. The entire team won't be needed for the project's duration; so individual personnel may be transferred among projects as needed. Often, a single person may perform more than one function.

A manager coordinates the project and provides administrative support. A system designer details the architecture and algorithms to use. A hardware engineer designs and debugs the circuitry. A software engineer or programmer writes and debugs the program. One or more technicians assemble circuits, edit programs, and perform other support functions. Larger design teams are less efficient because the problems of task division and communication among team members become very difficult. Large projects are best divided into as many independent subprojects as possible and assigned to small independent design teams. We'll examine this approach in a later section.

Build or Buy?

A great variety of preengineered microcomputer systems are available. Many resources, such as processor, ROM, RWM, and parallel and serial I/O, are commonly used. Manufacturers have designed complete printed circuit boards containing these resources. These printed circuit boards are commonly called *single-board computers* or *SBCs*. SBCs are tailored to a particular application by adding application software and peripherals. Several SBCs have become so popular that many manufacturers provide dozens of compatible printed circuit boards containing a variety of processors, memories, and peripheral interfaces. The decision to purchase an SBC, rather than manufacture your own system, is made on economic grounds. In fact, the same economic analysis applies to any purchased subassembly. The cost of a purchased SBC is often more than the direct cost of manufacturing that system yourself. However, your own system must be developed at a greater cost than that of developing an SBC system.

A prefabricated single board computer containing an 8085, and memory and I/O circuits. An 8041 or 8741 may be inserted into the empty socket at left and programmed to act like an auxiliary I/O processor to the 8085. (*Intel Corporation.*)

Figure 12-7 shows the total cost of manufacturing a number of systems. For small numbers of systems, lowered development costs make the SBC attractive. For large numbers of systems, indirect costs are a small fraction of total system cost, and the SBC is no longer attractive. Where is the break-even point? This break-even point varies not only with the system, but also with the existing resources of the manufacturer of the proposed system. A steel mill developing a microcomputer system would find the SBC attractive in almost any quantity. The steel mill would almost certainly not have any of the facilities needed to develop or manufacture microcomputer systems and would have to invest large sums of money to get those facilities. A manufacturer that already manufactures electronic, but not microcomputer, products might find the SBCs attractive only up to several hundred or even several

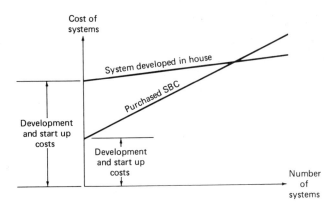

Figure 12-7 Cost of microcomputer systems for inhouse system and purchased SBC.

thousand systems. In any case, such a manufacturer might start using SBCs to minimize the amount of money risked at the beginning of a new product. If product volume increased sufficiently, a new system could be designed and manufactured in-house in order to reduce cost and increase profits with little risk. Finally, a manufacturer of automobiles, refrigerators, or TV games would never consider SBCs. Product volume is very large, and cost is very important.

You should know that the curves of Fig. 12-7 are simplified. The actual cost curves are not straight lines since the cost of electronic components decreases as the number purchased increases. The actual cost of components can vary tremendously in small quantities (e.g., less than a few hundred systems).

DISTRIBUTED ARCHITECTURES

Let's examine the *data logger* shown in Fig. 12-8. This data logger is a microcomputer-based system that periodically records temperatures, pressures, and other physical

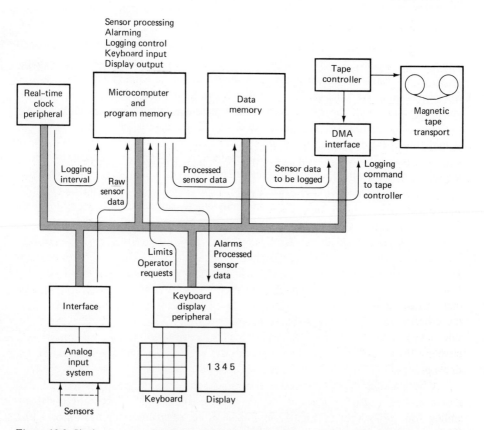

Figure 12-8 Single processor data logger. Excerpted from "Microcomputer Peripherals" by Murray and Wiatrowski appearing in *IEEE Transactions on Industrial Electronics and Control Instrumentation*, November 1978, Vol. IECI-25, No. 4, pp. 303–322.

A data logger (*John Fluke Mfg. Co., Inc.*).

variables on magnetic tape. A real-time clock keeps track of time for the logging interval. Interfaces to analog sensor inputs and to a magnetic-tape transport complete the primary data path. A keyboard and display interface allow the operator to monitor or change the operation of the data logger. For example, the operator may specify how often each sensor is to be logged and in what format. The operator may simply want to display the value of some temperature or pressure. This logger also incorporates an alarm function. If a pressure, temperature, or other physical variable moves outside normal limits of operation, an alarm is sounded. This alarm may be visual and audible and might also be programmed to log itself on the tape. Alarm limits are input via the keyboard. A high limit, a low limit, or both high and low limits may be specified for each sensor. One typical application of a data logger is monitoring the operation of a process in an industrial plant. Often, from 10 to 1000 sensors are used. Logging rates are relatively slow, usually measured in seconds, minutes, or even hours. The design of a data logger for such an application might look very much like Fig. 12-8. A single processor performs all the data logger's functions. If several thousand or more sensors must be logged or if logging or alarm checking rates must be very fast, the processor of Fig. 12-8 is liable to be insufficient. A larger, faster processor may be substituted in the logger, but performance will eventually be limited by the many data traveling over this single microcomputer's bus. In addition, the program for a large single processor is liable to be massive and difficult to write and debug.

A better alternative architecture for increasing the data logger's performance is shown in Fig. 12-9. The tasks of the single processor in Fig. 12-8 have been divided among four processors in Fig. 12-9. Furthermore, each processor has its own bus (heavy lines), and crowding is reduced on a single bus. For example, the sensor processor runs the analog input interface, corrects data for nonideal sensors, converts the corrected data to standard engineering units, and sends those data to the alarm processor. All the instruction fetches and intermediate data transfers associated with sensor processing appear *only* on the sensor processor's bus. Processing of sensor data occurs simultaneously with other functions performed by the other processor.

You might expect that four processors operating concurrently would be 4 times as fast as a single processor. This would be true if we had divided the tasks among the four processors so that each was equally busy. Some of the processors of Fig. 12-9 will be busier than others. For example, the console processor will stand idle most of the time. The console processor will only be used when an operator inputs new commands or limits or when an alarm must be displayed. We deliberately divided the tasks among the processors according to natural functions, even though the system will not operate as fast as theoretically possible. Division of tasks according to function reduces the dependence of one processor or another. Communication among processors is reduced. More importantly, each relatively independent processing system can be designed and debugged separately. Dividing tasks by function makes the system naturally modular. For example, additional sensors may be accommodated by adding another sensor processor. An easily added, remotely located sensor processor reduces wiring expense if many sensors are far from the logger. Adding a paper log only requires adding a logging and printer control processor. Adding or changing functions would not be so easy if we had assigned tasks among the processors solely on the basis of the time required for each task.

Before proceeding to another example, let's examine the advantages offered by the *distributed processing* system of Fig. 12-9. The multiple-processor system has higher performance than a single-processor system. We purposely sacrificed some of the potential performance increase to simplify development. The development of each processor system is an almost independent task that could be assigned to different product design teams in order to speed development. In any case, these smaller subsystems will be much easier to design and debug than one massive system. Finally, the natural modularity of our distributed system makes adding and changing functions easy.

Another distributed system is shown in Fig. 12-10. This system helps operate a manufacturing company. Five microcomputers are used. An order entry processor not only enters new orders, but also allows sales to check available inventory and to follow orders in progress. The order entry processor transmits shipping directives to the shipping and receiving processor. When an order is shipped or new parts are received, the inventory and scheduling processor is notified of changes in inventory. The shipping and receiving processor also notifies the receivables and payables processor so that invoices can be issued for products shipped to customers and invoices can be paid for parts received from suppliers. The inventory and scheduling processor is used by manufacturing to schedule production runs and by purchasing to order parts. Finally, a management information system processor allows managers to monitor orders, shipments, inventory, accounts, and other data needed to manage the company. Each of these subsystems is a fairly complex computer itself. As required, disks, printers, and terminals are part of each subsystem.

This distributed system illustrates some other advantages of multiprocessors. A failure of any of these processors affects only part of the whole system. For example,

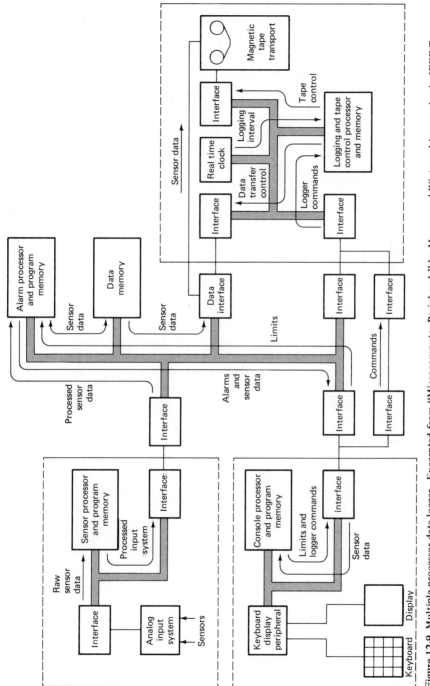

Figure 12-9 Multiple-processor data logger. Excerpted from "Microcomputer Peripherals" by Murray and Wiatrowski appearing in *IEEE Transactions on Industrial Electronics and Control Instrumentation*, November 1978, Vol. IECI-25, No. 4, pp. 303–322.

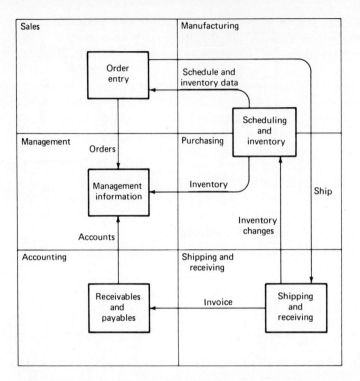

Figure 12-10 Distributed system for a manufacturing company.

a failure of the inventory processor will not affect order processing, shipping, or receivables. A manual (paper) backup system will keep track of inventory changes until the inventory processor is repaired. A single computer performing all these functions would be large with many peripherals. The probability of failure of such a single large complex system *might* be greater than the probability of failure of the distributed system. The reliability of both possible systems would have to be carefully calculated to determine which system was most reliable overall. For the same reason, the distributed system *might* be less costly than a centralized system. Now we've seen a few more advantages of distributed systems. Distributed systems are fail soft. That is, single failures do not incapacitate the system but merely reduce its performance. Distributed systems can be potentially more reliable and less costly than centralized systems. In fact, the benefits of distributed systems are all *potential* benefits. Systems must be carefully designed to achieve the desired benefits.

Distributed systems have disadvantages also. Important information concerning the operation of the manufacturing company of Fig. 12-10 is contained in most of the subsystems. This information is called a *data base* and is distributed among the subsystems of Fig. 12-10. A distributed data base might not be difficult to operate if all the data subsets were independent. In Fig. 12-10, a change in an order affects subsets of the data base in both the inventory and receivables processor. It would be easy enough to design a system that might miss or double count a data-base change in one or both of the data subsets. More importantly, it is difficult to prove that, under any circumstances, your system will not err in management of the data base.

A hardware or software error that propagates among the processors is difficult to find and repair. Such an error appears to be in every processor, even though only one has failed. A field service engineer might try disconnecting processors individually until the system works. Interactions might cause the system to start working when the order entry process is disconnected even though the shipping and receiving processor has caused the failure! Another reason to make the subsystems functionally independent is to minimize interactions that would make the diagnosis of the cause of a system failure difficult. These propagating failures have also caused our system to *fail hard*. A single malfunction has incapacitated the entire system.

We haven't enumerated all possible classes of architectures, nor have we included an in-depth analysis of what we've presented. Our purpose has only been to get you to think about system design alternatives. Because of the very low cost of microcomputers and memories, these alternatives are no longer just formalized configurations found in books on computer architecture. Any configuration is both possible and desirable if that architecture does the required task.

TESTING

All circuits and systems must be tested. Manufacturers of gates, ROMs, microprocessors, and other ICs test these components during manufacture. Often, purchasers test these components again before inserting them in printed circuit boards. The PC boards are tested during manufacture, as is the entire product composed of several PC boards, power supply, and other components.

Malfunctioning IC components are either returned to their manufacturer or simply discarded. The purchaser and seller of IC components often negotiate an agreement specifying who absorbs the cost of bad ICs. Malfunctioning assemblies, such as PC boards, must be tested to isolate bad components so that they may be replaced. The cost of reworking some malfunctioning assemblies may be much more than the cost of the assembly itself. Inexpensive assemblies could be discarded rather than repaired. Testing is very expensive. Expensive equipment is used, and each assembly may have to be tested for a long time. Many complex economic decisions have to be made. How often should an assembly be tested during manufacture? Testing too much is expensive. Testing too little may increase the costs of rework and scrap. How thorough should the test be? Very complete tests are expensive but are justified if reliability of the finished product is very important. The consequences of a malfunction may be an exploding refinery or a crashed spacecraft. Not testing for some malfunctions will increase product returns from customers. You must consider the expected frequency of occurrence of the malfunction, the savings resulting from not testing for that function, the costs of warranty service and customer returns, customer dissatisfaction from receiving an inoperative unit, and the consequences of a malfunction.

Figure 12-11 shows an idealized testing configuration. A sequence of algorithmic,

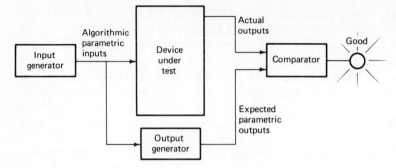

Figure 12-11 Idealized testing.

parametric inputs is generated and applied to the device under test or *DUT*. We call this sequence algorithmic because it was designed to implement a testing algorithm for the DUT. This sequence is parametric because timing, voltage, and other similar parameters are explicitly varied in the testing sequence. The actual outputs of the DUT are compared to the outputs expected from a correctly functioning unit. The configuration of Fig. 12-11 works for ICs or printed circuits, ASMs or microcomputers, and analog or digital circuits! Any actual tester limits the scope of the circuits to be tested to reduce the cost of that tester. Testing configurations may also be less than ideal in order to reduce costs. For example, most or all parametric testing may be eliminated in a digital circuit tester. Input patterns may be random rather than algorithmic. The savings in testing must be balanced against the costs of missing malfunctions.

Several methods have been developed for generating input sequences and expected output sequences. Input sequences may be pseudorandom. An ASM provides a pseudorandom bit pattern to the DUT. Although inexpensive to implement, pseudorandom patterns require long test times. Additionally, pseudorandom patterns may miss some malfunctions or apply invalid input combinations with unpredictable results. Algorithmic sequences may be manually planned, written, and stored in the tester's memory. Alternately, a very fast programmable ASM may execute a manually written testing program to generate a test sequence. This latter approach can be more flexible and require less memory. However, this *very fast* programmable ASM must be *much* faster than the DUT.

Expected outputs can be computed and stored in the tester's memory and compared with actual outputs. These outputs may be computed by observing the outputs of a good DUT, by manual calculation, or by inputting the input test sequence to a software simulator of the DUT. Outputs may be computed by a very fast ASM programmed to emulate the DUT. Although flexible, the *very fast* ASM must, again, be *much* faster than the DUT. A known good assembly, identical to the DUT, may be used to generate outputs to be compared. You must have a way to independently verify the operation of the known good assembly and ensure that it stays good! Parametric testing is seldom possible by comparison with a known good assembly.

Testers can be purchased that use all the input and output generation techniques in many useful combinations. Purchased testers are often used to test ICs and PC

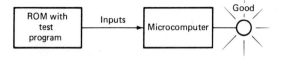

Figure 12-12 Microcomputer self-test.

boards. Sometimes, the right tester can't be purchased. The needed test functions may not be available, or a purchased tester may not be cost effective for a particular application. We'll discuss several variations of Fig. 12-11 that are often used with microprocessors that involve more than purchasing a tester.

Microcomputer Self-Test

Figure 12-12 shows the simplest test arrangement used to verify the operation of micro-processor ICs. Inputs are a test program stored in a ROM. The microcomputer executes this self-test program and indicates successful completion by lighting indicator lamps. Input sequences are not parametric; so timing, fan out, and other problems might not be discovered. Many microcomputer functions are left untested. No inputs are provided for interrupts, direct memory access, and other processor functions. The microcomputer itself functions as the output sequence comparator. Malfunctions in the microcomputer could cause an erroneous comparison and indicate a good IC. This testing method is often used on the assumption that most microprocessor malfunctions will be sufficiently serious to cause many instruction failures, if not catastrophic failure of the whole microcomputer.

Self-test is often used to verify operation of an entire system incorporating a microcomputer, as shown in Fig. 12-13. The microcomputer first performs a self-test on itself. If the microcomputer is functioning, it can supply input sequences to the rest of the system and verify correct outputs. The microcomputer may sum all the bytes of a ROM to check to see if they sum to the correct value. Data are transferred into and out of RWM and I/O ports to verify operation. Sequencing of peripheral ASMs is checked. Many products incorporate self-test. Each time power is applied to the system, it verifies its own correct operation. In a complex instrument (e.g., a logic

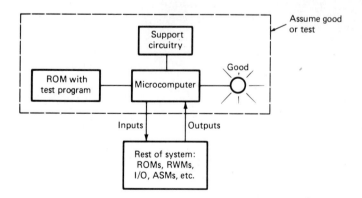

Figure 12-13 Self-test of a microcomputer system.

analyzer), self-test may be imperative. Otherwise, an operator would not be easily able to tell the difference between a malfunctioning instrument and a malfunctioning circuit being tested by that instrument! Finally, a complete self-test of a complex instrument may require an operator's assistance. At various points in the self-test program, the operator may be asked to press keys, observe displays, or even connect external jumper wires or signal sources.

Logic Analyzers

Many instruments, including most logic analyzers, have interfaces that allow them to be controlled by a computer or programmable calculator. Any computer-controlled instrument can potentially be used for production testing as well as for prototype debugging. A logic-*state* analyzer is combined with a self-test ROM to test a microcomputer in Fig. 12-14. The logic analyzer records the microcomputer's response to the test sequence stored in the ROM. These outputs are sent to a computer, which actually performs the comparison with expected outputs from a good microcomputer. The logic analyzer records the states of many signals; so a more complete test of the microcomputer is possible than the self-test of Fig. 12-12. Since the analyzer can be connected to signals like interrupt and DMA acknowledge, additional inputs to interrupt request, DMA request, and similar signals may be supplied. These signals can come from extra bits in the test ROM. A trigger signal from the test ROM identifies the beginning of the test program. The logic analyzer can use the trigger to find any place in the self-test program. Logic analyzers have a function called *digital delay* that enables them to delay recording data until a specified number of clock pulses have elapsed since a trigger signal. A logic analyzer with a small memory could be used to monitor thousands of outputs. A different group of outputs is recorded at each

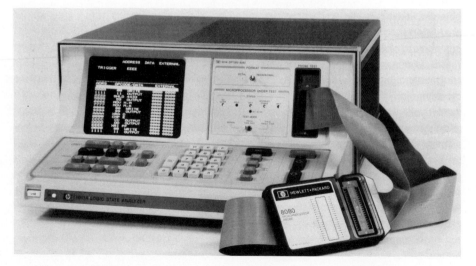

A logic analyzer designed to monitor microcomputer signals. (*Hewlett-Packard Co.*)

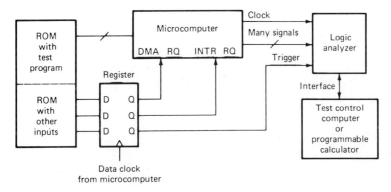

Figure 12-14 Testing with a logic analyzer.

execution of the self-test program by changing the digital delay. Logic *timing* analyzers record data at high speed *asynchronously*. Many data are recorded *between* microcomputer clock pulses; so timing may be measured and tested. Some analyzers include both state and timing analyzer functions configurable under computer control. Such an analyzer could perform functional *and* parametric testing in Fig. 12-14.

Finally, a logic analyzer could be used to monitor data from a microcomputer-based system as well as data from only the microcomputer IC. Unlike self-test of a system, the logic analyzer will provide some diagnostic information. If the microcomputer of Fig. 12-14 were replaced with a microcomputer system, the test control computer might be able to localize a malfunction to an individual component or, at least, a group of components.

Development Systems and Emulators

You'll notice that the test equipment in Fig. 12-14 is also contained in a microcomputer development system. Test programs stored in the development system may be connected to the system under test via the emulator cable. A logic analyzer monitors the microcomputer's signals as well as other signals. The development system's processor can sequence the testing as well as provide other inputs to the system under test via a general-purpose digital interface. In fact, even analog signals could be provided if needed. What differences exist between the test system of Fig. 12-14 and the development system of Fig. 12-15? The logic analyzers in development systems are often much simpler than separate logic analyzers. For example, timing analysis is seldom available in a development system. The emulator allows the development system to more closely control the system under test than the self-test ROM of Fig. 12-14 would allow. Of course, the microprocessor itself is not tested by the development system since it was removed to connect the emulator. Finally, the development system can provide external inputs to the system under test. These inputs can also be changed in response to the behavior of the system under test. A general-purpose interface could be added to the computer of Fig. 12-14 in order to provide this same capability to stimulate other inputs under computer control.

A microcomputer development system with integral CRT terminal and floppy disk drive. (*Intel Corporation.*)

Signature Analysis

All the test techniques we've discussed so far have been, at best, marginally useful for locating individual malfunctioning components. Analog circuits are often easy to troubleshoot. The analog circuit's schematic is annotated with dc voltage values and oscilloscope waveforms. By verifying these voltages and waveforms in an actual circuit, a technician can localize a faulty component. The inputs to a bad component will be correct, while its output will be incorrect. This technique is called *signal tracing.* Voltage measurements are not very useful in digital circuits since most signals are changing at high speed. If we try to draw digital timing diagrams for each circuit element output, we discover that those timing diagrams often involve thousands of clock cycles! In order to use a digital signal tracing technique, we'll need some way to compress a long sequence of data bits into a notation short enough to be easily recognizable. One alternative we might consider is counting the number of transitions of a digital signal during a specified time period. This number of transitions would become a compressed representation of that bit sequence. *Transition counting* is sometimes used for functional testing of PC boards. It has two disadvantages. Only the number of transitions are counted. Any digital signal having the same number of transitions will be

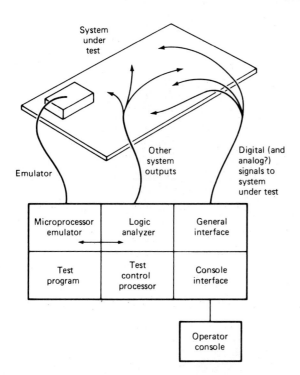

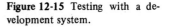

Figure 12-15 Testing with a development system.

interpreted as correct even if the transitions are in a completely different order. Errors are easily missed. The probability of finding errors is improved as longer data sequences are measured. Unfortunately, single measurements requiring seconds to minutes rule out transition counting as an economical digital signal tracing technique. The service technician must be able to quickly move a test probe among the various signals in the circuit.

We must be able to remember something about the *order* of the transitions as well as the number of transitions. Figure 12-16 shows an ASM that is commonly used

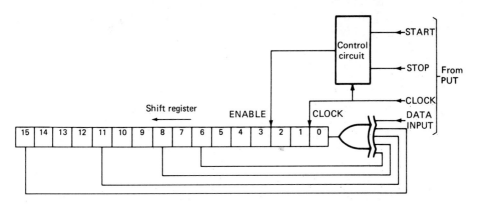

Figure 12-16 ASM for calculating signatures.

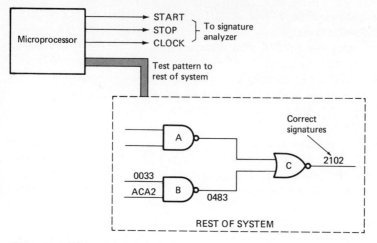

Figure 12-17 Using signature analysis.

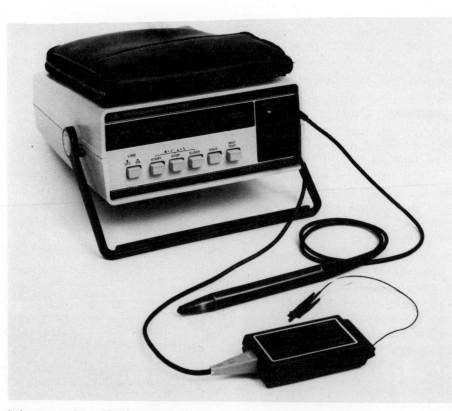

A signature analyzer. (*Hewlett-Packard Co.*)

for compressing sequences of digital bits. A shift register remembers 16 bits of data. Selected bits of the shift register are fed back to an exclusive OR gate at the register input. Some past history is combined with the current bit to preserve information about the order of the bits. Although a complete explanation of this circuit will not be given here, the 16 bits of the shift register are a much more useful compression of the data than was a transition count. Almost all errors (99.998%) are detected. Measurements require few bits and are almost instantaneous. The 16 shift-register bits are displayed as a four digit hex *signature*.

Figure 12-17 is a simplified example of using signature analysis. A self-test program in the product's microcomputer provides a repeated bit pattern to all the other circuitry. The microcomputer also provides start and stop signals to the signature analyzer to ensure that the same bit pattern is always measured. A technician probing gate B discovers signatures 0033 and ACA2 on gate B's inputs. The output of gate B has signature 8444 instead of 0483. Since gate B is receiving correct inputs but has an incorrect output, gate B has malfunctioned. Signature analysis is more complex than we've explained here. Before using signature analysis in a product, you should learn much more about signature analysis by reading appropriate literature.[1]

Field Service

As products became more complex, servicing those products became increasingly difficult. Even before microcomputers existed, many companies had started repairing complex systems by replacing entire PC boards. The malfunctioning PC board (or other subassembly) is found and exchanged for a working PC board. The bad board is returned to the factory for repair. Two problems arise from this technique. First, large amounts of money must be invested in spare PC boards. Second, the factory technicians often can't find the malfunction after the board is removed from its system. The malfunction was actually caused by interactions between the PC board and the *particular* system in which the board was installed!

Board exchange is imperative when malfunctions must be fixed quickly. For example, a large bank might be hopelessly behind if its malfunctioning computer wasn't repaired in a couple of hours. Sometimes, entire systems are exchanged. A refinery or other industrial plant might only tolerate a few minutes or even seconds of down time. Two computers are always kept running. If one fails, the other can be instantaneously switched to take the place of the malfunctioning unit.

Microprocessor emulators and logic and signature analyzers have made it possible to consider localizing bad components in the field. Emulators provide the capability of running test programs in a product, if they aren't designed into the product already. Logic analyzers localize complex faults to smaller subassemblies. Signature analysis can locate the malfunctioning component in one of these subassemblies. It sounds easy. It isn't. Careful technical and economic planning is required to set up an effective field service operation. A field service plan may involve many techniques. Board

---

[1] *A Designer's Guide to Signature Analysis, Application Note 222*, Hewlett-Packard Co., Palo Alto, Calif.

exchange, field repairs, local service depots, factory service, and other techniques may all be used in combination.

Other Topics for Study

Although you now have a firm foundation in digital system design, you have much to learn before you can effectively design complex systems. Some aspects of design can only be learned through experience but many other topics are worth studying in books or courses.

In the area of digital hardware, you need to learn more about electronics to better understand how to connect logic circuits together and to interface those circuits to sensors and actuators. You should learn more about testing circuits because testability is designed into systems and not added later. You should study the architectural alternatives available to you to construct large systems.

In the area of software, you need to learn much more about the structure of large programs. Learn about a variety of modern high-level languages. Real-time systems and operating systems as well as data structures deserve your attention. Testing and verifying software operation is important. You'll need to know more about economics, finance, manufacturing technology, applications, and other subjects not directly related to digital design.

You'll find learning this material natural and enjoyable, especially with your new background in digital systems. Digital circuits of all kinds, but especially microcomputers, are widely applied to interesting tasks. You've just started learning about one of the largest and most important areas of technology.

INDEX

INDEX